Honda GL1500 Gold Wing Owners Workshop Manual

by Alan Ahlstrand and John H Haynes
Member of the Guild of Motoring Writers

Models covered:
Honda GL1500 Gold Wing. 1502 cc.
1988 through 2000

(12C1 - 2225)

ABCDE
FGHIJ
KLMNO
PQRS

Haynes Publishing
Sparkford Nr Yeovil
Somerset BA22 7JJ England

Haynes North America, Inc
861 Lawrence Drive
Newbury Park
California 91320 USA

Acknowledgments

Special thanks to Honda of Milpitas, Milpitas, California, for providing the motorcycle used in these photographs; to Pete Sirett, service manager, for arranging the facilities and fitting the mechanical work into his shop's busy schedule; and to Bruce Farley, service technician, for doing the mechanical work and providing valuable technical information.

© **Haynes North America, Inc. 1997, 2000**
With permission from J.H. Haynes & Co. Ltd.

A book in the Haynes Owners Workshop Manual Series

Printed in the U.S.A.

ISBN 1 56392 406 4

Library of Congress Card Number 00-110004

British Library Cataloguing in Publication Data
A catalogue record for this book is available from the British Library

We take great pride in the accuracy of information given in this manual, but motorcycle manufacturers make alterations and design changes during the production run of a particular motorcycle of which they do not inform us. No liability can be accepted by the authors or publishers for loss, damage or injury caused by any errors in, or omissions from, the information given.

00-240

1998 GL 1500

Introduction to the Honda GL1500 Gold Wing

The GL1500 Gold Wing is Honda's top-of-the-line touring bike.

The engine on all models is a liquid-cooled, horizontally opposed six with single overhead camshafts and hydraulically operated lifters.

Fuel is delivered to two down-draft CV carburetors by an electric fuel pump.

The front suspension uses a pair of conventional damper rod forks with an anti-dive device built in.

The rear suspension uses a pair of air-adjustable shock absorbers and a swingarm, with an optional on-board compressor system to adjust air pressure in the shocks. Final drive is by a shaft.

The front brake uses dual discs and the rear brake uses a single disc. The front and rear brakes are interlinked; the brake pedal operates the left front brake as well as the rear brake. The right front brake is operated by the lever on the right handlebar independently of the rear and left front brakes.

Contents

About this manual

Its purpose

The purpose of this manual is to help you get the best value from your motorcycle. It can do so in several ways. It can help you decide what work must be done, even if you choose to have it done by a dealer service department or a repair shop; it provides information and procedures for routine maintenance and servicing; and it offers diagnostic and repair procedures to follow when trouble occurs.

We hope you use the manual to tackle the work yourself. For many simpler jobs, doing it yourself may be quicker than arranging an appointment to get the vehicle into a shop and making the trips to leave it and pick it up. More importantly, a lot of money can be saved by avoiding the expense the shop must pass on to you to cover its labor and overhead costs. An added benefit is the sense of satisfaction and accomplishment that you feel after doing the job yourself.

Using the manual

The manual is divided into Chapters. Each Chapter is divided into numbered Sections, which are headed in bold type between horizontal lines. Each Section consists of consecutively numbered paragraphs or steps.

At the beginning of each numbered Section you will be referred to any illustrations which apply to the procedures in that Section. The reference numbers used in illustration captions pinpoint the pertinent Section and the Step within that Section. That is, illustration 3.2 means the illustration refers to Section 3 and Step (or paragraph) 2 within that Section.

Procedures, once described in the text, are not normally repeated. When it's necessary to refer to another Chapter, the reference will be given as Chapter and Section number. Cross references given without use of the word 'Chapter' apply to Sections and/or paragraphs in the same Chapter. For example, 'see Section 8' means in the same Chapter.

References to the left or right side of the vehicle assume you are sitting on the seat, facing forward.

Motorcycle manufacturers continually make changes to specifications and recommendations, and these, when notified, are incorporated into our manuals at the earliest opportunity.

Even though we have prepared this manual with extreme care, neither the publisher nor the authors can accept responsibility for any errors in, or omissions from, the information given.

NOTE

A **Note** provides information necessary to properly complete a procedure or information which will make the procedure easier to understand.

CAUTION

A **Caution** provides a special procedure or special steps which must be taken while completing the procedure where the Caution is found. Not heeding a Caution can result in damage to the assembly being worked on.

WARNING

A **Warning** provides a special procedure or special steps which must be taken while completing the procedure where the Warning is found. Not heeding a Warning can result in personal injury.

Buying parts

Once you have found all the identification numbers, record them for reference when buying parts. Since the manufacturers change specifications, parts and vendors (companies that manufacture various components on the machine), providing the ID numbers is the only way to be reasonably sure that you are buying the correct parts.

Whenever possible, take the worn part to the dealer so direct comparison with the new component can be made. Along the trail from the manufacturer to the parts shelf, there are numerous places that the part can end up with the wrong number or be listed incorrectly.

The two places to purchase new parts for your motorcycle - the accessory store and the franchised dealer - differ in the type of parts they carry. While dealers can obtain virtually every part for your motorcycle, the accessory dealer is usually limited to normal high wear items such as shock absorbers, tune-up parts, various engine gaskets, cables, chains, brake parts, etc. Rarely will an accessory outlet have major suspension components, cylinders, transmission gears, or cases.

Used parts can be obtained for roughly half the price of new ones, but you can't always be sure of what you're getting. Once again, take your worn part to the wrecking yard (breaker) for direct comparison.

Whether buying new, used or rebuilt parts, the best course is to deal directly with someone who specializes in parts for your particular make.

Identification numbers

The frame number is stamped in the steering head . . .

. . . and is also displayed on a decal

The frame serial number is stamped into the steering head and printed on a label affixed to the frame. The engine number is stamped into the right side of the crankcase. Both of these numbers should be recorded and kept in a safe place so they can be furnished to law enforcement officials in the event of a theft.

The frame serial number, engine serial number and carburetor identification number should also be kept in a handy place (such as with your driver's license) so they are always available when purchasing or ordering parts for your machine.

The models covered by this manual are as follows:

Honda GL1500 Gold Wing, 1988 through 2000

Identifying model years

The procedures in this manual identify the bikes by model year. To determine which model year a given machine is, look for the following identification codes in the engine and frame numbers.

The engine number is stamped in the right side of the crankcase

Year	Frame numbers	Engine numbers
1988		
Except California	SC220*JA000001-JA010467	SC22E-2000137-2014618
California	SC221*JA000001-JA001461	SC22E-2000143-2009570
1989		
Except California	SC220*KA000001-KA110411	SC22E-2100101-2113825
California	SC221*KA000001-KA101412	SC22E-2100105-2111261
1990 (Interstate and Aspencade)		
Except California	SC220*LA000001-LA203608	SC22E-2200101-2206589
California	SC221*LA000001-LA200487	SC22E-2200106-2206691
1990 (SE)		
Except California	SC223*LA200001-LA202625	SC22E-2200101-2208675
California	SC224*LA200001-LA200366	SC22E-2200101-2207415
1991 (Interstate)		
Except California	SC226*MA300001 on	SC22E-2300101 on
California	SC227*MA300001 on	SC22E-2300101 on
1991 (Aspencade)		
Except California	SC220*MA300001 on	SC22E-2300101 on
California	SC227*MA300001 on	SC22E-2300101 on
1991 (SE)		
Except California	SC226*MA300001 on	SC22E-2300887 on
California	SC224*MA300001 on	SC22E-2301367 on

Year	Frame numbers	Engine numbers
1992 (Interstate)		
Except California	SC226*NA400001-NA400962	SC22E-22402757-2406705
California	SC227*NA400001-NA400183	SC22E-2402759-2406100
1992 (Aspencade)		
Except California	SC220*NA400003-NA401982	SC22E-2400114-2406485
California	SC221-NA400012-NA400243	SC22E-2401614-2405846
1992 (SE)		
Except California	SC223*NA400001-NA401340	SC22E-2400654-2406910
California	SC224-NA400003-NA400182	SC22E-2401434-2405510
1993 (Interstate)		
Except California	SC226*PA500001 on	SC22E-2500101 on
California	SC227*PA500001 on	SC22E-2500219 on
1993 (Aspencade)		
Except California	SC220*PA500001 on	SC22E-2500109 on
California	SC221*PA500012 on	SC22E-2500106 on
1993 (SE)		
Except California	SC223*PA500001 on	SC22E-2500564 on
California	SC224*PA500003 on	SC22E-2500104 on
1994 (Interstate)		
Except California	SC226*RA600001 on	SC22E-2602085-2609506
California	SC227*RA600001 on	SC22E-2600411 on
1994 (Aspencade)		
Except California	SC220*RA600001 on	SC22E-2600111 on
California	SC221-RA600012 on	SC22E-2600381 on
1994 (SE)		
Except California	SC223*RA600001 on	SC22E-2600894 on
California	SC224-RA600003 on	SC22E-2601494-2609246
1995 (Interstate)		
Except California	SC226*SA700001 on	SC22E-2700101 on
California	SC227*SA700001 on	SC22E- SC22E-2700101 on
1995 (Aspencade)		
Except California	SC220*SA700001 on	SC22E- SC22E-2700101 on
California	SC221*SA700001 on	SC22E- SC22E-2700101 on
1995 (SE)		
Except California	SC223*SA700001 on	SC22E- SC22E-2700101 on
California	SC224*SA700001 on	SC22E- SC22E-2700101 on
1996 (Interstate)		
Except California	SC226*TA800001 on	SC22E-2800101 on
California	SC227*TA800001 on	SC22E-2800101 on
1996 (Aspencade)		
Except California	SC220*TA800001 on	SC22E-2800101 on
California	SC221*TA800001 on	SC22E-2800101 on
1996 (SE)		
Except California	SC223*TA800001 on	SC22E-2800101 on
California	SC224*TA800001 on	SC22E-2800101 on
1997 (Aspencade)		
Except California	SC220*VA900001 on	SC22E-2900101 on
California	SC221*VA800001 on	SC22E-2900101 on
1997 (SE)		
Except California	SC223*VA900001 on	SC22E-2900101 on
California	SC224*VA900001 on	SC22E-2900101 on
1998 (Aspencade)		
Except California	SC220*WA000001	SC22E-3000001
California	SC221*WA000001	SC22E-3000001
1998 (SE)		
Except California	SC223*WA900001	SC22E-3000101
California	SC224*WA900001	SC22E-3000101
1999 (Aspencade)		
Except California	SC220*XA100001	SC22E-4000101
California	SC221*XA100001	SC22E-4000101
1999 (SE)		
Except California	SC223*XA100001	SC22E-4000101
California	SC224*XA100001	SC22E-4000101
2000 (Aspencade)		
Except California	SC220*YA200001	SC22E-5000101
California	SC221*YA000001	SC22E-5000101
2000 (SE)		
Except California	SC223*YA200001	SC22E-5000101
California	SC224*YA000001	SC22E-5000101

General specifications

Wheelbase
    1988 through 1993 .... 1700 mm (66.9 inches)
    1994 on .... 1690 mm (66.5 inches)
Overall length
    1988 through 1993 .... 2630 mm (103.5 inches)
    1994 on .... 2615 mm (103.0 inches)
Overall width .... 955 mm (37.6 inches)
Overall height
    1988 through 1993 .... 1525 mm (60.0 inches)
    1994 on .... 1495 mm (58.9 inches)
Seat height
    1988 through 1990 .... 770 mm (30.3 inches)
    1991 through 1993
        Aspencade and SE .... 770 mm (30.3 inches)
        Interstate .... 750 mm (29.5 inches)
    1994 on .... 740 mm (29.1 inches)
Ground clearance
    1988 through 1993 .... 135 mm (5.3 inches)
    1994 on .... 115 mm (4.5 inches)
Weight (with oil and full fuel tank)
    1988 and 1989
        US except California .... 390 kg (860 lbs)
        California .... 391 kg (862 lbs)
    1990
        Except SE
            US except California .... 392 kg (864 lbs)
            California .... 393 kg (865 lbs)
        SE
            US except California .... 396 kg (873 lbs)
            California .... 397 kg (875 lbs)
    1991 and 1992
        Interstate
            US except California .... 381 kg (840 lbs)
            California .... 384 kg (845 lbs)
        Aspencade
            US except California .... 398 kg (877 lbs)
            California .... 399 kg (880 lbs)
        SE
            US except California .... 402 kg (884 lbs)
            California .... 403 kg (887 lbs)
    1993 and 1994
        Interstate
            US except California .... 384 kg (847 lbs)
            California .... 385 kg (849 lbs)
        Aspencade
            US except California .... 398 kg (877 lbs)
            California .... 399 kg (880 lbs)
        SE
            US except California .... 404 kg (891 lbs)
            California .... 405 kg (893 lbs)
    1995-on
        Interstate
            US except California .... 385 kg (848 lbs)
            California .... 386 kg (851 lbs)
        Aspencade
            US except California .... 399 kg (880 lbs)
            California .... 400 kg (882 lbs)
        SE
            US except California .... 405 kg (893 lbs)
            California .... 406 kg (895 lbs)

Maintenance techniques, tools and working facilities

Basic maintenance techniques

There are a number of techniques involved in maintenance and repair that will be referred to throughout this manual. Application of these techniques will enable the amateur mechanic to be more efficient, better organized and capable of performing the various tasks properly, which will ensure that the repair job is thorough and complete.

Fastening systems

Fasteners, basically, are nuts, bolts and screws used to hold two or more parts together. There are a few things to keep in mind when working with fasteners. Almost all of them use a locking device of some type (either a lock washer, locknut, locking tab or thread adhesive). All threaded fasteners should be clean, straight, have undamaged threads and undamaged corners on the hex head where the wrench fits. Develop the habit of replacing all damaged nuts and bolts with new ones.

Rusted nuts and bolts should be treated with a penetrating oil to ease removal and prevent breakage. Some mechanics use turpentine in a spout type oil can, which works quite well. After applying the rust penetrant, let it -work for a few minutes before trying to loosen the nut or bolt. Badly rusted fasteners may have to be chiseled off or removed with a special nut breaker, available at tool stores.

If a bolt or stud breaks off in an assembly, it can be drilled out and removed with a special tool called an E-Z out (or screw extractor). Most dealer service departments and motorcycle repair shops can perform this task, as well as others (such as the repair of threaded holes that have been stripped out).

Flat washers and lock washers, when removed from an assembly, should always be replaced exactly as removed. Replace any damaged washers with new ones. Always use a flat washer between a lock washer and any soft metal surface (such as aluminum), thin sheet metal or plastic. Special locknuts can only be used once or twice before they lose their locking ability and must be replaced.

Tightening sequences and procedures

When threaded fasteners are tightened, they are often tightened to a specific torque value (torque is basically a twisting force). Over-tightening the fastener can weaken it and cause it to break, while under-tightening can cause it to eventually come loose. Each bolt, depending on the material it's made of, the diameter of its shank and the material it is threaded into, has a specific torque value, which is noted in the Specifications. Be sure to follow the torque recommendations closely.

Fasteners laid out in a pattern (i.e. cylinder head bolts, engine case bolts, etc.) must be loosened or tightened in a sequence to avoid warping the component. Initially, the bolts/nuts should go on finger tight only. Next, they should be tightened one full turn each, in a criss-cross or diagonal pattern. After each one has been tightened one full turn, return to the first one tightened and tighten them all one half turn, following the same pattern. Finally, tighten each of them one quarter turn at a time until each fastener has been tightened to the proper torque. To loosen and remove the fasteners the procedure would be reversed.

Disassembly sequence

Component disassembly should be done with care and purpose to help ensure that the parts go back together properly during reassembly. Always keep track of the sequence in which parts are removed. Take note of special characteristics or marks on parts that can be installed more than one way (such as a grooved thrust washer on a shaft). It's a good idea to lay the disassembled parts out on a clean surface in the order that they were removed. It may also be help-

ful to make sketches or take instant photos of components before removal.

When removing fasteners from a component, keep track of their locations. Sometimes threading a bolt back in a part, or putting the washers and nut back on a stud, can prevent mix-ups later. If nuts and bolts can't be returned to their original locations, they should be kept in a compartmented box or a series of small boxes. A cupcake or muffin tin is ideal for this purpose, since each cavity can hold the bolts and nuts from a particular area (i.e. engine case bolts, valve cover bolts, engine mount bolts, etc.). A pan of this type is especially helpful when working on assemblies with very small parts (such as the carburetors and the valve train). The cavities can be marked with paint or tape to identify the contents.

Whenever wiring looms, harnesses or connectors are separated, it's a good idea to identify the two halves with numbered pieces of masking tape so they can be easily reconnected.

Gasket sealing surfaces

Throughout any motorcycle, gaskets are used to seal the mating surfaces between components and keep lubricants, fluids, vacuum or pressure contained in an assembly.

Many times these gaskets are coated with a liquid or paste type gasket sealing compound before assembly. Age, heat and pressure can sometimes cause the two parts to stick together so tightly that they are very difficult to separate. In most cases, the part can be loosened by striking it with a soft-faced hammer near the mating surfaces. A regular hammer can be used if a block of wood is placed between the hammer and the part. Do not hammer on cast parts or parts that could be easily damaged. With any particularly stubborn part, always recheck to make sure that every fastener has been removed.

Avoid using a screwdriver or bar to pry apart components, as they can easily mar the gasket sealing surfaces of the parts (which must remain smooth). If prying is absolutely necessary, use a piece of wood, but keep in mind that extra clean-up will be necessary if the wood splinters.

After the parts are separated, the old gasket must be carefully scraped off and the gasket surfaces cleaned. Stubborn gasket material can be soaked with a gasket remover (available in aerosol cans) to soften it so it can be easily scraped off. A scraper can be fashioned from a piece of copper tubing by flattening and sharpening one end. Copper is recommended because it is usually softer than the surfaces to be scraped, which reduces the chance of gouging the part. Some gaskets can be removed with a wire brush, but regardless of the method used, the mating surfaces must be left clean and smooth. If for some reason the gasket surface is gouged, then a gasket sealer thick enough to fill scratches will have to be used during reassembly of the components. For most applications, a non-drying (or semi-drying) gasket sealer is best.

Hose removal tips

Hose removal precautions closely parallel gasket removal precautions. Avoid scratching or gouging the surface that the hose mates against or the connection may leak. Because of various chemical reactions, the rubber in hoses can bond itself to the metal spigot that the hose fits over. To remove a hose, first loosen the hose clamps that secure it to the spigot. Then, with slip joint pliers, grab the hose at the clamp and rotate it around the spigot. Work it back and forth until it is completely free, then pull it off (silicone or other lubricants will ease removal if they can be applied between the hose and the outside of the spigot). Apply the same lubricant to the inside of the hose and the out-side of the spigot to simplify installation.

If a hose clamp is broken or damaged, do not reuse it. Also, do not reuse hoses that are cracked, split or torn.

Spark plug gap adjusting tool

Feeler gauge set

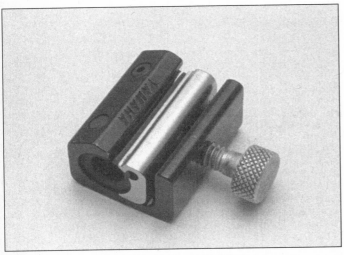

Control cable pressure luber

Hand impact screwdriver and bits

Tools

A selection of good tools is a basic requirement for anyone who plans to maintain and repair a motorcycle. For the owner who has few tools, if any, the initial investment might seem high, but when compared to the spiraling costs of routine maintenance and repair, it is a wise one.

To help the owner decide which tools are needed to perform the tasks detailed in this manual, the following tool lists are offered: *Maintenance and minor repair*, *Repair and overhaul* and *Special*. The newcomer to practical mechanics should start off with the *Maintenance and minor repair* tool kit, which is adequate for the simpler jobs. Then, as confidence and experience grow, the owner can tackle more difficult tasks, buying additional tools as they are needed. Eventually the basic kit will be built into the *Repair and overhaul* tool set. Over a period of time, the experienced do-it-yourselfer will assemble a tool set complete enough for most repair and overhaul procedures and will add tools from the *Special* category when it is felt that the expense is justified by the frequency of use.

Maintenance and minor repair tool kit

The tools in this list should be considered the minimum required for performance of routine maintenance, servicing and minor repair work. We recommend the purchase of combination wrenches (box end and open end combined in one wrench); while more expensive than

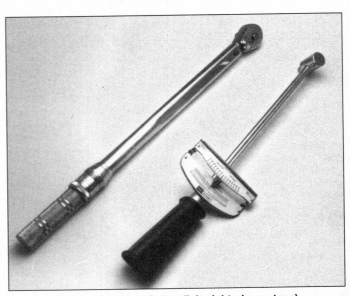

Torque wrenches (left - click; right - beam type)

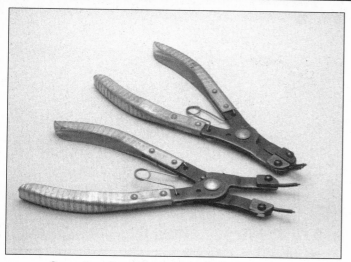

Snap-ring pliers (top - external; bottom - internal)

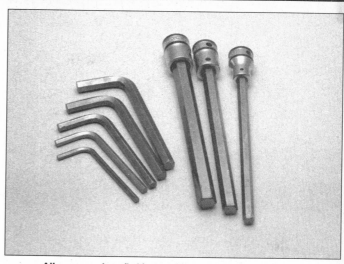

Allen wrenches (left), and Allen head sockets (right)

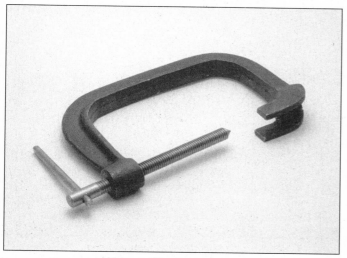

Valve spring compressor

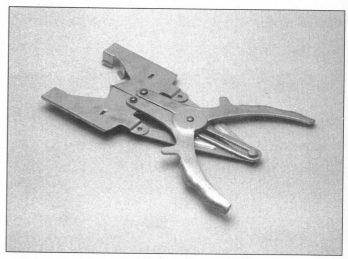

Piston ring removal/installation tool

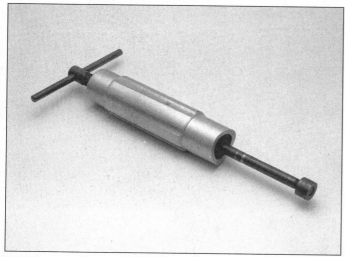

Piston pin puller

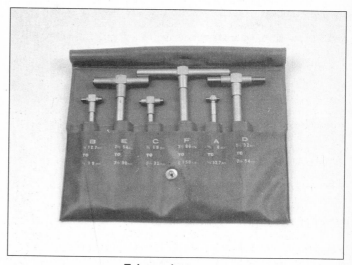

Telescoping gauges

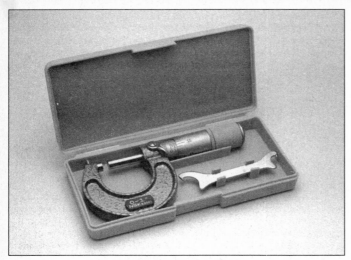

0-to-1 inch micrometer

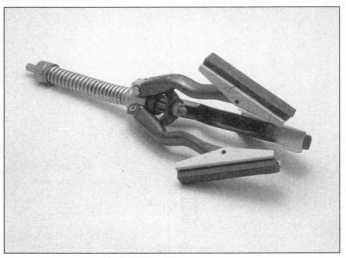

Cylinder surfacing hone

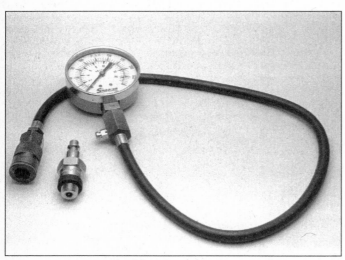

Cylinder compression gauge

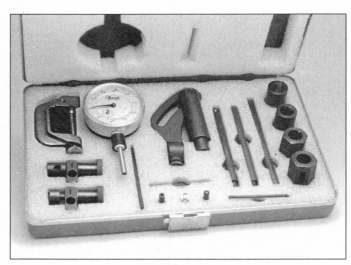

Dial indicator set

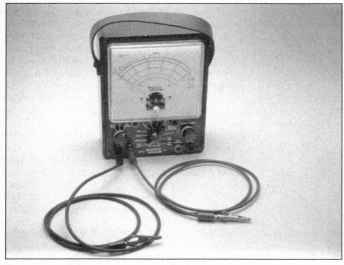

Multimeter (volt/ohm/ammeter)

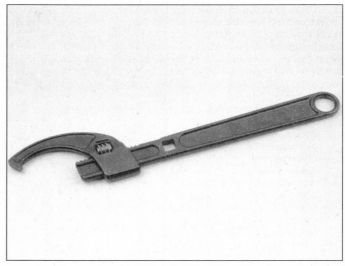

Adjustable spanner

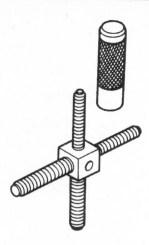

Alternator rotor puller

open-ended ones, they offer the advantages of both types of wrench.

>   Combination wrench set (6 mm to 22 mm)
>   Adjustable wrench - 8 in
>   Spark plug socket (with rubber insert)
>   Spark plug gap adjusting tool
>   Feeler gauge set
>   Standard screwdriver (5/16 in x 6 in)
>   Phillips screwdriver (No. 2 x 6 in)
>   Allen (hex) wrench set (4 mm to 12 mm)
>   Combination (slip-joint) pliers - 6 in
>   Hacksaw and assortment of blades
>   Tire pressure gauge
>   Control cable pressure luber
>   Grease gun
>   Oil can
>   Fine emery cloth
>   Wire brush
>   Hand impact screwdriver and bits
>   Funnel (medium size)
>   Safety goggles
>   Drain pan
>   Work light with extension cord

Repair and overhaul tool set

These tools are essential for anyone who plans to perform major repairs and are intended to supplement those in the Maintenance and minor repair tool kit. Included is a comprehensive set of sockets which, though expensive, are invaluable because of their versatility (especially when various extensions and drives are available). We recommend the 3/8 inch drive over the 1/2 inch drive for general motorcycle maintenance and repair (ideally, the mechanic would have a 3/8 inch drive set and a 1/2 inch drive set).

>   Alternator rotor removal tool
>   Socket set(s)
>   Reversible ratchet
>   Extension - 6 in
>   Universal joint
>   Torque wrench (same size drive as sockets)
>   Ball pein hammer - 8 oz
>   Soft-faced hammer (plastic/rubber)
>   Standard screwdriver (1/4 in x 6 in)
>   Standard screwdriver (stubby - 5/16 in)
>   Phillips screwdriver (No. 3 x 8 in)
>   Phillips screwdriver (stubby - No. 2)
>   Pliers - locking
>   Pliers - lineman's

>   Pliers - needle nose
>   Pliers - snap-ring (internal and external)
>   Cold chisel - 1/2 in
>   Scriber
>   Scraper (made from flattened copper tubing)
>   Center punch
>   Pin punches (1/16, 1/8, 3/16 in)
>   Steel rule/straightedge - 12 in
>   Pin-type spanner wrench
>   A selection of files
>   Wire brush (large)

Note: Another tool which is often useful is an electric drill with a chuck capacity of 3/8 inch (and a set of good quality drill bits).

Special tools

The tools in this list include those which are not used regularly, are expensive to buy, or which need to be used in accordance with their manufacturer's instructions. Unless these tools will be used frequently, it is not very economical to purchase many of them. A consideration would be to split the cost and use between yourself and a friend or friends (i.e. members of a motorcycle club).

This list primarily contains tools and instruments widely available to the public, as well as some special tools produced by the vehicle manufacturer for distribution to dealer service departments. As a result, references to the manufacturer's special tools are occasionally included in the text of this manual. Generally, an alternative method of doing the job without the special tool is offered. However, sometimes there is no alternative to their use. Where this is the case, and the tool can't be purchased or borrowed, the work should be turned over to the dealer service department or a motorcycle repair shop.

>   Paddock stand (for models not fitted with a centerstand)
>   Valve spring compressor
>   Piston ring removal and installation tool
>   Piston pin puller
>   Telescoping gauges
>   Micrometer(s) and/or dial/Vernier calipers
>   Cylinder surfacing hone
>   Cylinder compression gauge
>   Dial indicator set
>   Multimeter
>   Adjustable spanner
>   Manometer or vacuum gauge set
>   Small air compressor with blow gun and tire chuck

Buying tools

For the do-it-yourselfer who is just starting to get involved in motorcycle maintenance and repair, there are a number of options available when purchasing tools. If maintenance and minor repair is the extent of the work to be done, the purchase of individual tools is satisfactory. If, on the other hand, extensive work is planned, it would be a good idea to purchase a modest tool set from one of the large retail chain stores. A set can usually be bought at a substantial savings over the individual tool prices (and they often come with a tool box). As additional tools are needed, add-on sets, individual tools and a larger tool box can be purchased to expand the tool selection. Building a tool set gradually allows the cost of the tools to be spread over a longer period of time and gives the mechanic the freedom to choose only those tools that will actually be used.

Tool stores and motorcycle dealers will often be the only source of some of the special tools that are needed, but regardless of where tools are bought, try to avoid cheap ones (especially when buying screwdrivers and sockets) because they won't last very long. There are plenty of tools around at reasonable prices, but always aim to purchase items which meet the relevant national safety standards. The expense involved in replacing cheap tools will eventually be greater than the initial cost of quality tools.

It is obviously not possible to cover the subject of tools fully here. For those who wish to learn more about tools and their use, there is a book entitled *Motorcycle Workshop Practice Manual* (Book no. 1454) available from the publishers of this manual. It also provides an introduction to basic workshop practice which will be of interest to a home mechanic working on any type of motorcycle.

Care and maintenance of tools

Good tools are expensive, so it makes sense to treat them with respect. Keep them clean and in usable condition and store them properly when not in use. Always wipe off any dirt, grease or metal chips before putting them away. Never leave tools lying around in the work area.

Some tools, such as screwdrivers, pliers, wrenches and sockets, can be hung on a panel mounted on the garage or workshop wall, while others should be kept in a tool box or tray. Measuring instruments, gauges, meters, etc. must be carefully stored where they can't be damaged by weather or impact from other tools.

When tools are used with care and stored properly, they will last a very long time. Even with the best of care, tools will wear out if used frequently. When a tool is damaged or worn out, replace it; subsequent jobs will be safer and more enjoyable if you do.

Working facilities

Not to be overlooked when discussing tools is the workshop. If anything more than routine maintenance is to be carried out, some sort of suitable work area is essential.

It is understood, and appreciated, that many home mechanics do not have a good workshop or garage available and end up removing an engine or doing major repairs outside (it is recommended, however, that the overhaul or repair be completed under the cover of a roof).

A clean, flat workbench or table of comfortable working height is an absolute necessity. The workbench should be equipped with a vise that has a jaw opening of at least four inches.

As mentioned previously, some clean, dry storage space is also required for tools, as well as the lubricants, fluids, cleaning solvents, etc. which soon become necessary.

Sometimes waste oil and fluids, drained from the engine or cooling system during normal maintenance or repairs, present a disposal problem. To avoid pouring them on the ground or into a sewage system, simply pour the used fluids into large containers, seal them with caps and take them to an authorized disposal site or service station. Plastic jugs (such as old antifreeze containers) are ideal for this purpose.

Always keep a supply of old newspapers and clean rags available. Old towels are excellent for mopping up spills. Many mechanics use rolls of paper towels for most work because they are readily available and disposable. To help keep the area under the motorcycle clean, a large cardboard box can be cut open and flattened to protect the garage or shop floor.

Whenever working over a painted surface (such as the fuel tank) cover it with an old blanket or bedspread to protect the finish.

Safety first!

Professional mechanics are trained in safe working procedures. However enthusiastic you may be about getting on with the job at hand, take the time to ensure that your safety is not put at risk. A moment's lack of attention can result in an accident, as can failure to observe simple precautions.

There will always be new ways of having accidents, and the following is not a comprehensive list of all dangers; it is intended rather to make you aware of the risks and to encourage a safe approach to all work you carry out on your bike.

Essential DOs and DON'Ts

DON'T start the engine without first ascertaining that the transmission is in neutral.

DON'T suddenly remove the pressure cap from a hot cooling system - cover it with a cloth and release the pressure gradually first, or you may get scalded by escaping coolant.

DON'T attempt to drain oil until you are sure it has cooled sufficiently to avoid scalding you.

DON'T grasp any part of the engine or exhaust system without first ascertaining that it is cool enough not to burn you.

DON'T allow brake fluid or antifreeze to contact the machine's paint work or plastic components.

DON'T siphon toxic liquids such as fuel, hydraulic fluid or antifreeze by mouth, or allow them to remain on your skin.

DON'T inhale dust - it may be injurious to health (see *Asbestos* heading).

DON'T allow any spilled oil or grease to remain on the floor - wipe it up right away, before someone slips on it.

DON'T use ill fitting wrenches or other tools which may slip and cause injury.

DON'T attempt to lift a heavy component which may be beyond your capability - get assistance.

DON'T rush to finish a job or take unverified short cuts.

DON'T allow children or animals in or around an unattended vehicle.

DON'T inflate a tire to a pressure above the recommended maximum. Apart from over stressing the carcase and wheel rim, in extreme cases the tire may blow off forcibly.

DO ensure that the machine is supported securely at all times. This is especially important when the machine is blocked up to aid wheel or fork removal.

DO take care when attempting to loosen a stubborn nut or bolt. It is generally better to pull on a wrench, rather than push, so that if you slip, you fall away from the machine rather than onto it.

DO wear eye protection when using power tools such as drill, sander, bench grinder etc.

DO use a barrier cream on your hands prior to undertaking dirty jobs - it will protect your skin from infection as well as making the dirt easier to remove afterwards; but make sure your hands aren't left slippery. Note that long-term contact with used engine oil can be a health hazard.

DO keep loose clothing (cuffs, ties etc. and long hair) well out of the way of moving mechanical parts.

DO remove rings, wristwatch etc., before working on the vehicle - especially the electrical system.

DO keep your work area tidy - it is only too easy to fall over articles left lying around.

DO exercise caution when compressing springs for removal or installation. Ensure that the tension is applied and released in a controlled manner, using suitable tools which preclude the possibility of the spring escaping violently.

DO ensure that any lifting tackle used has a safe working load rating adequate for the job.

DO get someone to check periodically that all is well, when working alone on the vehicle.

DO carry out work in a logical sequence and check that everything is correctly assembled and tightened afterwards.

DO remember that your vehicle's safety affects that of yourself and others. If in doubt on any point, get professional advice.

IF, in spite of following these precautions, you are unfortunate enough to injure yourself, seek medical attention as soon as possible.

Asbestos

Certain friction, insulating, sealing and other products - such as brake pads, clutch linings, gaskets, etc. - contain asbestos. *Extreme care must be taken to avoid inhalation of dust from such products since it is hazardous to health*. If in doubt, assume that they *do* contain asbestos.

Fire

Remember at all times that gasoline (petrol) is highly flammable. Never smoke or have any kind of naked flame around, when working on the vehicle. But the risk does not end there - a spark caused by an electrical short-circuit, by two metal surfaces contacting each other, by careless use of tools, or even by static electricity built up in your body under certain conditions, can ignite gasoline (petrol) vapor, which in a confined space is highly explosive. Never use gasoline (petrol) as a cleaning solvent. Use an approved safety solvent.

Always disconnect the battery ground (earth) terminal before working on any part of the fuel or electrical system, and never risk spilling fuel on to a hot engine or exhaust.

It is recommended that a fire extinguisher of a type suitable for fuel and electrical fires is kept handy in the garage or workplace at all times. Never try to extinguish a fuel or electrical fire with water.

Fumes

Certain fumes are highly toxic and can quickly cause unconsciousness and even death if inhaled to any extent. Gasoline (petrol) vapor comes into this category, as do the vapors from certain solvents such as trichloroethylene. Any draining or pouring of such volatile fluids should be done in a well ventilated area.

When using cleaning fluids and solvents, read the instructions carefully. Never use materials from unmarked containers - they may give off poisonous vapors.

Never run the engine of a motor vehicle in an enclosed space such as a garage. Exhaust fumes contain carbon monoxide which is extremely poisonous; if you need to run the engine, always do so in the open air or at least have the rear of the vehicle outside the workplace.

The battery

Never cause a spark, or allow a naked light near the vehicle's battery. It will normally be giving off a certain amount of hydrogen gas, which is highly explosive.

Always disconnect the battery ground (earth) terminal before working on the fuel or electrical systems (except where noted).

If possible, loosen the filler plugs or cover when charging the battery from an external source. Do not charge at an excessive rate or the battery may burst.

Take care when topping up, cleaning or carrying the battery. The acid electrolyte, even when diluted, is very corrosive and should not be allowed to contact the eyes or skin. Always wear rubber gloves and goggles or a face shield. If you ever need to prepare electrolyte yourself, always add the acid slowly to the water; never add the water to the acid.

Electricity

When using an electric power tool, inspection light etc., always ensure that the appliance is correctly connected to its plug and that, where necessary, it is properly grounded (earthed). Do not use such appliances in damp conditions and, again, beware of creating a spark or applying excessive heat in the vicinity of fuel or fuel vapor. Also ensure that the appliances meet national safety standards.

A severe electric shock can result from touching certain parts of the electrical system, such as the spark plug wires (HT leads), when the engine is running or being cranked, particularly if components are damp or the insulation is defective. Where an electronic ignition system is used, the secondary (HT) voltage is much higher and could prove fatal.

Motorcycle chemicals and lubricants

A number of chemicals and lubricants are available for use in motorcycle maintenance and repair. They include a wide variety of products ranging from cleaning solvents and degreasers to lubricants and protective sprays for rubber, plastic and vinyl.

Contact point/spark plug cleaner is a solvent used to clean oily film and dirt from points, grime from electrical connectors and oil deposits from spark plugs. It is oil free and leaves no residue. It can also be used to remove gum and varnish from carburetor jets and other orifices.

Carburetor cleaner is similar to contact point/spark plug cleaner but it usually has a stronger solvent and may leave a slight oily reside. It is not recommended for cleaning electrical components or connections.

Brake system cleaner is used to remove grease or brake fluid from brake system components (where clean surfaces are absolutely necessary and petroleum-based solvents cannot be used); it also leaves no residue.

Silicone-based lubricants are used to protect rubber parts such as hoses and grommets, and are used as lubricants for hinges and locks.

Multi-purpose grease is an all purpose lubricant used wherever grease is more practical than a liquid lubricant such as oil. Some multi-purpose grease is colored white and specially formulated to be more resistant to water than ordinary grease.

Gear oil (sometimes called gear lube) is a specially designed oil used in transmissions and final drive units, as well as other areas where high-friction, high-temperature lubrication is required. It is available in a number of viscosities (weights) for various applications.

Motor oil, of course, is the lubricant specially formulated for use in the engine. It normally contains a wide variety of additives to prevent corrosion and reduce foaming and wear. Motor oil comes in various weights (viscosity ratings) of from 5 to 80. The recommended weight of the oil depends on the seasonal temperature and the demands on the engine. Light oil is used in cold climates and under light load conditions; heavy oil is used in hot climates and where high loads are encountered. Multi-viscosity oils are designed to have characteristics of both light and heavy oils and are available in a number of weights from 5W-20 to 20W-50.

Gas (petrol) additives perform several functions, depending on their chemical makeup. They usually contain solvents that help dissolve gum and varnish that build up on carburetor and intake parts. They also serve to break down carbon deposits that form on the inside surfaces of the combustion chambers. Some additives contain upper cylinder lubricants for valves and piston rings.

Brake fluid is a specially formulated hydraulic fluid that can withstand the heat and pressure encountered in brake systems. Care must be taken that this fluid does not come in contact with painted surfaces or plastics. An opened container should always be resealed to prevent contamination by water or dirt.

Chain lubricants are formulated especially for use on motorcycle final drive chains. A good chain lube should adhere well and have good penetrating qualities to be effective as a lubricant inside the chain and on the side plates, pins and rollers. Most chain lubes are either the foaming type or quick drying type and are usually marketed as sprays.

Degreasers are heavy duty solvents used to remove grease and grime that may accumulate on engine and frame components. They can be sprayed or brushed on and, depending on the type, are rinsed with either water or solvent.

Solvents are used alone or in combination with degreasers to clean parts and assemblies during repair and overhaul. The home mechanic should use only solvents that are non-flammable and that do not produce irritating fumes.

Gasket sealing compounds may be used in conjunction with gaskets, to improve their sealing capabilities, or alone, to seal metal-to-metal joints. Many gasket sealers can withstand extreme heat, some are impervious to gasoline and lubricants, while others are capable of filling and sealing large cavities. Depending on the intended use, gasket sealers either dry hard or stay relatively soft and pliable. They are usually applied by hand, with a brush, or are sprayed on the gasket sealing surfaces.

Thread cement is an adhesive locking compound that prevents threaded fasteners from loosening because of vibration. It is available in a variety of types for different applications.

Moisture dispersants are usually sprays that can be used to dry out electrical components such as the fuse block and wiring connectors. Some types can also be used as treatment for rubber and as a lubricant for hinges, cables and locks.

Waxes and polishes are used to help protect painted and plated surfaces from the weather. Different types of paint may require the use of different types of wax polish. Some polishes utilize a chemical or abrasive cleaner to help remove the top layer of oxidized (dull) paint on older vehicles. In recent years, many non-wax polishes (that contain a wide variety of chemicals such as polymers and silicones) have been introduced. These non-wax polishes are usually easier to apply and last longer than conventional waxes and polishes.

Troubleshooting

Contents

Engine doesn't start or is difficult to start

1 Starter motor does not rotate

1   Engine kill switch Off.
2   Fuse blown. Check fuse block (Chapter 9).
3   Battery voltage low. Check and recharge battery (Chapter 9).
4   Starter motor defective. Make sure the wiring to the starter is secure. Make sure the starter relay clicks when the start button is pushed. If the relay clicks, then the fault is in the wiring or motor.
5   Starter relay faulty. Check it according to the procedure in Chapter 9.
6   Starter button not contacting. The contacts could be wet, corroded or dirty. Disassemble and clean the switch (Chapter 9).
7   Wiring open or shorted. Check all wiring connections and harnesses to make sure that they are dry, tight and not corroded. Also check for broken or frayed wires that can cause a short to ground (see wiring diagram, Chapter 9).
8   Ignition switch defective. Check the switch according to the procedure in Chapter 9. Replace the switch with a new one if it is defective.
9   Engine kill switch defective. Check for wet, dirty or corroded contacts. Clean or replace the switch as necessary (Chapter 9).
10   Faulty starter lockout circuit. Check the wiring and the switch itself according to the procedures in Chapter 9.

2 Starter motor rotates but engine does not turn over

1   Starter motor clutch defective. Inspect and repair or replace (Chapter 2).
2   Damaged idler or starter gears. Inspect and replace the damaged parts (Chapter 2).

3 Starter works but engine won't turn over (seized)

Seized engine caused by one or more internally damaged components. Failure due to wear, abuse or lack of lubrication. Damage can include seized valves, valve lifters, camshaft, pistons, crankshaft, connecting rod bearings, or transmission gears or bearings. Refer to Chapter 2 for engine disassembly.

4 No fuel flow

1   No fuel in tank.
2   Fuel tap in off position.
3   Tank cap air vent obstructed. Usually caused by dirt or water. Remove it and clean the cap vent hole.
4   Inline fuel filter clogged. Replace the filter (Chapter 1).
6   Electric fuel pump not working. Test it according to the procedures in Chapter 4.
7   Fuel line clogged. Pull the fuel line loose and carefully blow through it.
8   Inlet needle valve clogged. For all of the valves to be clogged, either a very bad batch of fuel with an unusual additive has been used, or some other foreign material has entered the tank. Many times after a machine has been stored for many months without running, the fuel turns to a varnish-like liquid and forms deposits on the inlet needle valves and jets. The carburetors should be removed and overhauled if draining the float bowls doesn't solve the problem.

5 Engine flooded

1   Float level too high. Check and adjust as described in Chapter 4.

2   Inlet needle valve worn or stuck open. A piece of dirt, rust or other debris can cause the inlet needle to seat improperly, causing excess fuel to be admitted to the float bowl. In this case, the float chamber should be cleaned and the needle and seat inspected. If the needle and seat are worn, then the leaking will persist and the parts should be replaced with new ones (Chapter 4).
3   Starting technique incorrect. Under normal circumstances (i.e., if all the carburetor functions are sound) the machine should start with little or no throttle. When the engine is cold, the choke should be operated and the engine started without opening the throttle. When the engine is at operating temperature, only a very slight amount of throttle should be necessary. If the engine is flooded, turn the fuel tap off and hold the throttle open while cranking the engine. This will allow additional air to reach the cylinders. Remember to turn the fuel tap back on after the engine starts.

6 No spark or weak spark

1   Ignition switch Off.
2   Engine kill switch turned to the Off position.
3   Battery voltage low. Check and recharge battery as necessary (Chapter 9).
4   Spark plug dirty, defective or worn out. Locate reason for fouled plug(s) using spark plug condition chart and follow the plug maintenance procedures in Chapter 1.
5   Spark plug cap or secondary (HT) wiring faulty. Check condition. Replace either or both components if cracks or deterioration are evident (Chapter 5).
6   Spark plug cap not making good contact. Make sure that the plug cap fits snugly over the plug end.
7   ECM defective. Check the unit, referring to Chapter 5 for details.
8   Pulse generator(s) defective. Check the unit, referring to Chapter 5 for details.
9   Ignition coil(s) defective. Check the coils, referring to Chapter 5.
10   Ignition or kill switch shorted. This is usually caused by water, corrosion, damage or excessive wear. The switches can be disassembled and cleaned with electrical contact cleaner. If cleaning does not help, replace the switches (Chapter 9).
11   Wiring shorted or broken between:
   a)   *Ignition switch and engine kill switch (or blown fuse)*
   b)   *ECM and engine kill switch*
   c)   *ECM and ignition coil*
   d)   *Ignition coil and plug*
   e)   *ECM and pulse generator*
   Make sure that all wiring connections are clean, dry and tight. Look for chafed and broken wires (Chapters 5 and 9).
12   Bank angle sensor defective (Chapter 9).

7 Compression low

1   Spark plug loose. Remove the plug and inspect the threads. Reinstall and tighten to the specified torque (Chapter 1).
2   Cylinder head not sufficiently tightened down. If the cylinder head is suspected of being loose, then there's a chance that the gasket or head is damaged if the problem has persisted for any length of time. The head bolts should be tightened to the proper torque in the correct sequence (Chapter 2).
3   Improper valve clearance. This means that the valve is not closing completely and compression pressure is leaking past the valve. Inspect the hydraulic valve lifters and rocker assemblies (Chapter 1).
4   Cylinder and/or piston worn. Excessive wear will cause compression pressure to leak past the rings. This is usually accompanied by worn rings as well. A top end overhaul is necessary (Chapter 2).
5   Piston rings worn, weak, broken, or sticking. Broken or sticking piston rings usually indicate a lubrication or carburetion problem that causes excess carbon deposits or seizures to form on the pistons and rings. Top end overhaul is necessary (Chapter 2).

6   Piston ring-to-groove clearance excessive. This is caused by excessive wear of the piston ring lands. Piston replacement is necessary (Chapter 2).

7   Cylinder head gasket damaged. If the head is allowed to become loose, or if excessive carbon build-up on the piston crown and combustion chamber causes extremely high compression, the head gasket may leak. Retorquing the head is not always sufficient to restore the seal, so gasket replacement is necessary (Chapter 2).

8   Cylinder head warped. This is caused by overheating or improperly tightened head bolts. Machine shop resurfacing or head replacement is necessary (Chapter 2).

9   Valve spring broken or weak. Caused by component failure or wear; the spring(s) must be replaced (Chapter 2).

10 Valve not seating properly. This is caused by a bent valve (from over-revving or improper valve adjustment), burned valve or seat (improper carburetion) or an accumulation of carbon deposits on the seat (from carburetion or lubrication problems). The valves must be cleaned and/or replaced and the seats serviced if possible (Chapter 2).

8   Stalls after starting

1   Improper choke action. Make sure the choke rod is getting a full stroke and staying in the out position.

2   Ignition malfunction. See Chapter 5.

3   Carburetor malfunction. See Chapter 6.

4   Fuel contaminated. The fuel can be contaminated with either dirt or water, or can change chemically if the machine is allowed to sit for several months or more. Drain the tank and float bowls (Chapter 4).

5   Intake air leak. Check for loose carburetor-to-intake manifold connections, loose or missing vacuum gauge access port cap or hose, or loose carburetor top (Chapter 4).

6   Engine idle speed incorrect. Turn throttle stop screw until the engine idles at the specified rpm (Chapter 1).

9   Rough idle

1   Ignition malfunction. See Chapter 5.

2   Idle speed incorrect. See Chapter 1.

3   Carburetors not synchronized. Adjust carburetors with vacuum gauge or manometer set as described in Chapter 1.

4   Carburetor malfunction. See Chapter 4.

5   Fuel contaminated. The fuel can be contaminated with either dirt or water, or can change chemically if the machine is allowed to sit for several months or more. Drain the tank and float bowls (Chapter 5).

6   Intake air leak. Check for loose carburetor-to-intake manifold connections, loose or missing vacuum gauge access port cap or hose, or loose carburetor top (Chapter 4).

7   Air cleaner clogged. Service or replace air filter element (Chapter 1).

Poor running at low speed

10 Spark weak

1   Battery voltage low. Check and recharge battery (Chapter 9).

2   Spark plug fouled, defective or worn out. Refer to Chapter 1 for spark plug maintenance.

3   Spark plug cap or high tension wiring defective. Refer to Chapters 1 and 5 for details on the ignition system.

4   Spark plug cap not making contact.

5   Incorrect spark plug. Wrong type, heat range or cap configuration. Check and install correct plugs listed in Chapter 1. A cold plug or one with a recessed firing electrode will not operate at low speeds without fouling.

6   ECM defective. See Chapter 5.

7   Pulse generator defective. See Chapter 5.

8   Ignition coil(s) defective. See Chapter 5.

11 Fuel/air mixture incorrect

1   Pilot screw(s) out of adjustment (Chapters 1 and 4).

2   Pilot jet or air passage clogged. Remove and overhaul the carburetors (Chapter 4).

3   Air bleed holes clogged. Remove carburetor and blow out all passages (Chapter 4).

4   Air cleaner clogged, poorly sealed or missing.

5   Air cleaner-to-carburetor boot poorly sealed. Look for cracks, holes or loose clamps and replace or repair defective parts.

6   Fuel level too high or too low. Adjust the floats (Chapter 4).

7   Fuel tank air vent obstructed. Make sure that the air vent passage in the filler cap is open.

8   Carburetor intake manifolds loose. Check for cracks, breaks, tears or loose clamps or bolts. Repair or replace the rubber boots.

12 Compression low

1   Spark plug loose. Remove the plug and inspect the threads. Reinstall and tighten to the specified torque (Chapter 1).

2   Cylinder head not sufficiently tightened down. If the cylinder head is suspected of being loose, then there's a chance that the gasket and head are damaged if the problem has persisted for any length of time. The head bolts should be tightened to the proper torque in the correct sequence (Chapter 2).

3   Improper valve clearance. This means that the valve is not closing completely and compression pressure is leaking past the valve. Inspect the hydraulic lifters and rocker assemblies (Chapter 1).

4   Cylinder and/or piston worn. Excessive wear will cause compression pressure to leak past the rings. This is usually accompanied by worn rings as well. A top end overhaul is necessary (Chapter 2).

5   Piston rings worn, weak, broken, or sticking. Broken or sticking piston rings usually indicate a lubrication or carburetion problem that causes excess carbon deposits or seizures to form on the pistons and rings. Top end overhaul is necessary (Chapter 2).

6   Piston ring-to-groove clearance excessive. This is caused by excessive wear of the piston ring lands. Piston replacement is necessary (Chapter 2).

7   Cylinder head gasket damaged. If the head is allowed to become loose, or if excessive carbon build-up on the piston crown and combustion chamber causes extremely high compression, the head gasket may leak. Retorquing the head is not always sufficient to restore the seal, so gasket replacement is necessary (Chapter 2).

8   Cylinder head warped. This is caused by overheating or improperly tightened head bolts. Machine shop resurfacing or head replacement is necessary (Chapter 2).

9   Valve spring broken or weak. Caused by component failure or wear; the spring(s) must be replaced (Chapter 2).

10 Valve not seating properly. This is caused by a bent valve (from over-revving or improper valve adjustment), burned valve or seat (improper carburetion) or an accumulation of carbon deposits on the seat (from carburetion, lubrication problems). The valves must be cleaned and/or replaced and the seats serviced if possible (Chapter 2).

13 Poor acceleration

1   Carburetors leaking or dirty. Overhaul the carburetors (Chapter 5).

2   Timing not advancing. The pulse generator(s) or the ECM may be defective. If so, they must be replaced with new ones, as they can't be repaired.

3   Carburetors not synchronized. Adjust them with a vacuum gauge set or manometer (Chapter 1).

4   Engine oil viscosity too high. Using a heavier oil than that recommended in Chapter 1 can damage the oil pumps or lubrication system and cause drag on the engine.

5   Brakes dragging. Usually caused by debris which has entered the brake piston sealing boot, or from a warped disc or bent axle. Repair as necessary (Chapter 7).

Poor running or no power at high speed

14   Firing incorrect

1   Air filter restricted. Clean or replace filter (Chapter 1).

2   Spark plug fouled, defective or worn out. See Chapter 1 for spark plug maintenance.

3   Spark plug cap or secondary (HT) wiring defective. See Chapters 1 and 5 for details of the ignition system.

4   Spark plug cap not in good contact. See Chapter 5.

5   Incorrect spark plug. Wrong type, heat range or cap configuration. Check and install correct plugs listed in Chapter 1. A cold plug or one with a recessed firing electrode will not operate at low speeds without fouling.

6   ECM defective. See Chapter 5.

7   Ignition coil(s) defective. See Chapter 5.

15   Fuel/air mixture incorrect

1   Main jet clogged. Dirt, water or other contaminants can clog the main jets. Replace the fuel filter and clean the float bowl area, and the jets and carburetor orifices (Chapter 4).

2   Main jet wrong size. The standard jetting is for sea level atmospheric pressure and oxygen content.

3   Throttle shaft-to-carburetor body clearance excessive. Refer to Chapter 4 for inspection and part replacement procedures.

4   Air bleed holes clogged. Remove and overhaul carburetors (Chapter 4).

5   Air filter clogged, poorly sealed, or missing.

6   Air filter-to-carburetor boot poorly sealed. Look for cracks, holes or loose clamps, and replace or repair defective parts.

7   Fuel level too high or too low. Adjust the float(s) (Chapter 4).

8   Fuel tank air vent obstructed. Make sure the air vent passage in the filler cap is open.

9   Carburetor intake manifolds loose. Check for cracks, breaks, tears or loose clamps or bolts. Repair or replace the rubber boots (Chapter 4).

10   Fuel tap clogged. Remove the tap and clean it (Chapter 4).

11   Fuel line clogged. Pull the fuel line loose and carefully blow through it.

12   Fuel filter clogged. Replace it.

16   Compression low

1   Spark plug loose. Remove the plug and inspect the threads. Reinstall and tighten to the specified torque (Chapter 1).

2   Cylinder head not sufficiently tightened down. If the cylinder head is suspected of being loose, then there's a chance that the gasket and head are damaged if the problem has persisted for any length of time. The head bolts should be tightened to the proper torque in the correct sequence (Chapter 2).

3   Improper valve clearance. This means that the valve is not closing completely and compression pressure is leaking past the valve. Inspect the hydraulic valve lifters and rocker assemblies (Chapter 2).

4   Cylinder and/or piston worn. Excessive wear will cause compression pressure to leak past the rings. This is usually accompanied by worn rings as well. A top end overhaul is necessary (Chapter 2).

5   Piston rings worn, weak, broken, or sticking. Broken or sticking piston rings usually indicate a lubrication or carburetion problem that causes excess carbon deposits or seizures to form on the pistons and rings. Top end overhaul is necessary (Chapter 2).

6   Piston ring-to-groove clearance excessive. This is caused by excessive wear of the piston ring lands. Piston replacement is necessary (Chapter 2).

7   Cylinder head gasket damaged. If the head is allowed to become loose, or if excessive carbon build-up on the piston crown and combustion chamber causes extremely high compression, the head gasket may leak. Retorquing the head is not always sufficient to restore the seal, so gasket replacement is necessary (Chapter 2).

8   Cylinder head warped. This is caused by overheating or improperly tightened head bolts. Machine shop resurfacing or head replacement is necessary (Chapter 2).

9   Valve spring broken or weak. Caused by component failure or wear; the spring(s) must be replaced (Chapter 2).

10   Valve not seating properly. This is caused by a bent valve (from over-revving or improper valve adjustment), burned valve or seat (improper carburetion) or an accumulation of carbon deposits on the seat (from carburetion or lubrication problems). The valves must be cleaned and/or replaced and the seats serviced if possible (Chapter 2).

17   Knocking or pinging

1   Carbon build-up in combustion chamber. Use of a fuel additive that will dissolve the adhesive bonding the carbon particles to the crown and chamber is the easiest way to remove the build-up. Otherwise, the cylinder head will have to be removed and decarbonized (Chapter 2).

2   Incorrect or poor quality fuel. Old or improper grades of fuel can cause detonation. This causes the piston to rattle, thus the knocking or pinging sound. Drain old fuel and always use the recommended fuel grade.

3   Spark plug heat range incorrect. Uncontrolled detonation indicates the plug heat range is too hot. The plug in effect becomes a glow plug, raising cylinder temperatures. Install the proper heat range plug (Chapter 1).

4   Improper air/fuel mixture. This will cause the cylinder to run hot, which leads to detonation. Clogged jets or an air leak can cause this imbalance. See Chapter 4.

18   Miscellaneous causes

1   Throttle valve doesn't open fully. Adjust the cable slack (Chapter 1).

2   Clutch slipping. May be caused by loose or worn clutch components. Refer to Chapter 2 for clutch component replacement.

3   Timing not advancing.

4   Engine oil viscosity too high. Using a heavier oil than the one recommended in Chapter 1 can damage the oil pump or lubrication system and cause drag on the engine.

5   Brakes dragging. Usually caused by debris which has entered the brake piston sealing boot, or from a warped disc or bent axle. Repair as necessary.

Overheating

19   Engine overheats

1   Coolant level low. Check coolant level as described in Chapter 1. If coolant level is low, the engine will overheat.

2   Leak in cooling system. Check cooling system hoses and radiator for leaks and other damage. Repair or replace parts as necessary

(Chapter 3).

3   Thermostat stuck closed. Check and replace as described in Chapter 3.

4   Faulty radiator cap. Remove the cap and have it pressure checked.

5   Coolant passages clogged. Drain and flush the entire system, then refill with new coolant.

6   Water pump defective. Remove the pump and check the components.

7   Clogged radiator fins. Clean them by blowing compressed air through the fins from the back side.

8   Engine oil level low. Check and add oil (Chapter 1).

9   Wrong type of oil. If you're not sure what type of oil is in the engine, drain it and fill with the correct type (Chapter 1).

10   Air leak at carburetor intake manifold. Check and tighten or replace as necessary (Chapter 4).

11   Float level low. Check and adjust if necessary (Chapter 4).

12   Worn oil pump or clogged oil passages. Check oil pressure (Chapter 2). Replace pump or clean passages as necessary.

13   Clogged oil lines. Remove and check for foreign material (see Chapter 2).

14   Carbon build-up in combustion chambers. Use of a fuel additive that will dissolve the adhesive bonding the carbon particles to the piston crowns and chambers is the easiest way to remove the build-up. Otherwise, the cylinder head will have to be removed and decarbonized (Chapter 2).

20   Firing incorrect

1   Spark plug fouled, defective or worn out. See Chapter 1 for spark plug maintenance.

2   Incorrect spark plug (see Chapter 1).

3   Faulty ignition coil(s) (Chapter 5).

21   Fuel/air mixture incorrect

1   Main jet clogged. Dirt, water and other contaminants can clog the main jets. Clean the fuel tap filter, the float bowl area and the jets and carburetor orifices (Chapter 4).

2   Main jet wrong size. The standard jetting is for sea level atmospheric pressure and oxygen content.

3   Air filter poorly sealed or missing.

4   Air filter-to-carburetor boot poorly sealed. Look for cracks, holes or loose clamps and replace or repair.

5   Fuel level too low. Adjust the float(s) (Chapter 4).

6   Fuel tank air vent obstructed. Make sure that the air vent passage in the filler cap is open.

7   Carburetor intake manifold loose. Check for cracks, breaks, tears or loose fasteners. Replace the gaskets (Chapter 4).

22   Compression too high

1   Carbon build-up in combustion chamber. Use of a fuel additive that will dissolve the adhesive bonding the carbon particles to the piston crown and chamber is the easiest way to remove the build-up. Otherwise, the cylinder head will have to be removed and decarbonized (Chapter 2).

2   Improperly machined head surface or installation of incorrect gasket during engine assembly.

23   Engine load excessive

1   Clutch slipping. Can be caused by damaged, loose or worn clutch components. Refer to Chapter 2 for overhaul procedures.

2   Engine oil level too high. The addition of too much oil will cause pressurization of the crankcase and inefficient engine operation. Check Specifications and drain to proper level (Chapter 1).

3   Engine oil viscosity too high. Using a heavier oil than the one recommended in Chapter 1 can damage the oil pump or lubrication system as well as cause drag on the engine.

4   Brakes dragging. Usually caused by debris which has entered the brake piston sealing boot, or from a warped disc or bent axle. Repair as necessary.

24   Lubrication inadequate

1   Engine oil level too low. Friction caused by intermittent lack of lubrication or from oil that is overworked can cause overheating. The oil provides a definite cooling function in the engine. Check the oil level (Chapter 1).

2   Poor quality engine oil or incorrect viscosity or type. Oil is rated not only according to viscosity but also according to type. Some oils are not rated high enough for use in this engine. Check the Specifications section and change to the correct oil (Chapter 1).

3   Camshaft or journals worn. Excessive wear causing drop in oil pressure. Replace cam and/or cylinder head. Abnormal wear could be caused by oil starvation at high rpm from low oil level or improper weight or type of oil (Chapter 1).

4   Crankshaft and/or bearings worn. Same problems as paragraph 3. Check and replace crankshaft and/or bearings (Chapter 2).

25   Miscellaneous causes

Modification to exhaust system. Most aftermarket exhaust systems cause the engine to run leaner, which makes it run hotter. When installing an accessory exhaust system, always rejet the carburetors.

Clutch problems

26   Clutch slipping

1   Friction plates worn or warped. Overhaul the clutch assembly (Chapter 2).

2   Steel plates worn or warped (Chapter 2).

3   Clutch springs broken or weak. Old or heat-damaged springs (from slipping clutch) should be replaced with new ones (Chapter 2).

4   Worn or warped clutch plates. Replace (Chapter 2).

5   Clutch release mechanism defective. Replace any defective parts (Chapter 2).

6   Clutch boss or housing unevenly worn. This causes improper engagement of the plates. Replace the damaged or worn parts (Chapter 2).

27   Clutch not disengaging completely

1   Clutch lever play excessive (see Chapter 1). Air in clutch line or hydraulic system components worn. Bleed clutch or repair hydraulic components (Chapter 2).

2   Clutch plates warped or damaged. This will cause clutch drag, which in turn will cause the machine to creep. Overhaul the clutch assembly (Chapter 2).

3   Clutch spring tension uneven. Usually caused by a sagged or broken spring. Check and replace the springs (Chapter 2).

4   Engine oil deteriorated. Old, thin, worn out oil will not provide proper lubrication for the plates, causing the clutch to drag. Replace the oil and filter (Chapter 1).

5   Engine oil viscosity too high. Using a heavier oil than recommended in Chapter 1 can cause the plates to stick together, putting a drag on the engine. Change to the correct weight oil (Chapter 1).

6   Clutch housing seized on shaft. Lack of lubrication, severe wear or damage can cause the housing to seize on the shaft. Overhaul of the clutch, and perhaps transmission, may be necessary to repair the damage (Chapter 2).

7   Clutch release mechanism defective. Worn or damaged release mechanism parts can stick and fail to apply force to the pressure plate. Overhaul the release mechanism (Chapter 2).

8   Loose clutch hub nut. Causes housing and boss misalignment putting a drag on the engine. Engagement adjustment continually varies. Overhaul the clutch assembly (Chapter 2).

Gear shifting problems

28   Doesn't go into gear or lever doesn't return

1   Clutch not disengaging. See Section 26.

2   Shift fork(s) bent or seized. Often caused by dropping the machine or from lack of lubrication. Overhaul the transmission (Chapter 2).

3   Gear(s) stuck on shaft. Most often caused by a lack of lubrication or excessive wear in transmission bearings and bushings. Overhaul the transmission (Chapter 2).

4   Shift drum binding. Caused by lubrication failure or excessive wear. Replace the drum and bearing (Chapter 2).

5   Shift lever return spring weak or broken (Chapter 2).

6   Shift lever broken. Splines stripped out of lever or shaft, caused by allowing the lever to get loose or from dropping the machine. Replace necessary parts (Chapter 2).

7   Shift mechanism pawl broken or worn. Full engagement and rotary movement of shift drum results. Replace shaft assembly (Chapter 2).

8   Pawl spring broken. Allows pawl to float, causing sporadic shift operation. Replace spring (Chapter 2).

29   Jumps out of gear

1   Shift fork(s) worn. Overhaul the transmission (Chapter 2).

2   Gear groove(s) worn. Overhaul the transmission (Chapter 2).

3   Gear dogs or dog slots worn or damaged. The gears should be inspected and replaced. No attempt should be made to service the worn parts.

30   Overshifts

1   Pawl spring weak or broken (Chapter 2).

2   Shift drum stopper lever not functioning (Chapter 2).

3   Overshift limiter broken or distorted (Chapter 2).

Abnormal engine noise

31   Knocking or pinging

1   Carbon build-up in combustion chamber. Use of a fuel additive that will dissolve the adhesive bonding the carbon particles to the piston crown and chamber is the easiest way to remove the build-up. Otherwise, the cylinder head will have to be removed and decarbonized (Chapter 2).

2   Incorrect or poor quality fuel. Old or improper fuel can cause detonation. This causes the pistons to rattle, thus the knocking or pinging sound. Drain the old fuel and always use the recommended grade fuel (Chapter 4).

3   Spark plug heat range incorrect. Uncontrolled detonation indicates that the plug heat range is too hot. The plug in effect becomes a glow plug, raising cylinder temperatures. Install the proper heat range plug (Chapter 1).

4   Improper air/fuel mixture. This will cause the cylinders to run hot and lead to detonation. Clogged jets or an air leak can cause this imbalance. See Chapter 4.

32   Piston slap or rattling

1   Cylinder-to-piston clearance excessive. Caused by improper assembly. Inspect and overhaul top end parts (Chapter 2).

2   Connecting rod bent. Caused by over-revving, trying to start a badly flooded engine or from ingesting a foreign object into the combustion chamber. Replace the damaged parts (Chapter 2).

3   Piston pin or piston pin bore worn or seized from wear or lack of lubrication. Replace damaged parts (Chapter 2).

4   Piston ring(s) worn, broken or sticking. Overhaul the top end (Chapter 2).

5   Piston seizure damage. Usually from lack of lubrication or overheating. Replace the pistons and bore the cylinders, as necessary (Chapter 2).

6   Connecting rod upper or lower end clearance excessive. Caused by excessive wear or lack of lubrication. Replace worn parts.

33   Valve noise

1   Incorrect valve clearances. Adjust the clearances by referring to Chapter 1.

2   Valve spring broken or weak. Check and replace weak valve springs (Chapter 2).

3   Camshaft or cylinder head worn or damaged. Lack of lubrication at high rpm is usually the cause of damage. Insufficient oil or failure to change the oil at the recommended intervals are the chief causes. Since there are no replaceable bearings in the head, the head itself will have to be replaced if there is excessive wear or damage (Chapter 2).

34   Other noise

1   Cylinder head gasket leaking.

2   Exhaust pipe leaking at cylinder head connection. Caused by improper fit of pipe(s) or loose exhaust flange. All exhaust fasteners should be tightened evenly and carefully. Failure to do this will lead to a leak.

3   Crankshaft runout excessive. Caused by a bent crankshaft (from over-revving) or damage from an upper cylinder component failure.

4   Engine mounting bolts loose. Tighten all engine mount bolts to the specified torque (Chapter 2).

5   Crankshaft bearings worn (Chapter 2 or Chapter 3).

6   Camshaft chain tensioner defective. Replace according to the procedure in Chapter 2.

7   Camshaft chain, sprockets or guides worn (Chapter 2).

Abnormal driveline noise

35   Clutch noise

1   Clutch housing/friction plate clearance excessive (Chapter 2).

2   Loose or damaged clutch pressure plate and/or bolts (Chapter 2).

36 Transmission noise

1   Bearings worn. Also includes the possibility that the shafts are worn. Overhaul the transmission (Chapter 2).
2   Gears worn or chipped (Chapter 2).
3   Metal chips jammed in gear teeth. Probably pieces from a broken clutch, gear or shift mechanism that were picked up by the gears. This will cause early bearing failure (Chapter 2).
4   Engine oil level too low. Causes a howl from transmission. Also affects engine power and clutch operation (Chapter 1).

37 Final drive noise

1   Final drive oil level too low (see Chapter 1).
2   Final drive gear lash out of adjustment.
3   Final drive gear(s) damaged or worn.

Abnormal frame and suspension noise

38 Front end noise

1   Low fluid level or improper viscosity oil in forks. This can sound like spurting and is usually accompanied by irregular fork action (Chapter 6).
2   Spring weak or broken. Makes a clicking or scraping sound. Fork oil, when drained, will have a lot of metal particles in it (Chapter 6).
3   Steering head bearings loose or damaged. Clicks when braking. Check and adjust or replace as necessary (Chapter 6).
4   Fork clamps loose. Make sure all fork clamp pinch bolts are tight (Chapter 6).
5   Fork tube bent. Good possibility if machine has been dropped. Replace tube with a new one (Chapter 6).
6   Front axle loose. Tighten to the specified torque (Chapter 7).

39 Shock absorber noise

1   Fluid level incorrect. Indicates a leak caused by defective seal. Shock will be covered with oil. Replace shock (Chapter 6).
2   Defective shock absorber with internal damage. This is in the body of the shock and can't be remedied. The shock must be replaced with a new one (Chapter 6).
3   Bent or damaged shock body. Replace the shock with a new one (Chapter 6).

40 Brake noise

1   Squeal caused by pad shim not installed or positioned correctly (Chapter 7).
2   Squeal caused by dust on brake pads. Usually found in combination with glazed pads. Clean using brake cleaning solvent (Chapter 7).
3   Contamination of brake pads. Oil, brake fluid or dirt causing brake to chatter or squeal. Clean or replace pads (Chapter 7).
4   Pads glazed. Caused by excessive heat from prolonged use or from contamination. Do not use sandpaper, emery cloth, carborundum cloth or any other abrasive to roughen the pad surfaces as abrasives will stay in the pad material and damage the disc. A very fine flat file can be used, but pad replacement is suggested as a cure (Chapter 7).
5   Disc warped. Can cause a chattering, clicking or intermittent squeal. Usually accompanied by a pulsating lever and uneven braking. Replace the disc (Chapter 7).
6   Loose or worn wheel bearings. Check and replace as needed (Chapter 7).

Oil pressure light comes on

41 Engine lubrication system

1   Engine oil pump(s) defective (see Chapter 2).
2   Engine oil level low. Inspect for leak or other problem causing low oil level and add recommended oil (Chapters 1 and 2).
3   Engine oil viscosity too low. Very old, thin oil or an improper viscosity of oil used in the engine. Change to correct oil (Chapter 1).
4   Camshafts or journals worn. Excessive wear causing drop in oil pressure. Replace cams and/or heads. Abnormal wear could be caused by oil starvation at high rpm from low oil level or improper oil viscosity or type (see Chapter 1).

42 Electrical system

1   Oil pressure switch defective. Check the switch according to the procedure in Chapter 9. Replace it if it's defective.
2   Oil pressure indicator light circuit defective. Check for pinched, shorted, disconnected or damaged wiring (Chapter 9).

Excessive exhaust smoke

43 White smoke

1   Piston oil ring worn. The ring may be broken or damaged, causing oil from the crankcase to be pulled past the piston into the combustion chamber. Replace the rings with new ones (Chapter 2).
2   Cylinders worn, cracked, or scored. Caused by overheating or oil starvation. If worn or scored, the cylinders will have to be rebored and new pistons installed. If cracked, the cylinder block will have to be replaced (see Chapter 2).
3   Valve oil seal damaged or worn. Replace oil seals with new ones (Chapter 2).
4   Valve guide worn. Perform a complete valve job (Chapter 2).
5   Engine oil level too high, which causes the oil to be forced past the rings. Drain oil to the proper level (Chapter 1).
6   Head gasket broken between oil return and cylinder. Causes oil to be pulled into the combustion chamber. Replace the head gasket and check the head for warpage (Chapter 2).
7   Abnormal crankcase pressurization, which forces oil past the rings. Clogged breather or hoses usually the cause (Chapter 2).

44 Black smoke

1   Air filter clogged. Clean or replace the element (Chapter 1).
2   Main jet too large or loose. Compare the jet size to the Specifications (Chapter 4).
3   Choke stuck, causing fuel to be pulled through choke circuit (Chapter 4).
4   Fuel level too high. Check and adjust the float level as necessary (Chapter 4).
5   Inlet needle held off needle seat. Clean the float bowls and fuel line and replace the needles and seats if necessary (Chapter 4).

45 Brown smoke

1   Main jet too small or clogged. Lean condition caused by wrong size main jet or by a restricted orifice. Clean float bowl and jets and compare jet size to specifications (Chapter 4).
2   Fuel flow insufficient. Fuel inlet needle valve stuck closed due to chemical reaction with old fuel. Float level incorrect. Restricted fuel

line. Clean line and float bowl and adjust floats if necessary.
3   Carburetor intake manifolds loose (Chapter 4).
4   Air filter poorly sealed or not installed (Chapter 1).

Poor handling or stability

46   Handlebar hard to turn

1   Steering stem locknut too tight (Chapter 6).
2   Bearings damaged. Roughness can be felt as the bars are turned from side to side. Replace bearings and races (Chapter 6).
3   Races dented or worn. Denting results from wear in only one position (e.g., straight ahead), from a collision or hitting a pothole or from dropping the machine. Replace races and bearings (Chapter 6).
4   Steering stem lubrication inadequate. Causes are grease getting hard from age or being washed out by high pressure car washes. Disassemble steering head and repack bearings (Chapter 6).
5   Steering stem bent. Caused by a collision, hitting a pothole or by dropping the machine. Replace damaged part. Don't try to straighten the steering stem (Chapter 6).
6   Front tire air pressure too low (Chapter 1).

47   Handlebar shakes or vibrates excessively

1   Tires worn or out of balance (Chapter 7).
2   Swingarm bearings worn. Replace worn bearings by referring to Chapter 6.
3   Rim(s) warped or damaged. Inspect wheels for runout (Chapter 7).
4   Wheel bearings worn. Worn front or rear wheel bearings can cause poor tracking. Worn front bearings will cause wobble (Chapter 8).
5   Handlebar clamp bolts loose (Chapter 6).
6   Steering stem or fork clamps loose. Tighten them to the specified torque (Chapter 6).
7   Engine mount bolts loose. Will cause excessive vibration with increased engine rpm (Chapter 2).

48   Handlebar pulls to one side

1   Frame bent. Definitely suspect this if the machine has been dropped. May or may not be accompanied by cracking near the bend. Replace the frame (Chapter 6).
2   Wheel out of alignment. Caused by improper location of axle spacers or from bent steering stem or frame (Chapter 6).
3   Swingarm bent or twisted. Caused by age (metal fatigue) or impact damage. Replace the arm (Chapter 6).
4   Steering stem bent. Caused by impact damage or by dropping the motorcycle. Replace the steering stem (Chapter 6).
5   Fork leg bent. Disassemble the forks and replace the damaged parts (Chapter 7).
6   Fork oil level uneven. Check and add or drain as necessary (Chapter 6).

49   Poor shock absorbing qualities

1   Too hard:
a) Fork oil level excessive (Chapter 6).
b) Fork oil viscosity too high. Use a lighter oil (see the Specifications in Chapter 1).
c) Fork tube bent. Causes a harsh, sticking feeling (Chapter 6).
d) Shock shaft or body bent or damaged (Chapter 6).
e) Fork internal damage (Chapter 6).
f) Anti-dive O-ring swollen (Chapter 6).

g) Shock internal damage.
h) Tire pressure too high (Chapter 1).
2   Too soft:
a) Fork or shock oil insufficient and/or leaking (Chapter 6).
b) Fork oil level too low (Chapter 6).
c) Fork oil viscosity too light (Chapter 6).
d) Fork springs weak or broken (Chapter 6).

Braking problems

50   Brakes are spongy, don't hold

1   Air in brake line. Caused by inattention to master cylinder fluid level or by leakage. Locate problem and bleed brakes (Chapter 7).
2   Pad or disc worn (Chapters 1 and 7).
3   Brake fluid leak. See paragraph 1.
4   Contaminated pads. Caused by contamination with oil, grease, brake fluid, etc. Clean or replace pads. Clean disc thoroughly with brake cleaner (Chapter 7).
5   Brake fluid deteriorated. Fluid is old or contaminated. Drain system, replenish with new fluid and bleed the system (Chapter 7).
6   Master cylinder internal parts worn or damaged causing fluid to bypass (Chapter 7).
7   Master cylinder bore scratched by foreign material or broken spring. Repair or replace master cylinder (Chapter 7).
8   Disc warped. Replace disc (Chapter 7).

51   Brake lever or pedal pulsates

1   Disc warped. Replace disc (Chapter 7).
2   Axle bent. Replace axle (Chapter 7).
3   Brake caliper bolts loose (Chapter 7).
4   Brake caliper shafts damaged or sticking, causing caliper to bind. Lube the shafts or replace them if they are corroded or bent (Chapter 7).
5   Wheel warped or otherwise damaged (Chapter 7).
6   Wheel bearings damaged or worn (Chapter 7).

52   Brakes drag

1   Master cylinder piston seized. Caused by wear or damage to piston or cylinder bore (Chapter 7).
2   Lever balky or stuck. Check pivot and lubricate (Chapter 7).
3   Brake caliper binds. Caused by inadequate lubrication or damage to caliper shafts (Chapter 7).
4   Brake caliper piston seized in bore. Caused by wear or ingestion of dirt past deteriorated seal (Chapter 7).
5   Brake pad damaged. Pad material separated from backing plate. Usually caused by faulty manufacturing process or from contact with chemicals. Replace pads (Chapter 7).
6   Pads improperly installed (Chapter 7).
7   Front brake lever or rear brake pedal freeplay insufficient (Chapter 1).

Electrical problems

53   Battery dead or weak

1   Battery faulty. Caused by sulfated plates which are shorted through sedimentation or low electrolyte level. Also, broken battery terminal making only occasional contact (Chapter 9).
2   Battery cables making poor contact (Chapter 9).

3   Load excessive. Caused by addition of high wattage lights or other electrical accessories.

4   Ignition switch defective. Switch either grounds internally or fails to shut off system. Replace the switch (Chapter 9).

5   Regulator/rectifier defective (Chapter 9).

6   Alternator defective (Chapter 9).

7   Wiring faulty. Wiring grounded or connections loose in ignition, charging or lighting circuits (Chapter 9).

54 Battery overcharged

1   Regulator/rectifier defective. Overcharging is noticed when battery gets excessively warm or boils over (Chapter 9).

2   Battery defective. Replace battery with a new one (Chapter 9).

3   Battery amperage too low, wrong type or size. Install manufacturer's specified amp-hour battery to handle charging load (Chapter 9).

Chapter 1
Tune-up and routine maintenance

Contents

Specifications

Engine

Spark plugs
Type
    Standard .... NGK DPR7EA-9 or ND X22EPR-U9
    Cold weather (below 5-degrees C/41-degrees F) .... NGK DPR6EA-9 or ND X20EPR-U9
    Extended high-speed riding .... NGK DPR8EA-9 or ND X24EPR-U9
  Gap .... 0.8 to 0.9 mm (0.031 to 0.035 inch)
Engine idle speed .... 800 +/- 80 rpm
Cylinder compression pressure (at sea level) .... 185 to 242 psi
Carburetor synchronization - maximum vacuum
  difference between cylinders .... 40 mm Hg (1.6 inch Hg)
Cylinder numbering (from front to rear of bike)
  Right side 1-3-5
  Left side 2-4-6

Miscellaneous

Brake pad material minimum thickness	To wear groove - see text
Brake pedal position	10 mm (0.4 inch) above the top of the footpeg
Freeplay adjustments	
Throttle grip	5 to 8 mm (3/16 to 5/16 inch)
Clutch lever	Not adjustable
Front brake lever	Not adjustable
Battery electrolyte specific gravity	1.280 at 20-degrees C (68 degrees F)
Minimum tire tread depth	
Front	1.5 mm (0.06 inch)
Rear	2.0 mm (0.08 inch)
Tire pressures (cold)	
Front	33 psi
Rear	
Up to 90 kg (198 lbs)	36 psi
Above 90 kg (198 lbs)	41 psi
Tire sizes	
Front	130/70-18 63H
Rear	160/80-16 75H
Maximum load	185 kg (408 lbs)

Torque specifications

Engine oil drain plug	38 Nm (27 ft-lbs)
Oil filter	10 Nm (7 ft-lbs)
Spark plugs	16 Nm (12 ft-lbs)
Final drive filler and drain plugs	12 Nm (9 ft-lbs)

Recommended lubricants and fluids

Engine/transmission oil	
Type	API grade SF or SG
Viscosity	SAE 10W-40
Capacity	
With filter change	3.7 liters (4.0 qt)
Oil change only	3.5 liters (3.7 qt)
Coolant type	50/50 mixture of water and ethylene glycol antifreeze containing corrosion inhibitors for aluminum engines*
Final drive oil	
Type	SAE 80 hypoid gear oil
Capacity	140 cc (4.7 fl oz)
Coolant capacity	3.8 liters (4.1 qt)
Brake fluid	DOT 4
Fork oil	See Chapter 6

Miscellaneous

Wheel bearings	Medium weight, lithium-based multi-purpose grease
Swingarm pivot bearings	Medium weight, lithium-based multi-purpose grease
Cables and lever pivots	Chain and cable lubricant or 10W30 motor oil
Sidestand/centerstand pivots	Medium-weight, lithium-based multi-purpose grease
Brake pedal/shift lever pivots	Medium-weight, lithium-based multi-purpose grease
Throttle grip	Medium-weight, lithium-based multi-purpose grease

The silicate corrosion inhibitors used in automotive antifreeze/coolants may cause premature failure of the mechanical water pump seals. For this reason, be sure to use a silicate-free antifreeze, such as Honda HP coolant. Also, it's important to use only distilled water.

1 Honda GL1500 Routine maintenance intervals

Note: *The pre-ride inspection outlined in the owner's manual covers checks and maintenance that should be carried out on a daily basis. It's condensed and included here to remind you of its importance. Always perform the pre-ride inspection at every maintenance interval (in addition to the procedures listed). The intervals listed below are the shortest intervals recommended by the manufacturer for each particular operation during the model years covered in this manual. Your owner's manual may have different intervals for your model.*

Daily or before riding

Check the engine oil level
Check the coolant level
Check the fuel level and inspect for leaks
Check the operation of both brakes - also check the fluid level and look for leakage
Check the tires for damage, the presence of foreign objects and correct air pressure
Check the throttle for smooth operation and correct freeplay
Check the operation of the clutch - check the fluid level and look for leakage
Make sure the steering operates smoothly, without looseness and without binding
Check for proper operation of the headlight, taillight, brake light, turn signals, indicator lights, speedometer and horn
Make sure the sidestand returns to its fully up position and stays there under spring pressure
Make sure the engine kill switch works properly

After the initial 600 miles/1000 km

Perform all of the daily checks plus:
Check/adjust the engine idle speed
Change the engine oil and oil filter
Check the tightness of all fasteners
Check the steering
Check the brake fluid level
Check/adjust the brake pedal position
Check the operation of the brake light

Every 4000 miles/6000 km

Replace the spark plugs
Inspect the crankcase breather system
Check idle speed
Check the battery electrolyte level and specific gravity; inspect the breather tube
Check the brake fluid level
Check the brake discs and pads
Check the clutch for fluid level and leaks

Every 8000 miles/12000 km

Change the engine oil and filter
Clean the air filter element and replace it if necessary
Inspect the cooling system hoses
Check/adjust throttle cable free play
Check choke operation
Check/adjust the carburetor synchronization
Check/adjust the brake pedal position
Check the operation of the brake light
Lubricate the clutch and front brake lever pivots
Lubricate the throttle cables
Lubricate the shift/brake pedal pivots and the sidestand pivots
Check the operation of the sidestand switch
Check the steering for looseness or binding
Check the front forks for proper operation and fluid leaks
Check the tires, wheels and wheel bearings
Check the exhaust system for leaks and check the tightness of the fasteners
Check the cleanliness of the fuel system and the condition of the fuel lines and vacuum hoses
Inspect the evaporative emission control system (California models)
Inspect the secondary air induction system
Check rear suspension operation and swingarm play
Check all nuts, bolts and other fasteners for tightness
Inspect the air drier (on-board air compressor)

Every 12,000 miles/18,000 km

Replace the air filter element
Change the brake and clutch fluid*
Check the final drive oil level
Check headlight aim
Check operation of the reverse system (if equipped)

Every 16,000 miles/24,000 km

Clean the air pump element (onboard compressor system)

Every 24,000 miles (36,000 km)

Replace the cruise valve element (if equipped)

Every 100,000 miles/160,000 km

Replace the timing belt
Or every two years, whichever comes first.

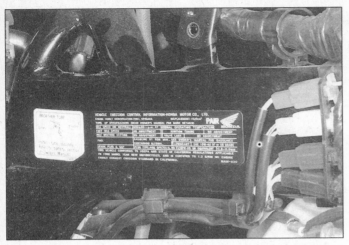

2.3a Maintenance information printed on decals includes tune-up data, battery vent tube routing . . .

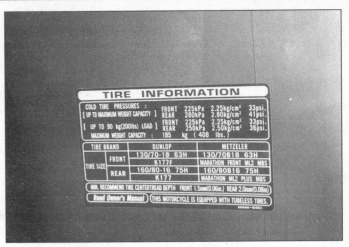

2.3b . . . tire pressure specifications . . .

2   Introduction to tune-up and routine maintenance

Refer to illustrations 2.3a, 2.3b, 2.3c and 2.3d

    This Chapter covers in detail the checks and procedures necessary for the tune-up and routine maintenance of your motorcycle. Section 1 includes the routine maintenance schedule, which is designed to keep the machine in proper running condition and prevent possible problems. The remaining Sections contain detailed procedures for carrying out the items listed on the maintenance schedule, as well as additional maintenance information designed to increase reliability.

    Since routine maintenance plays such an important role in the safe and efficient operation of your motorcycle, it is presented here as a comprehensive checklist. For the rider who does all his own maintenance, these lists outline the procedures and checks that should be done on a routine basis.

    Maintenance information is printed on labels attached to the motorcycle **(see illustrations)**. If the information on the labels differs from that included here, use the information on the label.

    Deciding where to start or plug into the routine maintenance schedule depends on several factors. If you have a motorcycle whose warranty has recently expired, and if it has been maintained according to the warranty standards, you may want to pick up routine maintenance as it coincides with the next mileage or calendar interval. If you have owned the machine for some time but have never performed any maintenance on it, then you may want to start at the nearest interval and include some additional procedures to ensure that nothing important is overlooked. If you

have just had a major engine overhaul, then you may want to start the maintenance routine from the beginning. If you have a used machine and have no knowledge of its history or maintenance record, you may desire to combine all the checks into one large service initially and then settle into the maintenance schedule prescribed.

    The Sections which outline the inspection and maintenance procedures are written as step-by-step comprehensive guides to the performance of the work. They explain in detail each of the routine inspections and maintenance procedures on the check list. References to additional information in applicable Chapters is also included and should not be overlooked.

    Before beginning any maintenance or repair, the machine should be cleaned thoroughly, especially around the oil filter, spark plugs, cylinder head covers, side covers, carburetors, etc. Cleaning will help ensure that dirt does not contaminate the engine and will allow you to detect wear and damage that could otherwise easily go unnoticed.

3   Fluid levels - check

Engine oil

Refer to illustrations 3.3 and 3.4

1   Run the engine and allow it to reach normal operating temperature. **Warning:** *Do not run the engine in an enclosed space such as a garage or shop.*

2   Stop the engine and allow the machine to sit undisturbed for about five minutes.

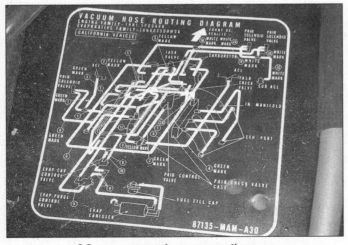

2.3c . . . vacuum hose connections . . .

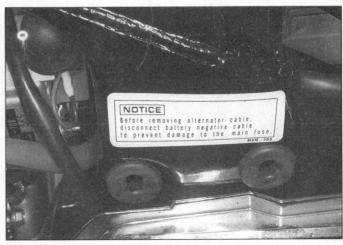

2.3d . . . and safety information

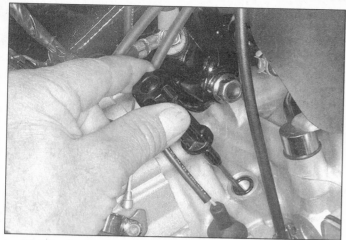

3.3 Check oil level on the dipstick; it should be between the Minimum and Maximum marks

3.4 The oil filler cap is located on the right side of the engine

3   Hold the motorcycle level. With the engine off, unscrew the dip-stick located at the right crankcase cover. Wipe the dipstick with a clean rag, reinsert it (don't screw it in; just let it rest on the threads). Pull the dipstick out and check the oil level; it should be between the Maximum and Minimum marks on the dipstick **(see illustration)**.

4   If the level is below the Minimum mark, remove the oil filler cap from the right side of the crankcase **(see illustration)** and add enough oil of the recommended grade and type to bring the level up to the Maximum mark. Do not overfill.

5   Inspect the filler cap and dipstick O-rings. Replace them if they're cut, flattened or deteriorated. Install the filler cap and dipstick and tighten them securely with fingers.

Brake and clutch fluid

6   In order to ensure proper operation of the hydraulic disc brakes and the hydraulic clutch if equipped, the fluid level in the master cylin-der reservoirs must be properly maintained.

Right front brake and clutch

Refer to illustrations 3.8 and 3.11

7   With the motorcycle on its centerstand, turn the handlebars until the top of the handlebar master cylinders are as level as possible.

8   Look closely at the inspection window in the master cylinder reservoirs. The right handlebar reservoir supplies the right front brake; the left handlebar reservoir supplies the clutch. Make sure that the fluid level is above the Lower mark on the reservoir **(see illustration)**.

9   If the level is low, the fluid must be replenished. Before removing the master cylinder cap, wrap the reservoir with a rag to protect the surrounding area from brake fluid spills (which will damage the paint) and remove all dust and dirt from the area around the cap.

10   To top up right front brake or clutch fluid, remove the screws and lift off the cap and rubber diaphragm. **Note:** *Do not operate the brakes or clutch with the cap removed.*

11   Add new, clean brake fluid of the recommended type until the level is up to the upper level line, which is cast inside the reservoir body **(see illustration)**. Do not mix different brands of brake fluid in the reservoir, as they may not be compatible.

12   Replace the rubber diaphragm and the cover. Tighten the screws evenly, but do not overtighten them.

13   Wipe any spilled fluid off the reservoir body. If the brake fluid level was low, inspect the brake or clutch system for leaks.

Left front and rear brakes

Refer to illustration 3.15

14   Remove the right rear side cover for access to the brake pedal reservoir (see Chapter 8). This reservoir supplies the left front brake and the rear brake.

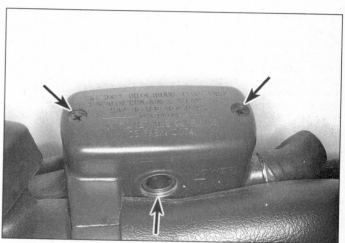

3.8 With the master cylinder in a level position, check fluid level in the inspection window (lower arrow) - this is the master cylinder for the right front brake; the clutch master cylinder, mounted on the left handlebar, has a similar inspection window - screws (upper arrows) secure the cover

3.11 The upper level line is cast inside the reservoir (arrow)

3.15 The fluid level in the rear brake master cylinder can be checked by looking through the plastic reservoir - fluid must be above the Lower mark

3.20 Coolant should be between the Low and Full marks on the dipstick

15   The fluid level should be visible through the translucent reservoir **(see illustration)**. If it's below the Lower mark, clean the area around the cap, then place rags around the reservoir to protect painted parts from brake fluid spills. Unscrew the cap.

16   Add new, clean brake fluid of the recommended type until the level is up to the Upper mark cast in the reservoir body. Do not mix different brands of brake fluid in the reservoir, as they may not be compatible.

17   Replace the cap. If the brake fluid level was low, inspect the brake system for leaks.

Coolant

Refer to illustration 3.20

18   The engine must be at normal operating temperature for the results to be accurate, so warm it up before performing this check. The measurement is taken with a dipstick which is located under the ignition switch cover.

19   Remove the ignition switch cover for access to the coolant dipstick (see Chapter 8).

20   Pull back the tab and lift the dipstick out of the filler hole (the dipstick is attached to the reservoir filler cap) **(see illustration)**. **Warning:** *Never remove the radiator cap when the engine is hot. Scalding coolant will spray out and may cause serious burns.*

21   The coolant level is satisfactory if it is between the Low and Full marks on the dipstick. If the level is at or below the Low mark, add the

recommended coolant mixture (see this Chapter's Specifications) until the Full level is reached. If the coolant level seems to be consistently low, check the entire cooling system for leaks.

Final drive oil

Refer to illustration 3.22

Warning: *Be sure the exhaust system is cool before starting this procedure. You'll be working close to the right muffler and touching it may cause serious burns.*

22   Place the motorcycle on its centerstand. Clean any dirt from around the filler plug, then unscrew the filler plug from the right side of the final drive **(see illustration)**. Look or reach into the filler hole and note the oil level. It should be up to the bottom of the hole.

23   If the oil level is low, add oil of the type recommended in this Chapter's Specifications, using a funnel with a flexible tube if necessary.

24   Thread the filler plug into the hole and tighten it to the torque listed in this Chapter's Specifications.

---

4   Battery electrolyte level/specific gravity - check

Refer to illustrations 4.3, 4.6, 4.11a and 4.11b

Caution: *Be extremely careful when handling or working around the battery. The electrolyte is very caustic and an explosive gas (hydrogen) is given off when the battery is charging.* **Note:** *The first Steps describe battery removal. If the electrolyte level is known to be sufficient it won't be necessary to remove the battery.*

1   This procedure applies to batteries that have removable filler caps, which can be removed to add water to the battery. This type is original equipment on the motorcycles covered in this manual. The sealed maintenance-free batteries used on some models can't be topped up.

2   Remove the right rear side cover for access to the battery (see Chapter 8).

3   The electrolyte level is visible through the translucent battery case - it should be between the upper and lower level marks **(see illustration)**.

4   If the electrolyte is low, remove the cell caps and fill each cell to the upper level mark with distilled water. Do not use tap water (except in an emergency), and do not overfill. The cell holes are quite small, so it may help to use a plastic squeeze bottle with a small spout to add the water. If the level is within the marks on the case, additional water is not necessary.

5   Next, check the specific gravity of the electrolyte in each cell with

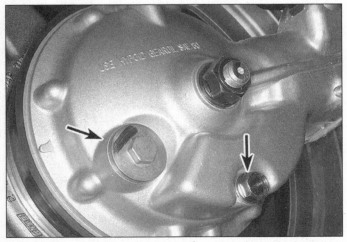

3.22 Final drive filler plug (left arrow) and drain plug (right arrow)

4.3 Battery electrolyte level can be seen through the battery case; it should be between the Upper level and Lower level marks

4.6 Check the specific gravity with a hydrometer

4.11a The battery vent tube slips over a fitting on the battery case (upper arrow); it's secured by a grommet to a clip on the battery box . . .

a small hydrometer made especially for motorcycle batteries. These are available from most dealer parts departments or motorcycle accessory stores.

6   Remove the caps, draw some electrolyte from the first cell into the hydrometer **(see illustration)** and note the specific gravity. Compare the reading to the Specifications listed in this Chapter. **Note:** *Add 0.004 points to the reading for every 10-degrees F above 20-degrees C (68-degrees F) - subtract 0.004 points from the reading for every 10-degrees below 20-degrees C (68-degrees F). Return the electrolyte to the appropriate cell and repeat the check for the remaining cells. When the check is complete, rinse the hydrometer thoroughly with clean water.*

7   If the specific gravity of the electrolyte in each cell is as specified, the battery is in good condition and is apparently being charged by the machine's charging system.

8   If the specific gravity is low, the battery is not fully charged. This may be due to corroded battery terminals, a dirty battery case, a malfunctioning charging system, or loose or corroded wiring connections. On the other hand, it may be that the battery is worn out, especially if the machine is old, or that infrequent use of the motorcycle prevents normal charging from taking place.

9   Be sure to correct any problems and charge the battery if necessary. Refer to Chapter 9 for additional battery maintenance and charging procedures.

10   Install the battery cell caps, tightening them securely.

11   Make sure the battery vent tube is secure in its retainers and is routed correctly **(see illustration 1.3a and the accompanying illustrations)**. Be very careful not to pinch or otherwise restrict the battery

vent tube, as the battery may build up enough internal pressure during normal charging system operation to explode.

12   Install the side cover.

5   Brake pads - wear check

Refer to illustrations 5.2a and 5.2b

1   The front and rear brake pads should be checked at the recommended intervals and replaced with new ones when worn beyond the limit listed in this Chapter's Specifications.

2   To check the brake pads, look at them from the edges **(see illustrations)**. There's a small gap between the edge of the friction material and the metal backing. If the friction material is worn near or all the way to the gap, the pads are worn excessively and must be replaced with new ones (see Chapter 7).

6   Brake system - general check

Refer to illustrations 6.3 and 6.6

1   A routine general check of the brakes will ensure that any problems are discovered and remedied before the rider's safety is jeopardized.

2   Check the brake lever and pedal for loose connections, excessive play, bends, and other damage. Replace any damaged parts with new ones (see Chapter 7).

1

4.11b . . . and by retainers on the crankcase

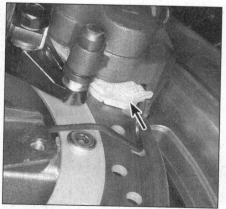

5.2a Inspect the groove between the friction material and the metal backing (arrow) (this is a front pad) . . .

5.2b . . . if the friction material is worn near the groove (arrow), replace the pads (this is a rear pad)

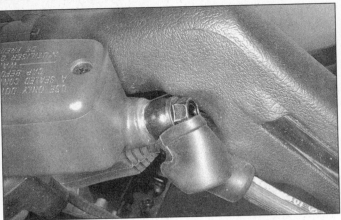

**6.3 Pull back the rubber cover and check the
hose fitting for leaks**

**6.6 Hold the switch body and turn the nut (arrow)
to adjust the switch**

3   Make sure all brake fasteners are tight. Check the brake pads for
wear (see Section 5) and make sure the fluid level in the reservoirs is
correct (see Section 3). Look for leaks at the hose connections and
check for cracks in the hoses **(see illustration)**. If the lever or pedal is
spongy, bleed the brakes as described in Chapter 7.
4   Make sure the brake light operates when the brake lever is
depressed. The front brake light switch is not adjustable. If it doesn't
work, check and replace it if necessary (see Chapter 9).
5   Press the brake pedal and make sure the brake light is activated

just as the brake takes effect.
6   If adjustment is necessary, remove the right chamber protector
(see Chapter 8). Hold the switch and turn the adjusting nut on the
switch body **(see illustration)** until the brake light is activated when
required (don't turn the switch body). If the switch doesn't operate the
brake lights, check it as described in Chapter 9.

7   Brake pedal position - check and adjustment

Refer to illustrations 7.1 and 7.2

1   The rear brake pedal should be positioned above the top of the
footpeg the distance listed in this Chapter's Specifications **(see illustration)**.
2   To adjust the position of the pedal, loosen the locknut on the
adjuster, turn the adjuster to set the pedal position and tighten the
locknut **(see illustration)**.
3   If necessary, adjust the brake light switch (see Section 6).

8   Tires/wheels - general check

Refer to illustrations 8.2a, 8.2b and 8.4

1   Routine tire and wheel checks should be made with the realiza-
tion that your safety depends to a great extent on their condition.
2   Check the tires carefully for cuts, tears, embedded nails or other
sharp objects and excessive wear. Operation of the motorcycle with
excessively worn tires is extremely hazardous, as traction and handling
are directly affected. Measure the tread depth at the center of the tire

**7.1 Pedal height should be the specified distance from
the top of the footpeg**

**7.2 To adjust pedal height, loosen the locknut (right arrow) and
turn the adjusting nut (left arrow)**

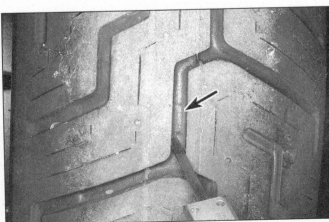

**8.2a Measure tread depth; if the raised wear indicators (arrow)
are even with the tread surface, the tire needs to be replaced . .**

8.2b . . . on some tires, there's also a wear indicator
on the side of the tread

8.4 Use an accurate gauge to check the air pressure in the tires

and replace worn tires with new ones when the tread depth is less than specified **(see illustrations)**.

3   Repair or replace punctured tires as soon as damage is noted. Do not try to patch a torn tire, as wheel balance and tire reliability may be impaired.

4   Check the tire pressures when the tires are cold and keep them properly inflated **(see illustration)**. Proper air pressure will increase tire life and provide maximum stability and ride comfort. Keep in mind that low tire pressures may cause the tire to slip on the rim or come off, while high tire pressures will cause abnormal tread wear and unsafe handling.

5   The cast wheels used on this machine are virtually maintenance free, but they should be kept clean and checked periodically for cracks and other damage. Never attempt to repair damaged cast wheels; they must be replaced with new ones.

6   Check the valve stem locknuts to make sure they are tight. Also, make sure the valve stem cap is in place and tight. If it is missing, install a new one made of metal or hard plastic.

9   Throttle and choke operation and freeplay - check and adjustment

Throttle

Refer to illustration 9.3

1   Make sure the throttle grip rotates easily from fully closed to fully open with the front wheel turned at various angles. The grip should return automatically from fully open to fully closed when released. If the throttle sticks, check the throttle cables for cracks or kinks in the hous-

ings. Also, make sure the inner cables are clean and well-lubricated.

2   Check for a small amount of freeplay at the grip and compare the freeplay to the value listed in this Chapter's Specifications. If adjustment is necessary, adjust idle speed first as described in Section 17.

3   To make fine adjustments, loosen the upper locknut on the handlebar cable adjuster **(see illustration)**. Turn the adjuster until the desired freeplay is obtained, then retighten the locknut.

4   To make major adjustments, loosen the lower locknut on the handlebar adjuster **(see illustration 9.3)**. Turn the adjuster until the desired freeplay is obtained, then retighten the locknut.

5   Make sure the throttle linkage lever contacts the idle adjusting screw when the throttle grip is in the closed throttle position. **Warning:** *Turn the handlebars all the way through their travel with the engine idling. Idle speed should not change. If it does, the cables may be routed incorrectly. Correct this condition before riding the bike.*

Choke

Refer to illustration 9.8

6   Operate the choke lever on the left handlebar. It should move smoothly, without sticking or binding. If it doesn't, check the choke cable for cracks or kinks in the housing. Also, make sure the inner cable is clean and well-lubricated.

7   Remove the air cleaner housing (see Chapter 4). Operate the choke lever and make sure the starting enrichment valve on the carburetor assembly moves smoothly from fully closed to fully open and back. If it doesn't, adjust the cable.

8   Loosen the locknut on the cable adjuster at the left handlebar **(see illustration)**. Turn the adjuster to get the correct enrichment valve travel, then tighten the locknut.

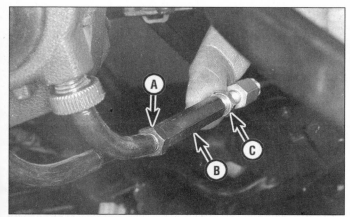

9.3 To make minor throttle cable adjustments, loosen the upper locknut (A) and turn the adjuster (B); to make major adjustments, loosen the lower locknut (C) and turn the adjuster (B)

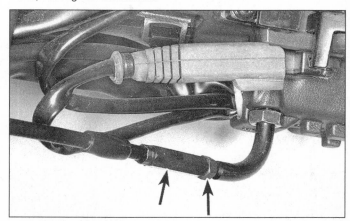

9.8 To adjust the choke lever, loosen the locknut (right arrow) and turn the adjuster (left arrow)

1

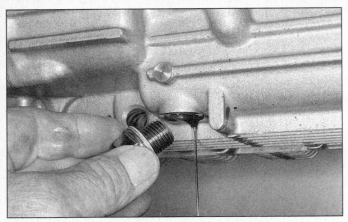

11.5 Remove the oil pan drain plug and sealing washer

11.6 Unscrew the oil filter with a filter wrench

10   Clutch - check and adjustment

1   The hydraulic clutch release mechanism eliminates the need for freeplay adjustment. No means of manual adjustment is provided.
2   Check the fluid level (see Section 3). Check for fluid leaks around the master cylinder on the left handlebar. Pull back the rubber cover and inspect the fluid line connection, then follow the fluid line to the release cylinder on the rear of the engine. If leaks are found, refer to Chapter 2 for repair procedures.
3   Start the bike, release the clutch and ride off, noting the position of the clutch lever when the clutch begins to engage. If it's too close to the handlebar, there may be air in the clutch fluid (the air compresses, rather than transmitting lever force to the release mechanism). Refer to Chapter 2 and bleed the system.

11   Engine oil/filter - change

Refer to illustrations 11.5, 11.6 and 11.7
1   Consistent routine oil and filter changes are the single most important maintenance procedure you can perform on a motorcycle. The oil not only lubricates the internal parts of the engine, transmission and clutch, but it also acts as a coolant, a cleaner, a sealant, and a protectant. Because of these demands, the oil takes a terrific amount of abuse and should be replaced often with new oil of the recommended grade and type. Saving a little money on the difference in cost between a good oil and a cheap oil won't pay off if the engine is damaged.
2   Before changing the oil and filter, warm up the engine so the oil will drain easily. Be careful when draining the oil, as the exhaust pipes, the engine, and the oil itself can cause severe burns.
3   Place the bike on its centerstand. Remove the oil filler cap to vent the crankcase and act as a reminder that there is no oil in the engine.
4   Remove the under cover from beneath the motorcycle (see Chapter 8).
5   Support the motorcycle securely over a clean drain pan. Remove the drain plug from the engine and allow the oil to drain into the pan **(see illustration)**. Discard the sealing washer on the drain plug; it should be replaced whenever the plug is removed.
6   Unscrew the filter with a wrench or socket and a filter wrench (Honda tool no. 07HAA-PJ70100 or equivalent) **(see illustration)**. Let the oil drain from the filter fitting.
7   Apply a film of oil to the gasket on the new filter **(see illustration)**. Thread the filter onto the fitting and tighten it to the torque listed in this Chapter's Specifications.
8   Slip a new sealing washer over the oil drain plug, then install and tighten it to the torque listed in this Chapter's Specifications. Avoid overtightening, as damage to the engine case will result.
9   Before refilling the engine, check the old oil carefully. If the oil was

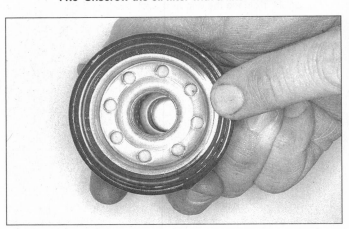

11.7 Apply a film of clean engine oil to the filter gasket

drained into a clean pan, small pieces of metal or other material can be easily detected. If the oil is very metallic colored, then the engine is experiencing wear from break-in (new engine) or from insufficient lubrication. If there are flakes or chips of metal in the oil, then something is drastically wrong internally and the engine will have to be disassembled for inspection and repair.
10   If there are pieces of fiber-like material in the oil, the clutch is experiencing excessive wear and should be checked.
11   If the inspection of the oil turns up nothing unusual, refill the crankcase to the proper level with the recommended oil and install the filler cap. Start the engine and let it idle for a few minutes (do not rev the engine). Shut it off, wait a few minutes, then check the oil level. If necessary, add more oil to bring the level up to the Maximum mark. Check around the drain plug and filter for leaks.
12   The old oil drained from the engine cannot be reused in its present state and should be disposed of. Check with your local refuse disposal company, disposal facility or environmental agency to see whether they will accept the used oil for recycling. Don't pour used oil into drains or onto the ground. After the oil has cooled, it can be drained into a suitable container (capped plastic jugs, topped bottles, milk cartons, etc.) for transport to one of these disposal sites.

12   Pulse air system - inspection

1   Remove the fairing lower and inner covers (see Chapter 8).
2   Reposition the system heat shield toward the front of the bike to gain access.
3   Using an inspection mirror where necessary, check the rubber hoses that connect the metal lines, check valves and control valve. Refer to Chapter 4 for complete details of the system.

**13.2a Release the clip to detach the duct from the
air cleaner housing . . .**

13.2b . . . unplug the temperature sensor connector . . .

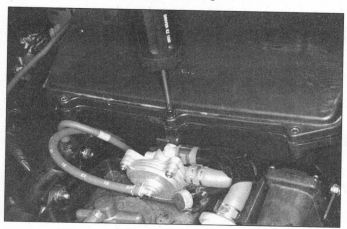

**13.2c . . . remove the cover screws and lift the
cover off the housing**

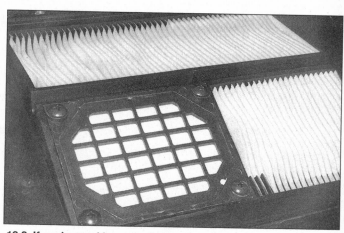

**13.3 If you're working on a California model, remove four screws
and detach the storage element; discard the main element
and reuse the storage element**

13 Air filter element - servicing

Refer to illustrations 13.2a, 13.2b, 13.2c and 13.3

1   Remove the top compartment (see Chapter 8).
2   Remove the air duct and the housing cover **(see illustrations)**.
3   If you're working on a California model, remove the screws and detach the evaporative emission storage element from the main air

cleaner element **(see illustration)**. Keep the storage element; it isn't replaced routinely.
4   Lift out the filter element and clean the inside of the filter housing.
5   Install the new filter element (and the storage element on California models) by reversing the removal procedure. Make sure the element is seated properly in the filter housing before installing the cover.
6   Install all components removed for access.

14 Crankcase breather - servicing

Refer to illustration 14.1

1   At the specified interval, squeeze the clamps at the bottoms of the drain tubes and slide them up the tubes **(see illustration)**.
2   Pull the plugs out of the tubes and let any accumulated deposits drain out, then reinstall the plugs and secure them with the clamps.

15 Cylinder compression - check

Refer to illustration 15.8

1   Among other things, poor engine performance may be caused by leaking valves, incorrect valve clearances, leaking head gaskets, or worn pistons, rings and/or cylinder walls. A cylinder compression check will help pinpoint these conditions and can also indicate the presence of excessive carbon deposits in the cylinder heads.

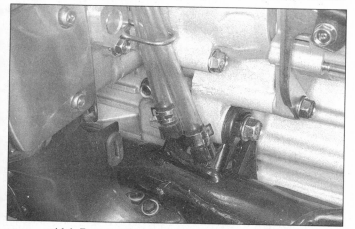

**14.1 Remove the plugs from the breather hoses
and let them drain**

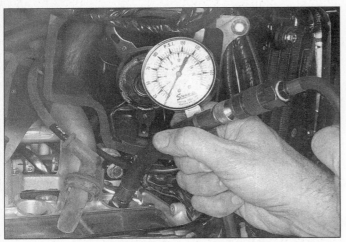

15.8 A compression gauge with a threaded fitting for the spark plug hole is preferred over the type that requires hand pressure to maintain the seal

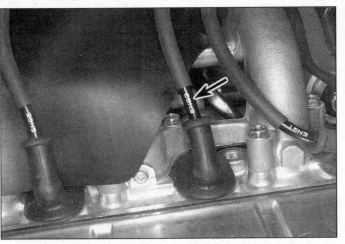

16.3a Rotate the spark plug caps back and forth to loosen them, then pull them off the plugs and check them for brittleness and cracking; there's a cylinder number on each wire (arrow)

2   The only tools required are a compression gauge and a spark plug wrench. Depending on the outcome of the initial test, a squirt-type oil can may also be needed.

3   Start the engine and allow it to reach normal operating temperature.

4   Place the bike on its centerstand.

5   Remove fairing lower covers for access to the spark plug holes (see Chapter 8).

6   Remove the spark plugs (see Section 16, if necessary). Work carefully - don't strip the spark plug hole threads and don't burn your hands.

7   Disable the ignition by unplugging the primary wires from the coils (see Chapter 5). Be sure to mark the locations of the wires before detaching them.

8   Install the compression gauge in one of the spark plug holes **(see illustration)**.

9   Hold or block the throttle wide open.

10   Crank the engine over a minimum of four or five revolutions (or until the gauge reading stops increasing) and observe the initial movement of the compression gauge needle as well as the final total gauge reading. Repeat the procedure for the other cylinders and compare the results to the value listed in this Chapter's Specifications.

11   If the compression in all cylinders built up quickly and evenly to

the specified amount, you can assume the engine upper end is in reasonably good mechanical condition. Worn or sticking piston rings and worn cylinders will produce very little initial movement of the gauge needle, but compression will tend to build up gradually as the engine spins over. Valve and valve seat leakage, or head gasket leakage, is indicated by low initial compression which does not tend to build up.

12   To further confirm your findings, add a small amount of engine oil to each cylinder by inserting the nozzle of a squirt-type oil can through the spark plug holes. The oil will tend to seal the piston rings if they are leaking. Repeat the test for the other cylinders.

13   If the compression increases significantly after the addition of the oil, the piston rings and/or cylinders are definitely worn. If the compression does not increase, the pressure is leaking past the valves or the head gasket. Leakage past the valves may be due to insufficient valve clearances, burned, warped or cracked valves or valve seats or valves that are hanging up in the guides.

14   If compression readings are considerably higher than specified, the combustion chambers are probably coated with excessive carbon deposits. It is possible (but not very likely) for carbon deposits to raise the compression enough to compensate for the effects of leakage past rings or valves. Remove the cylinder head and carefully decarbonize the combustion chambers (see Chapter 2).

16 Spark plugs - replacement

Refer to illustrations 16.3a, 16.3b, 16.7a and 16.7b

1   Make sure your spark plug socket is the correct size before attempting to remove the plugs.

2   Remove the fairing lower covers for access to the plugs (see Chapter 8).

3   Disconnect the spark plug caps from the spark plugs **(see illustration)**. If available, use compressed air to blow any accumulated debris from around the spark plugs. Remove the plugs **(see illustration)**.

4   Inspect the electrodes for wear. Both the center and side electrodes should have square edges and the side electrode should be of uniform thickness. Look for excessive deposits and evidence of a cracked or chipped insulator around the center electrode. Compare your spark plugs to the color spark plug reading chart. Check the threads, the washer and the ceramic insulator body for cracks and other damage.

5   If the electrodes are not excessively worn, and if the deposits can be easily removed with a wire brush, the plugs can be regapped and reused (if no cracks or chips are visible in the insulator). If in doubt concerning the condition of the plugs, replace them with new ones, as the expense is minimal.

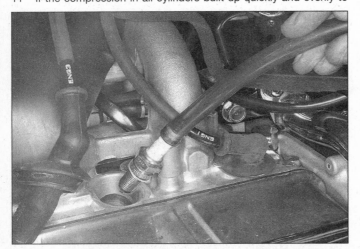

16.3b Use an extension and a deep socket (preferably one with a rubber insert to prevent damage to the plug) to remove the spark plugs; using a piece of flexible tubing to thread he plug into the hole will prevent cross-threading

16.7a Spark plug manufacturers recommend using a wire type gauge when checking the gap - if the wire doesn't slide between the electrodes with a slight drag, adjustment is required

16.7b To change the gap, bend the side electrode only, as indicated by the arrows, and be very careful not to crack or chip the ceramic insulator surrounding the center electrode

6   Cleaning spark plugs by sandblasting is permitted, provided you clean the plugs with a high flash-point solvent afterwards.

7   Before installing new plugs, make sure they are the correct type and heat range. Check the gap between the electrodes, as they are not preset. For best results, use a wire-type gauge rather than a flat gauge to check the gap (see illustration). If the gap must be adjusted, bend the side electrode only and be very careful not to chip or crack the insulator nose (see illustration). Make sure the washer is in place before installing each plug.

8   Since the cylinder head is made of aluminum, which is soft and easily damaged, thread the plugs into the heads by hand. Since the plugs are recessed, slip a short length of hose over the end of the plug to use as a tool to thread it into place (see illustration 16.3b). The hose will grip the plug well enough to turn it, but will start to slip if the plug begins to cross-thread in the hole - this will prevent damaged threads and the accompanying repair costs.

9   Once the plugs are finger-tight, the job can be finished with a socket. If a torque wrench is available, tighten the spark plugs to the torque listed in this Chapter's Specifications. If you do not have a torque wrench, tighten the plugs finger-tight (until the washers bottom on the cylinder head) then use a wrench to tighten them an additional 1/4 turn. Regardless of the method used, do not over-tighten them.

10   Reconnect the spark plug caps and reinstall all removed components.

17   Idle speed - check and adjustment

Refer to illustration 17.4

1   The idle speed should be checked and adjusted before and after the carburetors are synchronized and when it is obviously too high or too low. Before adjusting the idle speed, make sure the spark plug gaps are correct. Also, turn the handlebars back-and-forth and see if the idle speed changes as this is done. If it does, the accelerator cable may not be routed correctly, or it may be worn out. This is a dangerous condition that can cause loss of control of the bike. Be sure to correct this problem before proceeding.

2   The engine should be at normal operating temperature, which is usually reached after 10 to 15 minutes of stop and go riding. Place the motorcycle on its centerstand and make sure the transmission is in Neutral.

3   Open the top compartment cover for access to the throttle stop screw.

4   Turn the throttle stop screw (see illustration) until the idle speed listed in this Chapter's Specifications is obtained.

5   Snap the throttle open and shut a few times, then recheck the idle speed. If necessary, repeat the adjustment procedure.

6   If a smooth, steady idle can't be achieved, the fuel/air mixture may be incorrect. Refer to Chapter 4 for additional carburetor information.

18   Carburetor synchronization - check and adjustment

Refer to illustrations 18.9, 18.10a, 18.10b and 18.14

Warning 1: Gasoline (petrol) is extremely flammable, so take extra precautions when you work on any part of the fuel system. Don't smoke or allow open flames or bare light bulbs near the work area, and don't work in a garage where a natural gas-type appliance (such as a water heater or clothes dryer) is present. If you spill any fuel on your skin, rinse it off immediately with soap and water. When you perform any kind of work on the fuel system, wear safety glasses and have a class B type fire extinguisher on hand.

Warning 2: You'll need to work near the right cooling fan during this procedure. Be sure to keep your hands and tools out of the way. Don't wear loose clothing that might get caught in the fan if it comes on.

1   Carburetor synchronization is simply the process of adjusting the carburetors so they pass the same amount of fuel/air mixture to each cylinder. This is done by measuring the vacuum produced in each cylinder. Carburetors that are out of synchronization will result in decreased fuel mileage, increased engine temperature, less than ideal throttle response and higher vibration levels.

17.4 This knob is used to set idle speed

1

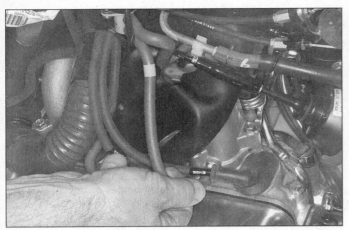

18.9 Detach the green-coded no. 6 hose from its fitting on the left side of the engine and attach the gauge setup to the fitting

18.10a On the right side, remove the screw and thread a vacuum hose fitting into the hole, then attach the gauge setup

2   To properly synchronize the carburetors, you will need some sort of vacuum gauge setup, preferably with a gauge for each cylinder, or a mercury manometer, which is a calibrated tube arrangement that utilizes columns of mercury to indicate engine vacuum. You'll also need an auxiliary fuel tank, since the bike's fuel tank must be removed for access to the vacuum fittings and synchronizing screws.

3   A manometer can be purchased from a motorcycle dealer or accessory shop and should have the necessary rubber hoses supplied with it for hooking into the vacuum hose fittings on the carburetors.

4   A vacuum gauge setup can also be purchased from a dealer or fabricated from commonly available hardware and automotive vacuum gauges.

5   The manometer is the more reliable and accurate instrument, and for that reason is preferred over the vacuum gauge setup; however, since the mercury used in the manometer is a liquid, and extremely toxic, extra precautions must be taken during use and storage of the instrument.

6   Because of the nature of the synchronization procedure and the need for special instruments, most owners leave the task to a dealer service department or a reputable motorcycle repair shop.

7   Remove both fairing lower covers and the right fairing inner cover (see Chapter 8).

8   Start the engine and let it run until it reaches normal operating temperature, then shut it off.

9   Disconnect the no. 6 vacuum hose (coded green) from the fitting on the left side of the engine near the rear spark plug **(see illustration)**.

10   On the right side of the bike, remove the screw from the vacuum

port and install a vacuum hose fitting in its place **(see illustration)**. Remove the rubber grommet from the right fan shroud to open up the access hole for the synchronizing screw **(see illustration)**.

11   Hook up the vacuum gauge set or the manometer according to the manufacturer's instructions. Make sure there are no leaks in the setup, as false readings will result.

12   Start the engine and make sure the idle speed is correct. If it isn't, adjust it (see Section 17).

13   The vacuum readings for both carburetors should be the same, or at least within the tolerance listed in this Chapter's Specifications. If the vacuum readings vary, adjust as necessary.

14   To perform the adjustment, synchronize the right carburetor to the left carburetor by turning the synchronizing screw, as needed, until the vacuum is identical or nearly identical for both cylinders **(see illustration)**. Snap the throttle open and shut 2 or 3 times, then recheck the adjustment and readjust as necessary.

15   When the adjustment is complete, recheck the vacuum readings and idle speed, then stop the engine. Remove the vacuum gauge or manometer and install the screw and vacuum hose.

16   Reinstall all components removed for access.

19 Lubrication - general

Refer to illustration 19.2a, 19.2b, 19.2c and 19.3

1   Since the controls, cables and various other components of a motorcycle are exposed to the elements, they should be lubricated

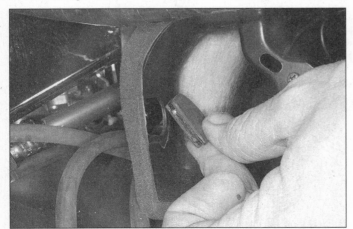

18.10b Pull the grommet out of the access hole in the fan shroud

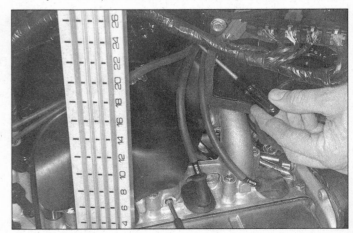

18.14 Insert a long screwdriver into the hole to turn the synchronizing screw

19.2a Ideally, the brake and clutch lever pivots should be removed and greased . . .

19.2b . . . and so should the pivot bushing . . .

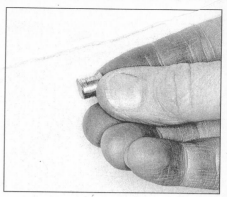

19.2c . . . unlubricated pivot bushings will wear severely, like this one

periodically to ensure safe and trouble-free operation.

2   The footpegs, clutch and brake lever, brake pedal, shift lever and sidestand pivots should be lubricated frequently. In order for the lubricant to be applied where it will do the most good, the component should be disassembled **(see illustrations)**. However, if chain and cable lubricant is being used, it can be applied to the pivot joint gaps and will usually work its way into the areas where friction occurs. If motor oil or light grease is being used, apply it sparingly as it may attract dirt (which could cause the controls to bind or wear at an accelerated rate). **Note:** *One of the best lubricants for the control lever pivots is a dry-film lubricant (available from many sources by different names).*

3   To lubricate the throttle and choke cables, disconnect the cable(s) at the lower end, then lubricate the cable with a pressure lube adapter **(see illustration)**.

4   The speedometer cable should be removed from its housing and lubricated with motor oil or cable lubricant.

5   Refer to Chapter 7 for the swingarm needle bearing lubrication procedures.

20 Fuel system - check and filter replacement

Warning: *Gasoline (petrol) is extremely flammable, so take extra precautions when you work on any part of the fuel system. Don't smoke or allow open flames or bare light bulbs near the work area, and don't work in a garage where a natural gas-type appliance (such as a water heater or clothes dryer) is present. If you spill any fuel on your skin, rinse it off immediately with soap and water. When you perform any kind of work on the fuel system, wear safety glasses and have a class B type fire extinguisher on hand.*

Check

Refer to illustration 20.5

1   Check the fuel tank, the tank breather hose, the fuel tap, the lines and the carburetors for leaks and evidence of damage.

2   If carburetor gaskets are leaking, the carburetors should be disassembled and rebuilt (see Chapter 4).

3   If the fuel tap is leaking, tightening the screws may help. If leakage persists, the tap should be disassembled and repaired or replaced with a new one.

4   If the fuel lines are cracked or otherwise deteriorated, replace them with new ones.

5   Check the fuel filter next to the filler cap for clogging **(see illustration)**. If there's visible sediment inside the filter, replace it. Honda doesn't specify a replacement interval for the filter.

Filter replacement

6   Remove the seat and the top compartment (see Chapter 8).

7   Disconnect the lines from the filter and remove it from its mounting band **(see illustration 20.5)**.

8   Install a new filter and reconnect the lines. Run the engine and check for leaks.

21 Evaporative emission control system (California models) - check

1   Periodic checking of this system consists of inspecting the lines and tubes for wear, cracking, brittleness and loose connections.

2   Check the canister, mounted behind the engine, for obvious damage such as cracks. For further details of the system refer to Chapter 4.

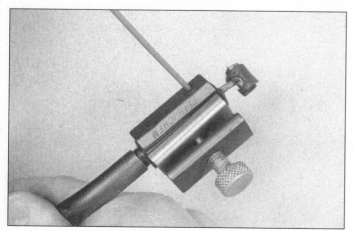

19.3 Lubricating a cable with a pressure lube adapter (make sure the tool seats around the inner cable)

20.5 The fuel filter is mounted next to the gas filler cap

23.1 If the desiccant in the window (upper arrow) is blue, it's in satisfactory condition; if it's clear, it needs to be replaced; the filter element is inside the rubber cover (lower arrow)

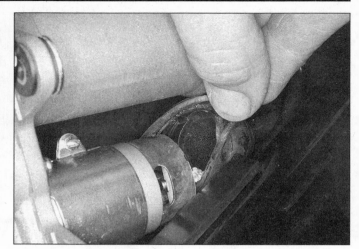

23.2 Pull the cover back and take the element out

22 Exhaust system - check

1   Periodically check all of the exhaust system joints for leaks and loose fasteners. The lower fairing panels will have to be removed to do this properly (see Chapter 8). If tightening the clamp bolts fails to stop any leaks, replace the gaskets with new ones (a procedure which requires disassembly of the system - see Chapter 4).

2   The exhaust pipe flange nuts at the cylinder heads are especially prone to loosening, which could cause damage to the head. Check them frequently and keep them tight.

23 On-board compressor system check and element cleaning

Refer to illustrations 23.1 and 23.2

1   The desiccant in the compressor should be inspected **(see illustration)**. For access, remove the seat (see Chapter 8). If the desiccant is blue, it is in good condition. If it's colorless, have it replaced by a Honda dealer or other qualified Gold Wing shop.

2   Pull back the rubber cover from the compressor and remove the filter element **(see illustration)**.

24.4 Grasp the front wheel or the bottom ends of the forks and try to pull the forks back and forth; if they move, the steering head bearings are loose and in need of adjustment

3   Clean the element in high flash point solvent, then squeeze it out thoroughly and let it dry completely. After the element has dried, soak it in the oil listed in this Chapter's Specifications, then squeeze out the excess.

4   Reverse the removal steps to reinstall the filter element.

24 Steering head bearings - check

Refer to illustration 24.4

1   This vehicle is equipped with tapered roller type steering head bearings which can become dented, rough or loose during normal use of the machine. In extreme cases, worn or loose steering head bearings can cause steering wobble that is potentially dangerous.

2   To check the bearings, support the motorcycle securely and block the machine so the front wheel is in the air.

3   Point the wheel straight ahead and slowly move the handlebars from side-to-side. Dents or roughness in the bearing races will be felt and the bars will not move smoothly.

4   Next, grasp the wheel and try to move it forward and backward **(see illustration)**. Any looseness in the steering head bearings will be felt as front-to-rear movement of the fork legs. If play is felt in the bearings, they should be adjusted, not a simple procedure on these models. Refer to Chapter 6 for details.

25 Fasteners - check

1   Since vibration of the machine tends to loosen fasteners, all nuts, bolts, screws, etc. should be periodically checked for proper tightness.

2   Pay particular attention to the following:
Spark plugs
Engine oil drain plug
Oil filter cover bolt and drain plug
Gearshift lever
Footpegs, sidestand and centerstand
Engine mount bolts
Exhaust system mounts
Shock absorber mount bolts
Rear suspension linkage bolts
Front axle and clamp bolt
Rear axle nut

3   If a torque wrench is available, use it along with the torque specifications at the beginning of this, or other, Chapters.

27.7 Inspect both cap gaskets (arrows)

26   Suspension - check

1   The suspension components must be maintained in top operating condition to ensure rider safety. Loose, worn or damaged suspension parts decrease the vehicle's stability and control.
2   While standing alongside the motorcycle, lock the front brake and push on the handlebars to compress the forks several times. See if they move up-and-down smoothly without binding. If binding is felt, the forks should be disassembled and inspected as described in Chapter 7.
3   Carefully inspect the area around the fork seals for any signs of fork oil leakage. If leakage is evident, the seals must be replaced as described in Chapter 6.
4   Check the tightness of all suspension nuts and bolts to be sure none have worked loose.
5   Inspect the rear shocks for fluid leakage and tightness of the mounting nuts. If leakage is found, the shocks should be replaced.
6   Support the bike securely so it can't be knocked over during this procedure. Grab the swingarm on each side, just ahead of the axle. Rock the swingarm from side to side - there should be no discernible movement at the rear. If there's a little movement or a slight clicking can be heard, make sure the pivot shaft nuts are tight. If the pivot nuts are tight but movement is still noticeable, the swingarm will have to be removed and the bearings replaced as described in Chapter 6.
7   Inspect the tightness of the rear suspension nuts and bolts.

27   Cooling system - inspection

Refer to illustrations 27.7 and 27.8
Warning: *The engine must be cool before beginning this procedure.*
Note: *Refer to Section 3 and check the coolant level before performing this check.*
1   The entire cooling system should be checked carefully at the recommended intervals. Look for evidence of leaks, check the condition of the coolant, check the radiator for clogged fins and damage and make sure the fans operate when required.
2   Remove fairing panels as necessary for access to the cooling system components (see Chapter 8).
3   Examine each of the rubber coolant hoses along its entire length. Look for cracks, abrasions and other damage. Squeeze each hose at various points. They should feel firm, yet pliable, and return to their original shape when released. If they are dried out or hard, replace them with new ones.
4   Check for evidence of leaks at each cooling system joint. Tighten the hose clamps careful to prevent future leaks. If coolant has been leaking from the joints of steel or aluminum coolant tubes, remove the tubes and replace the O-rings (see Chapter 3).
5   Check the radiators for evidence of leaks and other damage. Leaks in the radiators leave telltale scale deposits or coolant stains on

the outside of the core below the leak. If leaks are noted, remove the faulty radiator (see Chapter 3) and have it repaired by a radiator shop or replace it with a new one. **Caution:** *Do not use a liquid leak stopping compound to try to repair leaks.*
6   Check the radiator fins for mud, dirt and insects, which may impede the flow of air through the radiator. If the fins are dirty, force water or low pressure compressed air through the fins from the backside. If the fins are bent or distorted, straighten them carefully with a screwdriver.
7   Remove the pressure cap by turning it counterclockwise (anti-clockwise) until it reaches a stop. If you hear a hissing sound (indicating there is still pressure in the system), wait until it stops. Now, press down on the cap with the palm of your hand and continue turning the cap counterclockwise (anti-clockwise) until it can be removed. Check the condition of the coolant in the system. If it is rust colored or if accumulations of scale are visible, drain, flush and refill the system with new coolant. Check the cap gaskets for cracks and other damage **(see illustration)**. Have the cap tested by a dealer service department or replace it with a new one. Install the cap by turning it clockwise until it reaches the first stop, then push down on the cap and continue turning until it can turn no further.
8   Check the antifreeze content of the coolant with an antifreeze hydrometer **(see illustration)**. Sometimes coolant may look like it's in good condition, but might be too weak to offer adequate protection. If the hydrometer indicates a weak mixture, drain, flush and refill the cooling system (see Section 28).
9   Start the engine and let it reach normal operating temperature, then check for leaks again. As the coolant temperature increases, the fan should come on automatically and the temperature should begin to drop. If it doesn't, refer to Chapter 3 and check the fan and fan circuit carefully.
10   If the coolant level is consistently low, and no evidence of leaks can be found, have the entire system pressure checked by a Honda dealer service department, motorcycle repair shop or service station.

28   Cooling system - draining , flushing and refilling

Warning: *Allow the engine to cool completely before performing this maintenance operation. Also, don't allow antifreeze to come into contact with your skin or painted surfaces of the motorcycle. Rinse off spills immediately with plenty of water. Antifreeze is highly toxic if ingested. Never leave antifreeze lying around in an open container or in puddles on the floor; children and pets are attracted by its sweet smell and may drink it. Check with local authorities about disposing of used antifreeze. Many communities have collection centers which will see that antifreeze is disposed of safely. Antifreeze is also combustible, so don't store or use it near open flames.*

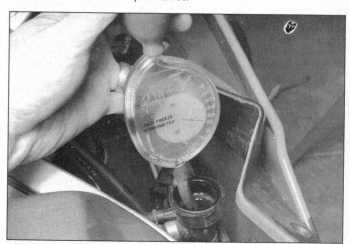

27.8 An antifreeze hydrometer is helpful in determining the condition of the coolant

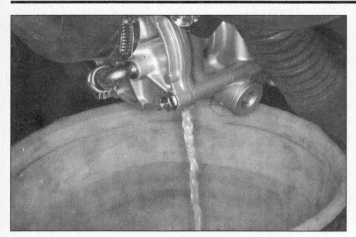

28.2 Remove the drain bolt from the water pump and let the coolant drain

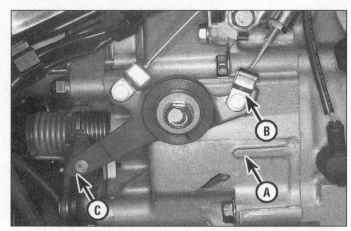

29.3 The cast pointer (A) should align with the indicator line in the lever (B - hidden behind the cable fitting); the indicator line on the other end of the lever (C) is used to check freeplay

Draining

Refer to illustration 28.2

1   Place a large, clean drain pan under the water pump at the left front corner of the engine.

2   Remove the drain bolt from the bottom of the water pump **(see illustration)** and allow the coolant to drain into the pan. After removing the drain bolt, remove the pressure cap to ensure that all of the coolant can drain. **Note:** *The coolant will rush out with considerable force as soon as the cap is removed, so position the drain pan accordingly.*

3   Drain the coolant reservoir. Refer to Chapter 3 for the reservoir removal procedure. Wash the reservoir out with water.

Flushing

4   Flush the system with clean tap water by inserting a garden hose in the radiator filler neck. Allow the water to run through the system until it is clear when it exits the drain bolt holes. If the radiator is extremely corroded, remove it (see Chapter 3) and have it cleaned at a radiator shop.

5   Honda recommends flushing the cooling system with a flushing compound compatible with aluminum engines. However, these compounds are generally toxic. Check with local authorities to see whether it's necessary to collect the drained compound and take it to a hazardous waste disposal facility.

6   Check the drain bolt gasket. Replace it with a new one if necessary.

7   Clean the drain hole, then install the drain bolt and tighten it securely, but don't overtighten it and strip the threads.

8   Fill the cooling system with clean water mixed with a flushing compound. Make sure the flushing compound is compatible with aluminum components, and follow the manufacturer's instructions carefully.

9   Start the engine and let it run for about ten minutes.

10   Stop the engine. Let the machine cool for a while, then cover the pressure cap with a heavy rag and turn it counterclockwise to the first stop, releasing any pressure that may be present in the system. Once the hissing stops, push down on the cap and remove it completely.

11   Drain the system once again.

12   Fill the system with clean water, then repeat Steps 8 through 11 two more times (that is, run the engine for 10 minutes, drain it, then run it with clean water again and drain it again).

Refilling

13   Fill the system with the proper coolant mixture (see this Chapter's Specifications). When the system is full (all the way up to the top of the radiator cap filler neck), start the engine. Watch the coolant and level as the engine runs, and add coolant when the level drops. When the coolant level stabilizes, shut the engine off.

14   Fill the system with coolant to the top of the filler neck.

15   Allow the engine to cool, then check the coolant level in the reservoir (see Section 3). If the coolant level is low, add the specified mix-

ture until it reaches the Full mark in the reservoir.

16   Check the system for leaks.

17   Do not dispose of the old coolant by pouring it down a drain. Instead, pour it into a heavy plastic container, cap it tightly and take it to an authorized disposal site or a service station.

29   Reverse system operation (Aspencade and Interstate) - check

Check

Refer to illustration 29.3

1   Make sure the ignition switch is in the Off position, then place the bike on its centerstand.

2   Remove the right front side cover (see Chapter 8).

3   Operate the reverse handle and make sure the reverse cables and pulley move smoothly **(see illustration)**. If they don't, disconnect and lubricate the cables (see Section 19 and Chapter 2).

4   Spin the rear wheel by hand. With the transmission in neutral and the reverse lever down (disengaged), the rear wheel should turn.

5   Pull the reverse lever up into the engaged position. It should now be impossible to turn the rear wheel by hand. If you can still turn the wheel, reverse gear isn't engaged and adjustment will be necessary.

6   Check the alignment of the pointer index mark with the cast pointer on the crankcase **(see illustration 29.3)**. They should align when reverse is engaged. Also, there should be a slight freeplay in the other end of the lever.

Adjustment

Refer to illustration 29.7

7   Start by aligning the index mark and pointer. To do this, loosen the locknut, turn the pointer adjuster, then tighten the locknut **(see illustration)**.

8   With the index marks aligned, adjust freeplay. To do this, loosen the locknut, turn the freeplay adjuster and tighten the locknut **(see illustration 29.7)**.

30   Cruise valve element (Aspencade and SE) - replacement

Refer to illustrations 30.2 and 30.3

1   Remove the left inner fairing cover (see Chapter 8).

2   Detach the filter housing from the cruise valve **(see illustration)**.

3   Pull out the element, install a new one and reinstall the housing **(see illustration)**.

4   Install the left inner fairing cover.

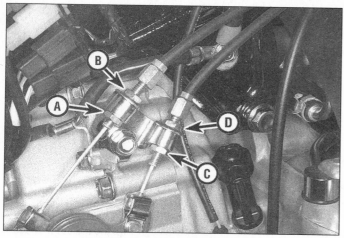

29.7 Reverse cable adjusting points

A Pointer indicator
    adjusting nut
B Pointer indicator locknut

C Freeplay adjusting nut
D Freeplay locknut

31 Final drive - oil change

1   Place the bike on its centerstand and place a drain pan beneath the final drive **(see illustration 3.22)**.
2   Remove the filler plug, then the drain plug and let the oil drain into the pan for 10 minutes or more.
3   Reinstall the drain plug and tighten it to the torque listed in this Chapter's Specifications.
4   Add oil of the type and amount listed in this Chapter's Specifications. **Note:** *The specified capacity is approximate. Fill the final drive until the oil is at the bottom of the filler hole.*
5   Install the filler plug and tighten it to the torque listed in this Chapter's Specifications.

32 Headlight aim - check and adjustment

The headlight aim should be adjusted periodically so it conforms with local regulations, for the safety of the rider as well as oncoming drivers. Some of the procedures require removal of the headlight trim or front grille ((see Chapter 8). For detailed adjustment procedures, refer to Chapter 9.

30.2 Detach the filter housing from the cruise valve . . .

30.3 . . . and pull out the element

Notes

Chapter 2
Engine, clutch and transmission

Contents

Specifications

Timing belts

Belt slack	5 to 7 mm (0.2 to 0.3 inch)

Camshaft holders

Rocker arm inside diameter
- Standard .... 25.000 to 25.021 mm (0.983 to 0.9851 inch)
- Limit .... 25.05 mm (0.986 inch)

Rocker arm shaft diameter
- Standard .... 11.966 to 11.984 mm (0.4711 to 0.4718 inch)
- Limit .... 11.95 mm (0.470 inch)

Rocker arm eccentric spindle inside diameter
- Standard .... 11.996 to 12.031 mm (0.4723 to 0.4724 inch)
- Limit .... 12.07 mm (0.475 inch)

Camshaft holders (continued)

Rocker arm eccentric spindle outside diameter
    Standard.. 20.945 to 20.980 mm (0.8246 to 0.8260 mm)
    Limit.. 20.93 mm (0.824 inch)
Lash adjuster stroke
    Standard.. Zero to 0.30 mm (zero to 0.12 inch)
    Limit.. 0.30 mm (0.12 inch)

Lash adjusters

Intake
    10.2 to 10.3 mm (0.402 to 0.406 inch) .... No shims
    10.3 to 10.4 mm (0.406 to 0.409 inch) .... 1 shim
    10.4 to 10.5 mm (0.409 to 0.413 inch) .... 2 shims
    10.5 to 10.66 mm (0.413 to 0.417 inch) .... 3 shims
Exhaust
    12.2 to 12.3 mm (0.480 to 0.484 inch) .... No shims
    12.3 to 12.4 mm (0.484 to 0.488 inch) .... 1 shim
    12.4 to 12.5 mm (0.488 to 0.492 inch) .... 2 shims
    12.5 to 12.6 mm(0.492 to 0.496 inch) .... 3 shims

Camshafts

Lobe height
    Standard.. 36.110 to 36.190 mm (1.4217 to 1.4284 inch)
    Minimum .... 35.9 mm (1.41 inch)
Bearing oil clearance
    Center journals
        Standard.. 0.045 to 0.087 mm (0.0018 to 0.0034 inch)
        Limit.. 0.14 mm (0.006 inch)
    Forward and rear journals
        Standard.. 0.030 to 0.072 mm (0.0012 to 0.0028 inch)
        Limit.. 0.014 mm (0.006 inch)
Journal diameter
    Center journals
        Standard.. 26.934 to 26.955 mm (1.0604 to 1.0612 inch)
        Limit.. 26.91 mm (1.059 inch)
    Forward and rear journals
        Standard.. 26.949 to 26.955 mm (1.0614 to 1.0612 inch)
        Limit.. 26.91 mm (1.059 inch)
Bearing bore
    Standard.. 27.000 to 27.021 mm (0.0630 to 0.0638 inch)
    Limit.. 27.05 mm (1.065 inch)
Camshaft runout limit (at center journals)............................... 0.10 mm (0.004 inch)

Cylinder head, valves and valve springs

Cylinder head warpage limit .... 0.10 mm (0.004 inch)
Valve stem bend limit .... Not specified
Valve stem diameter
    Standard
        Intake .... 5.475 to 5.490 mm (0.2156 to 0.2161 inch)
        Exhaust .... 5.455 to 5.470 mm (0.2148 to 0.2154 inch)
    Limit
        Intake .... 5.45 mm (0.215 inch)
        Exhaust .... 5.44 mm (0.214 inch)
Valve guide inside diameter (intake and exhaust)
    Standard.. 5.500 to 5.512 mm (0.2165 to 0.2170 inch)
    Limit.. 5.55 mm (0.179 inch)
Stem-to-guide clearance
    Intake
        Standard.. 0.010 to 0.037 mm (0.0004 to 0.0015 inch)
        Limit.. 0.08 mm(0.003 inch)
    Exhaust
        Standard.. 0.030 to 0.057 mm (0.0012 to 0.0022 inch)
        Limit.. 0.10 mm (0.004 inch)
Valve seat width (intake and exhaust) .... 1.2 mm (0.05 inch)
Valve face width (intake and exhaust) .... Not specified
Valve spring free length (intake and exhaust)
    Standard.. 44.6 mm (1.76 inch)
    Minimum.. 43.3 mm (1.70 inch)
Valve spring bend limit .... Not specified

Cylinders

Bore diameter
   Standard... 71.010 to 71.025 mm (2.7957 to 2.7963 inch)
   Maximum... 71.1 mm (2.8 inch)
   Bore measuring point... 40 mm (1.57 inch) from top of cylinder
Out-of-round limit.. 0.15 mm (0.006 inch)
Taper limit.. 0.05 mm (0.002 inch)
Surface warp limit.. 0.05 mm (0.002 inch)

Pistons

Piston diameter
   Standard... 70.960 to 70.990 mm (2.7937 to 2.7949 inch)
   Limit.. 70.85 mm (2.7789 inch)
Diameter measuring point.. 10 mm (0.4 inch) from bottom of skirt
Piston-to-cylinder clearance
   Standard... 0.015 to 0.065 mm (0.0006 to 0.0026 inch)
   Maximum... 0.10 mm (0.004 inch)
Ring side clearance
  Top ring
    Standard... 0.025 to 0.055 mm (0.0010 to 0.0022 inch)
    Maximum... 0.10 mm (0.004 inch)
  Second ring
    Standard... 0.015 to 0.045 mm (0.0006 to 0.0018 inch)
    Maximum... 0.10 mm (0.004 inch)
  Oil ring.. Not specified
Ring end gap
  Top and second rings... 0.15 to 0.30 mm (0.006 to 0.012 inch)
  Oil ring.. 0.20 to 0.70 mm (0.008 to 0.028 inch)

Reverse mechanism

Reverse stopper shaft installed height.................................. 6.7 to 7.3 mm (0.26 to 0.29 inch)

Primary gears

Primary driven gear boss needle bearing installed height...... 3.5 to 4.0 mm (0.14 to 0.16 inch)

Output shaft

Shaft diameter limit... 21.99 mm (0.866 inch)
Collar inside diameter limit.. 22.05 mm (0.868 inch)
Collar outside diameter limit.. 25.95 mm (1.022 inch)
Driven gear inside diameter limit... 26.03 mm (1.025 inch)

Crankshaft, connecting rods and bearings

Main bearing oil clearance
   Standard... 0.020 to 0.038 mm (0.0008 to 0.0015 inch)
   Maximum... 0.06 mm (0.002 inch)
Connecting rod side clearance
   Standard... 0.15 to 0.30 mm (0.006 to 0.012 inch)
   Maximum... 0.40 mm (0.016 inch)
Connecting rod bearing oil clearance
   Standard... 0.027 to 0.045 mm (0.0011 to 0.0018 inch)
   Maximum... 0.06 mm (0.002 inch)
Crankshaft runout limit.. 0.03 mm (0.001 inch)
Crankshaft journal taper limit.. 0.003 mm (0.0001 inch)
Crankshaft journal out-of-round limit..................................... 0.005 mm (0.0002 inch)
Connecting rod bearing selection
If crankcase ID number is I or 1
   With crankshaft journal ID letter A.................................... Yellow
   With crankshaft journal ID letter B.................................... Green
   With crankshaft journal ID letter C.................................... Brown
If crankcase ID number is II or 2
   With crankshaft journal ID letter A.................................... Green
   With crankshaft journal ID letter B.................................... Brown
   With crankshaft journal ID letter C.................................... Black
If crankcase ID number is III or 3
   With crankshaft journal ID letter A.................................... Brown
   With crankshaft journal ID letter B.................................... Black
   With crankshaft journal ID letter C.................................... Blue

2

Crankshaft, connecting rods and bearings (continued)

Main bearing selection
If crankcase ID number is I
    With crankshaft journal ID number 1 .... Yellow
    With crankshaft journal ID number 2 .... Green
    With crankshaft journal ID number 3 .... Brown
If crankcase ID number is II
    With crankshaft journal ID number 1 .... Green
    With crankshaft journal ID number 2 .... Brown
    With crankshaft journal ID number 3 .... Black
If crankcase ID number is III
    With crankshaft journal ID number 1 .... Brown
    With crankshaft journal ID number 2 .... Black
    With crankshaft journal ID number 3 .... Blue

Oil pumps

Inner to outer rotor clearance
    Standard .... Less than 0.15 mm (0.006 inch)
    Limit .... 0.35 mm (0.014 inch)
Outer rotor to housing clearance
    Standard .... 0.15 to 0.23 mm (0.006 to 0.009 inch)
    Limit .... 0.43 mm (0.017 inch)
Rotor to straightedge clearance
    Standard .... 0.02 to 0.07 mm (0.001 to 0.003 inch)
    Limit .... 0.12 mm (0.005 inch)

Clutch

Friction plate thickness
    Standard .... 3.72 to 3.88 mm (0.146 to 0.153 inch)
    Minimum .... 3.5 mm (0.14 inch)
Steel plate warpage limit .... 0.30 mm (0.012 inch)
Spring length
    Standard .... 5.38 mm (0.212 inch)
    Minimum .... 5.1 mm (0.20 inch)
Master cylinder bore diameter
    Standard .... 15.870 to 15.913 mm (0.6248 to 0.6265 inch)
    Limit .... 15.93 mm (0.627 inch)
Master cylinder piston diameter
    Standard .... 15.827 to 15.854 mm (0.6231 to 0.6242 inch)
    Limit .... 15.82 mm (0.623 inch)

Transmission

Countershaft gear inside diameter
    Standard .... 34.000 to 34.016 mm (1.3386 to 1.3392 inch)
    Limit .... 34.04 mm (1.340 inch)
Mainshaft gear inside diameter (1988 through 1996)
    Standard .... 34.000 to 34.016 mm (1.3386 to 1.3392 inch)
    Limit .... 34.04 mm (1.340 inch)
Mainshaft gear inside diameter (1997-on)
    Fourth gear
        Standard .... 31.000 to 31.025 mm (1.2205 to 1.2215 inch)
        Limit .... 31.04 mm (1.222 inch)
    Fifth gear
        Standard .... 30.000 to 30.021 mm (1.1811 to 1.1819 inch)
        Limit .... 30.04 mm (1.183 inch)
Countershaft bushing outside diameter
    Standard .... 33.940 to 33.965 mm (1.3362 to 1.3372 inch)
    Limit .... 33.92 mm (1.335 inch)
Mainshaft bushing outside diameter (1988 through 1996)
    Standard .... 33.940 to 33.965 mm (1.3362 to 1.3372 inch)
    Limit .... 33.92 mm (1.335 inch)
Mainshaft bushing outside diameter (1997-on)
    Fourth gear
        Standard .... 30.950 to 30.975 mm (1.2185 to 1.2195 inch)
        Limit .... 30.93 mm (1.218 inch)
    Fifth gear
        Standard .... 29.955 to 29.980 mm (1.1793 to 1.1803 inch)
        Limit .... 29.93 mm (1.178 inch)

Mainshaft bushing inside diameter (1997 and later only)
    Fourth gear
        Standard .... 28.000 to 28.021 mm (1.1024 to 1.1032 inch)
        Limit .... 28.04 mm (1.104 inch)
    Fifth gear
        Standard .... 23.000 to 23.021 mm (0.9055 to 0.9063 inch)
        Limit .... 23.03 mm (0.907 inch)
Mainshaft diameter (1997-on)
    At fourth gear
        Standard .... 27.974 to 27.987 mm (1.1013 to 1.1018 inch)
        Limit .... 27.95 mm (1.100 inch)
    At fifth gear
        Standard .... 22.947 to 22.987 mm (0.9045 to 0.0950 inch)
        Limit .... 22.95 mm (0.904 inch)
Countershaft gear to bushing clearance
    Standard .... 0.035 to 0.076 mm (0.0014 to 0.0030 inch)
    Limit .... 0.10 mm (0.004 inch)
Mainshaft gear to bushing clearance (1988 through 1996)
    Standard .... 0.035 to 0.076 mm (0.0014 to 0.0030 inch)
    Limit .... 0.10 mm (0.004 inch)
Mainshaft gear to bushing clearance (1997-on)
    Fourth gear
        Standard .... 0.035 to 0.076 mm (0.0014 to 0.0030 inch)
        Limit .... 0.10 mm (0.004 inch)
    Fifth gear
        Standard .... 0.020 to 0.066 mm (0.0008 to 0.0026 inch)
        Limit .... 0.09 mm (0.004 inch)
Shift forks
    Bore diameter
        Standard .... 14.000 to 14.021 mm (0.5512 to 0.5520 inch)
        Limit .... 14.04 mm (0.553 inch)
    Finger thickness
        Standard .... 5.93 to 6.00 mm (0.233 to 0.236 inch)
        Limit .... 5.6 mm (0.22 inch)
Fork shaft diameter
    Standard .... 13.966 to 13.984 mm (0.5498 to 0.5506 inch)
    Limit .... 13.90 mm (0.547 inch)

Torque specifications

Cylinder head main bolts .... 45 Nm (33 ft-lbs) (1)
Cylinder head sealing bolts .... 45 Nm (33 ft-lbs) (2)
Timing belt tensioner bolts .... 26 Nm (19 ft-lbs) (2)
Timing belt pulley bolts
    On crankshaft .... 75 Nm (54 ft-lbs)
    On camshafts .... 20 Nm (14 ft-lbs)
Camshaft holder bolts .... 20 Nm (14 ft-lbs)
Lash adjuster stopper plugs .... 30 Nm (22 ft-lbs)
Oil pressure switch .... 12 Nm (9 ft-lbs)
Oil filter mounting boss .... 17 Nm (12 ft-lbs) (2)
Clutch master cylinder clamp bolts .... 12 Nm (9 ft-lbs)
Clutch hose to metal tube union bolt .... 35 Nm (25 ft-lbs)
Slave cylinder bleed valve .... 9 Nm (7 ft-lbs)
Clutch bleed tube mounting bolt .... 12 Nm (9 ft-lbs)
Clutch center locknut .... 130 Nm (94 ft-lbs)
Clutch housing locknut .... 190 Nm (137 ft-lbs) (3)
Reverse shift shaft bolt .... 14 Nm (10 ft-lbs) (2)
Rear case cover bolts .... 30 Nm (22 ft-lbs)
Output shaft bearing holder bolts .... 30 Nm (22 ft-lbs)
Starter clutch bolt .... 75 Nm (54 ft-lbs)
Starter clutch Allen bolts (if equipped) .... 16 Nm (12 ft-lbs) (2)
Oil pump driven sprocket bolt .... 18 Nm (13 ft-lbs) (2)
Output shaft locknut .... 190 Nm (137 ft-lbs) (4)
Final drive gear locknut .... 190 Nm (137 ft-lbs) (3, 5)
Alternator drive gear bolts .... 27 Nm (20 ft-lbs) (6)
Shift arm return spring post .... 25 Nm (18 ft-lbs)
Shift arm lockbolt .... 25 Nm (18 ft-lbs)
Shift drum center bolt .... 28 Nm (20 ft-lbs)
Stopper arm bolt .... 12 Nm (9 ft-lbs) (2)

2

Torque specifications (continued)

Crankcase bolts
    10 mm shaft diameter .... 35 Nm (25 ft-lbs) (6)
    8 mm shaft diameter .... 26 Nm (19 ft-lbs)
    6 mm shaft diameter .... 12 Nm (9 ft-lbs)
Connecting rod cap nuts .... 32 Nm (23 ft-lbs) (6)
Main bearing cap bolts .... 70 Nm (51 ft-lbs) (6)
Mainshaft locknut .... 190 Nm (137 ft-lbs) (4, 5)

1   Apply molybdenum disulfide oil to the threads and the undersides of the bolt heads.
2   Apply non-permanent thread locking agent to the threads.
3   Apply non-permanent thread locking agent to the threads and stake the locknut in two places.
4   Stake the locknut in two places.
5   Left-hand threads (tighten counterclockwise).
6   Apply engine oil to the threads and the undersides of the bolt heads.

1   General information

The engine/transmission unit is a liquid-cooled, horizontally opposed six. The valves are operated by single overhead camshafts which are belt driven off the crankshaft. The engine/transmission assembly is constructed from aluminum alloy. The crankcase is divided vertically.

The crankcase incorporates a wet sump, pressure-fed lubrication system which uses two gear-driven oil pumps, an oil filter, relief valve and an oil pressure switch. The scavenge pump keeps the clutch well from filling with oil and the main pump supplies oil under pressure to friction points in the engine.

Power from the crankshaft is routed to the transmission via the clutch, which is of the diaphragm spring, wet multi-plate type and rides on the rear end of the crankshaft. The transmission is a five-speed, constant-mesh unit.

2   Operations possible with the engine in the frame

The components and assemblies listed below can be removed without having to remove the engine from the frame. If, however, a number of areas require attention at the same time, removal of the engine is recommended.

Starter motor
Alternator
Clutch assembly
Timing belts
Valve covers, rocker arms, camshafts and lifters
Cylinder heads

3   Operations requiring engine removal

It is necessary to remove the engine/transmission assembly from the frame and remove the rear engine cover or separate the crankcase halves to gain access to the following components:

Scavenging oil pump
Main oil pump
Starter clutch
Reverse system (if equipped)
Alternator gears
Primary gears
Output shaft and final drive gear
External and internal shift mechanisms
Crankshaft, connecting rods and bearings
Transmission shafts

4   Major engine repair - general note

1   It is not always easy to determine when or if an engine should be completely overhauled, as a number of factors must be considered.

2   High mileage is not necessarily an indication that an overhaul is needed, while low mileage, on the other hand, does not preclude the need for an overhaul. Frequency of servicing is probably the single most important consideration. An engine that has regular and frequent oil and filter changes, as well as other required maintenance, will most likely give many miles of reliable service. Conversely, a neglected engine, or one which has not been broken in properly, may require an overhaul very early in its life.

3   Exhaust smoke and excessive oil consumption are both indications that piston rings and/or valve guides are in need of attention. Make sure oil leaks are not responsible before deciding that the rings and guides are bad. Refer to Chapter 1 and perform a cylinder compression check to determine for certain the nature and extent of the work required.

4   If the engine is making obvious knocking or rumbling noises, the connecting rod and/or main bearings are probably at fault.

5   Loss of power, rough running, excessive valve train noise and high fuel consumption rates may also point to the need for an overhaul, especially if they are all present at the same time. If a complete tune-up does not remedy the situation, major mechanical work is the only solution.

6   An engine overhaul generally involves restoring the internal parts to the specifications of a new engine. During an overhaul the piston rings are replaced and the cylinder walls are bored and/or honed. If a rebore is done, then new pistons are also required. The main and connecting rod bearings are generally replaced with new ones and, if necessary, the crankshaft is also replaced. Generally the valves are serviced as well, since they are usually in less than perfect condition at this point. While the engine is being overhauled, other components

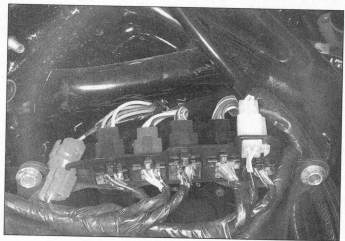

5.6 Unplug the connectors at the bracket on the right side of the engine

5.10 Disconnect the ground cable (upper arrow) and the reverse switch (if equipped) (lower arrow)

such as the carburetors and the starter motor can be rebuilt also. The end result should be a like-new engine that will give as many trouble free miles as the original.

7   Before beginning the engine overhaul, read through all of the related procedures to familiarize yourself with the scope and requirements of the job. Overhauling an engine is not all that difficult, but it is time consuming. Plan on the motorcycle being tied up for a minimum of two weeks. Check on the availability of parts and make sure that any necessary special tools, equipment and supplies are obtained in advance.

8   Most work can be done with typical shop hand tools, although a number of precision measuring tools are required for inspecting parts to determine if they must be replaced. Often a dealer service department or motorcycle repair shop will handle the inspection of parts and offer advice concerning reconditioning and replacement. As a general rule, time is the primary cost of an overhaul so it doesn't pay to install worn or substandard parts.

9   As a final note, to ensure maximum life and minimum trouble from a rebuilt engine, everything must be assembled with care in a spotlessly clean environment.

5   Engine - removal and installation

Note: *Engine removal and installation should be done with the aid of an assistant to avoid damage or injury that could occur if the engine is dropped. A hydraulic floor jack should be used to support and lower the engine if possible (they can be rented at low cost).*

Removal

Refer to illustrations 5.6, 5.10, 5.15, 5.17a, 5.17b, 5.17c, 5.18a through 5.18f and 5.20

1   Support the bike securely so it can't be knocked over during this procedure.

2   Disconnect the negative cable from the battery (see Chapter 1).

3   Remove the inner and lower fairing panels and the right footpeg (see Chapter 8).

4   Remove the air filter housing (see Chapter 5).

5   Drain the engine oil and coolant (see Chapter 1).

6   Locate the connector bracket on the right fan shroud **(see illustration)**. Unplug the black, white, red and blue connectors.

7   If the bike is equipped with a reverse system, disconnect the cables from the pulley and unplug the reverse switch connector (see Chapter 9).

8   Remove the left and right engine guards (see Chapter 8).

9   Remove the exhaust system (see Chapter 4).

10   Disconnect the engine ground cable from the right side of the

engine **(see illustration)**. Disconnect the crankcase breather tube from its retainers on the left side.

11   Remove the right timing belt cover (see Section 7).

12   Refer to Chapter 3 and remove or disconnect the following:

a) *Cooling fans*
b) *Radiator top hose, temperature sensor wire and ground wire from thermostat housing*
c) *Radiator bottom hose from water pump*

13   Refer to Chapter 9 and remove the starter and alternator. Disconnect the wires from the horn and sidestand switch.

14   Refer to Chapter 4 and remove the following:

a) *Air cleaner housing*
b) *Carburetors*
c) *Air and vacuum hoses from solenoids and air jet controller*

15   Refer to Section 13 and detach the clutch slave cylinder from the engine. **Note:** *It isn't necessary to disconnect the fluid line from the slave cylinder. However, to prevent the slave cylinder piston from being forced out of its bore, squeeze the clutch lever all the way to the handlebar and tie it securely* **(see illustration)**. *Don't release the clutch lever until the slave cylinder is reinstalled.*

16   Support the engine from below with a jack. **Note:** *At all times while the engine mounts and subframe are being unbolted, use the jack to relieve pressure on the mounts. You may need to raise or lower it slightly.*

17   On the right side of the engine, remove the bolts and nuts from

5.15 Tie the clutch lever to the handlebar before removing the slave cylinder so the piston won't fall out

2

5.17a Remove the lower right mounting bolt (left arrow) and the right sub-frame bolt(s) (right arrow) . . .

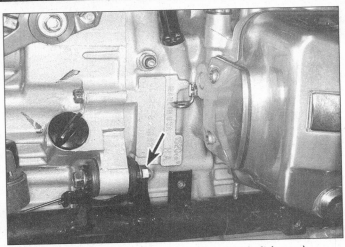

5.17b . . . remove the lower right mounting bolt (arrow) . . .

5.17c . . . and the upper right mounting bolt (arrow)

5.18a Remove the sub-frame forward Allen bolts . . .

the front and rear lower mounts and sub-frame, then from the front upper mount **(see illustrations)**.
18   On the left side of the bike, remove the sub-frame Allen bolts and the lower front and rear mounting bolts, then remove the sub-frame

(see illustrations). Remove the upper front mounting bracket, then remove the two short bolts and one through-bolt from the upper rear mounting bracket (the upper bolts also secure the cruise control actuator on models so equipped).

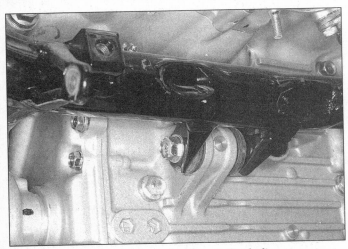

5.18b . . . the lower front mounting bolt . . .

5.18c . . . the lower rear mounting bolt (left arrow) and sub-frame rear Allen bolts (right arrows) . . .

5.18d . . . the upper left front bracket . . .

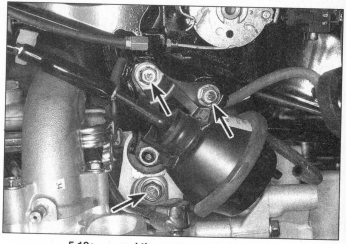

5.18e . . . and the upper rear bracket . . .

19   Make sure no wires or hoses are still attached to the engine assembly. **Warning:** *The engine weighs nearly 300 pounds and may cause injury if it falls. Be sure it's securely supported. Have an assistant help you steady the engine on the jack as you remove it.*

20   Slide the front end of the driveshaft off of the output shaft splines (see Chapter 6). Slowly and carefully lower the engine assembly to the floor, then guide it out from under the bike **(see illustration)**.

Installation

21   Installation is the reverse of removal. Note the following points.

22   Tighten all of the mounting bolts finger tight in the following order:

a) *Right rear lower*
b) *Right front lower*
c) *Right front upper*
d) *Left front and rear brackets*
e) *Upper rear (don't forget the collar)*
f) *Subframe Allen bolts*
g) *Subframe hex bolt on right side*
h) *Engine guards*
i) *Left lower rear*
j) *Left lower front*

23   Tighten the mounting bolts and nuts to the torque listed in this Chapter's Specifications, in the following order:

a) *Sub-frame Allen bolts (front and rear)*
b) *Sub-frame right side hex bolt*
c) *Lower right engine guard bolt*
d) *Left lower rear mounting bolt*

e) *Right lower rear mounting bolt*
f) *Left lower front mounting bolt*
g) *Right lower front mounting bolt*
h) *Left front and rear upper brackets to frame (but not to engine yet)*
i) *Left upper rear bracket through-bolt*
j) *Right upper front bracket bolt*
k) *Left upper front bracket to engine*

24   Use new gaskets at all exhaust pipe connections.

25   Adjust the throttle and choke cables following the procedures in Chapter 1.

26   Be sure to refill the cooling system and engine oil before starting the engine.

6   Engine disassembly and reassembly - general information

Refer to illustrations 6.2a, 6.2b and 6.3

1   Before disassembling the engine, clean the exterior with a degreaser and rinse it with water. A clean engine will make the job easier and prevent the possibility of getting dirt into the internal areas of the engine.

2   In addition to the precision measuring tools mentioned earlier, you will need a torque wrench, a valve spring compressor, oil gallery brushes, a piston ring removal and installation tool and special Honda piston ring compressors (which are described in Section 29). Some new, clean engine oil of the correct grade and type, some engine

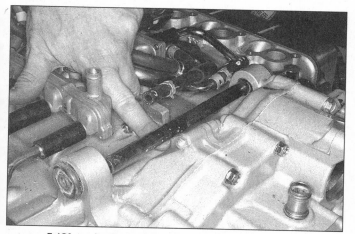

5.18f . . . its through-bolt passes through this tube

5.20 Use a jack to lower the engine and have an assistant help guide it out of the frame

assembly lube (or moly-based grease) and a tube of RTV (silicone) sealant will also be required. Although it may not be considered a tool, some Plastigage (type HPG-1) should also be obtained to use for checking bearing oil clearances **(see illustrations)**.

3   An engine support stand made from short lengths of 2 x 4's bolted together will facilitate the disassembly and reassembly procedures **(see illustration)**. The perimeter of the mount should be just big enough to accommodate the engine oil pan. If you have an automotive-type engine stand, an adapter plate can be made from a piece of plate, some angle iron and some nuts and bolts.

4   When disassembling the engine, keep "mated" parts together (including gears, cylinders, pistons, etc. that have been in contact with each other during engine operation). These "mated" parts must be reused or replaced as an assembly.

5   Engine/transmission disassembly should be done in the following general order with reference to the appropriate Sections.

Remove the timing belts
Remove the cylinder head covers
Remove the camshaft holders, rocker arms and camshafts
Remove the cylinder heads
Remove the front case cover
Remove the rear case cover
Remove the clutch
Remove the reverse mechanism (if equipped)
Remove the primary drive gears
Remove the scavenging oil pump
Remove the starter clutch and idle gears
Remove the external shift mechanism
Separate the crankcase halves
Remove the main oil pump
Remove the pistons and connecting rods
Remove the crankshaft and main bearings
Remove the transmission shafts/gears
Remove the shift drum/forks

6   Reassembly is accomplished by reversing the general disassembly sequence.

7   Timing belts - removal, inspection and installation

Note: *The timing belts can be removed with the engine in the frame. If the engine has been removed, ignore the steps which don't apply.*

Removal

Refer to illustrations 7.3, 7.4a, 7.4b, 7.4c, 7.5a, 7.5b and 7.6

1   Support the bike securely on its centerstand.
2   Remove the front and lower fairing panels (see Chapter 8).
3   Unbolt the timing belt covers from the engine **(see illustration)**.

6.3 An engine stand can be made from short lengths of 2 x 4 lumber and lag bolts or nails

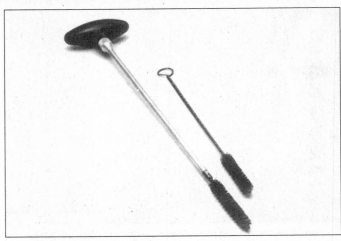

6.2a A selection of brushes is required for cleaning holes and passages in the engine components

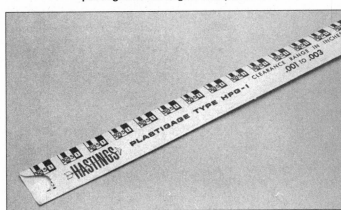

6.2b Type HPG-1 Plastigage is needed to check the crankshaft, connecting rod and camshaft oil clearances

4   Place a wrench on the crankshaft pulley and turn it counterclockwise (viewed from the front of the engine) until the line next to the 1-2 mark on the pulley aligns with the pointer cast in the front of the engine **(see illustration)**. The engine should be at top dead center on its compression stroke at this point. To verify that it is, check the UP marks on the timing belt pulleys; their index lines should be next to the pointers cast in the front of the engine **(see illustrations)**.

5   Using a felt pen, mark the belts with LEFT and RIGHT and an

7.3 Timing belt cover bolts

7.4a With the engine at top dead center on its compression stroke, the line next to the 1-2 mark on the crankshaft pulley will align with the triangular pointer cast in the cylinder head . . .

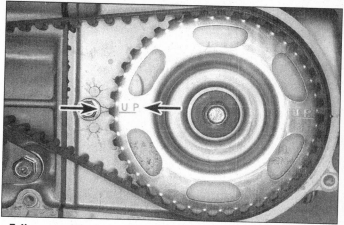

7.4b . . . and the index lines to the UP marks on each camshaft pulley will align with its triangular pointer in the cylinder head - this is the left camshaft pulley . . .

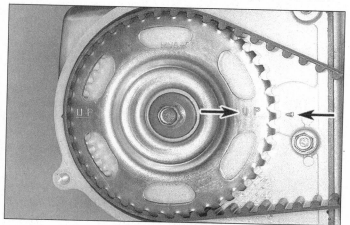

7.4c . . . and this is the right camshaft pulley

7.5a Label each belt with Left or Right marks and an arrow indicating direction of rotation

arrow to indicate their direction of rotation (counterclockwise, viewed from the front of the engine) **(see illustration)**. **Note:** *If you plan to remove the crankshaft pulley or either of the camshaft pulleys, loosen the pulley bolts now, before the belts are removed. If you decide to remove the pulleys later and the bolts haven't been loosened, you'll need a holder tool to keep the pulleys from turning while you loosen the bolts* **(see illustration).**

6   Loosen the tensioner mounting and adjusting bolts **(see illustra-**

tion). Slide the right timing belt off the pulleys with fingers only; don't pry it off or the belt may be damaged.

Caution: *Once either timing belt has been removed, don't turn the crankshaft pulley or either camshaft pulley. If this happens, the valves may be forced against the pistons, bending the valves.*

7   Refer to Chapter 5 and remove the pulse generators.
8   Slide the left timing belt off the pulleys.

7.5b A holder tool like this can be used to keep the camshaft pulley from turning while you loosen its bolt

7.6 There's a separate tensioner for each belt; they're secured by bolts (arrows)

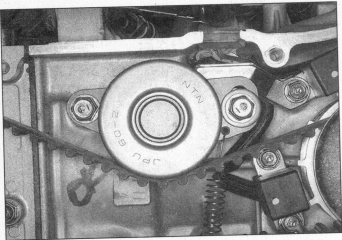

7.9 A new belt has evenly rounded teeth like this one, and its layers are securely attached to each other; with the belt removed, the tensioner pulley should spin freely

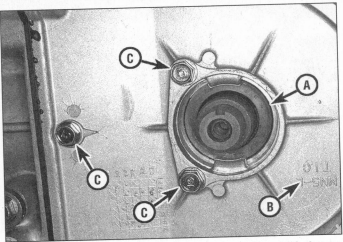

7.14 If oil has been leaking past the camshaft seal (A), the camshaft will need to be removed to install a new one; the left shield is marked MN5-L (B) and the right shield is marked MN-5R - each shield is secured by three bolts (C)

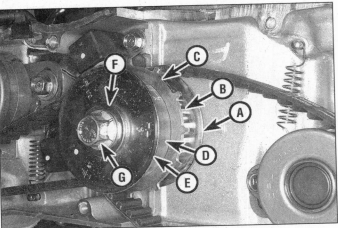

7.15 Crankshaft timing belt pulley details

A   *Inner guide plate (install with cupped side away from belt)*
B   *Left pulley*
C   *Pulse rotor (install with OUT SIDE mark away from engine)*
D   *Right pulley (with belt installed)*
E   *Outer guide plate (install with cupped side away from belt)*
F   *Washer*
G   *Bolt*

8.2 Remove the Allen bolts and take the rear cover off

Inspection

Refer to illustrations 7.9 and 7.14

9   Check the belts for worn, broken or missing teeth **(see illustration)**. If the teeth are worn more on one side that the other, replace the belt.

10   Look at both edges of the belt, all along the length, to see if the plies have separated. Replace the belt if there's any visible separation.

11   Check the pulley teeth for wear or damage. If the teeth are worn on one side, or if the plating is worn off, replace the pulleys. Try to rotate the pulleys on the crankshaft with fingers. If either pulley moves separately from the crankshaft, remove the pulleys and check their key slots for wear.

12   Spin the tensioners and make sure they rotate freely **(see illustration 7.9)**. If rotation is rough, loose, or noisy, or if a tensioner pulley binds, replace the tensioner. **Caution:** *Don't try to free a sticking tensioner by lubricating it. The lubricant will fly off and damage the timing belt. Also, don't clean the tensioners in solvent; it will break down the lubricant inside the tensioner.*

13   Check the tensioner springs for breakage or corrosion and replace them if any problems are found. Make sure the tensioner spring posts are securely attached to the engine.

14   Check for leaks around the camshaft seals **(see illustration)**. If oil has been leaking from one of the seals, remove the camshaft and install a new seal (see Section 9).

Installation

Refer to illustration 7.15

15   If you removed the pulleys and related components from the crankshaft, install them in the correct order **(see illustration)**. Be sure the cupped edges of the guide plates face away from the timing belt and the OUTSIDE mark on the pulse rotor faces away from the engine.

16   If the timing belt pulleys were removed, install them with their UP marks facing away from the engine. Install the washer on the pulley bolt with its chamfered side toward the bolt head, then thread the bolt into the camshaft. Keep the pulley from turning with a holder tool **(see illustration 7.5b)** and tighten the pulley bolt to the torque listed in this Chapter's Specifications.

17   Make sure the pulley timing marks are still aligned correctly **(see illustrations 7.4a, 7.4b and 7.4c)**.

18   Clean the threads of the left tensioner bolts, then coat them with non-permanent thread locking agent.

19   Install the left tensioner on the engine. The bolt with a washer goes in the hole closest to the center of the engine. Tighten the bolts just enough so the tensioner can still move in its slot. Install the tensioner spring with its hooked end at the tensioner facing away from the engine.

8.3a Pry the rubber plug out of the socket . . .

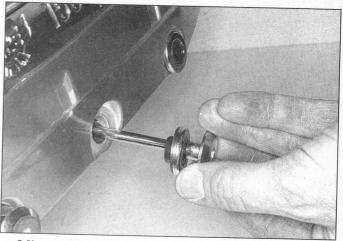

8.3b . . . and unscrew the cover bolts; replace the O-rings if they're brittle or deteriorated

20   Install the left timing belt. Place a wrench on the timing belt pulley and turn it clockwise (viewed from the front of the engine) so the loosest point of the belt will be at the tensioner. Don't tighten the tensioner bolts yet.

21   Refer to Chapter 5 and install the pulse generators.

22   Repeat Steps 17 through 20 above to install the right timing belt.

23   Place a wrench on the crankshaft pulley bolt. Turn the engine 1/4 turn clockwise, then 1/4 turn counterclockwise. Make sure all of the timing marks are still aligned correctly **(see illustrations 7.4a, 7.4b and 7.4c)**. If they aren't, find out why and fix the problem before continuing further; the valves could be bent if the engine is run while the timing marks are misaligned.

24   Tighten the tensioner bolts to the torque listed in this Chapter's Specifications. Tighten the bolt nearest the camshaft pulley first, then tighten the bolt nearest the crankshaft pulley.

25   Check belt tension by pressing down on the top run of the belt between the pulleys. Tension should be within the range listed in this Chapter's Specifications. **Note:** *If a right belt is loose, it will hit the cover and make a tapping noise when the engine idles. If either belt is too tight, it will whine.*

8   Cylinder head covers - removal and installation

Refer to illustrations 8.2, 8.3a, 8.3b, 8.4 and 8.10

1   Remove the engine guard from the side of the bike you'll be working on (see Chapter 8).

2   Remove the rear cover and gasket from the cylinder head cover **(see illustration)**.

3   Pry the rubber plugs out of the cover bolts with a pointed tool, then remove the bolts **(see illustrations)**.

4   Pull the cover off the engine **(see illustration)**. If it's stuck, tap it gently with a soft faced mallet. Don't pry between the cover and engine or the gasket surfaces will be damaged.

5   Peel the rubber gasket from the cover. If it's cracked, hardened, has soft spots or shows signs of general deterioration, replace it with a new one.

6   Clean the mating surfaces of the cylinder head and cover with lacquer thinner, acetone or brake system cleaner. Apply a thin film of RTV sealant to the gasket groove in the cover, but don't put any on the head.

7   Install the gasket to the cover. Make sure it fits completely into the cover groove.

8   Position the cover on the cylinder head, making sure the gasket doesn't slip out of place.

9   Check the rubber seals on the valve cover bolts, replacing them if necessary **(see illustration 8.3b)**. Coat the seals with engine oil, then install the bolts with their seals, tightening them evenly to the torque listed in this Chapter's Specifications.

10   Install the cover on the rear of the head cover, using a new gasket **(see illustration)**. Align the tabs on the gasket with the holes in the cover.

11   Install the engine guard.

2

8.4 Take the cover and gasket off the cylinder head

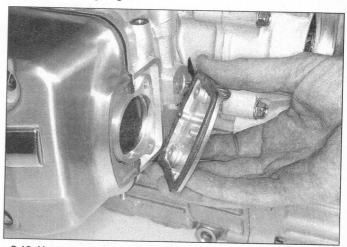

8.10 Use a new gasket on the rear cover and align its tabs with the holes in the cover

9.2 Take the timing belt shield off and clean away the old gasket

9.3a Remove the camshaft holder bolts (arrows) evenly in stages; the numbers 1 and 2 written on the holder refer to the number of lash adjuster shims installed

9   Camshafts, rocker arms and lash adjusters- removal, inspection and installation

Note: *This procedure can be performed with the engine in the frame.*

Camshafts

Removal

Refer to illustrations 9.2, 9.3a, 9.3b, 9.4 and 9.5

1   Remove the timing belt (Section 7) and cylinder head cover (Section 8).

2   Remove the timing belt shield bolts and remove the shield **(see illustration 7.14 and the accompanying illustration)**.

3   Unscrew the camshaft holder bolts in two or three stages in a criss-cross pattern **(see illustration)**. Take the holder off, together with the camshaft and rocker arms **(see illustration)**.

4   Locate the holder dowels **(see illustration)**. They may have come off with the holder or remained in the cylinder head.

5   Remove the camshaft from the holder, then remove the rubber plug and camshaft seal **(see illustration)**.

Inspection

Refer to illustrations 9.7a, 9.7b, 9.8, 9.9, 9.12a and 9.12b

Note: *Before replacing camshafts or the cylinder head and camshaft holder because of damage, check with local machine shops specializing in motorcycle engine work. In the case of the camshafts, it may be possible for cam lobes to be welded, reground and hardened, at a cost*

9.3b Take off the holder and camshaft (or remove the camshaft separately if it stays in the engine) the oil holes in holder and cylinder head (arrows) must be aligned on installation

far lower than that of a new camshaft. If the bearing surfaces in the cylinder head or holder are damaged, it may be possible for them to be bored out to accept bearing inserts. Due to the cost of a new cylinder head it is recommended that all options be explored before condemning it as trash!

9.4 The dowels (arrows) may stay in the cylinder head or come off with the holder

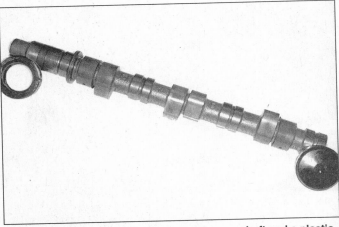

9.5 There's an oil seal on one end of the camshaft and a plastic cap on the other end

9.7a Check the lobes of the camshaft for wear - here's a good example of damage which will require replacement (or repair) of the camshaft

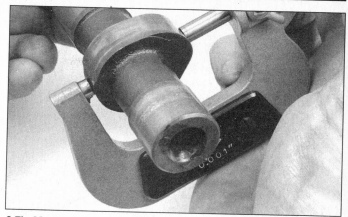

9.7b Measure the height of the camshaft lobes with a micrometer

9.8 Be sure the camshaft keyway (arrow) is up when the camshaft is installed

illustration) and compare the results to the minimum lobe height listed in this Chapter's Specifications. If damage is noted or wear is excessive, the camshaft must be replaced.

8   Next, check the camshaft bearing oil clearances. Clean the camshafts, the bearing surfaces in the cylinder head and the bearing caps with a clean, lint-free cloth, then lay the cams in place in the cylinder head. Be sure the keyways in the camshafts are upward **(see illustration)**.

9   Cut four strips of Plastigage (type HPG-1) and lay one piece on each bearing journal, parallel with the camshaft centerline **(see illustration)**.

10   Make sure the camshaft holder dowels are installed **(see illustration 9.4)**. Install the camshaft holder (see Step 3). Tighten the bolts in two or three steps to the torque listed in this Chapter's Specifications. **Caution:** *Tighten the holder bolts evenly to specifications, starting with the inner bolts and working outward. While tightening, DO NOT let the camshafts rotate!*

11   Now unscrew the bolts, a little at a time, and carefully lift off the camshaft holder. Be sure to start with the outer bolts and work inward.

12   To determine the oil clearance, compare the crushed Plastigage (at its widest point) on each journal to the scale printed on the Plastigage container **(see illustration)**. Compare the results to this Chapter's Specifications. If the oil clearance is greater than specified, measure the diameter of the cam bearing journal with a micrometer **(see illustration)**. If the journal diameter is less than the specified limit, replace the camshaft with a new one and recheck the clearance. If the clearance is still too great, replace the cylinder head and camshaft with new parts (see the Note that precedes Step 6).

6   Inspect the cam bearing surfaces of the head and the camshaft holder **(see illustration 9.4)**. Look for score marks, deep scratches and evidence of spalling (a pitted appearance).

7   Check the camshaft lobes for heat discoloration (blue appearance), score marks, chipped areas, flat spots and spalling **(see illustration)**. Measure the height of each lobe with a micrometer (see

9.9 Lay a strip of Plastigage lengthwise along each journal

9.12a Compare the width of the crushed Plastigage to the scale printed on the Plastigage container to obtain the clearance

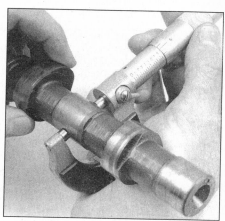

9.12b Measure the cam bearing journal diameter with a micrometer

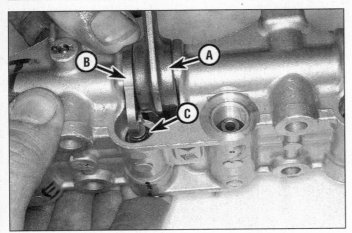

9.20 The rocker arms (A) ride on spindles (B),which ride on a shaft; the lever on the spindle contacts the lash adjuster (C)

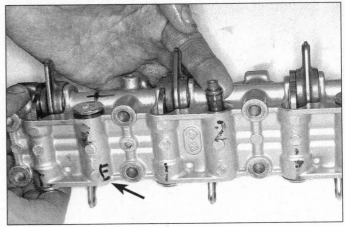

9.23 To prevent confusion, label the exhaust or intake side of the camshaft holder (arrow)

Installation

13   Make sure the crankshaft is still at no. 1 TDC (refer to Section 35).

14   If the camshaft holder dowels aren't in their holes, install them **(see illustration 9.4)**.

15   Make sure the bearing surfaces in the cylinder head and the camshaft holder are clean, then apply a light coat of engine assembly lube or moly-based grease to each of them.

16   Apply a coat of moly-based grease to the lobes of the camshaft. **Note:** *If you've removed both camshafts, be sure to install them on the correct sides of the engine. They're labeled R and L for right and left.* Install the seal over the front end of the camshaft with its open side facing the rear of the engine. Install the cap on the rear end. Wipe the outer circumferences of the seal and end cap with a thin layer of sealant.

17   Place the camshaft in the cylinder head bearing journals with the camshaft keyway straight up. Engage the seal and end cap with their bores in the cylinder head.

18   Position the camshaft holder on the cylinder head, making sure the oil holes in head and holder are lined up with each other **(see illustration 9.3b)**. Install the holder bolts and tighten them in two or three stages to the torque listed in this Chapter's Specifications, starting with the center bolts and working outward.

19   The remainder of installation is the reverse of removal.

Rocker arms and lash adjusters

Refer to illustration 9.20

20   The valves are opened and closed by rocker arms, which are operated directly by the camshafts. The rocker arms ride on eccentric spindles, which in turn ride on a shaft mounted in the camshaft holder. Valve clearance is controlled by hydraulic lash adjusters mounted in the camshaft holder. The adjusters extend, pressing against levers on the eccentric spindles, causing them to rotate around their shaft **(see illustration)**. As the spindles rotate, they raise or lower the pivot point of their rocker arm, so that valve clearance is maintained at zero. On later models, there's a needle roller bearing between each spindle and its rocker arm; on early models, the rocker arms ride directly on the spindles.

Removal

Refer to illustrations 9.23, 9.24a, 9.24b, 9.25a and 9.25b

21   Remove the camshaft holder following the procedure given above.

22   Make a holder with a separate section for each lash adjuster, spindle, rocker and needle roller bearing (if equipped) (a pair of egg cartons will work). Label the sections according to cylinder number (1 through 6), valve number (starting from the front of the engine) and whether the parts belong with an intake or exhaust valve. The parts form a wear pattern with each other and must be returned to their original locations if reused.

23   Label the camshaft holder intake and exhaust sides **(see illustration)**. Also, look for numbers indicating the number of shims used with each lash adjuster. It's important to install the same number of shims if the old parts are reinstalled (if parts are replaced with new ones, you'll need to select the number of shims as described below).

24   Unscrew the stopper plugs and remove them from the adjuster bores, together with their shims **(see illustration)**. Pull the adjusters out of the bores with a magnet. The intake valve adjusters have small caps that fit between the adjuster and its spindle lever **(see illustration)**; the exhaust adjusters don't have caps. If the adjusters are stuck, spray the area around them with carburetor cleaner and let it soak in. Place the adjusters in order in their holder.

25   Push the rocker shafts out of their bores and remove the rocker arms, together with their eccentric spindles (and bearings if equipped) **(see illustrations)**.

Inspection

Refer to illustrations 9.31 and 9.32

26   Check the needle roller bearings (later models) for wear or damage. Since needle roller bearing wear can be hard to see, it's a good idea to replace them if there's any doubt about their condition.

27   Check the contact surfaces of the rocker arms and their eccentric spindles for wear, scoring or pitting. If there's any visible damage, replace the worn parts.

28   Check the bores of the rocker arms and spindles, and the spindle contact surfaces on the shafts, for wear or scoring. If you have precision measuring equipment, measure the bore and shaft diameters and compare them to the values listed in this Chapter's Specifications. Replace worn or damaged parts.

9.24a Remove the stopper plugs and shims . . .

9.24b . . . and take the lash adjusters out of their bores; only the intake adjusters (shown) have caps

9.25a Pull out the shafts and remove the rocker arms and spindles

9.25b Later models use needle roller bearings between the rocker arms and spindles

29   Make sure the oil holes in the hydraulic adjusters are clear. Check the adjusters and their bores for wear, scuff marks, scratches or other damage. Also check the caps used on the intake valve adjusters. Honda doesn't provide specifications or wear tolerances for the adjusters or their bores. If wear or damage is found, replace the worn parts.

30   Adjuster performance can be tested, but it requires a dial indicator and a special Honda fixture for which there is no good substitute. The fixture holds open the adjuster check valve, allowing it to be bled of air. The procedure is described below, but you can have it done by a Honda dealer or motorcycle service shop if you don't have the equipment.

31   Place the adjuster in a tappet bleeder (Honda part no. 07973-MJ00000) **(see illustration)**. Immerse the fixture in a pan of kerosene with the adjuster in its upright position. Slowly compress and extend the bleeder until no more air bubbles can be seen coming from the adjuster.

32   Take the adjuster out of the fixture and place it on a workbench with a dial indicator contacting its end **(see illustration)**. Compress the adjuster suddenly with a finger and measure its stroke. If it's more than listed in this Chapter's Specifications, repeat Step 31 to bleed the adjuster, then measure the stroke again. If the stroke is still more than the specification, replace the adjuster.

Installation

Refer to illustration 9.34

33   Coat the inner bores of the rocker arms and the outer bores of the spindles with oil containing molybdenum disulfide. If you're working on a later model that has needle roller bearings, dip them in the oil. Assemble the spindle, bearing (if equipped) and rocker arms, keeping them with their mated parts if you're reusing the old ones.

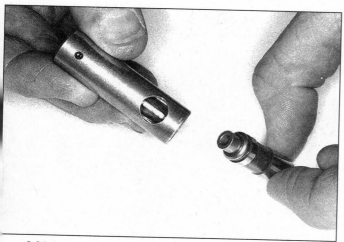

9.31 Insert the adjuster in the fixture, then immerse it in kerosene and bleed out the air

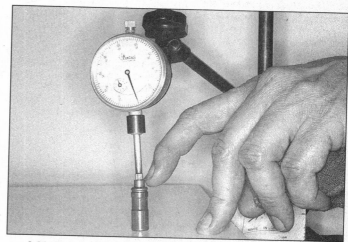

9.32 Place a dial indicator on the end of the adjuster, then compress it with a finger and measure the stroke

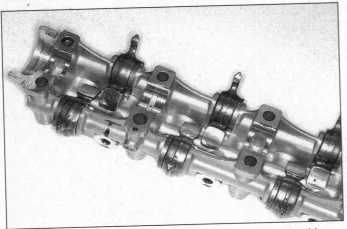

9.34 The assembled camshaft holder should look like this

9.39 Measure the distance from the gauge to the shim contact surface

34   Install the rocker arms and spindles in their spaces in the camshaft holder, then slip the rocker shafts through them **(see illustration)**. **Note:** *The intake side rocker shaft has a yellow paint mark.*
35   Coat the adjusters and their bores with clean engine oil. Install the caps on the intake valve adjusters, then install the adjusters in their bores. Install the stopper plugs with their shims and tighten them to the torque listed in this Chapter's Specifications.
36   To install the assembled camshaft holder on the engine, refer to Steps 13 through 19 above. If any parts were replaced, you'll need to select the correct number of shims as described below after the camshaft holder is installed.

Shim selection

Refer to illustration 9.39
37   This procedure requires a special Honda gauge and a vernier caliper. Have it done by a Honda dealer if you don't have the equipment.
38   Position the engine with no. 1 cylinder at top dead center on its compression stroke (see Section 7).
39   Starting with no. 1 cylinder, remove the stopper plugs, shims and adjusters. Insert the gauge in the adjuster bore **(see illustration)**. Make sure the rocker arm is touching the camshaft and the end of the gauge is touching the lever on the eccentric spindle. Measure the distance from the top of the gauge to the shim contact surface on the camshaft holder. Compare the measurement with the values listed in this Chapter's Specifications to determine how many shims are needed for that adjuster.
40   Measure the remaining cylinders in the same manner, following the engine's firing order (1-4-5-2-3-6). Before measuring for each cylinder, bring that cylinder to TDC on its compression stroke, referring to

the cylinder firing marks on the front of the crankshaft timing belt pulley **(see illustration 7.4a)**.

10 Cylinder heads - removal and installation

Caution: *The engine must be completely cool before beginning this procedure, or the cylinder head may become warped.*
Note: *This procedure can be performed with the engine in the frame. If the engine has been removed, ignore the steps which don't apply. If you're planning to remove the head just for gasket replacement, it can be removed as a unit with the camshaft holder.*

Removal

Refer to illustrations 10.8, 10.9, 10.11 and 10.12
1   Place the bike on its centerstand.
2   Drain the cooling system and disconnect the spark plug wires (see Chapter 1).
3   Remove the cylinder head cover (see Section 8).
4   Remove the timing belt(s) (see Section 7).
5   Remove the camshaft holder and camshaft (see Section 9).
6   Detach the exhaust manifold and air injection pipes from the head (see Chapter 4).
7   Detach the intake manifold from the head. Tie the manifold up so it won't be in the way and remove the manifold gasket (see Chapter 4).
8   Remove the single 6 mm bolt from beneath the cylinder head **(see illustration)**.
9   Loosen the main cylinder head bolts, 1/2 turn at a time, in the reverse of the tightening sequence **(see illustration)**. Once all of the

10.8 Remove the small bolt from the cylinder head

10.9 Main head bolts TIGHTENING sequence

10.11 Locate the dowels (arrows)

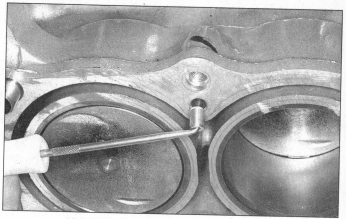

10.12 Lift the oil orifice out of its passage

bolts are loose, remove the bolts and washers.

10   Take the cylinder head off the crankcase. If the head is stuck, tap upward with a rubber mallet to jar it loose, or use two wooden dowels inserted into the intake or exhaust ports to rock the head back and forth slightly. Don't attempt to pry the head off by inserting a screwdriver between the head and the crankcase - you'll damage the sealing surfaces.

11   Lift the head gasket off the crankcase. Remove the dowel pins **(see illustration)**.

12   Lift the oil orifice out of its bore in the crankcase **(see illustration)**.

13   Check the cylinder head gasket and the mating surfaces on the cylinder head and block for leakage, which could indicate warpage. Refer to Section 12 and check the flatness of the cylinder head and its mating surface on the crankcase.

14   Clean all traces of old gasket material from the cylinder head and crankcase. Be careful not to let any of the gasket material fall into the crankcase, the cylinder bores or the coolant passages.

Installation

15   Install the oil orifice and dowels in the crankcase **(see illustrations 10.12 and 10.11)**.

16   Lay the new gasket in place on the crankcase. Never reuse the old gasket and don't use any type of gasket sealant.

17   Carefully place the cylinder head on the crankcase, making sure the coolant tube fits into the fitting on the side of the head toward the center of the engine.

18   Coat the threads of the main bolts and the undersides of the bolt heads with molybdenum disulfide oil. Install the main head bolts and washers. Starting with the inner bolts and working outward **(see illustration 10.9)**, tighten the bolts in three stages to the torque listed in this Chapter's Specifications.

19   Install the 6 mm bolt. Tighten it securely, but don't overtighten it and strip the threads.

20   The remainder of installation is the reverse of the removal steps.

21   Change the engine oil (see Chapter 1).

11   Valves/valve seats/valve guides - servicing

1   Because of the complex nature of this job and the special tools and equipment required, servicing of the valves, the valve seats and the valve guides (commonly known as a valve job) is best left to a professional.

2   The home mechanic can, however, remove and disassemble the head, do the initial cleaning and inspection, then reassemble and deliver the head to a dealer service department or properly equipped motorcycle repair shop for the actual valve servicing. Refer to Section 12 for those procedures.

3   The dealer service department will remove the valves and springs, recondition or replace the valves and valve seats, replace the valve

guides, check and replace the valve springs, spring retainers and keepers/collets (as necessary), replace the valve seals with new ones and reassemble the valve components.

4   After the valve job has been performed, the head will be in likenew condition. When the head is returned, be sure to clean it again very thoroughly before installation on the engine to remove any metal particles or abrasive grit that may still be present from the valve service operations. Use compressed air, if available, to blow out all the holes and passages.

12   Cylinder head and valves - disassembly, inspection and reassembly

1   As mentioned in the previous Section, valve servicing and valve guide replacement should be left to a dealer service department or motorcycle repair shop. However, disassembly, cleaning and inspection of the valves and related components can be done (if the necessary special tools are available) by the home mechanic. This way no expense is incurred if the inspection reveals that service work is not required at this time.

2   To properly disassemble the valve components without the risk of damaging them, a valve spring compressor is absolutely necessary. This special tool can usually be rented, but if it's not available, have a dealer service department or motorcycle repair shop handle the entire process of disassembly, inspection, service or repair (if required) and reassembly of the valves.

Disassembly

Refer to illustrations 12.7a, 12.7b, 12.7c and 12.7d

3   Remove the camshaft holder if you haven't already done so (see Section 9). Store the components in such a way that they can be returned to their original locations without getting mixed up.

4   Before the valves are removed, scrape away any traces of gasket material from the head gasket sealing surface. Work slowly and do not nick or gouge the soft aluminum of the head. Gasket removing solvents, which work very well, are available at most motorcycle shops and auto parts stores.

5   Carefully scrape all carbon deposits out of the combustion chamber area. A hand held wire brush or a piece of fine emery cloth can be used once the majority of deposits have been scraped away. Do not use a wire brush mounted in a drill motor, or one with extremely stiff bristles, as the head material is soft and may be eroded away or scratched by the wire brush.

6   Before proceeding, arrange to label and store the valves along with their related components so they can be kept separate and reinstalled in the same valve guides they are removed from (labeled plastic bags work well for this).

7   Compress the valve spring on the first valve with a spring compressor, then remove the keepers and the spring retainer from the

2

12.7a Compress the valve spring with a spring compressor . . .

12.7b . . . and remove the keepers with a magnet

valve assembly **(see illustration)**. Do not compress the springs any more than is absolutely necessary. Carefully release the valve spring compressor and remove the spring and the valve from the head **(see illustrations)**. If the valve binds in the guide (won't pull through), push it back into the head and deburr the area around the keeper groove with a very fine file or whetstone **(see illustration)**.

8   Repeat the procedure for the remaining valves. Remember to keep the parts for each valve together so they can be reinstalled in the same location.

9   Once the valves have been removed and labeled, pull off the valve stem seals with pliers and discard them (the old seals should never be reused), then remove the spring seats.

10   Next, clean the cylinder head with solvent and dry it thoroughly.

Compressed air will speed the drying process and ensure that all holes and recessed areas are clean.

11   Clean all of the valve springs, keepers, retainers and spring seats with solvent and dry them thoroughly. Do the parts from one valve at a time so that no mixing of parts between valves occurs.

12   Scrape off any deposits that may have formed on the valve, then use a motorized wire brush to remove deposits from the valve heads and stems. Again, make sure the valves do not get mixed up.

Inspection

Refer to illustrations 12.14a, 12.14b, 12.15, 12.16, 12.17, 12.18a, 12.18b, 12.19a and 12.19b

13   Inspect the head very carefully for cracks and other damage. If cracks are found, a new head will be required. Check the cam bearing surfaces for wear and evidence of seizure. Check the camshafts for wear as well (see Section 9).

14   Using a precision straightedge and a feeler gauge, check the head gasket mating surface for warpage. Lay the straightedge length-wise, across the head and diagonally (corner-to-corner), intersecting the head bolt holes, and try to slip a feeler gauge under it, on either side of each combustion chamber **(see illustration)**. The gauge should be the same thickness as the cylinder head warp limit listed in this Chapter's Specifications. If the feeler gauge can be inserted between the head and the straightedge, the head is warped and must either be machined or, if warpage is excessive, replaced with a new one. Minor surface imperfections can be cleaned up by sanding on a surface plate in a figure-eight pattern with 400 or 600 grit wet or dry sandpaper. Be sure to rotate the head every few strokes to avoid removing material unevenly. Also check the head mating surface on the cylinders **(see illustration)**.

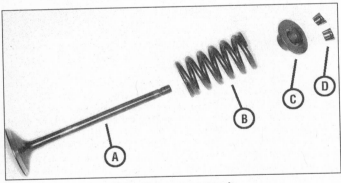

12.7c Valve components

A	Valve	C	Upper retainer (lower retainer not shown)
B	Spring	D	Keepers

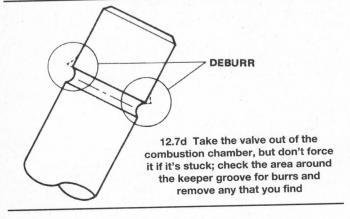

12.7d Take the valve out of the combustion chamber, but don't force it if it's stuck; check the area around the keeper groove for burrs and remove any that you find

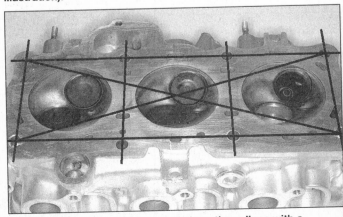

12.14a Measure the head along these lines with a feeler gauge and straightedge

12.14b Measure the top surface of the cylinders

12.15 Measure the valve seat width

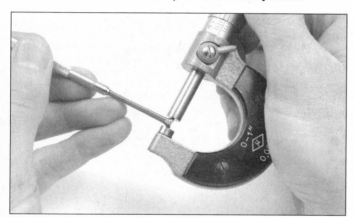

12.16 Measure the small hole gauge with a micrometer

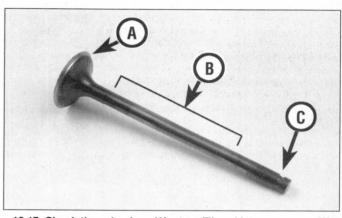

12.17 Check the valve face (A), stem (B) and keeper groove (C) for signs of wear and damage

2

15   Examine the valve seats in each of the combustion chambers. If they are pitted, cracked or burned, the head will require valve service that's beyond the scope of the home mechanic. Measure the valve seat width **(see illustration)** and compare it to this Chapter's Specifications. If it is not within the specified range, or if it varies around its circumference, valve service work is required.

16   Clean the valve guides to remove any carbon buildup, then measure the inside diameters of the guides (at both ends and the center of the guide) with a small hole gauge and a 0-to-1-inch micrometer **(see illustration)**. Record the measurements for future reference. These measurements, along with the valve stem diameter measurements, will enable you to compute the valve stem-to-guide clearance. This clearance, when compared to the Specifications, will be one factor that will determine the extent of the valve service work required. The guides are measured at the ends and at the center to determine if they are worn in a bell-mouth pattern (more wear at the ends). If they are, guide replacement is an absolute must.

17   Carefully inspect each valve face for cracks, pits and burned spots. Check the valve stem and the keeper groove area for cracks **(see illustration)**. Rotate the valve and check for any obvious indication that it is bent. Check the end of the stem for pitting and excessive wear and make sure the margin is not too thin. The presence of any of the above conditions indicates the need for valve servicing.

18   Measure the valve stem diameter **(see illustration)**. By subtracting the stem diameter from the valve guide diameter, the valve stem-to-guide clearance is obtained. If the stem-to-guide clearance is greater than listed in this Chapter's Specifications, the guides and valves will have to be replaced with new ones. Also check the valve stem for bending. Set the valve in a V-block with a dial indicator touching the middle of the stem **(see illustration)**. Rotate the valve and note the reading on the gauge. If the stem is bent, replace the valve.

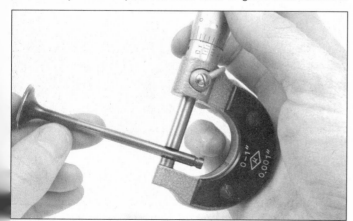

12.18a Measure the valve stem diameter with a micrometer

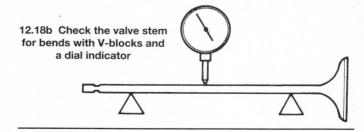

12.18b Check the valve stem for bends with V-blocks and a dial indicator

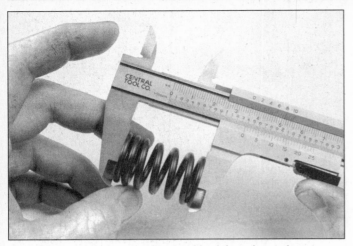

12.19a Measure the free length of the valve springs

19   Check the end of each valve spring for wear and pitting. Measure the free length (see illustration) and compare it to this Chapter's Specifications. Any springs that are shorter than specified have sagged and should not be reused. Stand the spring on a flat surface and check it for squareness (see illustration).
20   Check the spring retainers and keepers for obvious wear and cracks. Any questionable parts should not be reused, as extensive damage will occur in the event of failure during engine operation.
21   If the inspection indicates that no service work is required, the valve components can be reinstalled in the head.

Reassembly

Refer to illustrations 12.23, 12.24, 12.27, 12.28 and 12.29

22   Before installing the valves in the head, they should be lapped to ensure a positive seal between the valves and seats. This procedure requires coarse and fine valve lapping compound (available at auto parts stores) and a valve lapping tool. If a lapping tool is not available, a piece of rubber or plastic hose can be slipped over the valve stem (after the valve has been installed in the guide) and used to turn the valve.
23   Apply a small amount of coarse lapping compound to the valve face (see illustration), then slip the valve into the guide. **Note:** *Make sure the valve is installed in the correct guide and be careful not to get any lapping compound on the valve stem.*
24   Attach the lapping tool (or hose) to the valve and rotate the tool between the palms of your hands. Use a back-and-forth motion rather than a circular motion. Lift the valve off the seat and turn it at regular intervals to distribute the lapping compound properly. Continue the lapping procedure until the valve face and seat contact area is of uniform width and unbroken around the entire circumference of the valve face and seat (see illustration).
25   Carefully remove the valve from the guide and wipe off all traces of lapping compound. Use solvent to clean the valve and wipe the seat

12.19b Check the valve springs for squareness

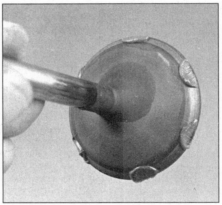

12.23 Apply the lapping compound very sparingly, in small dabs, to the valve face only

12.24 After lapping, the valve face should have a uniform, unbroken contact pattern (arrow)

12.27 Lay the spring seats on the head and install new seals on the guides

12.28 A small dab of grease will help hold the keepers in place on the valve spring while the spring is released

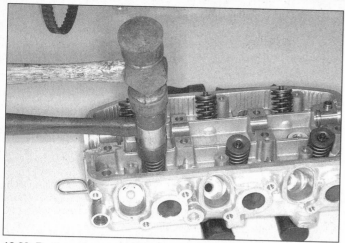

12.29 Rest one hammer on the end of the valve stem and tap on it with another hammer to settle the keepers

13.3 Pull back the rubber cap and place a vinyl tube on the clutch bleed valve

area thoroughly with a solvent soaked cloth.

26   Repeat the procedure with fine valve lapping compound, then repeat the entire procedure for the remaining valves.

27   Lay the spring seats in place in the cylinder head, then install new valve stem seals on each of the guides **(see illustration)**. Use an appropriate size deep socket to push the seals into place until they are properly seated. Don't twist or cock them, or they will not seal properly against the valve stems. Also, don't remove them again or they will be damaged.

28   Coat the valve stems with assembly lube or moly-based grease, then install one of them into its guide. Next, install the springs and retainers, compress the springs and install the keepers. **Note:** *When compressing the springs with the valve spring compressor, depress them only as far as is absolutely necessary to slip the keepers into place. Apply a small amount of grease to the keepers* **(see illustration)** *to help hold them in place as the pressure is released from the springs. Make certain that the keepers are securely locked in their retaining grooves.*

29   Support the cylinder head on blocks so the valves can't contact the workbench top, then very gently tap each of the valve stems with a soft-faced hammer **(see illustration)**. This will help seat the keepers in their grooves.

30   Once all of the valves have been installed in the head, check for

proper valve sealing by pouring a small amount of solvent into each of the valve ports. If the solvent leaks past the valve(s) into the combustion chamber area, disassemble the valve(s) and repeat the lapping procedure, then reinstall the valve(s) and repeat the check. Repeat the procedure until a satisfactory seal is obtained.

13   Clutch release mechanism - bleeding, removal, inspection and installation

Clutch bleeding

Refer to illustration 13.3

1   Place the motorcycle on its centerstand.

2   Remove the master cylinder cover and diaphragm. Place rags around the master cylinder to protect plastic and painted parts from being damaged by the clutch fluid. Top up the master cylinder with fluid to the upper level line cast inside the cylinder.

3   Remove the cap from the bleed valve **(see illustration)**. Place a box wrench over the bleed valve. Attach a vinyl tube to the valve fitting and put the other end of the tube in a container. Pour enough clean brake fluid into the container to cover the end of the tube.

4   Squeeze the clutch lever several times while you watch the bleed holes in the bottom of the reservoir. Once air bubbles stop rising from the bleed holes, hold the lever in. Tap on the master cylinder body several times to free any air bubbles that may be stuck to the sides of the fluid line. With the clutch lever held in, open the bleed valve 1/4-turn with the wrench, let air and fluid escape, then tighten the valve.

5   Slowly release the clutch lever.

6   Wait several seconds after releasing the lever, then repeat Steps 4 and 5 until there aren't any more bubbles in the fluid flowing into the container. Top off the master cylinder with fluid, then reinstall the diaphragm and cover and tighten the screws.

Master cylinder

Removal

Refer to illustration 13.9

7   Disconnect the electrical connector from the clutch switch beneath the master cylinder. If the bike has cruise control, disconnect the cruise cancel switch connector as well.

8   Place a towel under the master cylinder to catch any spilled fluid, then remove the union bolt from the master cylinder fluid line. **Caution:** *Brake fluid will damage paint. Wipe up any spills immediately and wash the area with soap and water.*

9   Pry the trim cap (if equipped) out of the master cylinder clamp **(see illustration)**. Remove the master cylinder clamp bolts and take the cylinder body off the handlebar.

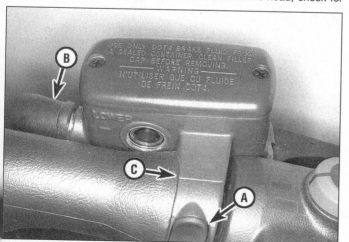

13.9 Pry off the trim cap (A) if equipped; the master cylinder bolts are under it; pull back the rubber cap (B) to expose the fluid line union bolt; on installation, the triangular mark on the handlebar trim (C) aligns with the split between the clamp and master cylinder

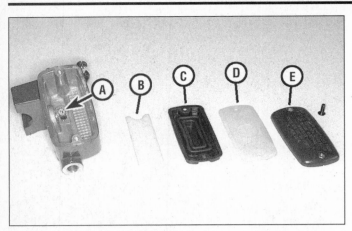

13.11 Clutch master cylinder cover details

A	Baffle	D	Plate
B	Float	E	Cover
C	Diaphragm		

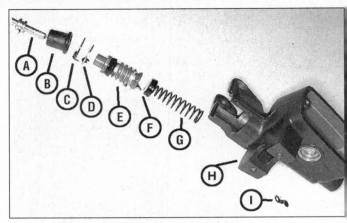

13.12 Clutch master cylinder piston details

A	Pushrod	F	Cup
B	Dust cover	G	Spring
C	Snap-ring	H	Master cylinder body
D	Retainer	I	Baffle
E	Piston		

Master cylinder

Overhaul

Refer to illustrations 13.11 and 13.12

10   Remove the lever pivot bolt and nut and take off the lever (**see illustration 19.2a** in Chapter 1).

11   Remove the cap, plate, rubber diaphragm and float from the reservoir (**see illustration**). Remove the baffle from the bottom of the master cylinder.

12   Remove the rubber boot, pushrod and spring from the master cylinder (**see illustration**).

13   Remove the snap ring and retaining ring, then dump out the piston and primary cup, secondary cup and spring (**see illustration 13.12**). If they won't come out, blow compressed air into the fluid line hole. **Warning:** *The piston may shoot out forcefully enough to cause injury. Point the piston at a block of wood or a pile of rags inside a box and apply air pressure gradually. Never point the end of the cylinder at yourself, including your fingers.*

14   Thoroughly clean all of the components in clean brake fluid (don't use any type of petroleum-based solvent).

15   Check the piston and cylinder bore for wear, scratches and rust. If the piston shows these conditions, replace it and both rubber cups as a set. If the cylinder bore has any defects, replace the entire master cylinder.

16   Install the spring in the cylinder bore, wide end first.

17   Coat a new cup with brake fluid and install it in the cylinder, wide side first.

18   Coat the piston with brake fluid and install it in the cylinder.

19   Install the retaining ring. Press the piston into the bore and install the snap ring to hold it in place.

20   Install the rubber boot, pushrod and spring.

21   When you install the lever, align the hole in the lever bushing with the pushrod.

Master cylinder

Installation

22   Installation is the reverse of the removal steps, with the following additions:

   a) *The split between the clamp and master cylinder aligns with the triangular mark on the handlebar cover (see illustration 13.9).*

   b) *Tighten the clamp bolts to the torque listed in this Chapter's Specifications.*

   c) *Fill and bleed the clutch hydraulic system.*

   d) *Operate the clutch lever and check for fluid leaks.*

Slave cylinder

Removal

Refer to illustrations 13.24a, 13.24b and 13.25

23   If the engine is in the frame, remove the front side covers (Chapter 8) and the evaporative emission canister (California models) (see Chapter 4).

24   Place rags and a container beneath the slave cylinder to catch spilled fluid. Unbolt the bleed valve tube on the left and remove the union bolt on the right (**see illustrations**). Place the end of the fluid hose in the container to let the fluid drain. **Caution:** *Brake fluid will damage paint. Wipe up any spills immediately and wash the area with soap and water.*

25   Remove the slave cylinder mounting bolts and take it off the rear cover, then locate the dowels (**see illustration**).

Slave cylinder

Overhaul

Refer to illustrations 13.26, 13.28 and 13.29

26   Remove the piston and spring (**see illustration**). If they won't come out, blow compressed air into the fluid line hole. **Warning:** *The piston may shoot out forcefully enough to cause injury. Point the piston at a block of wood or a pile of rags inside a box and apply air pressure gradually. Never point the end of the cylinder at yourself, including your fingers.*

27   Thoroughly clean all of the components in clean brake fluid (don't use any type of petroleum-based solvent).

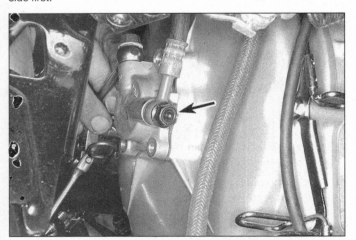

13.24a Remove the union bolt (arrow) . . .

13.24b . . . and the bleed valve tube bolt (arrow), then unbolt the cylinder . . .

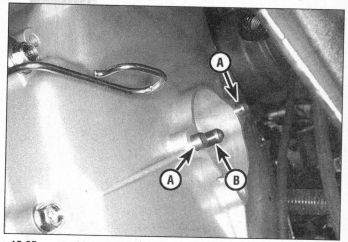

13.25 . . . and locate the dowels (A); they may stay in the engine or come off with the slave cylinder); on installation, make sure the pushrod (B) is in place

28   Check the piston and cylinder bore for wear, scratches and rust. If the piston shows these conditions, replace it and the seal as a set. If the cylinder bore has any defects, replace the entire slave cylinder. If the piston and bore are good, carefully remove the seal from the piston and install a new one **(see illustration)**.

29   Check the pushrod seal in the back of the piston and replace it if it's worn or damaged **(see illustration)**.

Slave cylinder

Installation

30   Installation is the reverse of the removal procedure, with the following additions:

a) *Use new sealing washers on the fluid line.*
b) *Tighten the cylinder mounting bolts and fluid line union bolt to the torques listed in this Chapter's Specifications.*
c) *Bleed the clutch (see above).*
d) *Operate the clutch and check for fluid leaks.*

---

14   Clutch - removal, inspection and installation

Note: *The clutch can be removed with the engine in the frame.*

Removal

Refer to illustrations 14.5, 14.6, 14.7, 14.8, 14.9a, 14.9b, 14.10, 14.11, 14.12, 14.13, 14.14a, 14.14b, 14.15, 14.16a and 14.16b

1   Place the bike on its centerstand and drain the engine oil (see Chapter 1).

2   Remove the front side cover (see Chapter 8).

3   Remove the exhaust pipe protector and exhaust heat shield from the left side of the bike (see Chapter 4). If you're working on a California model, remove the evaporative emission canister.

4   Refer to Section 13 and remove the slave cylinder.

13.26 Take the piston and spring out of the cylinder

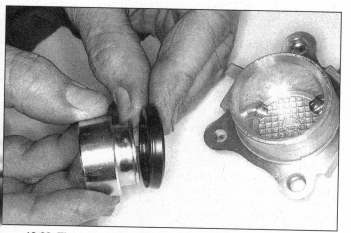

13.28 The wide side of the piston cup faces into the bore

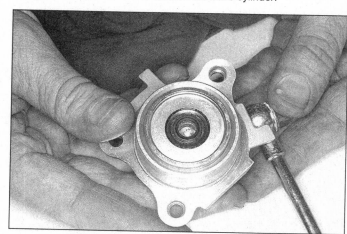

13.29 Replace the pushrod seal if it's worn or damaged

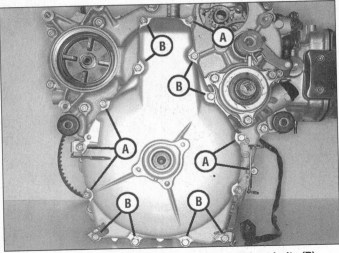

14.5 Remove the long cover bolts (A) and short bolts (B)

14.6 Locate the cover dowels (arrows) and remove the gasket

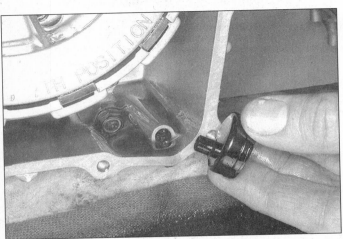

14.7 Pull the oil strainer out of its passage and make sure it's clear

14.8 Pull out the lifter rod and lifter piece, then remove the four bolts shown and take off the lifter plate

5   Unbolt the clutch cover from the rear of the engine (see illustration). If the cover is stuck, tap it gently with a soft-faced mallet to free it. Don't pry between the cover and engine or the gasket surfaces will be damaged.
6   Locate the cover dowels and remove the old gasket (see illustration).
7   Pull the oil pickup strainer out of its tube (see illustration).
8   Pull the lifter rod and lifter piece out of the clutch (see illustration). Loosen the lifter plate bolts evenly in a criss-cross pattern, then remove the lifter plate.

14.9a Bend the lockwasher away from the nut

14.9b Hold the clutch with a tool like this one and undo the nut

14.10 A pair of bolts make convenient handles to remove the clutch pack

14.11 Remove the spline washer and grind away both staked portions of the locknut (arrow); there's another staked portion hidden behind the washer

9   Bend back the lockwasher on the clutch nut **(see illustration)**. Remove the nut, using a special holding tool (Honda clutch center holder 07HGB-001000A or equivalent) to prevent the clutch housing from turning **(see illustration)**. Remove the lockwasher and discard it. Use a new one during installation. Remove the plain washer.

10   Thread a pair of bolts into two of the pressure plate posts and pull out the pressure plate, together with the clutch center and clutch plates **(see illustration)**. The bolts aren't strictly necessary, but do make convenient handles.

11   Take the spline washer off the transmission mainshaft and grind away the staked portions of the clutch housing locknut **(see illustration)**.

12   Hold the clutch center from turning with the same tool used to hold the clutch center **(see illustration 14.9)**. Undo the locknut with a 12-point 46 mm socket (Honda tool 07JMA-MN50100 or equivalent **(see illustration)**. **Note:** *This nut is secured with thread locking agent and tightened to an unusually high torque. For this reason, substitute tools aren't likely to work. You should be able to order the socket from your local Honda dealer; as an alternative, consider bringing the bike to the dealership and having the nut removed.*

13   Remove the lockwasher from behind the nut, then pull the clutch housing off **(see illustration)**.

14   Place the clutch center assembly in a vise. Tighten the vise just enough to take the pressure off the snap ring that secures the diaphragm spring, then remove the spring, washer and diaphragm spring **(see illustrations)**. **Caution:** *Don't compress the spring any more than necessary or it will lose tension.*

14.12 Because the nut is very tight and secured with thread locking agent, there's no good substitute for a 12-point 46 mm socket

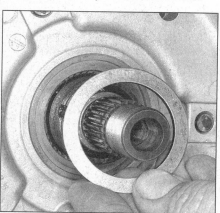

14.13 Remove the lockwasher from behind the nut; its OUT SIDE mark faces away from the engine on installation

14.14a Compress the clutch pack in a vise just enough to provide removal clearance for the snap-ring

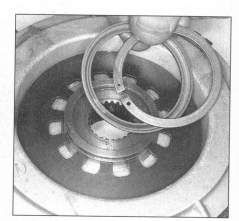

14.14b Remove the snap-ring, washer and diaphragm spring

2

14.15 Remove the stop ring from beneath the diaphragm spring

14.16a Take the pressure plate off the clutch pack . . .

15   Lift out the stop ring that the diaphragm spring rests on **(see illustration)**.
16   Lift the pressure plate out of the clutch center, then remove the clutch plates and damper **(see illustrations)**.

Inspection

Refer to illustrations 14.17, 14.18, 14.19, 14.20, 14.22, 14.23a and 14.23b

17   Examine the splines on both the inside and the outside of the clutch center **(see illustration)**. If any wear is evident, replace the clutch center with a new one. Check the friction surfaces on the clutch center and pressure plate for scoring, wear or signs of overheating.
18   Check the springs on the inside of the clutch housing for breakage **(see illustration)**. Check the splines for wear or damage. Check the edges of the slots in the clutch housing for indentations made by the friction plate tabs. If the indentations are deep they can prevent clutch release, so the housing should be replaced with a new one. If the indentations can be removed easily with a file, the life of the housing can be prolonged to an extent.
19   Measure the height of the diaphragm spring **(see illustration)**. Replace the spring if its free height is less than the value listed in this Chapter's Specifications.
20   If the lining material of the friction plates smells burnt or if it's glazed, new parts are required. If the metal clutch plates are scored or discolored, they must be replaced with new ones. Measure the thickness of each friction plate **(see illustration)** and compare the results to

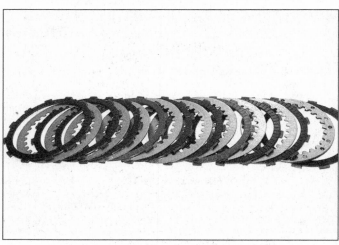

14.16b . . . then lift off the plates and clutch damper

this Chapter's Specifications. Replace the friction plates as a set if any are near the wear limit.
21   Check the tabs on the friction plates for excessive wear and mushroomed edges. They can be cleaned up with a file if the deformation is not severe.

14.17 Check the pressure plate and clutch center friction surfaces, as well as the clutch center splines

14.18 Check the clutch housing for worn splines or slots and broken springs

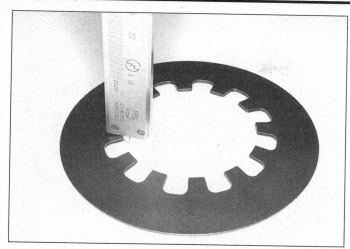

14.19 Measure the free height of the diaphragm spring

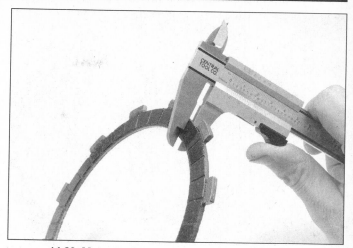

14.20 Measure the thickness of the friction plates

14.22 Check the metal plates for warpage

23   Check the clutch damper for warpage in the same manner as the metal plates **(see illustration)**. Also check the wave spring between the layers of the damper **(see illustration)**; if it's damaged, replace the damper.

24   Check the thrust washers and locknut for wear and damage. Replace any worn or damaged parts.

25   Make sure the clutch pushrod isn't bent (roll it on a perfectly flat surface or use V-blocks and a dial indicator). Check the pushrod and lifter piece for wear or damage and replace them if defects are visible.

26   Check the release bearing and lifter plate for wear, damage or roughness. Replace the bearing if its condition is uncertain or obviously bad. Drive it out with a bearing driver, then drive a new one in with a bearing driver or socket that presses against the outer race of the bearing. Don't apply pressure to the inner race or the bearing will be damaged.

27   Clean all traces of old gasket material from the clutch cover and its mating surface on the crankcase.

Installation

Refer to illustrations 14.29, 14.30, 14.31, 14.32 and 14.33

28   Clean all oil from the mainshaft splines and threads, then install the clutch housing on the engine. Install the lockwasher with its OUT SIDE mark facing away from the engine. Apply non-permanent thread locking agent to the threads of the nut, then tighten it to the torque listed in this Chapter's Specifications, using one of the methods described in Step 12. Stake the nut at two points, then install the spline washer next to it.

22   Lay the metal plates, one at a time, on a perfectly flat surface (such as a piece of plate glass) and check for warpage by trying to slip a feeler gauge between the flat surface and the plate **(see illustration)**. The feeler gauge should be the same thickness as the warpage limit listed in this Chapter's Specifications. Do this at several places around the plate's circumference. If the feeler gauge can be slipped under the plate, it is warped and should be replaced with a new one.

14.23a Check the clutch damper for warpage . . .

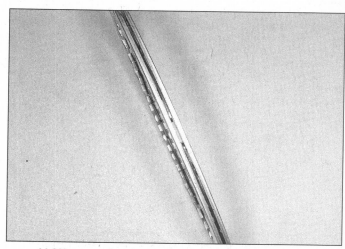

14.23b . . . and make sure its wave spring isn't broken

2

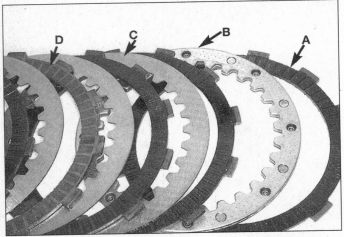

14.29 The first composite friction plate (A) has wider tabs than the others; the damper plate (B) goes next to the first composite plate; metal plates (C) go between the friction plates; the paper friction plates (D) have wider grooves in their friction material than the composite ones and when new, they're a lighter color

14.31 Be sure to install the plates in the correct order

A   Composite plate with wide tabs
B   Clutch damper
C   Paper plates (in fourth and seventh positions)

14.32 Align the O marks on clutch center and pressure plate (arrows)

14.30 Align the O marks (arrows) on damper plate and clutch center

29   Identify the friction plates. There are three different kinds. One has wider tabs than the others and two have paper friction material that looks different from the others **(see illustration)**. The remaining friction plates, which have composition material, are interchangeable with each other.

30   Coat the friction plates with clean engine oil. Install the friction plate with the wide tab on the clutch center. Install the clutch damper next to it, lining up the O marks on clutch damper and clutch center **(see illustration)**.

31   Install a composition friction plate, then a metal plate, then another composition plate, then another metal plate **(see illustration)**. Install a paper plate, then a metal plate, composition plate, metal plate, another composition plate and another metal plate. Install the last paper plate, then alternate the remaining metal and composition plates.

32   Install the clutch center on top of the last composition plate, aligning the O marks on clutch center and pressure plate **(see illustration)**.

33   Temporarily install the clutch pack in the clutch housing to align the friction plate tabs **(see illustration)**. Once the diaphragm spring is installed, it will difficult if not impossible to align the tabs, and if they aren't aligned they won't fit into the clutch housing slots. If you've got a pair of small coil springs and washers, it's a good idea to install them temporarily on two of the clutch center posts (secure them with two of the lifter plate bolts). This will keep the tabs from slipping out of alignment when the clutch pack is removed from the housing.

14.33 Temporarily install the clutch pack to align the tabs; a pair of small springs and washer will hold the tabs in alignment until the diaphragm spring can be installed

15.1a Pull the cover off the reverse lever . . .

15.1b . . . and remove the pivot bolt; pull the spring pin out of its hole as you pull the lever off

the torque listed in this Chapter's Specifications. Bend the lockwasher against the flats on the nut **(see illustration 14.9a)**.
36   Install the lifter plate. Tighten its bolts securely, but don't over-tighten them and strip the threads.
37   Lubricate the lifter piece and lifter rod with multipurpose grease, then install them in the engine.
38   Make sure the clutch cover dowels and the oil pickup strainer are in position, then install a new gasket. Install the cover and tighten its bolts evenly; tighten them securely, but don't strip the threads.
39   The remainder of installation is the reverse of the removal steps.
40   Fill the crankcase with the recommended type and amount of engine oil (see Chapter 1).

15   External reverse linkage - removal and installation

Cable replacement

Refer to illustrations 15.1a, 15.1b, 15.3, 15.4a, 15.4b and 15.5
1   Pull the cover off the reverse lever **(see illustration)**. Remove the pivot bolt and disengage the spring pin to take the lever off the drum **(see illustration)**.
2   Remove the fairing inner covers (see Chapter 8).
3   Unscrew the cable locknuts at the reverse drum and slip the cables out of their brackets **(see illustration)**.
4   Unbolt the cable retainer from the engine, then slip the cables out of the fittings on the reverse shift arm **(see illustrations)**.

15.3 Loosen the locknuts (left arrows) and slip the cables out of the brackets; on installation, grease the pivot area of the reverse drum (right arrow)

34   Install the clutch pack in a vise and reverse Steps 14 and 15 to install the diaphragm spring. Remove the clutch pack from the vise and take off the coil springs and washers (if used).
35   Install the clutch pack in the clutch housing. Install a new lock-washer with its oval hole over the tab on clutch center. Hold the clutch from turning with the tools described in Step 9 and tighten the nut to

15.4a Unbolt the cable bracket from the engine . . .

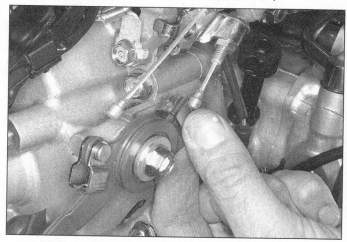

15.4b . . . this will create enough slack so the cables can be slipped out of their fittings

15.5 Slide the spring pin into its hole as you install the lever

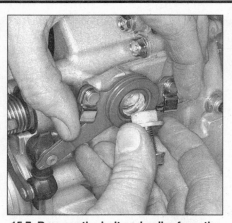

15.7 Remove the bolt and collar from the pivot on the side of the engine

15.8a Note how the ends of the spring engage the arm, then unbolt the pivot at the rear of the engine . . .

5   Installation is the reverse of the removal steps, with the following additions:
   a) *Lubricate the pivot area of the reverse drum with multi-purpose grease* **(see illustration 15.3)**.
   b) *Slide the spring pin into its hole as you install the lever* **(see illustration)**.
   c) *Refer to Chapter 1 and check the cable adjustment.*

15.8b . . . and remove the pivot collar, needle bearing and washer; replace the seal if it's been leaking

Linkage removal and installation

Refer to illustrations 15.7, 15.8a, 15.8b, 15.8c and 15.10

6   Disconnect the cables from the shift arm as described above.
7   Remove the bolt and collar from the reverse shift arm on the side of the engine **(see illustration)**.
8   Unbolt the shift arm from the rear of the engine. Remove the shift arm and its related components from the engine **(see illustrations)**.
9   Check all parts for wear and damage. Swivel the shift arm ball-joints and check them for looseness or rough movement. Replace any parts that have problems.
10   Installation is the reverse of the removal steps. Tighten the pivot bolts to the torques listed in this Chapter's Specifications **(see illustration)**.

---

16   Rear case cover - removal, bearing inspection and installation

---

Removal

Refer to illustrations 16.4a, 16.4b, 16.6a, 16.6b, 16.6c, 16.7a and 16.7b

1   Remove the engine from the motorcycle (see Section 5).
2   Remove the external reverse linkage and the clutch (see Sections 15 and 14).
3   Remove the alternator (including the alternator drive coupling) and starter (see Chapter 9).
4   Unbolt the output shaft bearing holder from the engine **(see illustrations)**.

15.8c Reverse shift arm details

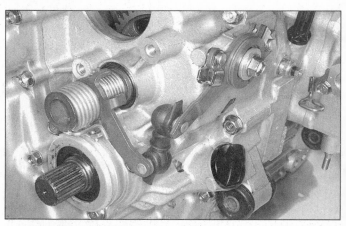

15.10 The assembled reverse linkage should look like this

16.4a Unbolt the output shaft bearing holder . . .

16.4b . . . and take it off the rear cover; use a new O-ring on installation

16.6a Grind away the staked portions of the nut without damaging the output shaft threads

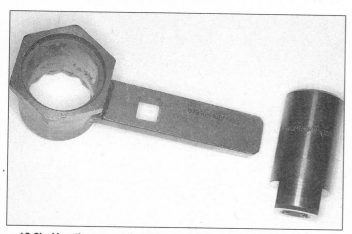

16.6b Use these tools to hold the mainshaft and undo the nut

16.6c Place the mainshaft holder on the end of the mainshaft and hold it with a wrench; place the 12-point socket on the nut and turn the lever with a breaker bar

5   If the shift pedal was removed, reinstall it temporarily and shift the transmission into a gear (not neutral). This is necessary so the mainshaft can be used to hold the output shaft from turning.
6   Grind away the two staked portions of the output shaft locknut **(see illustration)**. Lock the output shaft by placing the mainshaft holder (Honda tool 07JMB-MN50200 or equivalent) over the end of the mainshaft and holding it with a wrench **(see illustration)**. Place a

12-point 30 mm socket (Honda tool 07916-MB00001 or equivalent) over the output shaft locknut, then undo the locknut with a breaker bar **(see illustration)**.
7   Undo the rear case cover bolts **(see illustration)**. Tap the cover loose and take it off the engine, then locate the dowel pins and remove the old gasket **(see illustration)**.

16.7a Remove the rear cover bolts and tap the cover loose

16.7b Locate the dowels (A) and remove the gasket; on installation, apply a dab of sealant at the crankcase parting lines (B), then install the gasket over the sealant

2

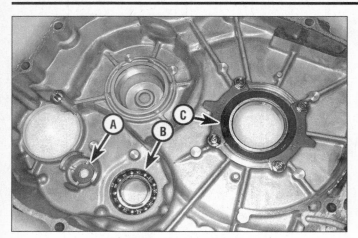

16.9 Rear case cover bearings

A   *Reverse shifter shaft needle bearing and thrust washer*
B   *Output shaft bearing*
C   *Mainshaft bearing and retainer plates*

Inspection

Refer to illustration 16.9

8   Check the cover for obvious problems, such as warpage, cracks or a damaged gasket surface, and replace it if problems are found.
9   Rotate the bearings in the cover and check them for roughness, looseness or noise **(see illustration)**. If the bearings are in bad or doubtful condition, replace them.
10   The mainshaft bearing is held in place by a pair of retainers bolted to the cover. To replace it, unbolt the retainers and tap the bearing out of its bore with a bearing driver or a socket the same diameter as the bearing outer race. Drive in a new bearing, using the same tool. Apply non-permanent thread locking agent to the retainer bolts. Place the retainers on the bearing with their OUT SIDE marks facing away from the rear cover, then install the bolts. Tighten them securely, but don't overtighten them and strip the threads.
11   The reverse shifter shaft bearing and output shaft bearing are interference (tight) fits in the cover. If either bearing needs to be replaced, tap the bearing out of its bore with a bearing driver or a socket the same diameter as the bearing outer race. Drive in a new bearing, using the same tool.

Installation

12   Apply a dab of sealant to each of the crankcase parting lines **(see illustration 16.6b)**. Be sure the dowels are in position, then install a

17.2 Remove the starter idle gear

new gasket.
13   Place the cover on the engine and finger-tighten its bolts. Then tighten the bolts evenly in stages to the torque listed in this Chapter's Specifications.
14   If the transmission is in neutral, place it in a gear. Hold the mainshaft with the tool described in Step 7 and install a new locknut. Tighten the locknut to the torque listed in this Chapter's Specifications, then stake it at two opposite points.
15   Coat a new output shaft bearing holder O-ring with engine oil and install it in the holder **(see illustration 16.4b)**. Install the holder on the engine and tighten its bolts to the torque listed in this Chapter's Specifications.
16   The remainder of installation is the reverse of the removal steps.

17 Reverse gears and shifter shaft - removal, inspection and installation

Removal

Refer to illustrations 17.2, 17.3, 17.4a and 17.4b

1   Remove the rear case cover (see Section 16).
2   Pull the starter idle gear out of the case **(see illustration)**.
3   Pull the reverse shifter shaft assembly out of the case **(see illustration)**.
4   Unbolt the starter drive gear holder from the case, then take it off and locate the dowels **(see illustrations)**.

17.3 Pull out the reverse shifter shaft assembly; on installation, the OUT mark on the reverse idle gear (arrow) faces away from the engine

17.4a Unbolt the starter drive gear holder (arrows) . . .

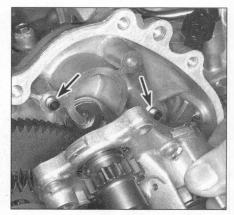

17.4b . . . then pull it off and locate the dowels

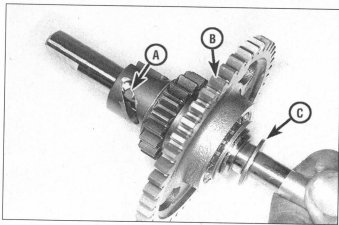

17.5 Pull out the roller pin (A) and slide off the reverse idle gear (B) and the washer (C)

Inspection

Refer to illustrations 17.5, 16.6a, 17.6b, 17.8a and 17.8b

5 Take the roller pin out of the shifter shaft **(see illustration)**. Slide

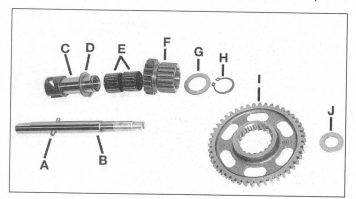

17.6b Reverse shifter shaft assembly details

A Roller pin	F Shift gear
B Reverse shifter shaft	G Washer
C Reverse shifter	H Snap-ring
D Washer	I Reverse idle gear
E Needle roller bearings	J Washer

17.8a Check the bearings in the starter drive gear holder for roughness, looseness or noise

17.6a Remove the snap-ring and washer and separate the shift gear from the reverse shifter

the washer, reverse idle gear and combined shift gear and reverse shifter off.

6 Remove the snap-ring and washer and separate the reverse shifter from the shift gear, then remove the washer and bearings **(see illustrations)**.

7 Thoroughly clean all parts in high flash point solvent and check them for wear or damage. Since needle roller bearing wear can be difficult to see, the bearings should be replaced if there's any doubt about their condition.

8 Spin the bearings in the starter drive gear holder and check them for wear or damage **(see illustration)**. The bearings can be replaced with a press and the appropriate size drivers. Before replacing the needle bearing, drive the stopper shaft and collar out of the holder with a hammer and punch **(see illustration)**. When installing the stopper shaft, make sure its installed height is within the range listed in this Chapter's Specifications.

Installation

9 Installation is the reverse of the removal steps, plus the following additions:

a) Lubricate the roller pin with grease.
b) Lubricate the other parts with oil containing molybdenum disulfide.
c) Install the reverse idle gear with its OUT mark facing away from the engine.

2

17.8b Drive out the stopper shaft (arrow) so the needle roller bearing can be removed; on installation, its installed height must be within the Specifications

18.2 Hold the starter clutch with a tool like this one and undo the bolt

18.3 Pull off the bearing, then remove the starter clutch together with the starter driven gear (arrows)

18.5 The driven gear should only rotate clockwise when viewed from this side

18 Starter clutch - removal, inspection and installation

Removal

Refer to illustrations 18.2 and 18.3

1   Remove the rear case cover (see Section 16).
2   Hold the starter clutch with a universal holder (Honda tool 07725-0030000 or equivalent) **(see illustration)**. Remove the starter clutch bolt.
3   Pull off the bearing, then the starter clutch **(see illustration)**.

18.6a Lift the driven gear out of the starter clutch and remove the needle roller bearing (arrow)

Inspection

Refer to illustrations 18.5, 18.6a, 18.6b and 18.6c

4   Spin the starter clutch bearing with fingers. Replace it if it's rough, loose or noisy.
5   Hold the starter clutch with one hand and try to rotate the driven gear in both directions **(see illustration)**. It should turn only clockwise (viewed from the gear side). If it turns both ways or neither way, the starter clutch rollers are damaged. If it turns only in the wrong direction, the rollers and installed backwards.
6   To disassemble the starter clutch, lift out the driven gear and the needle roller bearing **(see illustration)**. Remove the six T-30 Torx bolts or the large snap-ring and take out the rollers **(see illustrations)**.
7   Replace worn or damaged parts, then reverse the disassembly steps to reassemble the starter clutch. If it's held together with Torx bolts, place non-permanent thread locking agent on the bolt threads and tighten them to the torque listed in this Chapter's Specifications.
8   Repeat Step 4 to make sure the rollers are installed correctly.

Installation

9   Installation is the reverse of the removal steps.

19 Alternator gears, primary gears and oil pump sprocket - removal, inspection and installation

Removal

Refer to illustrations 19.1, 19.2, 19.3, 19.4 and 19.5

1   Take the alternator driven gear out of its bearing **(see illustration)**.
2   Slip the spline washer off the crankshaft **(see illustration)**.

18.6b Some starter clutches are held together by six T-30 Torx bolts, which go in these holes . . .

18.6c . . . others are held together by a snap-ring

19.1 Pull the alternator drive gear out of its bearing

19.2 Slide the spline washer off the crankshaft

19.3 Align the primary drive gear halves with a screwdriver and pull the driven gear (arrow) off the mainshaft

19.4 Remove the oil pump sprocket bolt (A); for access to the reverse lockout linkage or scavenge oil pump, remove the bolts (B) and baffle plate

19.5 The sprocket on the driven gear boss drives the scavenge oil pump through a chain; the flats in the sprocket center hole fit over mating flats on the oil pump shaft

3   The primary drive gear is made in two halves, which are spring loaded to keep the teeth slightly separated. This reduces gear noise. To disengage the primary driven gear from the drive gear, insert a screwdriver into the drive gear teeth and twist it to relieve the spring

19.6 The alternator drive gear is bolted to the crankshaft

tension (see illustration). Slide the driven gear off the mainshaft, then take the drive gear off the crankshaft.

4   Hold the crankshaft so it won't turn while you remove the oil pump sprocket bolt (see illustration). One way to do this is to temporarily reinstall the clutch housing, then use the holder tool used for clutch removal to keep the clutch housing from turning. The clutch housing will hold the driven gear boss, which will hold the oil pump chain, which in turn will hold the sprocket.

5   Once the sprocket bolt is removed, remove the holding tools. Disengage the sprocket from the oil pump shaft and slide the driven gear boss off the mainshaft (see illustration).

Inspection

Refer to illustrations 19.6 and 19.9

6   The alternator drive gear can be inspected without removing it from the crankshaft (see illustration). If it needs to be replaced due to wear or damage, or if the crankshaft will be removed from the engine, unbolt the gear and take it off.

7   Check the remaining gear teeth for wear or damage. The drive and driven gears should be replaced as a set if one of them needs to be replaced.

8   Check the oil pump chain for looseness between the links. If the chain flops sideways when you hold it up, replace it. If the sprocket teeth are damaged, replace the sprocket and the driven gear boss.

2

19.9 Press the new bearing into the driven gear boss

20.2 Pull the output shaft out of the engine

9   Inspect the needle roller bearing inside the driven gear boss **(see illustration)**. The bearing can be pressed out and a new one pressed in, using appropriate drifts. The installed height of the new bearing should be within the range listed in this Chapter's Specifications.

10   Spin the alternator bearing and check it for roughness, looseness or noise **(see illustration 19.1)**. If problems are found, remove the bearing with a slide hammer puller, then tap in a new one, using a bearing driver or socket that applies pressure to the bearing outer race. Tapping against the inner race will damage the bearing.

Installation

11   Installation is the reverse of the removal steps, with the following additions:

a) *Install the oil pump sprocket with its OUT mark facing away from the engine.*

b) *Tighten the sprocket bolt to the torque listed in this Chapter's Specifications.*

20 Output shaft and final drive gear - removal, inspection and installation

Removal

Refer to illustrations 20.2, 20.3, 20.5 and 20.6

1   Remove the primary gears (see Section 19).

2   Pull the output shaft out of the engine **(see illustration)**.

3   Grind away the staked portions of the final drive gear locknut without damaging the countershaft threads **(see illustration)**.

4   Temporarily reinstall the shift pedal and place the transmission in any gear except neutral. This will hold the countershaft to the locknut can be removed.

5   Turn the locknut clockwise to loosen (it has left-hand threads). Remove the washer from behind the locknut and pull the final drive gear off **(see illustration)**.

6   Unbolt the countershaft bearing retainer from the crankcase **(see illustration)**.

Inspection

Refer to illustration 20.8

7   Check the gears for worn or damaged teeth and replace them if problems are found.

8   Check the output shaft for wear or damage, such as a broken spring. Spin the bearing on the end of the output shaft and check it for roughness, looseness or noise **(see illustration)**.

9   If problems are found, remove the snap-ring, retainer and keepers from the end of the output shaft. Place the shaft in a press and press it out of the bearing, then remove the collar, final driven gear, washer, damper lifter, spring and reverse driven gear from the shaft. **Note:** *If you don't have a press, take the shaft to a Honda dealer for disassembly and parts replacement.*

10   Measure the free length of the damper spring. Also measure the output shaft diameter at the snap-ring end, the inner and outer diameters of the collar, and the inside diameter of the reverse driven gear. If

20.3 Grind away the staked portions of the nut and unscrew it . . .

20.5 . . . then take off the washer and final drive gear; on installation, the OUT SIDE mark on the washer faces away from the engine

20.6 Remove the retainer for access to the countershaft bearing; on installation, the OUT SIDE mark on the retainer faces away from the engine

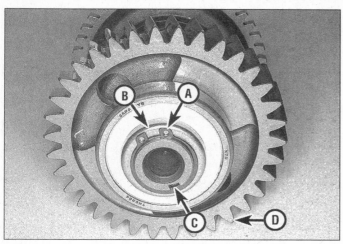

20.8 Output shaft details

A	Snap-ring	C	Keyway
B	Retainer	D	Reverse driven gear

21.2b Note how the return spring is installed . . .

any of these measurements are not within the range listed in this Chapter's Specifications, replace the affected part.

11   Reverse Step 9 to reassemble the shaft. The dished side of the reverse driven gear faces the output shaft spring. The tab on the inner diameter of the retainer goes opposite the keyway in the shaft. The

21.2c . . . then unbolt the arm from the engine

21.2a The assembled reverse lockout system should look like this

A	Rod	C	Drum
B	Lockout arm and lever		

sealed side of the ball bearing faces away from the gear.

12   Check the small oil hole in the inner diameter of the final drive gear (between the splines). Make sure it's not clogged.

13   Inspect the countershaft ball bearing in the crankcase. If it's rough, loose or noisy when you spin it, pull it out and install a new one.

Installation

14   Installation is the reverse of the removal steps, with the following additions:

a) *Install the countershaft bearing retainer with its OUT SIDE mark facing away from the crankcase and tighten its bolts to the torque listed in this Chapter's Specifications.*

b) *Coat the threads of a new locknut with non-permanent thread locking agent. Tighten the nut to the torque listed in this Chapter's Specifications, then stake it in two places.*

21   Reverse lockout system - removal and installation

Refer to illustrations 21.2a, 21.2b and 21.2c

1   Remove the rear case cover, starter clutch, primary driven gear, oil pump chain and sprockets and oil pump chain guide (see Sections 16 through 19). If necessary for access, remove the output shaft and final drive gear (see Section 20).

2   Note how the system is installed **(see illustrations)**. Remove the lock arm bolt, collar and return spring from the rear of the crankcase **(see illustration)**. Slide the upper end of the lock rod out of the case and remove the assembly from the engine.

3   Check all parts for wear and damage. If necessary, unbolt the drum from the engine **(see illustration 21.2b)**.

4   Installation is the reverse of the removal steps. Apply non-permanent thread locking agent to the bolt threads and tighten it to the torque listed in this Chapter's Specifications.

22   Scavenging oil pump - removal, inspection and installation

Removal

Refer to illustrations 22.5a and 22.5b

1   The scavenging oil pump, which picks up oil from the clutch cavity to lubricate the primary gears, can be removed without separating the crankcase halves.

2   Remove the engine from the motorcycle (see Section 5).

2

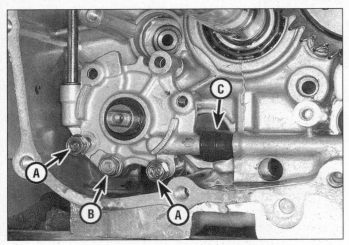

22.5a Scavenging pump installation

A   Pump mounting bolts   C   Rubber grommet
B   Pump assembly bolt

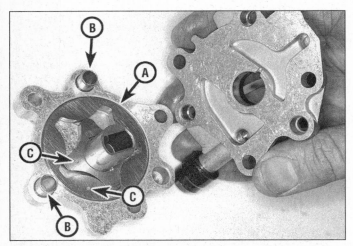

22.6 Lift the cover off the pump; after it's cleaned, measure the gap between outer rotor and pump body (A) - on assembly, make sure the dowels (B) are in position and the punch marks on both rotors (C) face the same direction

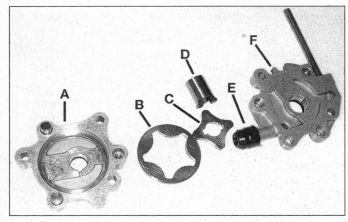

22.7 Scavenging oil pump details

A   Pump body   D   Drive guide
B   Outer rotor   E   Rubber grommet
C   Inner rotor   F   Pump cover

22.5b Remove the pump and locate its dowel (arrow); it may stay in the engine or come off with the pump

3   Remove the clutch (see Section 14).
4   Remove the rear case cover, primary driven gear, oil pump chain and sprockets and oil pump chain guide (see Sections 16 through 19).
5   Unbolt the scavenging pump from the engine and pull it off the pump drive shaft **(see illustrations)**.

Inspection

Refer to illustrations 22.6, 22.7, 22.9a, 22.9b and 22.10

6   Remove the pump assembly bolt and separate the pump halves **(see illustration)**.
7   Take the rotors and drive guide out of the pump **(see illustration)**. Wash the oil pump in solvent, then dry it off.
8   Check the pump body and rotors for scoring and wear. If any damage or uneven or excessive wear is evident, replace the pump (individual parts aren't available). If you are rebuilding the engine, it's a good idea to install a new oil pump.
9   Measure the clearance between the inner and outer rotor tips and between the outer rotor and housing **(see illustration)**. Place a straightedge across the pump body and measure the gap between the straightedge and rotors with a feeler gauge **(see illustration)**. Replace the pump if any of the clearances is excessive.
10   Inspect the pump shaft seal and the rubber grommet **(see illustration)**. Since there's a good deal of labor required to remove the pump, it's a good idea to replace the grommet and seal whenever the pump is removed.
11   If the pump is good, reverse the disassembly steps to reassemble it. Make sure the pin is centered in the rotor shaft so it will align with the slot in the inner rotor.

22.9a Measure the gap between inner and outer rotors

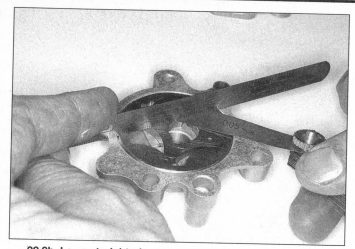

22.9b Lay a straightedge across the rotors and pump body and measure the gap

22.10 It's a good idea to replace the pump seal and grommet (arrows) whenever the pump is removed

Installation

12   Before installing the pump, prime it by pouring oil into it while turning the shaft by hand - this will ensure that it begins to pump oil quickly.

13   Installation is the reverse of removal, with the following additions:

a) *Align the flat on the pump drive shaft with the flat in the drive guide.*

b) *Be sure the pump-to-engine dowel and rubber grommet are in position.*

c) *Tighten the mounting bolts securely, but don't overtighten them and strip the threads.*

23   Front case cover - removal and installation

Refer to illustrations 23.5, 23.6a, 23.6b, 23.7, 23.8a, 23.8b and 23.10

1   Place the transmission in neutral.

2   Drain the engine oil and coolant (see Chapter 1).

3   Remove the fairing front cover and under cover (see Chapter 8).

4   Refer to Chapter 3 and remove the water pump.

5   Loosen the screw and detach the connector from the oil pressure switch **(see illustration)**. Follow the gear position sensor harness from the rubber grommet in the cover to the electrical connector and unplug it.

6   Remove the cover bolts and take the cover off the engine, locate the dowels and remove the gasket **(see illustrations)**.

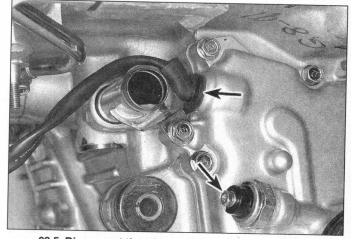

23.5 Disconnect the wire from the oil pressure switch (lower arrow); follow the harness (upper arrow) to its connector and unplug it

2

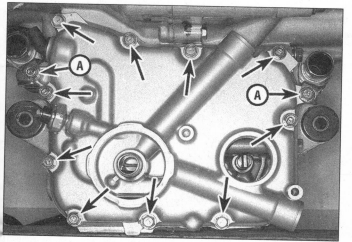

23.6a Remove the cover bolts; two of the cover bolts (A) secure coolant tubes

23.6b Take the cover off and remove the gasket; locate the dowel and replace the two O-rings (arrows)

23.7 Pull out the oil pump tube and replace its O-rings

7   Pull out the oil pump tube **(see illustration)**. Replace its O-rings with new ones if there's any doubt about their condition. It's a good idea to replace these O-rings, as well as the cover dowel O-rings, whenever the cover is removed.
8   Unbolt the bearing holder from the front of the crankcase **(see illustration)**. If the countershaft bearing is rough, loose or noisy **(see illustration)**, pull it out and install a new one. Install the bearing holder and tighten the bolts securely, but don't overtighten them and damage the threads.
9   Thoroughly clean the gasket from the cover and crankcase.
10   Turn the pin on the gearshift position sensor to align with the tab on the switch **(see illustration)**.
11   Make sure all O-rings and the wiring harness grommet are in position. Install the oil tube in the crankcase.
12   Place a quarter-inch wide dab of sealant across the crankcase parting lines at top center and bottom center of the gasket surface, then install a new gasket over the dowel.
13   Position the cover on the engine and install its bolts. Tighten the bolts evenly, in two or three stages, in a criss-cross pattern. Tighten the bolts securely, but don't overtighten them and damage the threads.

---

24   External shift mechanism - removal, inspection and installation

Shift pedal - removal and installation

Refer to illustrations 24.2, 24.3a, 24.3b and 24.4
1   Place the bike on its centerstand.
2   Look for alignment marks on the shift pedal and its outer shaft

23.8a Unbolt the bearing holder . . .

23.8b . . . check the countershaft bearing (left) and replace it if it's worn or damaged

23.10 Align the pin and tab of the gear position switch (A); on installation, fit the pin into the notch in the shift drum (B)

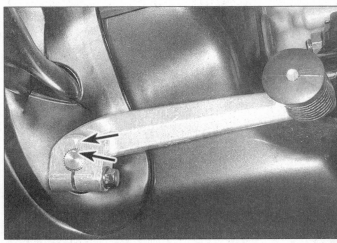

24.2 Check for alignment marks on the pedal and shaft, then remove the pinch bolt and take the pedal off

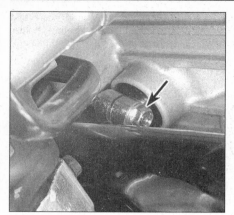

24.3a Remove the pinch bolt (arrow) . . .

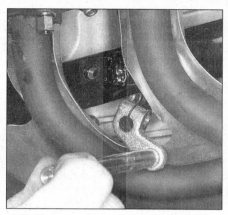

24.3b . . . and take the outer shaft off

24.4 Check the shift shaft seal and
replace it if it leaks

(see illustration). If there aren't any, make your own. Remove the
pinch bolt and take the pedal of the shaft.

3   For access to the pedal shaft pinch bolt, remove fairing panels as

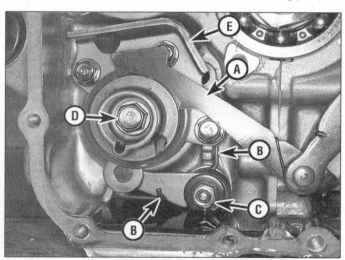

24.7 External shift linkage details

A	Shift arm pawl	D	Drum center bolt
B	Stopper arm spring ends	E	Bearing retainer
C	Stopper arm nut		

necessary from the lower left side of the bike (see Chapter 8). Look for
alignment marks on the outer and inner shafts and make your own if
there aren't any. Remove the shaft pinch bolt and take the outer shaft
off (see illustrations).

4   Check the shaft seal for leakage (see illustration). It it's been
leaking, pry it out and tap in a new one with a socket the same diameter as the seal. You may need to remove the left side of the exhaust
system for access (see Chapter 4).

5   Installation is the reverse of the removal steps. Tighten the pinch
bolts securely, but don't overtighten them and strip the threads.

Shift mechanism

Removal

Refer to illustrations 24.7, 24.8a, 24.8b and 24.9

6   The stopper arm, shift drum center and cam plate are the only
parts of the external shift linkage that can be removed without disassembling the crankcase. The shift arm, generally considered part of the
external linkage, is bolted to components on the inside of the
crankcase, so the crankcase must be disassembled to remove it.
Remove the front engine case (see Section 23).

7   Lift the shift arm to disengage it from the shift drum center (see
illustration).

8   Remove the nut and washer from the stopper lever, then remove
the stopper lever, collar and spring (see illustrations).

9   Remove the drum center bolt and take the drum center off (see
illustration 24.7 and the accompanying illustration).

24.8a Remove the stopper arm washer . . .

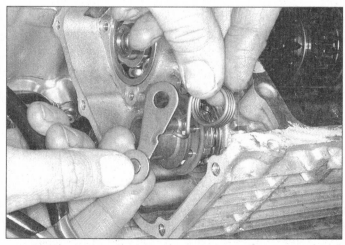

24.8b . . . and take off the stopper arm, collar and spring

Inspection

10   Check the condition of the stopper lever and spring. Replace the stopper lever if it's worn where it contacts the shift drum. Replace the spring if it's distorted.

11   Inspect the pins on the end of the shift drum **(see illustration 24.9)**. If they're worn or damaged, replace them. If their holes in the end of the shift drum are enlarged, you'll have to disassemble the crankcase to replace the shift drum.

12   If the shift drum bearing is worn, remove the bearing retainer **(see illustration 24.7)**. Take the bearing out of the case and install a new one.

Installation

Refer to illustration 24.13

13   If the drum center was removed from the shift drum, install it. Be sure to reinstall the dowel pins. Align the pin on the shift drum with the notch in the cam plate **(see illustration)**. Tighten the drum center bolt to the torque listed in this Chapter's Specifications.

14   Apply non-permanent thread locking agent to the threads of the stopper lever bolt, then install the stopper lever and return spring. Make sure the stopper lever engages the neutral detent in the shift drum. Tighten the bolt securely, but don't overtighten it and damage the threads.

15   The remainder of installation is the reverse of the removal steps, plus the following additions:

a) *Before installing the front case cover, operate the shift linkage by hand to make sure it works properly.*

b) *Fill the engine with oil and coolant (see Chapter 1).*

25   Crankcase - disassembly and reassembly

1   To examine and repair or replace the pistons, connecting rods, bearings, main oil pump, crankshaft, internal shift linkage or transmission components, the crankcase must be split into two parts. Before you start, read through the procedure, paying special attention to the Honda piston ring compressor used for assembly. Experienced Honda mechanics consider this tool essential. Even for experienced professional mechanics who use the special tool and have an assistant to help, it often takes more than one try to get the case halves together.

Disassembly

Refer to illustrations 25.6a, 25.6b, 25.6c, 25.7a, 25.7b, 25.7c, 25.8a and 25.8b

2   Remove the engine from the motorcycle (see Section 5).

3   Refer to Chapter 4 and remove the pulse air system.

4   Refer to Chapter 3 and remove the coolant tubes.

5   Remove the timing belts, clutch, rear case cover, scavenging oil

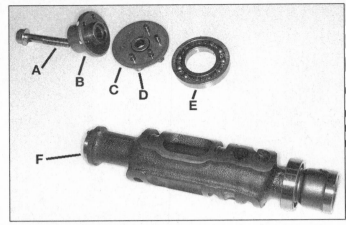

24.9 The drum center components can be removed from the drum without disassembling the crankcase; to remove the shift drum from the engine, the crankcase must be disassembled

A   Bolt
B   Drum center
C   Plate

D   Cam plate and dowels
E   Bearing
F   Shift drum

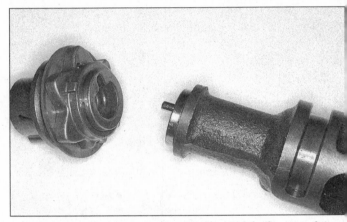

24.13 Align the shift drum pin with the notch in the cam plate

pump, front engine cover and the bearing retainer inside it (see Sections 7, 14, 16, 22 and 23). You can remove just the left cylinder head if you're not planning to work on the right cylinder head (see Section 10).

6   Remove the 22 crankcase bolts **(see illustrations)**. All eight of the

25.6a Remove the upper crankcase bolts . . .

25.6b . . . the lower crankcase bolts . . .

25.6c . . . and one at the top rear of the engine

25.7a Lift the left crankcase half off the right half . . .

25.7b . . . pulling the shift arm out of the way as you lift

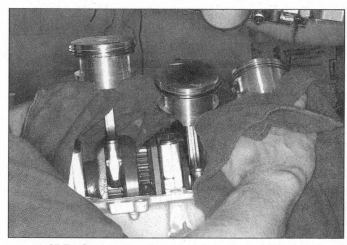

25.7c Support the pistons so they aren't damaged

10 mm bolts, and four of the 8 mm bolts, have sealing washers. The sealing washers on the two forward 10 mm bolts are copper colored and have a smaller outside diameter than the others.

7   Carefully separate the crankcase halves, guiding the external shift linkage pawl clear of the drum center as you do so **(see illustrations)**. If they won't separate easily, make sure all fasteners have been

removed. Don't pry against the crankcase mating surfaces or they will leak.

8   Look for the O-rings and the dowels **(see illustrations)**. If they're not in one of the crankcase halves, locate them.

9   Refer to Sections 26 through 38 for information on the internal components of the crankcase.

25.8a There's a single dowel with O-ring on the lower side of the case . . .

25.8b . . . and three dowels, one with an O-ring, on the upper side

2

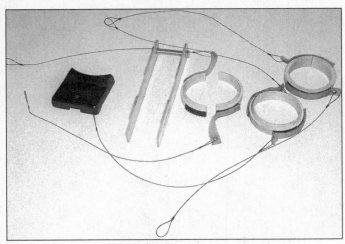

25.15a This set of ring compressors is necessary to reassemble the case halves

25.15b Insert the white plastic supports under the no. 4 and no. 6 pistons and the black rubber support under the no. 2 piston

Reassembly

Refer to illustrations 25.15a, 25.15b, 25.17, 25.20a, 25.20b, 25.21 and 25.26

10   Make sure the transmission shafts are correctly positioned in the right crankcase half (see Section 36). Make sure the crankshaft is fully installed, with all connecting rods, pistons and rings. The timing belt pulley must be installed on the end of the crankshaft.

11   You'll need a pair of supports later in the procedure. Either make a pair of wooden support blocks (3-3/8 by 1-1/2 by 1-1/2 inches), or use a pair of deep sockets about 3-3/8 inches long.

12   Set the crankcase assembly on a workbench with the right side downward. Rotate the crankshaft so the T-1-2 timing mark is straight up (toward the left side of the engine).

13   Remove all traces of sealant from the crankcase mating surfaces. Be careful not to let any fall into the case as this is done. Check to make sure the dowel pins and O-rings are in place **(see illustrations 25.8a and 25.8b)**.

14   Cover the transmission gears and the shift drum with a clean rag.

15   Twist the two sides of the white plastic piston base away from each other, so their notches face away from each other. Work the piston base under the no. 6 and no. 4 pistons, then release it so the pistons are supported **(see illustrations)**.

16   Place the black rubber piston base under no. 1 piston **(see illustration 25.15b)**.

17   Place a ring compressor over each piston and secure it with Velcro strips **(see illustration)**. Be sure to position the removal cords and the gaps in the ring compressors as shown, so the cords will pull the Velcro strips off after the left crankcase half is installed over the pistons. If the cords are placed on the wrong side of the engine or the gaps are in the wrong place, it will be impossible to separate the ring compressor halves.

18   Place the supports from Step 11 on diagonally opposite corners of the engine, at the dowel locations, to support the left case half. Once the case half is on far enough that the no. 2 piston rings are in their cylinder, you'll need to stop lowering it so you can remove part of the ring compressor. This will be much easier if the case half has something to rest on. **Note:** *If you use support blocks, you'll need to remove the dowel and O-ring on the timing belt end of the engine. If you use deep sockets, the dowel can be left in position.*

19   Tie the shift arm out of the way with wire **(see illustration 25.7b)**.

20   Lower the crankcase half straight onto the no. 2 piston until it rests on the supports **(see illustration)**. Once it reaches the supports, remove the black rubber piston base **(see illustration)**. Be very careful not to force the ring compressors off of the pistons, or you'll have to lift up the case and start over.

21   Pull the strings of the no. 2 piston's ring compressor to detach the Velcro strips. Take the ring compressor halves out of the crankcase **(see illustration)**.

25.17 Be sure to align the gaps in the ring compressors and position the removal cords as shown here, or you won't be able to get the compressors off the pistons

25.20a Lower the left case half onto no. 2 piston . . .

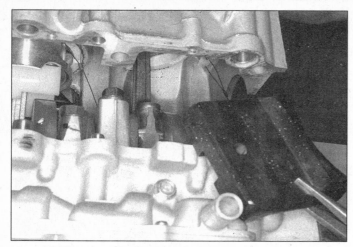

25.20b . . . and pull the black rubber support out from under no. 2 piston

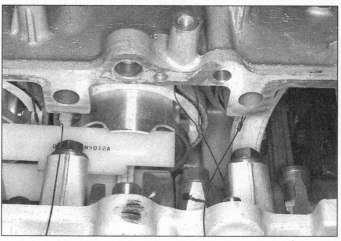

25.21 Pull the removal cords to undo the Velcro and take the compressor halves off no. 2 piston

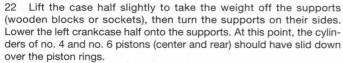

22   Lift the case half slightly to take the weight off the supports (wooden blocks or sockets), then turn the supports on their sides. Lower the left crankcase half onto the supports. At this point, the cylinders of no. 4 and no. 6 pistons (center and rear) should have slid down over the piston rings.

23   Twist the tops of the white plastic piston tool toward each other to get removal clearance, then pull the tool out of the engine.

24   Pull the rear (no. 6) piston's ring compressor down until it's clear of the cylinder, then pull on its removal cords to separate the ring compressor halves and take the ring compressor out of the engine.

25   Finally, twist the lower side of the left crankcase half away from the transmission as far as possible without pulling the no. 2 and no. 6 cylinders off their piston rings. This will provide space for removing the last ring compressor. Pull the release cords and work the ring compressor out of the engine.

26   Apply a thin, even bead of sealant to the crankcase mating surfaces. This isn't easy to do with the crankcase halves so close together, but it's necessary to do it now (rather than earlier) to ensure that the sealant doesn't cure before the case halves are fitted together. Be sure to coat the two surfaces next to the center main bearing caps **(see illustration)**.

27   Lubricate the threads of the 10 mm bolts with clean engine oil. Install the case bolts **(see illustrations 25.6a, 25.6b and 25.6c)**. The two longer 10 mm bolts go toward the front of the engine. Tighten the 10 mm bolts first, in two or three stages and a criss-cross pattern, to

the torque listed in this Chapter's Specifications. Then tighten the remaining bolts evenly to their specified torques.

28   Turn the mainshaft to make sure it turns freely. Also make sure the crankshaft turns freely.

29   The remainder of assembly is the reverse of disassembly.

26   Crankcase components - inspection and servicing

Refer to illustration 26.2

1   After the crankcases have been separated and the crankshaft, shift cam and forks and transmission components removed, the crankcases should be cleaned thoroughly with new solvent and dried with compressed air.

2   Remove any oil passage plugs that haven't already been removed **(see illustration)**. All oil passages should be blown out with compressed air.

3   All traces of old gasket sealant should be removed from the mating surfaces. Minor damage to the surfaces can be cleaned up with a fine sharpening stone or grindstone. **Caution:** *Be very careful not to nick or gouge the crankcase mating surfaces or leaks will result. Check both crankcase halves very carefully for cracks and other damage.*

4   If any damage is found that can't be repaired, replace the crankcase halves as a set.

25.26 Coat the mating surfaces with sealant; don't miss the areas that are hard to reach (arrows)

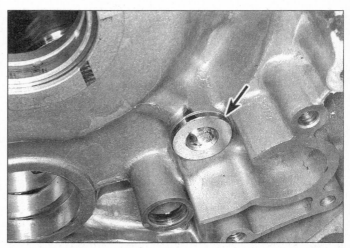

26.2 Oil passage plugs should be removed so the passages can be cleaned

27.2a Unbolt the oil pump . . .

27.2b . . . then lift it up and locate the dowels (arrows); they may come off with the pump or stay in the case

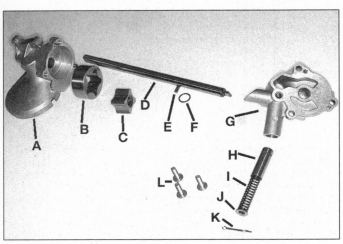

27.3 Main oil pump details

A	Pump body	G	Pump cover
B	Outer rotor	H	Relief valve
C	Inner rotor	I	Spring
D	Shaft	J	Washer
E	Drive pin	K	Cotter pin
F	Spacer	L	Pump cover screws

27.4 Check the oil strainer screen for clogging

27 Main oil pump - removal, inspection and installation

Refer to illustrations 27.2a, 27.2b, 27.3, 27.4 and 27.7

1   Refer to Section 25 and disassemble the crankcase.
2   Unbolt the pump from the left crankcase half and locate its dowels **(see illustrations)**.
3   Remove the pump assembly bolts and disassemble the pump **(see illustration)**.
4   Make sure the strainer is clean **(see illustration)**.
5   Check the pressure relief valve for scoring or wear and replace the pump if problems are found.
6   The remainder of inspection is the same as for the scavenging oil pump (see Section 22).
7   Assembly is the reverse of disassembly. Make sure the drive pin engages the inner rotor **(see illustration)**. Use a new cotter pin to secure the relief valve.
8   Installation is the reverse of the removal steps. Tighten the mounting bolts securely, but don't overtighten them and strip the threads.

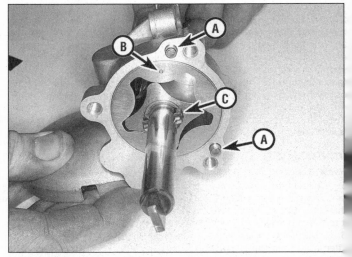

27.7 Make sure the cover dowels (A) are in position, the outer rotor punch mark (B) faces the pump cover, and the drive pin (C) engages the slots in the inner rotor

28.2 Bend back the lockwasher tab (arrow) and
undo the shift arm bolt

28.3a The ends of the return spring fit on either side of the post

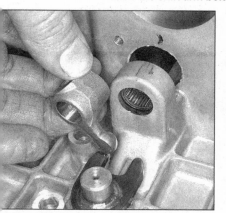

28.3b Lift out the inner shaft arm and
inspect the needle bearing

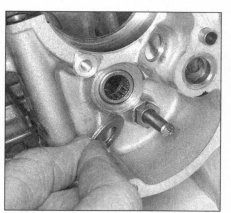

28.3c Lift off the thrust washer and
inspect the needle bearing

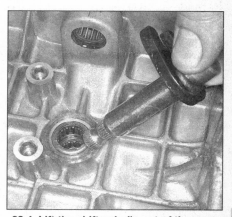

28.4 Lift the shift spindle out of the case
and inspect its needle bearing

2

28 Internal shift linkage - removal, inspection and installation

Removal

Refer to illustrations 28.2, 28.3a, 28.3b, 28.3c and 28.4

Refer to Section 25 and disassemble the crankcase.

In the left case half, bend back the lockwasher tab and remove the shift arm bolt (see illustration).

On the outside of the case at the front, note how the return spring ends fit over the return spring post (see illustration). Pull the outer shift arm shaft partway out of the case and lift out the inner shift arm (see illustration). Then pull the outer shift arm shaft the rest of the way out and remove the thrust washer (see illustration).

If you haven't already done so, remove the outer shift shaft from the shift spindle (see Section 24). Lift the shift spindle out of the case (see illustration).

Inspection

Refer to illustration 28.6

Inspect the return spring post (see illustration 28.3a). If it's worn or damaged, replace it. If it's loose, unscrew it, apply a non-permanent thread locking compound to the threads, reinstall the post and tighten to the torque listed in this Chapter's Specifications.

Check the shift arm shaft for bends. If the shaft is bent, you can attempt to straighten it. Inspect the pawls and springs on the shift shaft and replace the shaft if they're worn or damaged (see illustration).

Check the inner shift arm and shift spindle for wear at their contact points (see illustration 28.6). Replace worn parts.

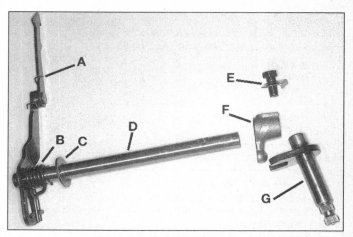

28.6 Internal shift linkage details

A	Shift pawl spring	E	Bolt and lockwasher
B	Return spring	F	Inner shift arm
C	Thrust washer	G	Shift spindle
D	Outer shift arm		

8 Check the shift shaft and shift spindle needle roller bearings in the crankcase (see illustrations 28.3b, 28.3c and 28.4). If any of them are worn or damaged, remove it with a slide hammer puller and tap in a new one. To prevent damage to the new bearing, you'll need a shouldered drift with a small diameter the same size as the bearing inner diameter.

29.2 Measure connecting rod side clearance with a feeler gauge

29.3a Mark the cylinder number on each connecting rod

Installation

9   Installation is the reverse of the removal steps. Use a new lock-washer on the shift arm bolt. Tighten the bolt to the torque listed in this Chapter's Specifications and bend the lockwasher tab against the bolt.

29 Piston/connecting rod assemblies - removal, connecting rod inspection and installation

Removal

Refer to illustrations 29.2, 29.3a, 29.3b, 29.4a, 29.4b and 29.6

1   Remove both cylinder heads and disassemble the crankcase (Sections 10 and 25).

2   Before removing the connecting rods from the crankshaft, measure the side clearance of each rod with a feeler gauge **(see illustration)**. If the clearance on any rod is greater than that listed in this Chapter's Specifications, that rod will have to be replaced with a new one. If the clearance is still excessive after replacing the rod, the crankshaft will have to be replaced.

3   There aren't any cylinder numbers marked on the connecting rods and caps, and it's important to reinstall them in their original locations. Using a felt pen or a center punch, mark the cylinder number on each rod and cap **(see illustration)**. Number the pistons as well; if

29.3b Label the pistons as well; its' a good idea to wrap them in padding so the skirts won't be damaged

they're reused, they must be returned to their original cylinders **(see illustration)**.

4   Unscrew the left side bearing cap nuts, separate the caps from the rods, then detach the rods from the crankshaft **(see illustrations)**. If the cap is stuck, tap on the ends of the rod bolts with a soft face hammer to free them.

29.4a Lay the left side connecting rods down so the nuts are accessible, then remove them (arrows; no. 2 cylinder shown)

29.4b Separate the caps from the connecting rods; the lines on the rod and cap (left arrow) are a Roman numeral that indicates a bearing selection code; the letter (right arrow) is a weight grade

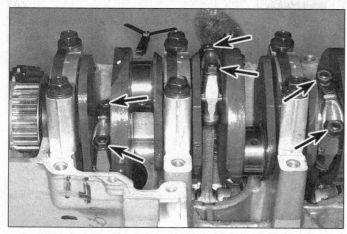

29.6 Remove the cap nuts from the right connecting rods (arrows)

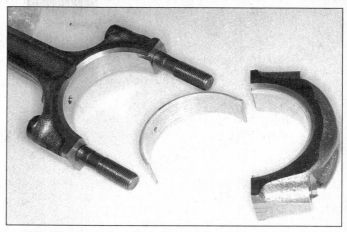

29.8 Align the rod and bearing oil holes. Fit the bearing tabs into the notches

5   Temporarily reassemble the rods to the caps so the rods and caps don't get mixed up.

6   Unscrew the right side bearing cap nuts and separate the caps from the rods **(see illustration)**. If the engine is still on a workbench with its right side facing down, lay it flat. Tap gently on the studs of the connecting rods with a wooden hammer handle to push the pistons out of their bores, then carefully remove the rods without scratching the cylinders. Temporarily reassemble the rods to the caps so the rods and caps don't get mixed up.

Connecting rod inspection

7   Check the connecting rods for cracks and other obvious damage. Have the rods checked for twisting and bending at a dealer service department or other motorcycle repair shop.

Installation

Refer to illustrations 29.8, 29.10 and 29.11

8   Wipe off the bearing inserts, connecting rods and caps. Install the inserts into the rods and caps, using your hands only, making sure the tabs on the inserts engage with the notches in the rods and caps **(see illustration)**. When all the inserts are installed, lubricate them with engine assembly lube or moly-based grease. Don't get any lubricant on the mating surfaces of the rod or cap.

9   Place short pieces of vinyl hose over the connecting rod studs to prevent them from damaging the crankshaft.

10   On the right side of the engine, place the ring compressors over

the rings **(see illustration)**. Insert the connecting rods into the correct bores, making sure the oil holes and piston top marks are in the correct relationship **(see illustration 31.17)**. Assemble each connecting rod to its proper journal, referring to the previously applied cylinder numbers. The lines present at the rod/cap seam on one side of the connecting rod should fit together perfectly when the rod and cap are assembled **(see illustration 29.4b)**. If it doesn't, the wrong cap is on the rod. Fix this problem before assembling the engine any further.

11   When you're sure the rods are positioned correctly, lubricate the threads of the rod bolts and the undersides of the rod nuts with molybdenum disulfide grease and tighten the nuts to the torque listed in this Chapter's Specifications **(see illustration)**. **Note:** *Snug both nuts evenly, in several stages, to the specified torque.*

12   Turn the rods on the crankshaft. If any of them feel tight, tap on the bottom of the connecting rod caps with a hammer - this should relieve stress and free them up. If it doesn't, recheck the bearing clearance.

13   As a final step, recheck the connecting rod side clearances (see Step 1). If the clearances aren't correct, find out why before proceeding with engine assembly.

30   Cylinders - inspection

1   Don't attempt to separate the liners from the cylinder block.

2   Check the cylinder walls carefully for scratches and score marks.

3   Using the appropriate precision measuring tools, check each

29.10 Gently tap the pistons in with a wooden hammer handle

29.11 Tighten rod cap nuts to the specified torque

2

cylinder's diameter. Measure parallel to the crankshaft axis and across the crankshaft axis, at the top, center and bottom of the cylinder. Average the measurements and compare the results to this Chapter's Specifications. If the cylinder walls are tapered, out-of-round, worn beyond the specified limits, or badly scuffed or scored, have them rebored and honed by a dealer service department or a motorcycle repair shop. If a rebore is done, oversize pistons and rings will be required as well.

4   As an alternative, if the precision measuring tools are not available, a dealer service department or motorcycle repair shop will make the measurements and offer advice concerning servicing of the cylinders.

5   If they are in reasonably good condition and not worn to the outside of the limits, and if the piston-to-cylinder clearances can be maintained properly, then the cylinders do not have to be rebored; honing is all that is necessary.

6   To perform the honing operation you will need the proper size flexible hone with fine stones, or a ìbottle brushî type hone, plenty of light oil or honing oil, some shop towels and an electric drill motor. Hold the crankcase half in a vise (cushioned with soft jaws or wood blocks) when performing the honing operation. Mount the hone in the drill motor, compress the stones and slip the hone into the cylinder. Lubricate the cylinder thoroughly, turn on the drill and move the hone up and down in the cylinder at a pace which will produce a fine crosshatch pattern on the cylinder wall with the crosshatch lines intersecting at approximately a 60-degree angle. Be sure to use plenty of lubricant and do not take off any more material than is absolutely necessary to produce the desired effect. Do not withdraw the hone from the cylinder while it is running. Instead, shut off the drill and continue moving the hone up and down in the cylinder until it comes to a complete stop, then compress the stones and withdraw the hone. Wipe the oil out of the cylinder and repeat the procedure on the remaining cylinders. Remember, do not remove too much material from the cylinder wall. If you do not have the tools, or do not desire to perform the honing operation, a dealer service department or motorcycle repair shop will generally do it for a reasonable fee.

7   Next, the cylinders must be thoroughly washed with warm soapy water to remove all traces of the abrasive grit produced during the honing operation. Be sure to run a brush through the bolt holes and coolant passages and flush them with running water. After rinsing, dry the cylinders thoroughly and apply a coat of light, rust-preventative oil to all machined surfaces.

31 Pistons - inspection, removal and installation

1   The pistons on early models are attached to the connecting rods with piston pins that are a slip fit in the pistons and rods. On later models, the pistons are pressed into the connecting rods and are a slip fit in the pistons.

2   Refer to Section 29 and remove the piston/connecting rod assemblies.

Inspection

Refer to illustrations 31.12

3   Before the inspection process can be carried out, the pistons must be cleaned and the old piston rings removed.

4   Using a piston ring installation tool, carefully remove the rings from the pistons. Do not nick or gouge the pistons in the process.

5   Scrape all traces of carbon from the tops of the pistons. A hand-held wire brush or a piece of fine emery cloth can be used once most of the deposits have been scraped away. Do not, under any circumstances, use a wire brush mounted in a drill motor to remove deposits from the pistons; the piston material is soft and will be eroded away by the wire brush.

6   Use a piston ring groove cleaning tool to remove any carbon deposits from the ring grooves. If a tool is not available, a piece broken off the old ring will do the job. Be very careful to remove only the carbon deposits. Do not remove any metal and do not nick or gouge the sides of the ring grooves.

7   Once the deposits have been removed, clean the pistons with solvent and dry them thoroughly. Make sure the oil return holes below the oil ring grooves are clear.

8   If the pistons are not damaged or worn excessively and if the cylinders are not rebored, new pistons will not be necessary. Normal piston wear appears as even, vertical wear on the thrust surfaces of the piston and slight looseness of the top ring in its groove. New piston rings, on the other hand, should always be used when an engine is rebuilt.

9   Carefully inspect each piston for cracks around the skirt, at the pin bosses and at the ring lands.

10   Look for scoring and scuffing on the thrust faces of the skirt, holes in the piston crown and burned areas at the edge of the crown. If the skirt is scored or scuffed, the engine may have been suffering from overheating and/or abnormal combustion, which caused excessively high operating temperatures. The oil pump and cooling system should be checked thoroughly. A hole in the piston crown, an extreme to be sure, is an indication that abnormal combustion (pre-ignition) was occurring. Burned areas at the edge of the piston crown are usually evidence of spark knock (detonation). If any of the above problems exist, the causes must be corrected or the damage will occur again.

11   Measure the piston ring-to-groove clearance by laying a new piston ring in the ring groove and slipping a feeler gauge in beside it. Check the clearance at three or four locations around the groove. Be sure to use the correct ring for each groove; they are different. If the clearance is greater than specified, new pistons will have to be used when the engine is reassembled.

12   Check the piston-to-bore clearance by measuring the bore (see Section 30) and the piston diameter. Make sure that the pistons and cylinders are correctly matched. Measure the piston across the skirt on the thrust faces at a 90-degree angle to the piston pin, at the distance from the bottom of the skirt listed in this Chapter's Specifications **(see illustration)**. Subtract the piston diameter from the bore diameter to obtain the clearance. If it is greater than specified, the cylinders will have to be rebored and new oversized pistons and rings installed. If the appropriate precision measuring tools are not available, the piston-to-cylinder clearances can be obtained, though not quite as accurately, using feeler gauge stock. Feeler gauge stock comes in 12-inch lengths and various thicknesses and is generally available at auto parts stores. To check the clearance, select a feeler gauge of the same thickness as the piston clearance listed in this Chapter's Specifications and slip it into the cylinder along with the appropriate piston. The cylinder should be upside down and the piston must be positioned exactly as it normally would be. Place the feeler gauge between the piston and cylinder on one of the thrust faces (90-degrees to the piston pin bore). The piston should slip through the cylinder (with the feeler gauge in place) with moderate pressure. If it falls through, or slides through easily, the clearance is excessive and a new piston will be required. If the

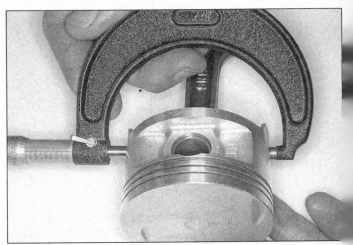

31.12 Measure the piston diameter with a micrometer

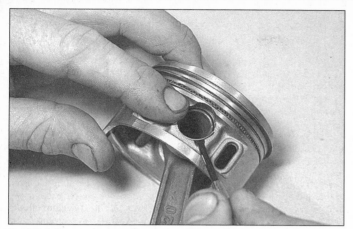

31.13 Wear eye protection and pry the circlip out of its groove with a pointed tool

31.14a Push the piston pin partway out, then pull it the rest of the way

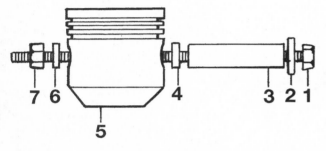

31.14b The piston pins should come out with hand pressure - if they don't, this removal tool can be fabricated with readily available parts

1	Bolt	7	Nut (B)
2	Washer	A	Large enough for piston
3	Pipe (A)		pin to fit inside
4	Padding (A)	B	Small enough to fit
5	Piston		through piston pin bore
6	Washer (B)		

piston binds at the lower end of the cylinder and is loose toward the top, the cylinder is tapered, and if tight spots are encountered as the feeler gauge is placed at different points around the cylinder, the cylinder is out-of-round. Repeat the procedure for the remaining pistons

and cylinders. Be sure to have the cylinders and pistons checked by a dealer service department or a motorcycle repair shop to confirm your findings before purchasing new parts.

Removal

Clip-type pistons

Refer to illustrations 31.13, 31.14a, 31.14b, 31.15a and 31.15b

13   Support the piston, grasp the circlip with a pointed tool or needle-nose pliers and remove it from the groove **(see illustration)**.

14   Push the piston pin out from the opposite end to free the piston from the rod **(see illustration)**. You may have to deburr the area around the groove to enable the pin to slide out (use a triangular file for this procedure). If the pin won't come out, remove the remaining circlip. Fabricate a piston pin removal tool from threaded stock, nuts, washers and a piece of pipe **(see illustration)**. Repeat the procedure for the other pistons.

15   Apply clean engine oil to the pin, insert it into the piston and check for freeplay by rocking the pin back-and-forth **(see illustration)**. If the pin is loose, new pistons and pins must be installed. Also check the play of the piston pin in the connecting rod **(see illustration)**.

Press fit pistons

16   If the pistons don't have clips, they're secured in the rods by a press fit. Separating the pistons from the rods requires a press and special tools and should be done by a Honda dealer or motorcycle service shop.

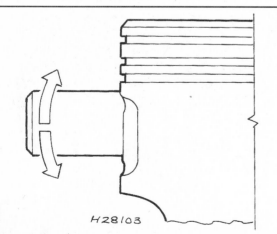

31.15a Slip the pin into the piston and try to wiggle it back-and-forth; if it's loose, replace the piston and pin

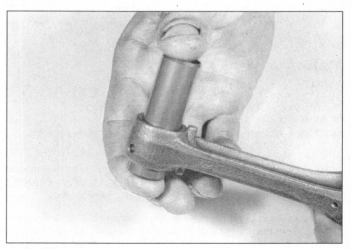

3.15b Slip the piston pin into the rod and try to rock it back-and-forth to check for looseness

2

31.17 When the piston/connecting rod assembly is installed, the connecting rod oil hole (left arrow) goes downward and the piston intake mark (right arrow) goes upward

Installation

Refer to illustrations 31.17 and 31.18

17   Install the pistons on the connecting rods so that when the assembly is installed in the engine, the connecting rod oil jets will face down and the L-IN or R-IN marks will be upward **(see illustration)**.

18   If you're working on a bike with clip-type pistons, lubricate the pins and the rod bores with clean engine oil. Install new circlips in the grooves in the inner sides of the pistons (don't reuse the old circlips). Push the pins into position from the opposite side and install new circlips. Compress the circlips only enough for them to fit in the piston. Make sure the clips are properly seated in the grooves **(see illustration)**.

32 Piston rings - installation

Refer to illustrations 32.3, 32.5, 32.9a, 32.9b, 32.11 and 32.15

1   Before installing the new piston rings, the ring end gaps must be checked.

2   Lay out the pistons and the new ring sets so the rings will be matched with the same piston and cylinder during the end gap measurement procedure and engine assembly.

3   Insert the top (No. 1) ring into the bottom of the first cylinder and square it up with the cylinder walls by pushing it in with the top of the

32.3 Check the ring end gap near the bottom of the cylinder

31.18 Make sure both piston pin circlips are securely seated in their grooves

piston. The ring should be about one inch above the bottom edge of the cylinder. To measure the end gap, slip a feeler gauge between the ends of the ring **(see illustration)** and compare the measurement to the Specifications.

4   If the gap is larger or smaller than specified, double check to make sure that you have the correct rings before proceeding.

5   If the gap is too small, it must be enlarged or the ring ends may come in contact with each other during engine operation, which can cause serious damage. The end gap can be increased by filing the ring ends very carefully with a fine file **(see illustration)**. When performing this operation, file only from the outside in.

6   Excess end gap is not critical unless it is greater than the limits listed in this Chapter's Specifications. Again, double check to make sure you have the correct rings for your engine.

7   Repeat the procedure for each ring that will be installed in the first cylinder and for each ring in the remaining cylinders. Remember to keep the rings, pistons and cylinders matched up.

8   Once the ring end gaps have been checked and corrected, the rings can be installed on the pistons.

9   The oil control ring (lowest on the piston) is installed first. It is composed of three separate components. Slip the expander into the groove, then install the upper side rail **(see illustrations)**. Do not use a piston ring installation tool on the oil ring side rails as they may be damaged. Instead, place one end of the side rail into the groove between the spacer expander and the ring land. Hold it firmly in place and slide a finger around the piston while pushing the rail into the

32.5 If the end gap is too small, clamp a file in a vise and file the ring ends (from the outside in only) to enlarge the gap slightly

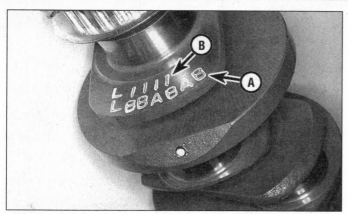

34.7a The six letters on the end of the crankshaft (A) are used to select connecting rod bearings; the four numbers (B) are used to select main bearings

34.7b The bearing color codes are on the edge of the bearing near the tang (arrow)

35.2a Each main cap is numbered 1-2-3-4, with a punch mark next to the number of the cap (A); the arrow mark on each cap (B) points to the top of the engine

35.2b If the cap numbers aren't readily visible, make your own marks

Connecting rod bearing selection

Refer to illustrations 34.7a and 34.7b

7   Each connecting rod has a Roman numeral or an Arabic number stamped across its parting line, ranging from 1 to 3 **(see illustration 29.4b)**. There's a corresponding letter on the end of the crankshaft **(see illustration)**. Using the letter and number together, refer to this Chapter's Specifications to select the correct bearing color code for each connecting rod. The color codes are stamped on the edge of the bearing near the locating tab **(see illustration)**.

8   Repeat the bearing selection procedure for the remaining connecting rods.

Installation

9   Refer to Section 29 for bearing and connecting rod installation.

35 Crankshaft and main bearings - removal, inspection, main bearing selection and installation

Removal

Refer to illustrations 35.2a, 35.2b, 35.4a, 35.4b, 35.5a, 35.5b and 35.6

1   Before removing the crankshaft check the endplay, using a dial indicator mounted in-line with the crankshaft. Honda doesn't provide endplay specifications, but if the endplay is excessive (more than a few thousandths of an inch), replace the thrust bearings.

2   Look for main bearing cap number marks **(see illustration)**. If you don't see any, make your own **(see illustration)**.

3   Unbolt the connecting rods from the crankshaft (see Section 29). The right connecting rods and pistons don't need to be removed from the cylinders.

4   Unbolt the main bearing caps. Use the bolts as levers to rock the caps from side-to-side to free them from the engine, then lift

35.4a Lift the bolts to this point and use them to rock the caps free of the crankcase

35.4b The dowels should come off with the caps (arrows)

35.5a Lift the crankshaft out of the bearing saddles

35.5b The right-side connecting rods can be left in place

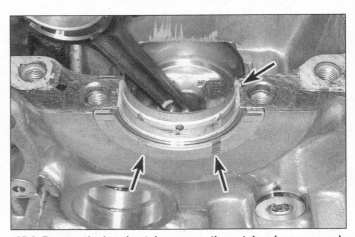

35.6 Be sure the bearing tabs engage the notches (upper arrow) and the thrust bearing oil grooves face away from the crankcase (lower arrow)

them out **(see illustration)**. Note the locations of the cap dowels **(see illustration)**.

5   Lift the crankshaft out and set it on a clean surface **(see illustrations)**.

6   The main bearing inserts can be removed from their saddles by pushing their centers to the side, then lifting them out **(see illustration)**. Keep the bearing inserts in order. The main bearing oil clearance should be checked, however, before removing the inserts (see Step 8).

Inspection

Refer to illustrations 35.9, 35.10, 35.11, 35.13, 35.16a, 35.16b

7   Clean the crankshaft with solvent, using a rifle-cleaning brush to scrub out the oil passages. If available, blow the crank dry with compressed air. Check the main and connecting rod journals for uneven wear, scoring and pits. Rub a copper coin across the journal several times - if a journal picks up copper from the coin, it's too rough. Replace the crankshaft.

35.9 Measure the main bearing journals at several points to check for out-of-roundness and at both ends to check for taper

35.10 Measure the inside diameter of the assembled bearing with a bore gauge

35.11 Rotate the crankshaft and check runout

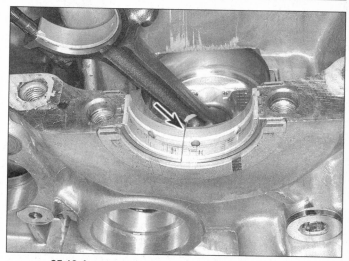

35.13 Lay a strip of Plastigage along the bearing

8   Check the crankshaft for cracks and other damage. It should be magnafluxed to reveal hidden cracks - a dealer service department or motorcycle machine shop will handle the procedure.

9   Steps 9 though 11 require precision measuring equipment. You can have the measurements done by a dealer or motorcycle repair shop. Measure the main bearing journals with a micrometer **(see illustration)**. Compare the readings with the values listed in this Chapter's Specifications.

10   Assemble the main caps and bearings and tighten them to the specified torque. Measure the inside diameter of the bearing bore with a bore gauge **(see illustration)**.

11   Set the crankshaft on V-blocks and check the runout with a dial indicator touching each of the main journals, comparing your findings with this Chapter's Specifications **(see illustration)**. If the runout exceeds the limit, replace the crank.

12   Wipe the main bearing inserts, saddles and bearing caps clean, using a lint-free cloth.

13   Install the bearing inserts in the saddles and caps. Make sure the tab on the bearing engages with the notch in the rod or cap **(see illustration 35.6)**. Lay a strip of Plastigage (type HPG-1) across each bearing insert (in the saddle, not in the cap), parallel with the journal axis **(see illustration)**.

14   Wipe off the main bearing journals with a lint-free cloth.

15   Lay the crankshaft in the saddles, then install the main bearing caps (with their steel plates). Tighten the rod caps to the torque listed in this Chapter's Specifications, but don't allow the crankshaft to rotate at all.

16   Unscrew the bolts and remove the caps and crankshaft, being very careful not to disturb the Plastigage. Compare the width of the crushed Plastigage to the scale printed in the Plastigage envelope to determine the bearing oil clearance **(see illustrations)**.

17   If the clearance is within the range listed in this Chapter's Specifications and the bearings are in perfect condition, they can be reused. If the clearance is beyond the standard range, replace the bearing inserts with new inserts that have the same color code, then check the oil clearance once again. Always replace all of the inserts at the same time.

18   The clearance should be within the range listed in this Chapter's Specifications.

Main bearing selection

Refer to illustrations 35.20a and 35.20b

19   The clearance should be within the range listed in this Chapter's Specifications.

20   Use the number marks on the crankshaft and on the case to determine the bearing sizes required. The first four numbers on the

35.16a The Plastigage will flatten out where the bearing contacts it

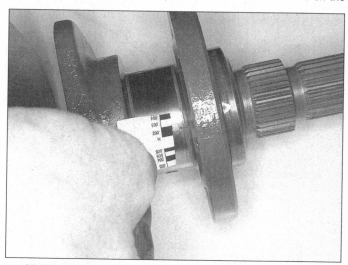

35.16b Measure the widest point with the Plastigage scale

35.20a The Arabic numerals indicate the journal number; the Roman numerals above them are used, together with the crankshaft numbers, to select main bearings

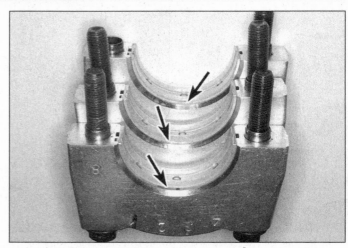

35.20b The bearing color codes are painted on the sides of the bearings (arrows)

36.2 Lift the mainshaft bearings (arrows) out of their saddles

36.3a The shift forks are labeled F, C and R for front, center and rear (arrows); the marks face the front of the engine

crankshaft are the main journal numbers, starting with the front journal **(see illustration 34.7a)**. These correspond with the numbers on the front of the left crankcase half **(see illustration)**. Use these numbers and this Chapter's Specifications to determine the correct bearing color code for each journal. The color codes are painted on the edges of the bearings **(see illustration)**.

Installation

21   Clean the bearing saddles in the case halves, then install the bearing inserts and thrust bearings in the case **(see illustration 35.7a)**. When installing the bearings, use your hands only - don't tap them into place with a hammer.
22   Lubricate the bearing inserts and thrust bearings with engine assembly lube or moly-based grease.
23   Install the seal on the end of the crankshaft.
24   Carefully lower the crankshaft into place **(see illustration 35.5a)**.
25   Make sure the main bearing cap dowels are in position. Install the caps in their correct locations, referring to the number marks **(see illustrations 35.2a and 35.2b)**. Be sure the arrow marks on the caps point to the top of the engine.
26   Install the steel plate on top of each cap. Lubricate the threads and the underside of the bolt heads with clean engine oil, then finger-tighten the bolts.
27   Tighten the bolts in several stages, in a criss-cross pattern, to the

torque listed in this Chapter's Specifications.
28   Turn the crankshaft. If should turn easily by hand. If it doesn't, there's a problem; find and fix it before assembling the engine further. You may have forgotten to lubricate the bearing inserts; the bearings may be the wrong size; or a bearing cap may be in the wrong location or installed backwards (with its arrow pointing to the bottom of the engine). Any of these can cause bearing damage when the engine is first started, or may prevent it from turning at all.
29   If the crankshaft turns freely, continue with assembly.

36 Transmission shafts, shift drum and forks - removal and installation

Refer to illustrations 36.2, 36.3a, 36.3b, 36.3c, 36.4, 36.5, 36.6a, 36.6b and 36.6c

Removal

1   Remove the engine and separate the case halves (see Sections 5 and 25). Remove the external shift linkage, shift drum bearing retainer, the final drive gear and its bearing retainer (Sections 20 and 24).
2   Lift out the mainshaft **(see illustration)**. If it's stuck, use a soft-face hammer and gently tap on the bearings on the ends of the shaft to free it.
3   Note the position marks (F, C and R for front, center and rear) on the shift forks **(see illustration)**. Grip the inside of the fork shaft with

36.3b Pull the fork shaft out of the forks and lift the forks out

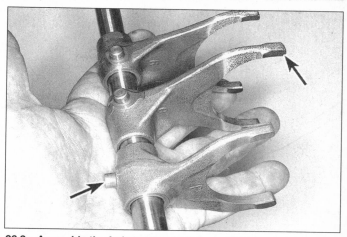

36.3c Assemble the forks to the shaft so you'll remember how they go; the fork fingers and pins (arrows) are common wear points

36.4 Pull the shift drum out of the case

36.5 Pull the front countershaft bearing out of the case; its recessed side faces the mainshaft on installation

snap-ring pliers or a similar tool, pull it out of the crankcase and lift the forks away from the gears **(see illustration)**. It's a good idea to reassemble the forks to the shaft right away so you don't forget how they go **(see illustration)**.

4   Pull the shift drum forward out of the case **(see illustration)**.
5   Pull the front countershaft bearing out of the case **(see illustration)**.

6   Pull the countershaft forward to clear its rear bearing, then tilt it and lift it out of the case **(see illustration)**. Remove the countershaft rear thrust washer and the rear bearing **(see illustrations)**.
7   Refer to Section 37 for information pertaining to shift drum and fork inspection and Section 38 for information pertaining to the shift cam and forks.

36.6a Pull the countershaft forward to clear the case, then lift it out

36.6b There's a thrust washer at the rear of the countershaft . . .

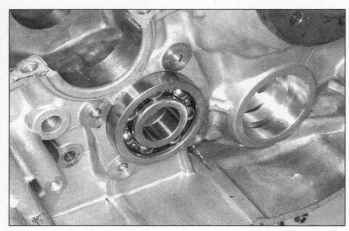

36.6c . . . as well as a ball bearing

36.10 Engage the fork fingers with the gear grooves (upper arrows); engage the pins with the shift drum grooves (lower arrows)

36.11 Engage the front fork fingers with the mainshaft groove (upper arrow) and the pin with the shift drum groove (lower arrow)

37.1 Check the shift drum grooves for wear

Installation

Refer to illustrations 36.10 and 36.11

8   Place the countershaft thrust washer in its bore **(see illustration 36.6a)**. Lower the countershaft into the case, insert its rear end through the thrust washer and install the rear bearing **(see illustration 36.6c)**. Install the front bearing with its recessed side toward the countershaft **(see illustration 36.5)**.

9   Install the shift drum **(see illustration 36.4)**.

10   Place the shift forks on the shaft. Refer to the F, C and R marks to place the forks in the correct positions on the shaft. The marks face the front of the engine. Slide the fork shaft into its bores and engage the center and rear forks with their gear grooves on the countershaft **(see illustration)**.

11   Lay the mainshaft in its bearing journals and engage the front shift fork with its gear groove **(see illustration)**.

12   The remainder of installation is the reverse of removal.

13   Make sure the gears are in the neutral position. When they are, it will be possible to rotate the transmission shafts independently of each other.

37 Shift drum and forks - inspection

Refer to illustrations 37.1 and 37.3

1   Check the edges of the grooves in the shift drum for signs of excessive wear **(see illustration)**. If the grooves are worn, replace the shift drum.

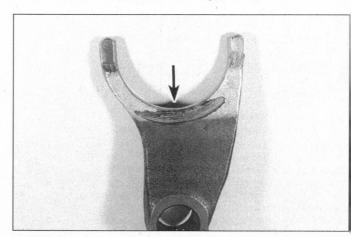

37.3 An arc-shaped burn mark like this means the fork was rubbing against a gear, probably due to bending or worn fork ears

2   Check the pins on the front end of the shift drum, and the reverse lockout drum on the rear end, for wear and damage. Spin the bearing on each and check for roughness, looseness or noise. If problems are found, unbolt the drum center or reverse lockout drum from the shift drum and replace the worn or damaged components **(see illustration 24.9)**.

3   Check the shift forks for distortion and wear, especially at the fork fingers and pins **(see illustration 36.3c and the accompanying illus-**

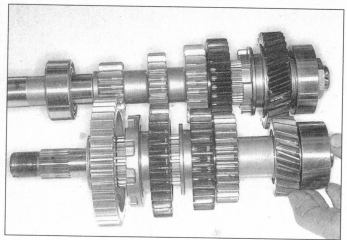

38.2 The assembled mainshaft (top) and countershaft (bottom) should look like this; the front ends of the shafts are on the right

38.3 Grand away the staked portion of the nut without damaging the mainshaft threads

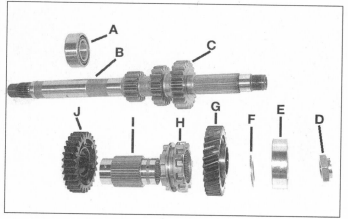

38.4 Mainshaft details

A	Bearing	H	Fourth/fifth gear bushing
B	Mainshaft		(1988 through 1996; see
C	Mainshaft third gear		text for details of later
D	Locknut		models)
E	Bearing	I	Front shifter
F	Washer	J	Mainshaft fourth gear
G	Mainshaft fifth gear		

38.6 Measure the gear inside diameters

tration). If they are discolored or severely worn they are probably bent. If damage or wear is evident, check the shift fork groove in the corresponding gear as well. Inspect the shaft bore for excessive wear and replace any defective parts with new ones.

4   Check the shift fork shaft for evidence of wear, galling and other damage **(see illustration 36.3)**. Make sure the shift forks move smoothly on the shaft. If the shaft is worn or bent, replace it with a new one.

---

38   Transmission shafts - disassembly, inspection and reassembly

Refer to illustration 38.2

Note: *When disassembling the transmission shafts, place the parts on a long rod or thread a wire through them to keep them in order and facing the proper direction.*

1   Remove the shafts from the case (see Section 36).

2   Before you start, mesh the assembled shafts, noting how they're assembled and how they fit together **(see illustration)**.

Mainshaft

Disassembly

Refer to illustrations 38.3 and 38.4

3   Grind away the staked portions of the mainshaft nut **(see illustration)**. Place the mainshaft in a padded vise and unscrew the nut.

4   Slide the parts off the mainshaft, keeping them in order **(see illustration)**. On 1988 through 1996 models, no snap-rings are used on the mainshaft. The bearings will slide off, but they may tilt sideways and jam. On 1997 models, the combined fourth-fifth gear bushing has been replaced by a separate fifth gear bushing and washer, a snap-ring, a spline washer and separate fourth gear bushing.

Inspection

Refer to illustrations 38.6, 38.7 and 38.8

5   Wash all of the components in clean solvent and dry them off. Rotate the bearings, feeling for tightness, rough spots and excessive looseness and listening for noises. If any of these conditions are found, replace the bearing.

6   Check the gear teeth for cracking and other obvious damage. Check the gear bushings and the surface in the inner diameter of each gear for scoring or heat discoloration. If the gear or bushing is damaged, replace it. If you have precision measuring equipment, measure the inside diameters of the removable gears and compare the measurements with the values listed in this Chapter's Specifications **(see illustration)**. Replace worn gears.

2

38.7 Check the slots (left arrow) and dogs (right arrow) for wear, especially at the edges; rounded corners can cause the transmission to jump out of gear - new gears (bottom) have sharp corners

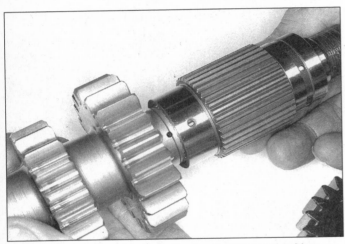

38.11 Align the oil holes in the fourth-fifth gear bushing with those in the mainshaft

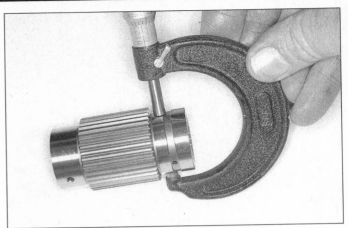

38.8 Measure the outside diameter of the shifter smooth sections

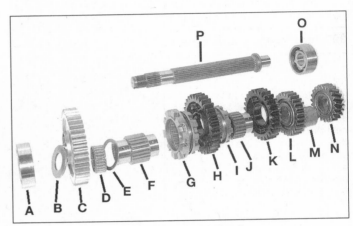

38.12 Countershaft details

A	Bearing	I	Center shifter
B	Washer	J	Third gear bushing
C	Countershaft first gear	K	Countershaft third gear
D	Needle roller bearing	L	Countershaft fourth gear
E	Washer	M	Collar
F	First/second gear bushing	N	Countershaft fifth gear
G	Rear shifter	O	Bearing
H	Countershaft second gear	P	Countershaft

7   Inspect the dogs and the dog holes in the gears for excessive wear **(see illustration)**. Replace worn or damaged gears as a set with their mating gear on the countershaft.

8   Measure the bushing outside diameters at the smooth sections **(see illustration)**. Use this measurement, together with the gear inside diameter, to calculate gear-to-bushing clearance.

9   Place the shaft in V-blocks and check runout with a dial indicator. Replace the shaft if runout exceeds the value listed in this Chapter's Specifications.

Reassembly

Refer to illustration 38.11

10   Lubricate the components with engine oil before assembling them.

11   Assembly is the reverse of the disassembly procedure with the following additions:

    a) *Align the oil holes in the mainshaft bushing with the holes in the shaft* **(see illustration)**.

    b) *Install the bearings with their marked sides facing away from the mainshaft.*

    c) *Install a new mainshaft locknut and tighten it to the torque listed in this Chapter's Specifications. Turn counterclockwise to tighten the nut; it has left-hand threads.*

    d) *Stake the nut into the mainshaft at two points* **(see illustration 38.3)**.

Countershaft

Disassembly

Refer to illustration 38.12

12   Slide the parts off the end of the shaft and place them in order **(see illustration)**. No snap-rings are used. The bearings will slide off, but can easily tilt sideways and jam.

Inspection

13   Refer to Steps 5 through 9 above to inspect the countershaft components.

Reassembly

Refer to illustration 38.14

14   Assembly is the reverse of the disassembly procedure. Lubricate the components with engine oil before assembling them. Align the oil holes in each bushing with the corresponding oil hole in the shaft **(see illustration)**.

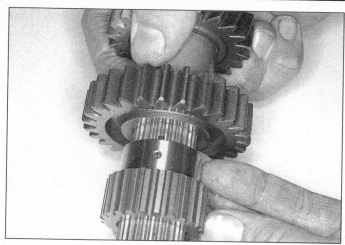

38.14 Align the oil holes in the shaft and in the bushing

39 Initial start-up after overhaul

1   Make sure the engine oil level is correct and the cooling system is full, then remove the spark plugs from the engine. Place the engine kill switch in the Off position and unplug the primary wires from the coils.
2   Turn on the key switch and crank the engine over with the starter several times to build up oil pressure. Reinstall the spark plugs, connect the wires and turn the switch to On.
3   Make sure there is fuel in the tank, then turn the fuel tap to the On position and operate the choke.
4   Start the engine and allow it to run at a moderately fast idle until it reaches operating temperature.
5   Check carefully for oil leaks and make sure the transmission and

controls, especially the brakes, function properly before road testing the machine. Refer to Section 40 for the recommended break-in procedure.

40 Recommended break-in procedure

1   Any rebuilt engine needs time to break in, even if parts have been installed in their original locations. For this reason, treat the machine gently for the first few miles to make sure oil has circulated throughout the engine and any new parts installed have started to seat.
2   Even greater care is necessary if the cylinders have been rebored or a new crankshaft has been installed. In the case of a rebore, the engine will have to be broken in as if the machine were new. This means greater use of the transmission and a restraining hand on the throttle until at least 500 miles have been covered. There's no point in keeping to any set speed limit - the main idea is to keep from lugging the engine and to gradually increase performance until the 500 mile mark is reached. These recommendations can be lessened to an extent when only a new crankshaft is installed. Experience is the best guide, since it's easy to tell when an engine is running freely. The following recommendations, which Honda provides for new motorcycles, can be used as a guide:

   a) *Don't lug the engine (full throttle at low engine speeds).*
   b) *0 to 600 miles (0 to 1000 km): Keep sustained engine speed below 4,000 rpm.*
   c) *600 to 1000 miles (1000 to 1600 km): Don't run the engine for long periods above 5000 rpm, or at all above 5500 rpm. Rev the engine freely through the gears, but use full throttle only for very short periods. Change engine speeds often.*
   d) *Above 1000 miles (1600 km): Full throttle can be used. Don't exceed maximum recommended engine speed (redline).*

3   If a lubrication failure is suspected, stop the engine immediately and try to find the cause. If an engine is run without oil, even for a short period of time, severe damage will occur.

2

Notes

Chapter 3   Cooling system

Contents

3

Specifications

General

Coolant type	See Chapter 1
Mixture ratio	See Chapter 1
Cooling system capacity	See Chapter 1
Radiator cap pressure rating	
1988 through 1996	11 to 15 psi
1997	16 to 20 psi
Thermostat rating	
Opening temperature	80 to 84-degrees C (176 to 183-degrees F)
Fully open at	93 to 97-degrees C (199 to 206-degrees F)
Valve travel (when fully open)	Not less than 8 mm (5/16 inch)
Fan thermoswitch continuity	
Below 98 to 102-degrees C (208 to 216-degrees F)	No continuity
Above 98 to 102-degrees C (208 to 216-degrees F)	Continuity
Gauge temperature sensor resistance	
60-degrees C (140-degrees F)	104 ohms
85-degrees C (185-degrees F)	44 ohms
110-degrees C (230-degrees F)	20 ohms
120-degrees C (248-degrees F)	16 ohms

Torque specifications

Cooling fan thermoswitch	28 Nm (20 ft-lbs)
Ignition timing temperature sensor	28 Nm (20 ft-lbs)
Temperature gauge sensor	12 Nm (9 ft-lbs)

1   General information

The models covered by this manual are equipped with a liquid cooling system which utilizes a water/antifreeze mixture to carry away excess heat produced during the combustion process. The cylinders are surrounded by water jackets, through which the coolant is circulated by the water pump. Coolant passages beneath the intake manifolds and carburetors control the temperature of the fuel mixture entering the engine. The coolant passes through hoses and tubes, around the cylinders and to the thermostat. When the engine is warm, the thermostat opens and allows coolant to flow down into the radiators, where it is cooled by the passing air, routed through another hose and back to the water pump, where the cycle is repeated. The water pump is mounted to the left front corner of the crankcase and driven by the oil pump shaft.

Two electric fans, mounted one behind each radiator and automatically controlled by a thermostatic switch, provide a flow of cooling air through the radiators when the motorcycle is not moving.

The coolant temperature sender unit, threaded into the thermostat housing, senses the temperature of the coolant and controls the coolant temperature gauge on the instrument cluster.

The entire system is sealed and pressurized. The pressure is controlled by a valve which is part of the radiator cap. By pressurizing the coolant, the boiling point is raised, which prevents premature boiling of the coolant. An overflow hose, connected between the radiator and reservoir tank, directs coolant to the tank when the radiator cap valve is opened by excessive pressure. The coolant is automatically siphoned back to the radiator as the engine cools.

Many cooling system inspection and service procedures are considered part of routine maintenance and are included in Chapter 1.

Warning 1: *Do not allow antifreeze to come in contact with your skin or painted surfaces of the motorcycle. Rinse off spills immediately with plenty of water. Antifreeze is highly toxic if ingested. Never leave antifreeze lying around in an open container or in puddles on the floor; children and pets are attracted by its sweet smell and may drink it. Check with local authorities about disposing of used antifreeze. Many communities have collection centers which will see that antifreeze is disposed of safely.*

Warning 2: *Do not remove the pressure cap from the thermostat housing when the engine and radiator are hot. Scalding hot coolant and steam may be blown out under pressure, which could cause serious injury. To open the pressure cap, remove the right side panel on the inside of the fairing. When the engine has cooled, lift up the panel and place a thick rag, like a towel, over the radiator cap; slowly rotate the cap counterclockwise to the first stop. This procedure allows any residual pressure to escape. When the steam has stopped escaping, press down on the cap while turning counterclockwise and remove it.*

2   Radiator cap - check

If problems such as overheating and loss of coolant occur, check the entire system as described in Chapter 1. The radiator cap opening pressure should be checked by a dealer service department or service station equipped with the special tester required to do the job. If the cap is defective, replace it with a new one.

3   Coolant reservoir - removal and installation

Refer to illustration 3.4

1   Remove the carburetors (see Chapter 4). If you're only planning to remove the coolant reservoir, it isn't necessary to disconnect the carburetor coolant hoses or throttle cables.
2   Unbolt the ignition coils and lower them to provide removal access for the reservoir tank (see Chapter 5).
3   Disconnect the coolant hose and breather tube from the reservoir and catch any escaped coolant. Plug the end of the reservoir hose so it doesn't siphon coolant from the system.

3.4 Unbolt the reservoir and lift it out of its two lower grommets

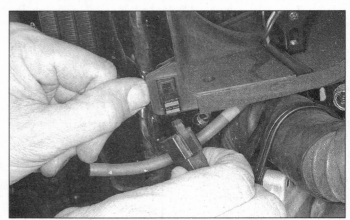

4.3 The fan connectors fit into the fan housings like this

4   Remove the reservoir mounting screw and take it out **(see illustration)**.
5   Installation is the reverse of the removal steps. Position the tabs on the bottom of the reservoir in their grommets.

4   Cooling fan and thermostatic switch - check and replacement

1   The fans have a common thermostatic switch and fuses. If neither fan works, the problem is most likely in the fuses, fan switch or ignition switch. If only one fan works, the problem is most likely in the wiring to that fan motor or the motor itself.

Check

Refer to illustrations 4.3 and 4.5

2   If the engine is overheating and the cooling fans aren't coming on, first remove the left rear side cover and check the fan and main fuses. If a fuse is blown, check the fan circuit for a short to ground (see the *Wiring diagrams* at the end of this book). Check that the battery is fully charged.
3   If the fuses and battery are good, follow the wiring harness from each fan motor in turn to the electrical connector and unplug the connector **(see illustration)**. Using two jumper wires, apply battery voltage to the terminals in the fan motor side of the electrical connector. If the fan doesn't work, replace the motor.
4   If the fan does come on, the problem lies in the fan switch or the wiring that connects the components. Remove the jumper wires and reconnect the electrical connector to the fan.
5   Remove the fairing front cover (see Chapter 8). Unplug the black

4.5 The fan switch is mounted in the underside of the left radiator (arrow)

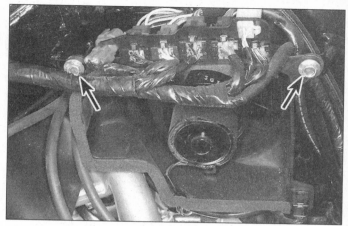

4.11a Remove the fan housing bolts (arrows)

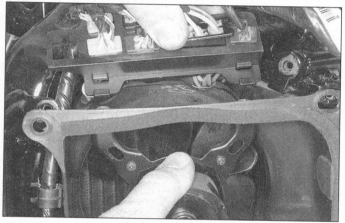

4.11b Detach the connector bracket from the right fan housing; it's held by two tabs

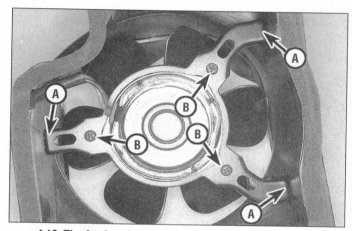

4.12 The fan bracket and motor are secured by screws

A   Bracket screws (on outside of housing)
B   Motor screws

wire's connector from the fan thermoswitch on the radiator **(see illustration)**. Connect the disconnected wire to ground (nearby bare metal). If the fan comes on, the circuit to the motor is good and the switch is defective.

6   Before replacing the switch, test it as described below.

7   **Warning:** *Antifreeze is poisonous. DO NOT use a cooking pan for this test!* Refer to Chapter 1 and drain the cooling system. Unscrew the switch and suspend it in a pan of coolant (50/50 mixture of antifreeze and water) so just the switch threads are covered. Don't let the switch body sink into the coolant and don't let the switch touch the sides of the pan. Connect an ohmmeter between the terminal and switch body.

8   Heat the water to the switch operating temperature listed in this Chapter's Specifications. Hold the temperature at this range for three minutes before checking continuity. Let the water cool and note the ohmmeter readings as it cools. If the readings aren't within the specified ranges, replace the switch.

9   If the switch is good, refer to Chapter 9 and test the ignition switch.

Replacement

Fan motor

Refer to illustrations 4.11a, 4.11b, 4.12 and 4.13

Warning: *The engine must be completely cool before beginning this procedure.*

10   Disconnect the cable from the negative terminal of the battery. Unbolt the radiator and lift it out of its grommets, but you don't need to disconnect the radiator hoses or drain the coolant (see Section 7).

11   Remove the bolts securing the fan shroud to the frame **(see illustrations)**. Separate the fan and bracket from the radiator.

12   Remove three bracket screws from the outside of the fan shroud **(see illustration)**. Take the fan motor bracket out of the shroud together with the motor and fan.

13   To separate the fan from the motor, remove the nut, fan and washer from the motor shaft **(see illustration)**.

14   Installation is the reverse of the removal steps.

4.13 Remove the nut to detach the fan from the motor; there's a washer behind the fan

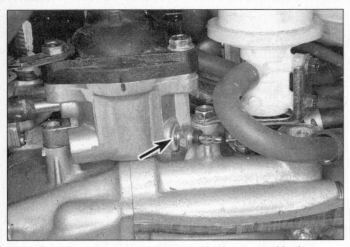

5.4 The temperature gauge sender is mounted in the thermostat housing (arrow)

6.3 Remove the bolts (arrows) . . .

Thermoswitch

Warning: *The engine must be completely cool before beginning this procedure.*

15   Prepare the new switch by wrapping the new threads with Teflon tape or by coating the threads with RTV sealant.

16   Disconnect its electrical connector and unscrew the switch from the thermostat housing or radiator.

17   Quickly install the new switch, tightening it to the specified torque.

18   Connect the electrical connector to the switch. Check, and if necessary, add coolant to the system (see Chapter 1).

5   Coolant temperature gauge and sender unit - check and replacement

Check

1   If the engine has been overheating but the coolant temperature gauge hasn't been indicating a hotter than normal condition, begin with a check of the coolant level (see Chapter 1). If it's low, add the recommended type of coolant and be sure to locate the source of the leak.

2   Check the fuses and ignition switch (see Chapter 9) and replace them if necessary. Check that the battery is fully charged.

Temperature gauge test

Refer to illustration 5.4

3   Remove the left fan and shroud (see Section 4). This will provide access to the coolant temperature sensor, which is mounted in the thermostat housing.

4   Locate the temperature sensor **(see illustration)**. Make a short jumper with a terminal that will plug into the temperature sensor wire when it's disconnected.

5   **Caution:** *During this step, don't leave the jumper wire connected for more than a few seconds or the temperature gauge will be damaged.* Disconnect the wire from the temperature sensor. Connect the jumper wire between the disconnected wire and ground. Turn the ignition key to the On position and watch the gauge; it should move all the way to the Hot side. Quickly disconnect the jumper wire; the gauge should move all the way to the Cold side.

6   If the gauge passes both of these tests, but doesn't operate correctly under normal riding conditions, the temperature sender unit is probably defective and must be replaced. Before replacing, test the sender in the same way as the fan thermoswitch (see Section 4) and compare the ohmmeter readings to those listed in this Chapter's Specifications.

7   If the gauge didn't respond to the tests properly, either the wire to the gauge is bad or the gauge itself is defective.

Replacement

Sender unit

Warning: *The engine must be completely cool before beginning this procedure.*

8   Prepare the new sender unit by wrapping the threads with Teflon tape or coating them with silicone sealant.

9   Disconnect its electrical connector and unscrew the sender unit from the thermostat housing and quickly install the new unit, tightening it to the specified torque.

10   Connect the electrical connector to the sender unit. Check, and if necessary, add coolant to the system (see Chapter 1).

Temperature gauge

11   Refer to Chapter 9 for the coolant temperature gauge replacement procedure.

6   Thermostat - removal, check and installation

Warning: *The engine must be completely cool before beginning this procedure.*

Removal

Refer to illustrations 6.3 and 6.4

1   If the thermostat is functioning properly, the coolant temperature gauge should rise to the normal operating temperature quickly and then stay there, only rising above the normal position occasionally when the engine gets abnormally hot. If the engine does not reach normal operating temperature quickly, or if it overheats, the thermostat should be removed and checked, or replaced with a new one.

2   Refer to Chapter 1 and drain the cooling system. If necessary for access, remove the radiator (see Section 7).

3   Remove the thermostat housing cover **(see illustration)**. Note that the forward bolt secures a bracket.

4   Lift out the thermostat **(see illustration)**.

Check

5   Remove any coolant deposits, then visually check the thermostat for corrosion, cracks and other damage. If it was open when it was removed, the thermostat is defective.

6   To check the thermostat operation, submerge it in a container of water along with a thermometer. The thermostat should be suspended so it does not touch the sides of the container. **Warning:** *Antifreeze is poisonous. DO NOT use a cooking pan to test the thermostat!*

7   Gradually heat the water in the container with a hot plate or stove and check the temperature when the thermostat first starts to open.

6.4 . . . and lift off the thermostat cover for access
to the thermostat

8   Compare the opening temperature to the values listed in this Chapter's Specifications.
9   Continue heating the water until the valve is fully open.
10   Measure how far the thermostat valve has opened and compare to the value listed in this Chapter's Specifications.
11   If these specifications are not met, or if the thermostat doesn't open while the water is heated, replace it with a new one.

Installation

12   Install the thermostat into the housing.
13   If you're working on a model with a separate O-ring, install a new one in the groove.
14   Place the cover on the housing and install the bolts, tightening them securely.
15   The remainder of installation is the reverse of the removal steps. Fill the cooling system with the recommended coolant (see Chapter 1).

7   Radiator - removal and installation

Warning: *The engine must be completely cool before beginning this procedure.*
Refer to illustrations 7.5a through 7.5e, 7.6 and 7.8
1   Place the bike on its centerstand.
2   Drain the cooling system (see Chapter 1).
3   Remove the radiator shroud and the front and lower fairing covers (see Chapter 8).
4   Follow the wiring from the fan motor to the electrical connector and disconnect it (see Section 4).
5   Loosen the radiator hose clamps. Each radiator has a large hose at the top inside corner facing the rear of the bike, a small hose near these hoses, and a large hose at the bottom **(see illustrations)**. Work the hoses free from the fittings, taking care not to damage the fittings in the process.

7.5b . . . and from the upper inner corner
of the right radiator; the vertical branch
of the hose (arrow) . . .

7.5c . . . extends upward to the pressure
cap fitting

7.5a Disconnect the hose from the upper inner corner of the left radiator (arrow) . . .

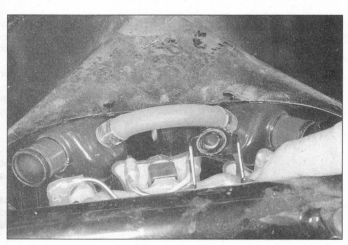

7.5d Disconnect the crossover hose from the upper
corners of the radiators

7.5e Disconnect the hose from the bottoms
of the radiators (arrows)

3

7.6 Remove the upper mounting bolts and the cruise control bracket (if equipped)

7.8 Don't forget the pad between the cruise control accumulator (if equipped) and the radiator

6   Remove the mounting bolt from the outer upper corner of each radiator **(see illustration)**. Lift the radiator out of its grommet and remove it from the motorcycle.
7   Inspect the radiator mounting grommets. Replace them if they're cracked or deteriorated.
8   Installation is the reverse of the removal steps, with the following additions:
   a) *If the bike has cruise control, be sure to reinstall the pad between the radiator and the vacuum accumulator* **(see illustration)**.
   b) *Don't forget to connect the fan switch ground wire.*
   c) *Fill the cooling system with the recommended coolant* (see Chapter 1).

8   Water pump - check, removal, disassembly, inspection and installation

Warning: *The engine must be completely cool before beginning this procedure.*

Check and removal

Refer to illustrations 8.1, 8.6 and 8.7
1   Visually check the area around the water pump for coolant leaks. Try to determine if the leak is simply the result of a loose hose clamp or deteriorated hose. Coolant dripping from the telltale hole behind the

drain plug indicates a leaking mechanical seal; in this case the pump will have to be replaced with a new one **(see illustration)**.
2   Place the bike on its centerstand.
3   Remove the fairing under cover (see Chapter 8).
4   Drain the engine oil and coolant following the procedure in Chapter 1.
5   Disconnect the radiator lower hose and two coolant tubes from the water pump **(see illustration 8.1)**.
6   Loosen the two cover bolts and remove the two mounting bolts. Disconnect the water pump hose from the pump **(see illustration)**.
7   Pull the pump out of the engine **(see illustration)**.

Disassembly and inspection

Refer to illustration 8.9
8   Check the shaft seal for leaks (indicate by coolant leaking from the telltale hole). Replace the water pump if the seal has been leaking.
9   Remove the pump cover bolts and take the cover off **(see illustration)**.
10   Try to wiggle the pump impeller back-and-forth and in-and-out. Check the impeller blades for corrosion. If you can feel movement or the impeller blades are heavily corroded, the water pump must be replaced.
11   If the impeller blades are heavily corroded, flush the system thoroughly (it would also be a good idea to check the internal condition of the radiator).

8.1 If coolant leaks from the small hole behind the drain bolt (arrow), it's time for a new water pump

8.6 Disconnect the water pump hose from the rear fitting on the water pump (left arrow); the hose connects to metal tubes on each side of the engine (right arrow)

8.7 Pull the water pump out of the engine; use a new O-ring on installation

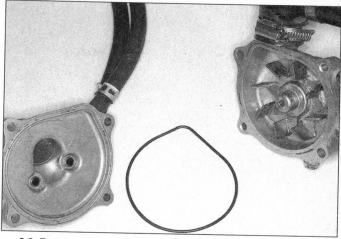

8.9 Remove the cover and take the O-ring out of its groove

12   Remove the O-ring from its groove with a pointed tool and install a new one **(see illustration 8.9)**.
13   Install the cover and tighten the bolts securely, but don't over-tighten them and strip the threads.

Installation

Refer to illustration 8.14

14   Installation is the reverse of the removal steps with the following additions:

a) *Align the slot in the water pump shaft with the drive tooth in the oil pump shaft* **(see illustration)**.

b) *Tighten the mounting bolts securely, but don't overtighten them and strip the threads.*

---

9   Metal coolant tubes - removal and installation

Warning: *The engine must be completely cool for this procedure.*
Refer to illustrations 9.2a, 9.2b and 9.3

1   Refer to Chapter 1 and drain the cooling system.
2   To remove the two tubes that connect the water pump hose to the engine, disconnect the hose **(see illustration 8.6 and the accompanying illustration)**. Pull the tube out of the engine and remove its O-rings **(see illustration)**.
3   You'll need to remove the carburetors and intake manifolds for

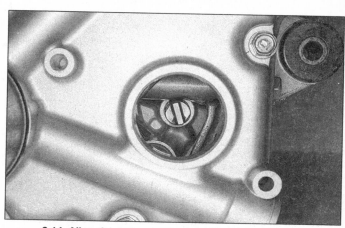

8.14 Align the water pump slot with the tang on the oil pump drive shaft

access to the tubes on top of the engine (see Chapter 4). To remove the tubes, undo their mounting bolts and work the tubes free of their bores in the thermostat housing **(see illustration)**.
4   Installation is the reverse of the removal steps, with the following addition: Use new O-rings and lubricate them with multi-purpose grease.

9.2a There's a metal fitting at each end of the water pump hose (arrow) . . .

9.2b . . . remove their mounting bolts (arrows) and pull the fittings out of the engine; be sure to install a new O-ring on each end of the fitting

9.3 The tubes on top of the engine fit into the thermostat housing

3

Notes

Chapter 4
Fuel and exhaust systems

Contents

4

Specifications

Carburetor
Carburetor type	36 mm CV (two)
Idle speed	See Chapter 1
Pilot screw setting	2 turns out
Float level	8 mm (5/16 inch)

Fuel pump
Flow rate	640 cc (21.6 fl oz) per minute
Reserve sensor resistance	0.9 to 1.3 ohms

Carburetor coolant valve
Starts to close at:
California models	78 to 82-degrees C (172 to 180-degrees F)
Except California models	58 to 62-degrees F (136 to 144-degrees F)

Tightening torques
Carburetor insulator screws	5 Nm (43 inch-lbs)
Exhaust pipe clamp bolts	10 Nm (7 ft-lbs)

2.3 Unscrew the fuel filler cap and disconnect the hose from the corner of the fuel tray (arrow)

2.4 Unclip the throttle stop screw from its bracket and disconnect the fuel line from the auto fuel valve

1   General information

The fuel system consists of the fuel tank, the fuel tap and filter, the carburetors and the connecting lines, hoses and control cables and an electric fuel pump.

The carburetors used on these motorcycles are two Mikunis with butterfly-type throttle valves and accelerator pumps. For cold starting, an enrichment circuit is actuated by a cable and the choke lever mounted on the left handlebar.

The exhaust system is a six-into-two design.

Many of the fuel system service procedures are considered routine maintenance items and for that reason are included in Chapter 1.

2   Fuel tank - removal and installation

2.5 Unbolt the cruise valve assembly (arrows)

Refer to illustrations 2.3, 2.4, 2.5 and 2.6

Warning: *Gasoline is extremely flammable, so take extra precautions when you work on any part of the fuel system. Don't smoke or allow open flames or bare light bulbs near the work area, and don't work in a garage where a natural gas-type appliance (such as a water heater or clothes dryer) is present. If you spill any fuel on your skin, rinse it off immediately with soap and water. When you perform any kind of work on the fuel system, wear safety glasses and have a fire extinguisher suitable for class B fires on hand.*

1   The fuel tank is mounted beneath the seat and is held in place at the rear end by two bolts. At the front, cups on each side of the tank fit over rubber mounts on the frame.

2   Remove the seat, rear fender and inner fairing covers (see Chapter 8). Disconnect the cable from the negative terminal of the battery.

3   Remove the cap from the fuel tank and disconnect the hose from the left rear corner of the fuel tray **(see illustration)**.

4   Unclip the throttle stop screw from its bracket and detach the fuel inlet line from the auto fuel valve **(see illustration)**. If you're working on a California model, disconnect the canister hose as well.

5   If the bike has cruise control, unbolt the cruise control valve from the left side of the tank **(see illustration)**.

6   Unplug the electrical connectors for the fuel pump (and the fuel level sensor if equipped) **(see illustration)**. Disconnect the two-pin black connector at the left side of the tank and remove the connector bracket from the bike.

7   Remove the rear wheel (see Chapter 7).

8   Remove the two mounting bolts at the top rear of the tank.

9   Remove the fuel tray, then pull the tank back and down so the cups clear the mounts. Pull the tank out to the rear.

10   Before installing the tank, check the condition of the hoses and rubber mounting dampers - if they're hardened, cracked, or show any

other signs of deterioration, replace them.

11   If necessary, refer to Section 4 and remove the fuel pump.

12   When replacing the tank, reverse the above procedure. Make sure the tank seats properly and does not pinch any control cables or wires. If difficulty is encountered when trying to slide the tank onto the dampers, a small amount of light oil should be used to lubricate them.

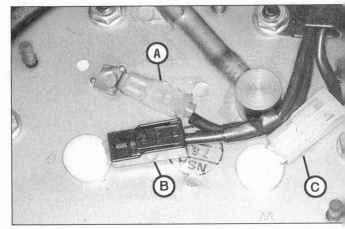

2.6 Disconnect the fuel pump ground connector (A), power connector (B) and the fuel reserve sensor connector (C); the colors of the connectors (not the wires) are stamped in the fuel pump flange

4.3a Lift the pump flange off the studs

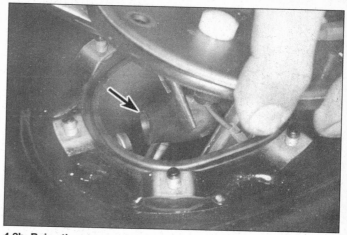

4.3b Raise the pump part way and disconnect the air hose (arrow)

3 Fuel tank - cleaning and repair

1   All repairs to the fuel tank should be carried out by a professional who has experience in this critical and potentially dangerous work. Even after cleaning and flushing of the fuel system, explosive fumes can remain and ignite during repair of the tank.
2   If the fuel tank is removed from the vehicle, it should not be placed in an area where sparks or open flames could ignite the fumes coming out of the tank. Be especially careful inside garages where a natural gas-type appliance is located, because the pilot light could cause an explosion.

4 Fuel pump and filter screen - removal and installation

Refer to illustrations 4.3a, 4.3b, 4.3c, 4.4a and 4.4b
1   Remove the seat (see Chapter 8).
2   Disconnect the fuel line at the pump and unplug the electrical connectors **(see illustration 2.6)**.
3   Remove the mounting nuts and lift the pump off the studs **(see illustration)**. Hold the pump part way up, reach into the opening and disconnect the air hose **(see illustration)**. Lift the rest of the way, rotating the pump backwards so it clears the opening and lift it out **(see illustration)**.
4   The rear cover, motor and strainer can be separated for inspection, but parts aren't available separately. Disconnect the electrical

4.3c Rotate the pump backward to clear the opening and take it out

connectors **(see illustration)**. Detach the fuel and air hoses from the pump, unclip the rear cover and take the cover, grommet and motor off the strainer **(see illustration)**. The fuel reserve sensor can be tested; remove it from the pump and connect an ohmmeter between the wiring terminal and the pump body. If the resistance is not within the range listed in this Chapter's Specifications, replace the sensor.

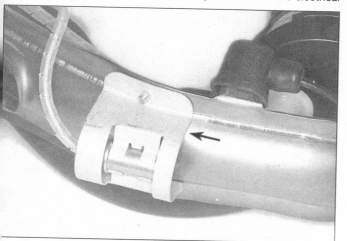

4.4a Disconnect the electrical connectors; detach the fuel reserve sensor (arrow) for testing

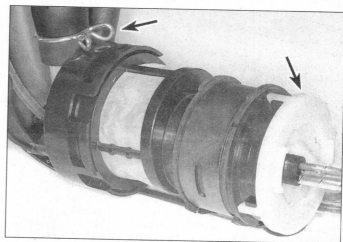

4.4b Undo the clip (right arrow) and disconnect the hoses (left arrow)

4

5.2a Disconnect the vacuum hose from the air duct diaphragm

5.2b Unclip the duct and lift it out

5.4 Remove the six housing screws and two tube joint screws (arrows)

5.5a Disconnect the vacuum tube from the bottom left of the air cleaner housing . . .

5   Installation is the reverse of the removal steps, with the following additions:

   a) *Use a new pump gasket if the old one is compressed, brittle or deteriorated.*

   b) *Be sure the PUSH marks molded into the connectors on top of the pump are upward when the connectors are attached to the terminals. You should be able to see the terminal colors (B for black, G for green and W for white) stamped into the top of the pump, but if they're not visible,* **refer to illustration 2.6***.*

5   Air filter housing - removal and installation

Refer to illustrations 5.2a, 5.2b, 5.4, 5.5a, 5.5b, 5.5c, 5.6a and 5.6b

1   Remove the top compartment (see Chapter 9).
2   Disconnect the hose from the air duct actuator, then undo the clip and remove the duct **(see illustrations)**.
3   Remove the housing cover and the air filter (see Chapter 1).
4   Remove the tube joint screws and housing screws **(see illustration)**. The tube joint will stay on the engine when the housing is lifted off.

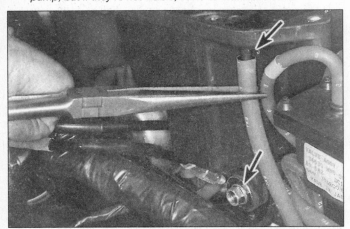

5.5b . . . and from the left rear corner (upper arrow); loosen the mounting bolt on each side (lower arrow) . . .

5.5c . . . and lift the air cleaner housing free of the mounting grommets

5.6a Use new O-rings in the air horn grooves

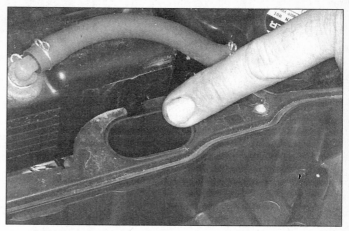

5.6b Engage the hot air duct with its slot in the housing

Disconnect the two hoses from the left underside of the air cleaner housing **(see illustrations)**. Disconnect the remaining hose from the right rear underside and lift the air cleaner off of the grommets (there's one on each side) **(see illustration)**.

Installation is the reverse of the removal steps, with the following additions:

a) *Use new O-rings in the air horn* **(see illustration)**.
b) *Be sure the duct fits into its slot in the housing* **(see illustration)**. *Take care not to pinch the duct hose as you install the housing, or the engine may run erratically.*

Idle fuel/air mixture adjustment

Refer to illustration 6.3

Due to the increased emphasis on controlling motorcycle exhaust emissions, certain governmental regulations have been formulated which directly affect the carburetion of this machine. A special tool is required to turn the pilot screws, and setting them requires a tachometer which can accurately indicate changes of 50 rpm or less.

If the engine runs extremely rough at idle or continually stalls, and all of the non-carburetor problems listed in Step 3 of Section 7 have been eliminated, try adjusting the pilot screws as described below.

Turn the pilot screws with Honda tool 07LMA-MT8010A or equivalent **(see illustration)**.

Turn the screws clockwise until they seat lightly, then back them out the number of turns listed in this Chapter's Specifications. **Caution:** *Don't bottom the screws hard or their tips will be damaged, resulting in an unstable idle mixture.*

6.3 Turn the mixture screws (arrows) with the Honda special tool

5   Warm the engine to normal operating temperature (stop-and-go riding for about 10 minutes should be enough). Park the bike, shut it off and connect a tune-up tachometer following the tachometer manufacturer's instructions.

6   Start the engine and let it idle. Adjust idle speed, using the procedure and specifications listed in Chapter 1.

7   Turn both of the pilot screws counterclockwise 1/2 turn and note the reading on the tachometer. If it increases by 50 rpm or more, bring it back down by turning the pilot screws (not the throttle stop screw). Turn the screws out evenly, 1/2 turn at a time, until engine speed drops (but don't drop it more than 50 rpm).

8   Readjust idle speed to the Chapter 1 Specifications, using the throttle stop screw.

9   Turn the pilot screw on the left carburetor clockwise just enough to reduce engine speed by 50 rpm. Turn it counterclockwise exactly one turn. This will cause the idle speed to change, so you'll need to reset it to the Chapter 1 Specifications with the throttle stop screw.

10   Repeat Step 9 on the pilot screw for the right carburetor. At this point, the engine should idle smoothly, at the rpm listed in the Chapter 1 Specifications.

7   Carburetor overhaul - general information

1   Poor engine performance, hesitation, hard starting, stalling, flooding and backfiring are all signs that major carburetor maintenance may be required.

2   Keep in mind that many so-called carburetor problems are really not carburetor problems at all, but mechanical problems within the engine or ignition system malfunctions. Try to establish for certain that the carburetors are in need of maintenance before beginning a major overhaul.

3   Check the fuel filter, the fuel lines, the fuel tank cap vent (if equipped), the intake manifold hose clamps, the vacuum hoses, the air filter element, the cylinder compression, the spark plugs, the carburetor synchronization and the fuel pump before assuming that a carburetor overhaul is required.

4   Most carburetor problems are caused by dirt particles, varnish and other deposits which build up in and block the fuel and air passages. Also, in time, gaskets and O-rings shrink or deteriorate and cause fuel and air leaks which lead to poor performance.

5   When the carburetor is overhauled, it is generally disassembled completely and the parts are cleaned thoroughly with a carburetor cleaning solvent and dried with filtered, unlubricated compressed air. The fuel and air passages are also blown through with compressed air to force out any dirt that may have been loosened but not removed by the solvent. Once the cleaning process is complete, the carburetor is reassembled using new gaskets, O-rings and, generally, a new inlet needle valve and seat.

4

6   Before disassembling the carburetors, make sure you have a carburetor rebuild kit (which will include all necessary O-rings and other
parts), some carburetor cleaner, a supply of rags, some means of
blowing out the carburetor passages and a clean place to work. It is
recommended that only one carburetor be overhauled at a time to
avoid mixing up parts.

7   Don't separate the carburetors from each other unless one of the
joints between them is leaking. The carburetors can be overhauled
completely without being separated, and reconnecting them properly
can be difficult.

8   Carburetors - removal and installation

Warning: *Gasoline is extremely flammable, so take extra precautions
when you work on any part of the fuel system. Don't smoke or allow
open flames or bare light bulbs near the work area, and don't work in a
garage where a natural gas-type appliance (such as a water heater or
clothes dryer) is present. If you spill any fuel on your skin, rinse it off
immediately with soap and water. When you perform any kind of work
on the fuel system, wear safety glasses and have a class B type fire
extinguisher (flammable liquids) on hand.*

Removal

Refer to illustrations 8.5, 8.6, 8.7, 8.8, 8.9 and 8.10

1   You'll need to disconnect some coolant fittings to remove the carburetors, but draining the system isn't usually necessary. If the radiator
cap is left on - and there aren't any leaks in the cooling system - only a
few drops of coolant will spill.

2   Remove the fairing inner covers (see Chapter 8).

3   Remove the air filter housing (see Section 5).

**8.5 Loosen the screws on the carburetor insulator clamps
(carburetors removed for clarity)**

4   Disconnect the fuel line at the auto fuel valve - you can also disconnect it at the T-fitting where it branches off to the carburetors, but
the metal fitting at the auto fuel valve is less likely to break. Unclip the
throttle stop screw cable from its bracket **(see illustration 2.4)**.

5   Loosen the clamp screws on the insulators (the rubber tubes that
connect the carburetors to the intake manifold) **(see illustration)**. Pull
the carburetors up until the insulators separate from the carburetors or
intake manifold.

6   Follow the drain tubes and air vent tubes from the carburetors to
their T-fittings, then disconnect the single tube from each fitting **(see
illustration)**.

7   Refer to Section 14 and disconnect the throttle and choke cables.
If the bike has cruise control, disconnect the cruise control throttle

**8.6 Disconnect the drain and vent tubes
from their T-fittings**

**8.7 Disengage the cruise control throttle
cable from its pulley**

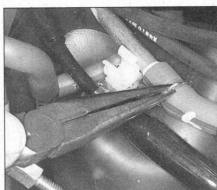

**8.8 Disconnect the hose from
the metal tube**

**8.9 On California bikes, disconnect the no. 5 hose (A)
and no. 11 hose (B)**

8.10 Disconnect the coolant hoses (arrows)

8.14 Remove the insulators; on installation, fit the tab on the intake manifold (arrow) into the insulator notch

9.1a Carburetor assembly - front view (carburetors shown inverted)

9.1b Carburetor assembly - rear view (carburetors shown inverted)

9.1c Carburetor assembly - right end view (carburetors shown inverted)

cable from its pulley **(see illustration)**.

8   Follow the metal tube back to its rubber hose and disconnect it **(see illustration)**.

9   If you're working on a California model, follow the no. 5 and no. 11 hoses back to their fittings and disconnect them **(see illustration)**.

10   Disconnect the carburetor coolant hoses **(see illustration)**.

11   At the right front corner of the carburetor assembly, locate the no. 18 and no. 19 hoses. Follow them back to their fittings and disconnect

them (you can also disconnect them at the T-fittings on the carburetor assembly).

12   After the carburetors have been removed, stuff clean rags into the insulators to prevent the entry of dirt or other objects.

13   Inspect the insulators **(see illustration 8.5)**. If they're cracked or brittle, replace them.

Installation

Refer to illustration 8.14

14   If the insulators were removed from the intake manifold, install them, aligning the insulator notches with the tabs on the manifold **(see illustration)**.

15   Place the carburetors in their installed position, but don't push them into the insulators yet. Connect the coolant hoses to their fittings. The left hose is marked with yellow tape; the fitting it connects to is marked with a dab of yellow paint.

16   The remainder of installation is the reverse of the removal steps.

17   Adjust the throttle grip freeplay (see Chapter 1).

18   Check and, if necessary, adjust the idle speed and carburetor synchronization (see Chapter 1).

9   Carburetors - separation and reconnection

Refer to illustrations 9.1a, 9.1b, 9.1c, 9.1d, 9.2, 9.3, 9.4a, 9.4b, 9.5a, 9.5b, 9.6, 9.7, 9.8, 9.9a, 9.9b, 9.10a, 9.10b, 9.11 and 9.12

1   Refer to Section 8 and remove the carburetor assembly from the engine. Before you start separating the carburetors, study the assembled views **(see illustrations)**.

9.1d Carburetor assembly - left end view (carburetors shown inverted)

9.2 Remove the four heat riser screws (arrows)

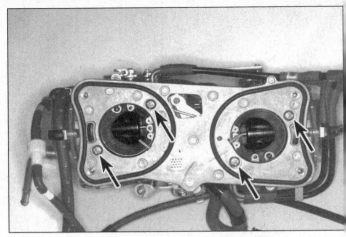

9.3 Loosen the airhorn screws (arrows), but don't remove them yet

2   Remove four screws and lift the heat riser off the assembly **(see illustration)**.
3   Turn the assembly over. If you haven't already removed the airhorn O-rings, do it now. Loosen the airhorn screws, but don't remove them yet **(see illustration)**.
4   Remove the accelerator pump screws **(see illustration)**. Lift the pump away from its mounting surface and pull the fuel tube out of the

airhorn **(see illustration)**.
5   Remove the choke rod lever screw, lockwasher and washer from the airhorn **(see illustration)**. Slip the lever off its pivot, then reinstall the washer, lockwasher and screw so they won't be lost **(see illustration)**. **Note:** *As an alternative, you can remove the cotter pin, washer and bushing from each choke rod where it joins its carburetor, then detach the choke rods from the carburetors.*

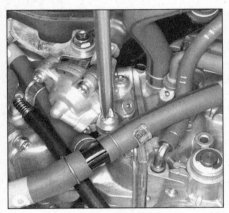

9.4a Remove the accelerator pump screws . . .

9.4b . . . move the pump out of the way and pull its fuel tube out of the airhorn bore (arrow)

9.5a Remove the choke lever screw (arrow) and pull the lever off the pivot . . .

9.5b . . . then reinstall the washer, lockwasher and screw (arrow) (airhorn removed for clarity)

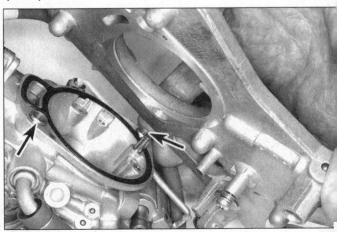

9.6 Remove the airhorn from the carburetors and locate the dowels (arrows)

9.7 Locate the accelerator pump dowels and O-ring (arrows)

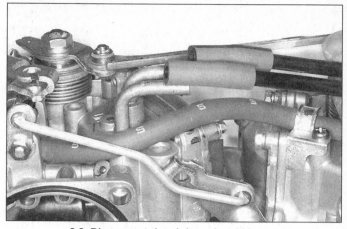

9.8 Disconnect the air jet solenoid hoses

6　Remove the airhorn screws that were loosened earlier and take the airhorn off the carburetors **(see illustration)**. Locate the airhorn dowels; they may have come off with the airhorn or stayed in the carburetors.

7　Locate the accelerator pump dowels and O-ring **(see illustration)**.

8　Disconnect the air jet solenoid hoses from their fittings **(see illustration)**.

9　Remove the cotter pin, brass washer and plastic washer from one end of the throttle linkage rod, then slip the rod off the throttle lever **(see illustrations)**.

10　Disconnect the fuel hose from the left carburetor **(see illustration)**. Disconnect one carburetor's no. 6 hose from the T-fitting **(see illustration)**.

9.9a Remove the cotter pin, brass washer and plastic washer from one end of the throttle linkage rod . . .

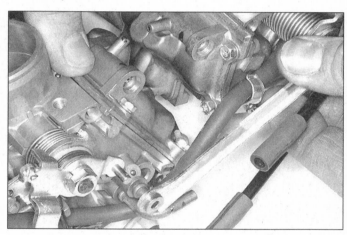

9.9b . . . and slip the rod off its pivot

4

9.10a Disconnect the fuel hose from the left carburetor . . .

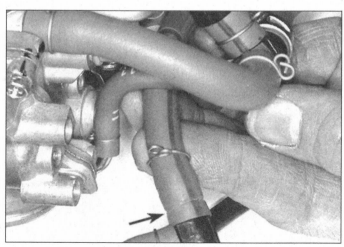

9.10b . . . and from the T-fitting where it branches to the right carburetor (arrow)

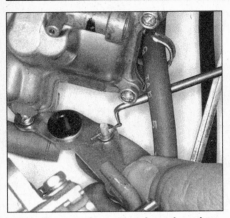

9.11 Remove the cotter pin and washer and detach one of the choke rods from the lever

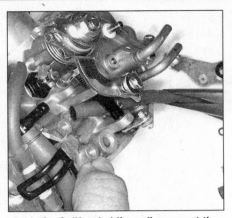

9.12 On California bikes, disconnect the no. 5 hose from the T-fitting and pull it out from behind the choke shaft

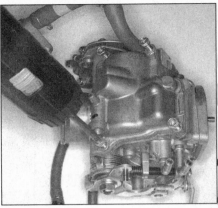

10.2a Remove the float chamber cover screws . . .

11   Remove the cotter pin and washer and slip one of the choke rods out of the pivot lever **(see illustration)**. Place the washer back on the rod and install the cotter pin so they won't be lost.

12   If you're working on a California bike, disconnect the no. 5 hose from the T-fitting and pull it out from behind the choke shaft **(see illustration)**.

13   Reconnection is the reverse of the separation steps, with the following additions:

  a) *Use new O-rings on the accelerator pump, its fuel tube and the air horn.*
  b) *Replace any removed cotter pins with new ones.*
  c) *Install the air horn screws loosely, then install the heat riser and tighten its screws securely before tightening the air horn screws.*
  d) *Make sure the choke and throttle linkages operate smoothly.*

10 Carburetors - disassembly, cleaning and inspection

Warning: *Gasoline is extremely flammable, so take extra precautions when you work on any part of the fuel system. Don't smoke or allow open flames or bare light bulbs near the work area, and don't work in a garage where a natural gas-type appliance (such as a water heater or clothes dryer) is present. If you spill any fuel on your skin, rinse it off immediately with soap and water. When you perform any kind of work on the fuel system, wear safety glasses and have a fire extinguisher suitable for class B fires (flammable liquids) on hand.*

Disassembly

Refer to illustrations 10.2a through 10.2l

1   Remove the carburetors from the motorcycle as described in Section 8, then separate them as described in Section 9. Set the assembly on a clean working surface. **Note:** *Work on one carburetor at a time to avoid getting parts mixed up.*

2   Refer to the accompanying illustrations to disassemble the carburetor **(see illustrations)**.

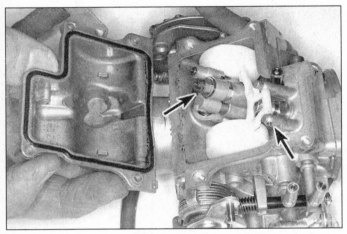

10.2b . . . and lift off the cover with its O-ring; pull out the float pivot pin (lower arrow), remove the floats with the needle valve and unscrew the main jet (upper arrow)

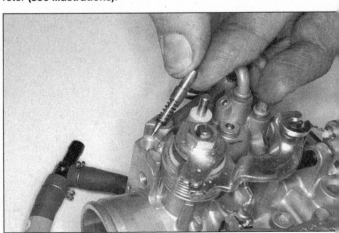

10.2c Lift off the main jet holder and unscrew the slow jet (arrow)

10.2d Remove the pilot screw, spring, washer and O-ring

10.2e Remove the nut and washer and detach the lever from the end of the choke shaft

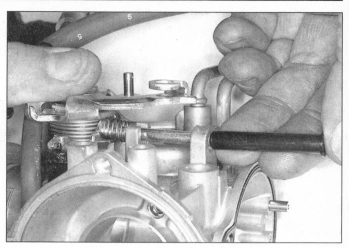

10.2f Remove the choke shaft

10.2g Disengage the choke arm groove from the slot on the end of the choke valve

10.2h Unscrew the choke valve and pull it out of the carburetor body

4

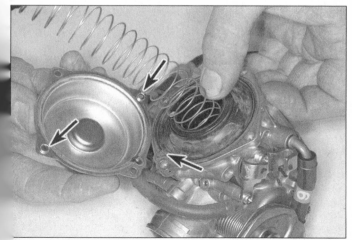

10.2i Remove the vacuum chamber cover screws, lift off the cover, and note the locations of the dowels and diaphragm tab (arrows); lift the diaphragm out of the carburetor

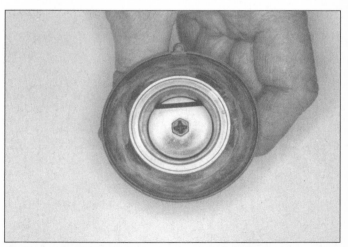

10.2j Use an 8 mm socket to press the jet needle retainer into the piston and turn it 1/4 turn counterclockwise . . .

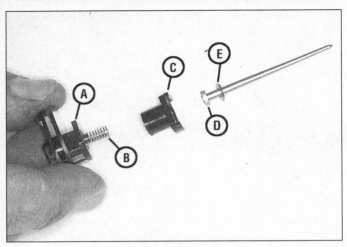

10.2k . . . then lift out the retainer (A), spring (B), spring holder (C), jet needle (D) and washer (E)

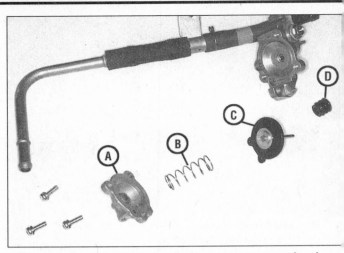

10.2l Remove the screws, accelerator pump cover and spring, then pull out the diaphragm

A Cover   C Diaphragm
B Spring   D Diaphragm rod seal

Inspection

3 Check the tip of the needle valve. If it has grooves or scratches in it, it must be replaced. Push in on the rod in the other end of the needle valve, then release it - if it doesn't spring back, replace the valve needle.
4 Check the operation of the choke plunger. If it doesn't move smoothly, replace it, along with the return spring. Inspect the needle on the end of the choke plunger and replace it if it's worn.
5 Check the tapered portion of the pilot screw for wear or damage. Replace the pilot screw if necessary.
6 Check the carburetor body, float chamber cover and vacuum chamber cover for cracks, distorted sealing surfaces and other damage. If any defects are found, replace the faulty component, although replacement of the entire carburetor will probably be necessary (check with your parts supplier for the availability of separate components).
7 Check the diaphragm for splits, holes and general deterioration. Holding it up to a light will help to reveal problems of this nature.
8 Insert the throttle piston in the carburetor body and see that it moves up-and-down smoothly. Check the surface of the piston for wear. If it's worn excessively or doesn't move smoothly in the bore, replace the carburetor.
9 Check the jet needle for straightness by rolling it on a flat surface (such as a piece of glass). Replace it if it's bent or if the tip is worn.
10 Operate the throttle shaft to make sure the throttle butterfly valve

opens and closes smoothly. If it doesn't, replace the carburetor.
11 Check the floats for damage. This will usually be apparent by the presence of fuel inside one of the floats. If the floats are damaged, they must be replaced.

Cleaning

Caution: *Use only a petroleum based solvent for carburetor cleaning. Don't use caustic cleaners.*
12 Submerge the metal components in the solvent for approximately thirty minutes (or longer, if the directions recommend it).
13 After the carburetor has soaked long enough for the cleaner to loosen and dissolve most of the varnish and other deposits, use a brush to remove the stubborn deposits. Rinse it again, then dry it with compressed air. Blow out all of the fuel and air passages in the main body. **Caution:** *Never clean the jets or passages with a piece of wire or a drill bit, as they will be enlarged, causing the fuel and air metering rates to be upset.*

11 Carburetors - reassembly and float level adjustment

Caution: *When installing the jets, be careful not to overtighten them; they're made of soft material and can strip or shear easily.*
Note: *When reassembling the carburetors, be sure to use the new O-rings, gaskets and other parts supplied in the rebuild kit.*

Reassembly

1 Assembly is the reverse of the disassembly steps, with the following additions.
2 Install the pilot screw (if removed) along with its spring, washer and O-ring, turning it in until it seats lightly. Now, turn the screw out the number of turns that was previously recorded. Refer to Section 6 and adjust the fuel mixture.
3 Be sure to place the diaphragm tab in its groove when installing the vacuum chamber cover **(see illustration 10.2i)**.

Float level adjustment

4 With the float chamber cover removed, make sure the needle valve is fully seated and hold the carburetor so the float hangs down. Position the carburetor so the float arm just touches the needle valve, then measure the distance from the float chamber gasket surface to the bottom of the floats. If it differs from the value listed in this Chapter's Specifications, bend the float arm, in very small amounts, to change it.

12.2 Lift the heat shield off the manifolds

12.4 Disconnect the vacuum lines; stick-on labels like this will make reconnection easier

12.5 Disconnect the coolant hoses from the heat risers (arrow)

12.6 Unplug the temperature sensor electrical connector

12 Intake manifold - removal and installation

Refer to illustrations 12.2, 12.4, 12.5, 12.6, 12.7a, 12.7b and 12.7c

1 Drain the cooling system (see Chapter 1).
2 Remove the air cleaner housing and the carburetors (Sections 5 and 8). Detach the carburetor insulators from the manifold, then pull off the heat shield **(see illustration)**.

3 Refer to Section 16 and remove the pulse secondary air (PAIR) valve.
4 Disconnect the intake manifold vacuum hoses (no. 1 green, no. 1 orange, no. 3 orange, no. 6 green and no. 11 yellow) **(see illustration)**.
5 Disconnect the coolant hoses from the heat risers. There's one cast into the underside of each side of the manifold, for a total of four fittings **(see illustration)**.
6 Disconnect the engine coolant temperature sensor **(see illustration)**.
7 Unbolt each manifold from the engine, lift it off and remove the gasket **(see illustrations)**.
8 Installation is the reverse of the removal steps, with the following additions:

   a) *Use new gaskets.*
   b) *Be sure to install the manifolds on the correct sides of the engine; they're labeled R and L for right and left.*
   c) *Tighten the manifold bolts evenly, in several stages. Tighten the bolts securely, but don't overtighten them and strip the threads.*
   d) *Refer to Chapter 1 and refill the cooling system.*

13 Carburetor coolant valve - removal, testing and installation

Refer to illustration 13.2

1 You'll need to remove the intake manifolds for access to the carburetor coolant valve (see Section 12).
2 Remove the valve mounting bolts and detach it from its hoses **(see illustration)**.

12.7a Remove the right side manifold bolts . . .

12.7b . . . and the left side manifold bolts; some of the bolts secure hose retainers and tube brackets

12.7c Lift up the manifolds and remove the gaskets

13.2 The carburetor coolant valve (arrow) is located under the intake manifold

14.2 Loosen the locknuts (left arrows), slip the cables out of the brackets and disengage their ends from the pulleys (right arrows)

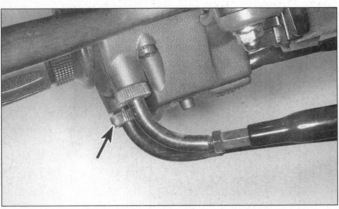

14.3 Loosen the locknuts (arrow)

14.5 Lift up the upper switch housing and disengage the cable ends from the pulley (arrows)

3   Attach a vacuum/pressure pump to one end of the valve. Suspend the valve in a pan of water so it doesn't touch the sides or bottom of the pan. **Warning:** *Antifreeze is poisonous. DO NOT use a cooking pan for this test.*
4   Start heating the water and apply light pressure from the pump to the valve. As the temperature rises to the valve listed in this Chapter's Specifications, the valve should close, allowing pressure to build up. If the valve closes too soon or not at all, replace it.

14   Throttle and choke cables - removal, installation and adjustment

Throttle cables

Refer to illustrations 14.2, 14.3 and 14.5
1   Remove the fairing inner covers (see Chapter 8).
2   Loosen the accelerator cable mounting nuts and slip the cables out of their brackets **(see illustration)**. Rotate the cables so they align with the slots in the pulley and slip them out.
3   Loosen the cable locknuts at the throttle grip **(see illustration)**.
4   Remove the handlebar switch mounting screws and separate the halves of the handlebar switch (see Chapter 9).
5   Detach the accelerator and decelerator cables from the throttle grip pulley **(see illustration)**. Remove the cables, noting how they are routed.
6   Take the throttle grip off the handlebar. Clean the handlebar and apply a light coat of multi-purpose grease.
7   Route the cables into place. Make sure they don't interfere with

14.13a Loosen the bracket screw and slip the choke cable out of the bracket . . .

any other components and aren't kinked or bent sharply.
8   Lubricate the ends of the accelerator and decelerator cables with multi-purpose grease and connect them to the throttle pulleys at the carburetors and at the throttle grip.
9   Follow the procedure outlined in Chapter 1, *Throttle operation/grip freeplay - check and adjustment*, to adjust the cables.

14.13b . . . then turn the cable to align it with the lever slot and slip the cable out of the lever

14.14 Lift up the upper switch housing and disengage the choke cable from the pulley (arrow)

15.2a Support the mufflers from below and remove the muffler-to-frame bolts

15.2b At the exhaust chamber, loosen the clamps that secure the mufflers to the rear fittings and the exhaust pipes to the front fittings, then pull the mufflers off . . .

A   *Chamber to muffler clamp*
B   *Chamber to exhaust pipe clamp*
C   *Exhaust chamber mounting bolts and nuts*

13   Loosen the choke cable bracket screw and slip the cable out of the bracket **(see illustration)**. Rotate the end of the cable to align with the slot in the choke arm and slip the cable out **(see illustration)**.
14   Remove the screws from the underside of the left handlebar switch. Lift off the top half of the switch housing and detach the choke cable from its pulley **(see illustration)**.
15   Installation is the reverse of the removal steps. Lubricate the ends of the cable with multi-purpose grease.

15.2c . . . DO NOT touch the spun metal gaskets with fingers, as they'll leave metal splinters; use pliers or wear heavy leather gloves to remove them

10   Turn the handlebars back and forth to make sure the cables don't cause the steering to bind. With the engine idling, turn the handlebars back and forth and make sure idle speed doesn't change. If it does, find and fix the cause before riding the motorcycle.
11   Install components removed for access.

Choke cables

Refer to illustrations 14.13a, 14.13b and 14.14
12   Remove the air cleaner housing (Section 5).

15 Exhaust system - removal and installation

Removal

1   Refer to Chapter 8 and remove the following panels:
  a) *Rider's footrest trim panels*
  b) *Exhaust chamber protector panels*
  c) *Fairing front cover*
  d) *Fairing under cover*
  e) *Front and rear exhaust pipe protectors*
  f) *Exhaust pipe protector lid*

Exhaust system

Refer to illustrations 15.2a through 15.2f
2   Refer to the accompanying illustrations to remove the exhaust system **(see illustrations)**.

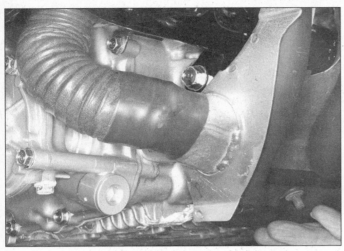

15.2d   Disconnect the air tube from the hot air chamber on the left side

15.2e   Remove the exhaust pipe holder nuts at each cylinder head, lower the pipe assemblies off the mounting studs and pull them off the exhaust chamber

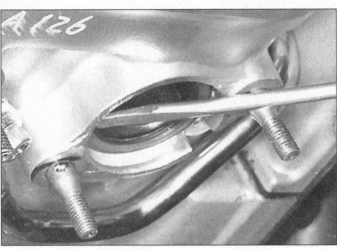

15.2f   Carefully pry the gaskets out of the exhaust ports without scratching the cylinder heads

15.3a   Unbolt the heat shield from the inside of each pipe assembly

15.3b   Remove three bolts (A) and the left rear heat shield; the remaining bolt (B) secures the left side of the exhaust chamber heat shield

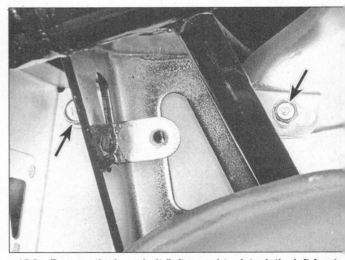

15.3c   Remove the large bolt (left arrow) to detach the left front heat shield from the frame; the small bolt (right arrow) secures it to the exhaust chamber heat shield

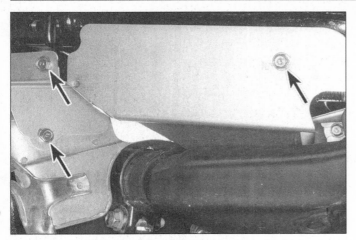

15.3d Remove the right front and rear heat shield bolts (arrows) . . .

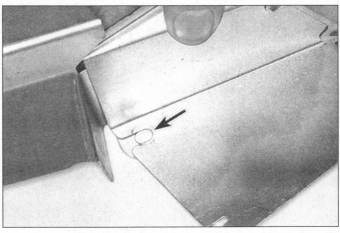

15.3e . . . the front bolt holds the two heat shields together (arrow)

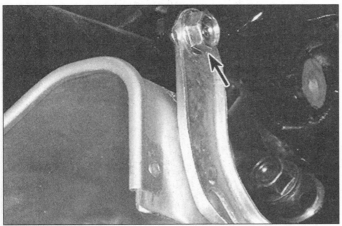

15.3f Remove the bolt from each side of the center heat shield . . .

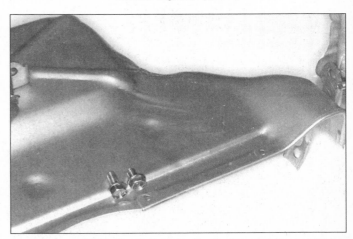

15.3g . . . and the two bolts from the top bracket (heat shield removed for clarity)

Heat shields

Refer to illustrations 15.3a through 15.3g

3   Refer to the accompanying illustrations to remove the heat shields **(see illustrations)**.

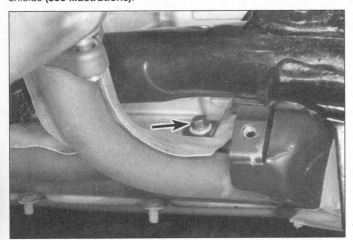

15.7 It's easier to install the forward bolt in the left exhaust pipe protector (arrow) before the pipe assembly is raised to the cylinder head

Installation

Refer to illustration 15.7

4   If the exhaust chamber heat shield was removed, install it.
5   Install the exhaust chamber loosely, then install new spun metal gaskets on its fittings. DO NOT touch the gaskets with fingers, as they'll cause metal splinters. Slip the rear ends of the pipe assemblies into the chamber and let the pipe assemblies hang down. **Note:** *If the assemblies catch in the spun metal gaskets, lubricate them with WD-40 or equivalent.*
6   Install new gaskets in the exhaust ports. Install the left rear exhaust pipe protector, raise the left pipe assembly into the cylinder head studs and attach it loosely.
7   Install the forward bolt that secures the left rear exhaust pipe protector to the left pipe assembly and heat shield **(see illustration)**.
8   Raise the left pipe assembly into its final installed position, then tighten the nuts securely.
9   Install the right rear heat shield, but don't install its bolts yet. Install the front bolt partway, then slide the slot of the right front heat shield over the bolt shaft **(see illustration 15.3e)**. Install the remaining three bolts, then tighten all four bolts **(see illustration 15.3d)**.
10   Install the left front heat shield, then the left rear.
11   Install the left pipe assembly in the exhaust chamber, then raise it to the cylinder head and tighten its nuts.
12   Tighten the exhaust chamber bolts.
13   Attach the mufflers to the exhaust chamber and tighten their mounting bolts.

4

16.1 The carburetor air jet system consists of two solenoids (upper arrows), a filter (lower arrow) and connecting hoses

16.3 Remove the cover for access to the filter element

16.4 Main components of the shot air system are the shot air valve (A) and check valve (B) (later models); the PAIR control valve (C) is part of the pulse secondary air system

16.8a Pry the hose fittings out of the top of the cylinder head; use new O-rings on installation

16 Emission control systems - inspection and component replacement

Carburetor air jet system

Refer to illustrations 16.1 and 16.3

1   This system uses a pair of solenoids to regulate the flow of air to main air jets 2 and 3 in the carburetors **(see illustration)**. One or both solenoids may open, depending on riding conditions. Opening and closing of the solenoids is controlled by the carburetor control unit mounted in the upper right part of the fairing. Maximum rich mixture occurs when both solenoids are closed; maximum lean mixture occurs when both are open.

2   The system's hoses should be checked occasionally for cracking, brittleness or deterioration. Hoses with problems should be replaced.

3   To inspect the filter, open its case and remove the foam element **(see illustration)**. Clean the element in solvent and let it dry thoroughly. If the foam has deteriorated, replace the element with a new one.

Shot air system

Refer to illustration 16.4

4   This system pulls fresh air into the intake manifold on deceleration

to compensate for the over-rich mixture that occurs when the throttle is closed. Its main component is a shot air valve **(see illustration)**.

5   If the bike backfires on deceleration, check the system's hoses (they're coded yellow) for leaks, damage or deterioration. Replace any hoses that have problems. If there's no obvious sign of trouble, have the system components individually checked by a Honda dealer or other shop familiar with Gold Wing 1500 emission controls.

Pulse secondary air injection (PAIR) system

Refer to illustrations 16.8a, 16.8b, 16.10 and 16.11

6   The PAIR system uses exhaust gas pulses to suck fresh air into the exhaust ports, where it mixes with hot combustion gases. The additional oxygen provided by the fresh air allows combustion to continue for a longer time, reducing unburned hydrocarbons in the exhaust. Reed valves allow the flow of air into the ports and prevent exhaust gas from flowing into the system **(see illustration 16.4)**. There are two sets of three reed valves, one for each cylinder head. The PAIR control valve shuts off the flow of air into the system during deceleration to prevent backfiring. The PAIR solenoid valve regulates the function of the PAIR control valve.

7   Check the hoses for loose connections, damage and deterioration. Tighten or replace loose or damaged hoses.

8   Access to the components generally requires removal of the carburetors and intake manifolds (see Sections 8 and 12). To remove air

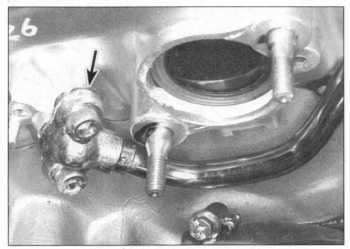

16.8b Remove the Allen bolts to detach the hose fittings from the bottom of the cylinder heads; use a new gasket on installation

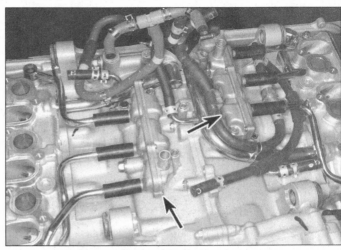

16.10 The reed valves are enclosed in housings on top of the engine (arrows)

16.11 The PAIR solenoid is mounted within the left side of the fairing

16.13a The canister is mounted forward of the swingarm

tubes from the cylinder heads, carefully pry them loose from the top or unbolt them from the bottom **(see illustrations)**. Use new O-rings and gaskets when you reconnect the tubes.

9 · To replace the PAIR control valve, remove the mounting bolts and disconnect the hoses **(see illustration 16.4)**.

10 To replace reed valves, remove the mounting bolts and disconnect the hoses **(see illustration)**. Remove the reed case assembly bolts and separate the halves to expose the reeds.

11 To replace the PAIR solenoid, locate it inside the left side of the fairing **(see illustration)**. Disconnect its electrical connector and hoses, detach it from the motorcycle and take it out.

12 Installation is the reverse of the removal steps.

Evaporation control system (California models)

Refer to illustrations 16.13a, 16.13b, 16.13c, 16.15a and 16.15b

13 The evaporation control system used on California models prevents fuel vapor from escaping into the atmosphere. When the engine isn't running, the vapor is stored in a canister, then routed into the combustion chambers for burning when the engine starts **(see illustrations)**.

14 The hoses should be checked periodically for loose connections, damage and deterioration. Tighten or replace the hoses as needed.

15 To remove the canister, disconnect the hoses. Remove the

16.13b The purge control valve is mounted within the left side of the fairing

4

16.13c The air vent control valve (right arrow) is located in the left side of the fairing; on bikes with cruise control, it's just behind the cruise control actuator (left arrow)

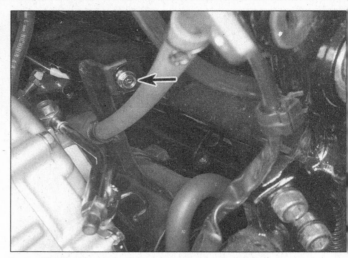

16.15a Remove the canister mounting bolt (arrow) . . .

16.15b . . . and disengage the mounting hooks from their slots

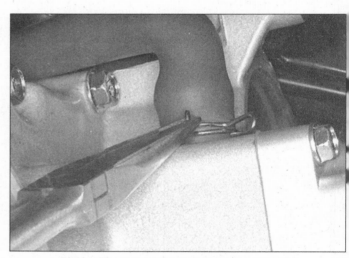

16.19a Disconnect the breather hose from the top of the crankcase . . .

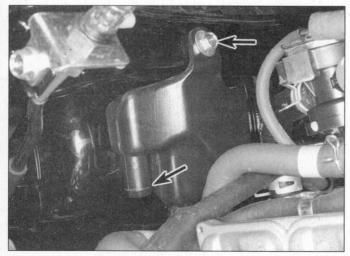

16.19b . . . and from the fitting on the storage tank (arrow); remove the bolt (arrow) to detach the tank from the bike

mounting bolt and lift the mounting tabs out of the pockets on the frame **(see illustration 16.13a and the accompanying illustrations)**.

16 Inspect the rubber mounting bushings and replace them if they're cracked or deteriorated. Bolt the canister to its bracket and reconnect the hoses.

Crankcase breather system

Refer to illustrations 16.19a and 16.19b

17 The breather system allows air into the crankcase. Its storage tank traps deposits.

18 The storage tank should be removed occasionally and any accumulated deposits cleaned out.

19 Disconnect the breather hose from the top of the engine near the alternator **(see illustration)**. Disconnect the upper end of the breather hose from the fitting on the storage tank **(see illustration)**. Disconnect the drain hose (smaller diameter, clear vinyl) from the other fitting on the bottom of the tank and disconnect the air cleaner hose form the fitting on the top. Remove the tank mounting bolt and lift it out.

20 Dump out any accumulated deposits.

21 Reinstall the storage tank and reconnect the hoses.

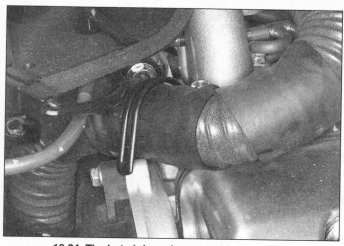

16.24 The hot air hose is secured by a retainer

Intake air temperature control system

Refer to illustration 16.24

22   This system warms the air coming into the carburetors when the engine is cold, so that the engine can run on a lean fuel mixture. It draws hot air from around the left exhaust manifold (which heats up very quickly) and mixes it with cold air coming through the normal air intake. The hot air is collected by a tube that connects to a fitting on the manifold heat shield **(see illustration 15.2d)**. The hot and cold air are mixed by a vacuum-operated duct at the front of the air cleaner housing (see Section 5).

23   Check the flap in the duct for free movement and make sure the vacuum hose hasn't been pinched by the fairing. Replace the duct if the valve is jammed and replace the vacuum hose if it has been pinched.

24   Make sure the hot air hose is secured in its retainer **(see illustration)**.

4

Notes

Chapter 5   Ignition system

Contents

Specifications

Ignition coil primary resistance..	2.6 to 3.2 ohms at 20-degrees C (68-degrees F)
Ignition coil secondary resistance	11,700 to 14,300 ohms at 20-degrees C (68-degrees F)
Arcing distance...	6 mm (1/4 inch)
Pulse generator resistance	400 to 500 ohms at 20-degrees C (68-degrees F)
Ignition timing	Not adjustable
Spark plugs...	See Chapter 1

5

1   General information

This motorcycle is equipped with a battery operated, fully transistorized, breakerless ignition system. The system consists of the following components:

Engine control module
Pulse generators and timing rotor
Battery and fuse
Ignition coils
Spark plugs
Ignition (main) and engine kill (stop) switches
Primary and secondary circuit wiring

The transistorized ignition system functions on the same principle as a breaker point DC ignition system with the pulse generators, timing rotor and engine control module performing the tasks previously associated with the breaker points and mechanical advance system. As a result, adjustment and maintenance of ignition components is eliminated (with the exception of spark plug replacement).

All models use a digital microprocessor and a pair of pulse generators. The digital microprocessor system also controls ignition timing, taking into account engine rpm, coolant and air temperature, intake manifold vacuum and transmission gear position.

Because of their nature, the individual ignition system components can be checked but not repaired. If ignition system troubles occur, and the faulty component can be isolated, the only cure for the problem is to replace the part with a new one. Keep in mind that most electrical parts, once purchased, can't be returned. To avoid unnecessary expense, make very sure the faulty component has been positively identified before buying a replacement part.

2   Ignition system - check

Refer to illustrations 2.5 and 2.13
Warning: *Because of the very high voltage generated by the ignition system, extreme care should be taken when these checks are performed.*

1   If the ignition system is the suspected cause of poor engine performance or failure to start, a number of checks can be made to isolate the problem.

2   Make sure the engine kill switch is in the Run position.

2.5 Connect an ohmmeter between each coil's pair of spark plug wires to check secondary resistance

2.13 A simple spark gap testing fixture can be made from a block of wood, a large alligator clip, two nails, a screw and a piece of wire

Engine will not start

3   Disconnect one of the spark plug wires, connect the wire to a spare spark plug and lay the plug on the engine with the threads contacting the engine. If necessary, hold the spark plug with an insulated tool. Crank the engine over and make sure a well-defined, blue spark occurs between the spark plug electrodes. **Warning:** *Don't remove one of the spark plugs from the engine to perform this check - atomized fuel being pumped out of the open spark plug hole could ignite, causing severe injury*!

4   If no spark occurs, the following checks should be made:

5   Unscrew the spark plug caps from the plugs and check the resistance between the secondary terminals of each ignition coil pair with an ohmmeter **(see illustration)**. The pairs are cylinders 1 and 2; 3 and 4; and 5 and 6. If the resistance is not within Specifications, test the coil secondary resistance without the plug wires as described below.

6   Make sure all electrical connectors are clean and tight. Check all wires for shorts, opens and correct installation.

7   Check the battery voltage with a voltmeter and - on models equipped with batteries having removable filler caps - check the specific gravity with a hydrometer (see Chapter 1). If the voltage is less than 12-volts or if the specific gravity is low, recharge the battery.

8   Check the ignition fuse and the fuse connections. If the fuse is blown, replace it with a new one; if the connections are loose or corroded, clean or repair them.

9   Refer to Chapter 9 and check the ignition switch, engine kill switch, neutral switch and sidestand switch.

10   Refer to Section 3 and check the ignition coil primary and secondary resistance.

11   Refer to Section 4 and check the pulse generator resistance.

Engine starts but misfires

12   If the engine starts but misfires, make the following checks before deciding that the ignition system is at fault.

13   The ignition system must be able to produce a spark across a six millimeter (1/4-inch) gap (minimum). A simple test fixture **(see illustration)** can be constructed to make sure the minimum spark gap can be jumped. Make sure the fixture electrodes are positioned six millimeters apart.

14   Connect one of the spark plug wires to the protruding test fixture electrode, then attach the fixture's alligator clip to a good engine ground/earth.

15   Crank the engine over (it will probably start and run on the remaining cylinders) and see if well-defined, blue sparks occur between the test fixture electrodes. If the minimum spark gap test is positive, the ignition coil for that cylinder (and its companion cylinder) is functioning properly. Repeat the check on one of the spark plug wires that is connected to the other coils. If the spark will not jump the

gap during either test, or if it is weak (orange colored), refer to Steps 5 through 11 of this Section and perform the component checks described.

3   Ignition coils - check, removal and installation

Check

Refer to illustrations 3.4, 3.5 and 3.6

1   In order to determine conclusively that the ignition coils are defective, they should be tested by an authorized Honda dealer service department which is equipped with the special electrical tester required for this check.

2   However, the coils can be checked visually (for cracks and other damage) and the primary and secondary coil resistances can be measured with an ohmmeter. If the coils are undamaged, and if the resistances are as specified, they are probably capable of proper operation.

3   To check the primary resistances, remove the right fairing inner cover (see Chapter 8) and unplug the primary circuit electrical connector (four-pin white connector inside the right fairing).

4   Place the ohmmeter selector switch in the Rx1 position. Attach one ohmmeter lead to the black/white terminal in the primary connector, then connect the other ohmmeter lead to the other primary terminals (yellow/white, yellow/blue and yellow/red) in turn **(see illustra-**

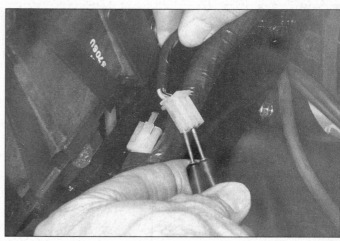

3.4 To test the coil primary resistance, connect the ohmmeter leads between the primary terminals in the coil connector

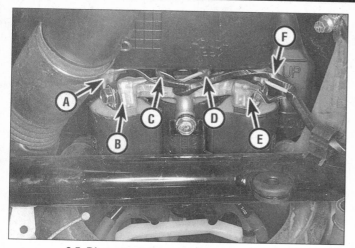

3.5 Disconnect the coil primary connectors

A	Black-white wire	D	Yellow/blue wire
B	Yellow/red wire	E	Black/white wire
C	Black/white wire	F	Yellow/white wire

**3.6 Unscrew the spark plug wires from the coils (arrows) -
wires 1 and 5 shown**

tion). Compare each measured resistance to the value listed in this Chapter's Specifications.

5   If the primary resistance isn't as specified, you'll need to isolate the problem to the wiring harness or the coils themselves. Remove the carburetors (see Chapter 4) and the coolant reserve tank (see Chapter 3). Disconnect the primary (small) wires from the coil that didn't meet the Specifications and repeat the test between the primary terminals on the coil **(see illustration)**. If the reading is now within specifications, the problem is in the wiring harness. If the reading still isn't correct, the coil is defective and must be replaced as described below.

6   If the coil primary resistance is as specified, check the coil secondary resistance. Unscrew the spark plug wires from the bottoms of the coils **(see illustration)** and connect the ohmmeter leads between the pair of spark plug wire terminals on each coil.

7   Place the ohmmeter selector switch in the Rx100 position and compare the measured resistance to the values listed in this Chapter's Specifications.

8   If the resistances are not as specified, the coil is probably defective and should be replaced with a new one.

Removal and installation

Refer to illustration 3.10

9   To remove the coils, remove the carburetors (Chapter 4) and the

coolant reserve tank (Chapter 3). Disconnect the spark plug wires from the plugs and unscrew them from the coils. After labeling them with tape to aid in reinstallation, unplug the coil primary circuit electrical connectors **(see illustration 3.5)**.

10   Support the coils with one hand and remove the coil bracket bolts and grommets **(see illustration)**. Lift the coil assembly out and unbolt the individual coil(s) from the bracket.

11   Installation is the reverse of removal. Make sure the primary circuit electrical connectors are attached to the proper terminals and the plug wires to the correct plugs.

4   Pulse generators - check, removal and installation

Check

Refer to illustration 4.2

1   Remove the right lower fairing cover (see Chapter 8).

2   Locate the pulse generator connector (it's in the upper front hole in the connector bracket), then unplug it **(see illustration)**.

3   Probe the terminals in the pickup coil connector with an ohmmeter and compare the resistance readings with the value listed in this Chapter's Specifications.

4   If either pulse generator has a resistance reading outside the specified range, replace it.

5

3.10 Remove the cool bracket bolts and grommets

**4.2 Connect an ohmmeter between the specified pairs of
terminals to check pulse generator resistance**

4.7 Remove two bolts to undo each pulse generator (lower arrows) and work the harness grommet out of its notch (upper arrow)

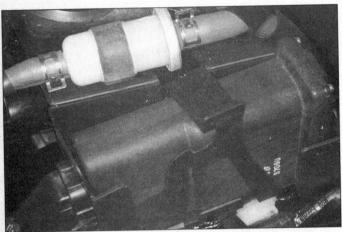

5.3 Unplug the electrical connector(s) and unhook the strap to free the engine control module

Removal

Refer to illustration 4.7

5   Remove the fairing front cover and under cover (see Chapter 8).
6   Remove the timing belt covers and the right timing belt (see Chapter 2).
7   Remove the pulse generator mounting bolts. Work the wiring harness grommet free of the crankcase and remove the pulse generators **(see illustration)**.

---

5   Engine control module - check, removal and installation

Check

1   The ECM is checked by process of elimination (when all other possible causes have been checked and eliminated, the ECM is at fault). Because the ECM is expensive and can't be returned once purchased, consider having a Honda dealer test the ignition system before you buy a new ECM.

Removal and installation

Refer to illustration 5.3

2   Remove the inner fairing cover on the right side of the bike (see Chapter 8).
3   Unplug the electrical connectors (early models) or single connector (later models). Unhook the retaining strap and take the ECM out **(see illustration)**.
4   Installation is the reverse of the removal steps.

Chapter 6
Steering, suspension and final drive

Contents

Specifications

Fork spring length (1988 through 1994)
    Short spring
        Standard .... 192.9 mm (7.59 inches)
        Limit .... 189.0 mm (7.44 inches)
    Long spring
        Standard .... 386.3 mm (15.21 inches)
        Limit .... 378.6 mm (14.91 inches)
Fork spring length (1995-on)
    Standard .... 390.6 mm (15.38 inches)
    Limit .... 382.8 mm (15.07 inches)
Fork oil capacity (1988 through 1994)
    Left fork .... 325 cc (10.9 fl oz)
    Right fork .... 320 cc (10.8 fl oz)
Fork oil capacity (1995-on)
    Left fork
        Interstate .... 361 cc (12.2 fl oz)
        Aspencade and SE .... 372 cc (12.6 fl oz)
    Right fork .... 377 cc (12.7 fl oz)
Fork oil level (fully compressed)
    1988 through 1994 .... 239 mm (9.4 inches) below top of fork tube
    1995-on .... 194 cc (7.6 fl oz)
Fork tube runout limit .... 0.2 mm (0.01 inch)

6

Torque specifications

Handlebar bracket bolts	25 Nm (18 ft-lbs) (1)
Front fork caps	23 Nm (17 ft-lbs)
Fork damper rod Allen bolt	20 Nm (14 ft-lbs) (2)
Steering stem upper nut (above triple clamp)	100 Nm (72 ft-lbs)
Steering stem adjusting nut	
Initial torque	40 Nm (29 ft-lbs)
Final torque	19 Nm (14 ft-lbs)
Rear shock absorber bolts	
Upper	23 Nm (17 ft-lbs)
Lower (right shock)	23 Nm (17 ft-lbs)
Lower (left shock)	70 Nm (51 ft-lbs)
Air hoses	
To air pump	6 Nm (48 inch-lbs)
To air distributor	
End with spring and steel ball	15 Nm (11 ft-lbs)
End without spring and steel ball	6 Nm (48 inch-lbs)
Shock absorber air hose (both ends)	6 Nm (48 inch-lbs)
Final drive unit mounting nuts	65 Nm (47 ft-lbs)
Swingarm pivot bolts	
Right side	100 Nm (72 ft-lbs)
Left side	19 Nm (14 ft-lbs)
Swingarm pivot bolt locknut	
Indicated torque with special tool	90 Nm (65 ft-lbs)
Actual applied torque	100 Nm (72 ft-lbs)

1   General information

The steering system on these models consists of a one-piece handlebar and a steering stem, which rides in a steering head attached to the front portion of the frame. All models use tapered roller bearings in the steering head.

The front suspension consists of conventional coil spring, hydraulically damped telescopic forks with antidive units. Air pressure in the forks is adjustable.

The rear suspension consists of twin shock absorbers and a swingarm. The shock absorber air pressure is adjustable on all models. Interstate models have an air fitting so air can be pumped in from an outside source; Aspencade and SE models have an on-board compressor system that allows air pressure to be changed at the touch of a switch.

The final drive uses a shaft and bevel gears to transmit power from the transmission to the rear wheel.

2   Handlebars - removal and installation

Refer to illustrations 2.1, 2.2 and 2.4

1   If you're working on an Aspencade or SE, pull off the handlebar center cover **(see illustration)**.

2   If the handlebars must be removed for access to other components, such as the forks or the steering head, simply remove the brackets and lift the handlebar off the upper triple clamp **(see illustration)**. It's not necessary to disconnect the cables, wires or hoses, but it is a good idea to support the assembly with a piece of wire or rope, to avoid unnecessary strain on the cables, wires and the brake or clutch hose.

3   If the handlebars are to be removed completely, refer to Chapter 2 for clutch master cylinder removal procedures, Chapter 7 for the brake master cylinder removal procedures, Chapter 5 for the throttle cable removal procedure and Chapter 9 for the switch removal procedure.

4   Check the handlebars for cracks and distortion and replace them if any undesirable conditions are found. When installing the handle-

2.1 Lift the cover from the center of the handlebar

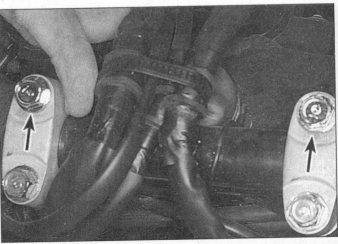

2.2 The bracket punch marks (arrows) face forward

2.4 Align the punch mark in the handlebar (arrow) with the lower rear corner of the right or left bracket

bars, align the punch mark on the handlebar with the lower inner corner of the bracket **(see illustration)**. Tighten the bolts to the torque listed in this Chapter's Specifications.

3 Forks - removal and installation

Removal

Refer to illustrations 3.8a, 3.8b, 3.9a and 3.9b

1   Support the bike securely so it can't be knocked over during this procedure.

2   Place a jack under the engine and raise it slightly to lift the front tire off the ground.

3   Remove the brake calipers and front wheel (see Chapter 7).

4   Remove the front fender (see Chapter 8).

5   Loosen the clamp bolts in the handlebar bosses, then lift the handlebars off the forks and support them from above (see Section 2).

6   Remove any wiring harness clamps or straps from the fork tubes and detach the speedometer cable retainer.

7   If the fork will be disassembled after removal, read through the disassembly procedure (see Section 4), paying special attention to the damper rod bolt removal steps. If you don't have the necessary special tool or a substitute for it, you can loosen the damper rod bolt before the fork is disassembled, while the spring tension will keep the damper rod from spinning inside the fork tube.

8   If you're working on an Interstate model and you plan to

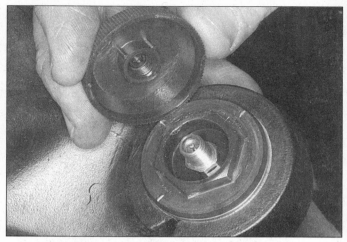

3.8a Unscrew the cover from the top of the fork

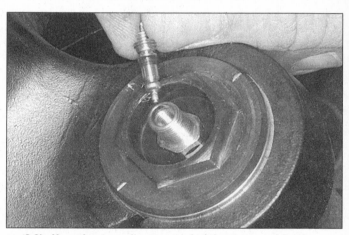

3.8b If you have a valve core tool of the type used for tires, you can unscrew the core from the air valve; if not, unscrew the air valve from the fork cap

disassemble the forks after removal, loosen the fork caps. If you're working on an Aspencade or SE, remove the air valve caps **(see illustrations)**.

9   Loosen the fork upper and lower triple clamp bolts **(see illustrations)**, then slide the fork tubes down and remove the forks from the motorcycle.

3.9a Loosen the fork cap, then loosen the upper triple clamp bolt (arrow) . . .

3.9b . . . and the lower triple clamp bolts

6

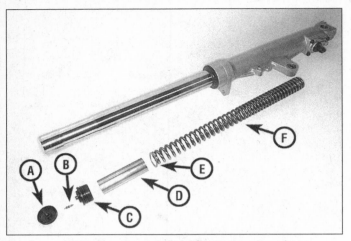

4.2 Fork spring details (single spring shown)

A	Fork cap cover	D	Spacer
B	Air valve core	E	Spring seat
C	Fork cap	F	Fork spring

Installation

10   Slide each fork leg into the lower triple clamp.

11   Slide the fork legs up, installing the tops of the tubes into the upper triple clamp. Position the top of the fork tube flush with the top of the upper triple clamp.

12   The remainder of installation is the reverse of the removal procedure. Tighten all fasteners to the torques listed in this Chapter's Specifications and the Chapter 7 Specifications.

13   Pump the front brake lever several times to bring the pads into contact with the discs.

---

4   Forks - disassembly, inspection and reassembly

Disassembly

Refer to illustrations 4.2, 4.4, 4.5, 4.6, 4.7, 4.8, 4.12a, 4.12b and 4.12c

1   Remove the forks following the procedure in Section 3. Work on one fork leg at a time to avoid mixing up the parts.

2   **Warning:** *The fork cap is under spring tension. Be sure to point the end of the fork away from yourself while you remove the cap.* Remove the fork cap (it should have been loosened before the forks

4.6 Unscrew the Allen bolt and remove the sealing washer; use a new sealing washer on assembly

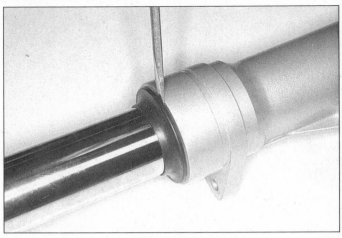

4.4 Pry the dust seal from its bore

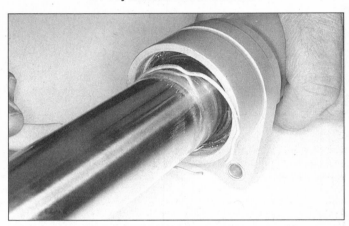

4.5 Pry the retainer from its bore without scratching the fork tubes

were removed) **(see illustration)**. Remove the spacer, spring seat(s) and spring(s). **Note:** *Early models have two fork springs and two spring seats, with the shorter spring on top of the longer spring.*

3   Invert the fork assembly over a container and extend and compress it several times to drain the oil.

4   Pry the dust seal from the outer tube **(see illustration)**.

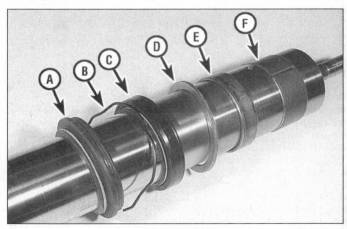

4.7 Seal and bushing details

A	Dust seal	D	Backup ring
B	Retainer	E	Outer tube bushing
C	Oil seal	F	Inner tube bushing

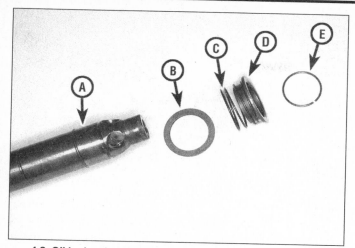

4.8 Oil lock valve details (Aspencade and SE left fork leg)

A	Damper piston	D	Oil lock valve
B	Spring seat	E	Stopper ring
C	Spring		

5   Pry the retaining ring from its groove in the outer tube (see illustration).

6   Unscrew the Allen bolt at the bottom of the outer tube and remove the copper washer (see illustration).

7   Hold the outer tube and yank the inner tube away from it, repeatedly (like a slide hammer), until the seal and outer tube guide bushing pop loose (see illustration).

8   If you're working on an Aspencade or SE left fork, remove the stopper ring, oil lock valve, spring and spring seat from the damper rod (see illustration).

9   If you're working on an Aspencade or SE right fork, remove the stopper ring, oil lock piece, second stopper ring and spring from the end of the damper rod.

10   If you're working on an Interstate (either fork), remove the stopper ring, oil lock piece and spring from the damper rod.

11   Slide the oil seal, backup ring and slider bushing (larger bushing) from the inner tube.

12   If you're working on an Aspencade or SE left fork, remove the antidive unit (see illustrations).

Inspection

Refer to illustration 4.18

13   Clean all parts in solvent and blow them dry with compressed air, if available. Check the inner and outer fork tubes and the damper rod for score marks, scratches, flaking of the chrome and excessive or abnormal wear. Look for dents in the tubes and replace them if any are found. Check the fork seal seat for nicks, gouges and scratches. If damage is evident, leaks will occur around the seal-to-outer tube junction. Replace worn or defective parts with new ones.

14   Check the bushings for scoring, scratches or excessive wear. Replace them if they're scored or scratched, or if the Teflon coating has worn away from more than three-quarters of the surface, exposing the copper. If the bushings need to be replaced, pry them apart at the slit and take them off the fork tube. Install new ones, prying them just enough so they fit over the tube.

15   Check the inner circumference of the backup ring and replace it if it looks bent or distorted.

16   Have the inner fork tube checked for runout at a dealer service department or other repair shop. Warning: *If it is bent, it should not be straightened; replace it with a new one.*

17   Measure the overall length of the fork spring(s) and check for cracks and other damage. Compare the length to the minimum length listed in this Chapter's Specifications. If it's defective or sagged, replace the springs in both forks with new ones. Never replace the spring(s) in only one fork.

4.12a Remove the Allen bolts . . .

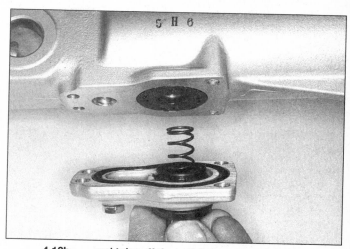

4.12b . . . and take off the antidive cover and spring

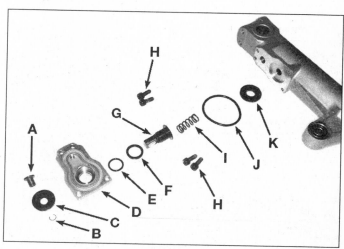

4.12c Antidive unit details

A	Pivot collar	G	Piston
B	Stopper ring	H	Allen bolts
C	Boot	I	Spring
D	Cover	J	Cover O-ring
E	O-ring	K	Seal
F	Seal		

6

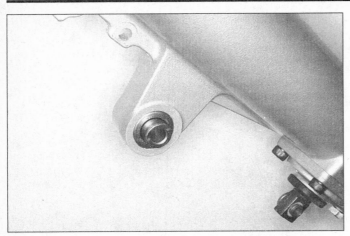

4.18 Pull the collar out to inspect the needle bearing

18   Slide the collar out of the anti-dive bearing (Aspencade and SE left fork legs) **(see illustration)**. Check the needle bearing for wear or damage and replace it if necessary. To install the new bearing without damaging it, you'll need a hydraulic press and a shouldered bearing driver with a small diameter the same diameter as the inside of the bearing, and a large diameter the same as the bearing outer diameter. If you don't have the necessary equipment, a machine shop or Honda dealer service department can press the bearing for you.

19   Check the Teflon rings on the damper rod and replace them if they're worn or damaged.

20   If the fork has an anti-dive unit, inspect the components for wear or damage **(see illustration 4.12)**. **Note:** *A swollen anti-dive O-ring can freeze the unit, causing a very harsh ride.*

Reassembly

Refer to illustrations 4.27a, 4.27b, 4.28 and 4.32

21   Install the rebound spring on the damper rod. Install the damper rod in the inner fork tube, then let it slide slowly down until it protrudes from the bottom of the inner fork tube.

22   If you're working on an Interstate, install the oil lock piece and stopper ring on the damper rod.

23   If you're working on an Aspencade or SE, install the upper stopper ring, oil lock piece and second stopper ring on the end of the damper rod.

24   If you're working on an Aspencade or SE left fork, install the spring seat, spring, oil lock valve and stopper ring on the damper rod **(see illustration 4.8)**.

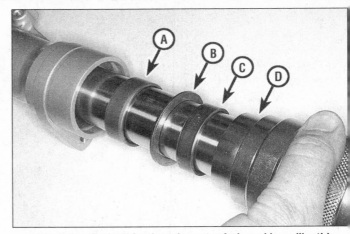

4.27a Drive the bushing into the outer fork seal bore like this

A   New bushing   C   Old bushing (used as a
B   Backup ring   spacer)
                               D   Fork seal driver

25   Install the inner fork tube in the outer fork tube.

26   Temporarily install the fork spring and cap bolt. Apply non-permanent thread locking agent to the damper rod bolt, then install the bolt and tighten it to the torque listed in this Chapter's Specifications.

27   Slide the slider bushing down the inner tube, then slide the backup ring on behind it. Using a fork seal driver (Honda tool 07947-KA50100 and FK00100 or equivalent) and a used slider bushing placed on top of the slider bushing being installed, drive the bushing into place until it's fully seated **(see illustration)**. If you don't have access to one of these tools, it is highly recommended that you take the assembly to a Honda dealer service department or other motorcycle repair shop to have this done. It is possible, however, to drive the bushing into place using a section of pipe and an old guide bushing **(see illustration)**. Wrap tape around the ends of the pipe to prevent it from scratching the fork tube. Once you've installed the new bushing, remove the old one that was used as a spacer.

28   Lubricate the lips and the outer diameter of the oil seal with the recommended fork oil (see Chapter 1) and slide it down the inner tube, with the seal lip facing into the outer fork tube. Drive the seal into place with the same tool used to drive in the slider bushing **(see illustration)**. If you don't have access to these, it is recommended that you take the assembly to a Honda dealer service department or other motorcycle repair shop to have the seal driven in. If you are very careful, the seal can be driven in with a hammer and a drift punch. Work around the

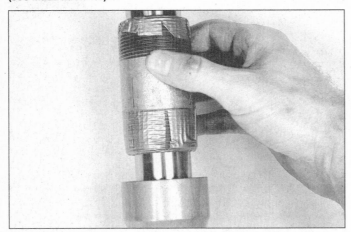

4.27b If you don't have a seal driver, a section of pipe can be used the same way the seal driver would be used - as a slide hammer (be sure to tape the ends of the pipe so it doesn't scratch the fork tube)

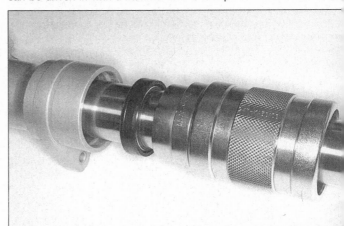

4.28 Drive the oil seal in with the same tool used to install the bushing

4.32 Measure fork oil level with a vernier caliper, ruler or steel tape measure

circumference of the seal, tapping gently on the outer edge of the seal until it's seated. Be careful - if you distort the seal, you'll have to disassemble the fork again and end up taking it to a dealer anyway!

29　Install the retainer ring, making sure it's completely seated in its groove.

30　Install the dust seal, making sure it seats completely. The same tool used to drive in the oil seal can be used for the dust seal.

31　Install the anti-dive assembly (if equipped).

32　Add the recommended type and amount of fork oil. Pump the fork up and down several times, then measure oil level with the spring removed and the fork fully compressed **(see illustration)**.

33　Install the fork spring, with the closer-wound coils at the bottom. Install the spring seat and spacer.

34　Install the O-ring and fork cap.

35　Install the fork by following the procedure outlined in Section 3. If you won't be installing the fork right away, store it in an upright position.

5　Steering head bearings - adjustment and lubrication

Adjustment

Refer to illustrations 5.2, 5.3, 5.4a, 5.4b, 5.7a, 5.7b, 5.9a, 5.9b, 5.9c and 5.10

1　This procedure is shown with the fairing removed for clarity. It can be done without removing the fairing.

2　Remove two screws and detach the under cover from the steering stem **(see illustration)**.

3　Release the ends of the wiring harness retainers in front of the ignition switch, but don't remove them from the frame or you'll need new ones **(see illustration)**.

4　If you're working on an Aspencade or SE, pull the rubber grommet off the top of the steering stem. Lubricate the wiring harness with soapy water, then slide the grommet down the harness to the white tape **(see illustrations)**.

5.2 Remove two screws and the steering stem under cover

5.3 Unwrap the wiring harness retainers, but don't detach them from the frame or you'll need new ones

5.4a Pull the grommet off the steering stem . . .

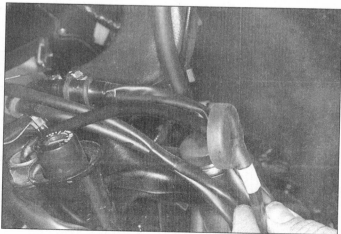

5.4b . . . and slide it down the harness to the white tape

6

5.5a Unscrew the self-canceling turn signal unit

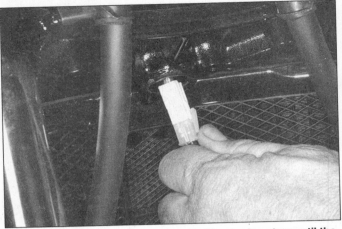

5.5b Push the harness down through the steering stem until the connector is exposed, then unplug it

5.7a Release the harnesses from the retainer on top of the triple clamp . . .

5.7b . . . then undo the steering stem upper nut and lift the triple clamp off

5   Remove two screws and undo the turn signal self-canceling unit from the bottom of the steering stem **(see illustration)**. Push the wiring harness into the top of the steering stem until the grommet reaches it; this will provide enough slack so you can unplug the self-canceling unit's electrical connector **(see illustration)**. Once the connector's unplugged, pull the harness out the top of the steering stem.

6   Refer to Section 2 and remove the handlebars.

7   Release the wiring harnesses from the retainer on top of the upper triple clamp, then remove the steering stem upper nut **(see illustrations)**.

8   Remove the upper triple clamp pinch bolts (Section 3) and remove the upper triple clamp.

9   Bend back the lockwasher tabs and unscrew the steering stem locknut **(see illustrations)**.

5.9a Bend the lockwasher tabs away from the locknut . . .

5.9b . . . then undo the locknut with this special tool or an adjustable spanner wrench . . .

5.9c . . . and take the locknut and lockwasher off

5.10 Undo or tighten the steering stem nut with the same tool used on the locknut

6.5a Lower the steering stem out the bottom of the steering head . . .

6.5b . . . and lift the upper bearing out of the top

10   Carefully tighten the steering stem nut to the initial torque listed in this Chapter's Specifications **(see illustration)**. Turn the steering stem from full left lock to full right lock five times to seat the bearings. Loosen the nut just until it's handtight (not all the way) and retighten to the final torque listed in this Chapter's Specifications.

11   Once again, turn the steering stem from lock-to-lock five times,

then loosen it until handtight and retighten to the final torque.

12   A third time, turn the steering stem from lock-to-lock five times. This time, don't loosen the nut; finish by tightening to the final torque.

13   Turn the steering from lock-to-lock and check for binding. If there is any, remove the bearings for inspection (Section 6).

14   If the steering operates properly, install a new lockwasher with its tabs in the slots of the steering stem nut. Tighten the locknut with fingers only (don't use tools) so its slots align with those of the steering stem nut (don't allow the steering stem nut to turn). **Note:** *The lockwasher tabs are offset. If you can't get the locknut slots to align with the tabs, try removing the nut and turning the lockwasher over.*

15   Bend two of the lockwasher tabs into locknut slots.

16   Recheck the steering head bearings for play as described in Chapter 1. If necessary, repeat the adjustment procedure. Reinstall all parts previously removed. Tighten the steering stem nut, triple clamp bolts and handlebar bolts to the torques listed in this Chapter's Specifications.

Lubrication

17   Periodic cleaning and repacking of the steering head bearings is recommended by the manufacturer. Refer to Section 6 for steering head bearing lubrication and replacement procedures.

6   Steering head bearings - replacement

Refer to illustrations 6.5a, 6.5b, 6.5c, 6.8, 6.9, 6.11 and 6.14

1   If the steering head bearing adjustment (Section 5) does not remedy excessive play or roughness in the steering head bearings, the entire front end must be disassembled and the bearings and races replaced with new ones.

2   Remove the front wheel (Chapter 7), the front forks (Section 3), the handlebars (Section 2) and the front fender (Chapter 8).

3   Refer to Section 5 and remove the upper triple clamp, steering stem locknut and steering stem lockwasher.

4   Remove the steering stem nut and bearing cover **(see illustration 5.10)**.

5   Lower the steering stem and lower triple clamp assembly out of the steering head, then remove the upper bearing **(see illustrations)**. If it's stuck, gently tap on the top of the steering stem with a plastic mallet or a hammer and a wood block.

6   Clean all the parts with solvent and dry them thoroughly, using compressed air, if available. If you do use compressed air, don't let the bearings spin as they're dried - it could ruin them. Wipe the old grease out of the frame steering head and bearing races.

7   Examine the races in the steering head for cracks, dents, and pits. If even the slightest amount of wear or damage is evident, the races should be replaced with new ones.

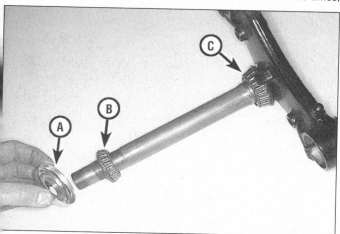

6.5c The bearings fit on the steering stem like this

A   Cover
B   Upper bearing
C   Lower bearing and grease seal

6

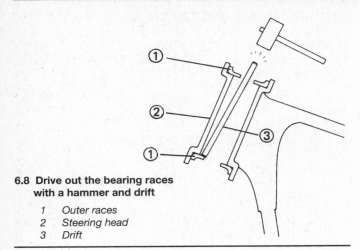

6.8 Drive out the bearing races with a hammer and drift

1   Outer races
2   Steering head
3   Drift

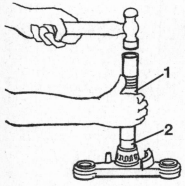

6.11 Drive the grease seal and bearing lower race on with a hollow driver (or an equivalent piece of pipe)

1   Driver
2   Bearing and grease seal

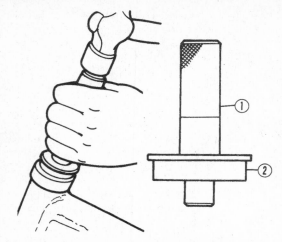

6.9 Drive in the bearing races with a bearing driver or socket the same diameter as the bearing race

1   Bearing driver handle   2   Bearing driver

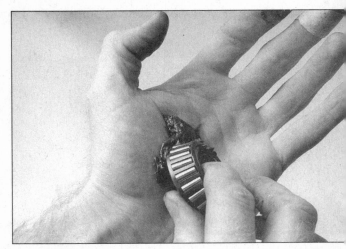

6.14 Work the grease completely into the rollers or balls

8   To remove the bearing races, drive them out of the steering head with a hammer and long rod **(see illustration)**. A slide hammer with the proper internal-jaw puller will also work.

9   Since the races are an interference fit in the frame, installation will be easier if the new races are left overnight in a refrigerator. This will cause them to contract and slip into place in the frame with very little effort. When installing the races, tap them gently into place with a hammer and a bearing driver, punch or a large socket **(see illustration)**. Do not strike the bearing surface or the race will be damaged.

10   Check the bearings for wear. Look for cracks, dents, and pits in the races and flat spots on the bearings. Replace any defective parts with new ones. If a new bearing is required, replace both of them as a set.

11   Don't remove the lower bearing unless it, or the grease seal underneath, must be replaced. To remove the bearing from the steering stem, carefully tap between the bearing and steering stem with a hammer and punch. You can also use a bearing splitter and puller setup (these can be rented). Tap the lower bearing on with a hammer and piece of pipe the same diameter as the bearing inner race **(see illustration)**. Don't tap against the rollers or outer race or the bearing will be ruined. As an alternative, take the steering stem to a Honda dealer or motorcycle repair shop for bearing replacement.

12   Check the grease seal under the lower bearing and replace it with a new one if necessary.

13   Inspect the steering stem/lower triple clamp for cracks and other damage. Do not attempt to repair any steering components. Replace them with new parts if defects are found.

14   Pack the bearings with high-quality grease (preferably a moly-based grease) **(see illustration)**. Coat the outer races with grease also.

15   Insert the steering stem/lower triple clamp into the steering head. Install the upper bearing and steering stem nut. Refer to Section 5 and adjust the bearings.

16   The remainder of installation is the reverse of removal.

7   Rear shock absorbers - removal, inspection and installation

Removal

Refer to illustrations 7.3a, 7.3b, 7.4a, 7.4b and 7.5

1   Place the bike on its centerstand. Remove the rear wheel (Chapter 7) and the right saddlebag (Chapter 8).

2   Support the swingarm so it can't drop.

3   If you're working on an Aspencade or SE, note the routing of the air hose over the right shock absorber **(see illustration)**. Place an open-end wrench on the flats of the air hose fitting, then undo the union bolt with another wrench **(see illustration)**.

4   Remove the shock absorber lower bolt and nut **(see illustrations)**.

5   Remove the shock absorber upper bolt and washer **(see illustration)**. Take the shock absorber out. **Caution:** *If you're going to re-use the shocks, store them upright to prevent fluid loss.*

Inspection

6   Check the shock for signs of oil leaks. The oil seal can be replaced, but this is a job for a Honda dealer or service department

7.3a If the bike has an on-board compressor, note the routing of the air hose to the right shock absorber . . .

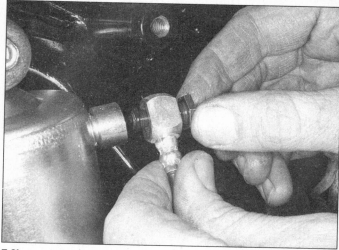

7.3b . . . then hold the fitting with a wrench and unscrew the bolt - there's an O-ring on each end of the bolt

7.4a The lower left shock absorber bolt is threaded near its head . . .

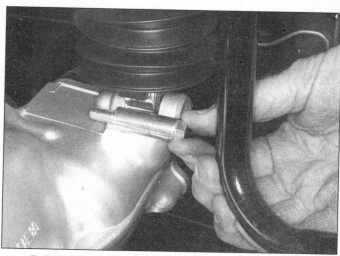

7.4b . . . the lower right bolt is threaded on its end and has a thick shaft

a motorcycle repair shop having the necessary special equipment.

7   Inspect the pivot hardware at the top and bottom of the shock and replace any worn or damaged parts.

Installation

8   Installation is the reverse of the removal procedure, with the following additions:

a) Use new O-rings on the air hose union bolt (if equipped). Lubricate them with Pro Honda suspension fluid or equivalent.

b) Install the upper and lower shock absorber bolts and nuts and the air hose union bolt (if equipped), then tighten them to the torque values listed in this Chapter's Specifications.

8   On-board air compressor - removal and installation

Air pump

Refer to illustration 8.2

1   Remove the rear mounting bolt from the rear fender. Remove the left saddlebag and the trunk (see Chapter 8).

2   Follow the wiring harness from the air pump to its connector, then

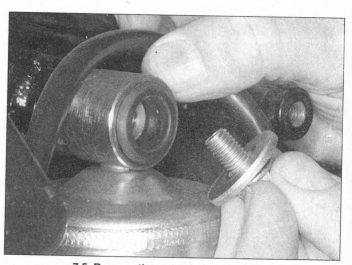

7.5 Remove the upper bolt and washer

6

**8.2 The air compressor is mounted behind
the left shock absorber**

8.7 Air distributor mounting details

A	*Outlet air hose*	*C*	*Air pressure sensor*
B	*Inlet air hose*	*D*	*Solenoids*

unplug the connector **(see illustration)**.
3   Remove the air pump mounting bolts and collars **(see illustration
8.2)**. Lift the pump out for access and disconnect the air hoses. **Note:**
Don't remove the screw from the end of the pump.
4   To test the pump motor, connect it directly to the battery with a
pair of jumper wires. If the pump doesn't run, replace it.
5   Installation is the reverse of the removal steps, with the following
additions:
  a) *Use new O-rings on the air hose fittings and lubricate them with
     Pro Honda suspension fluid or equivalent.*
  b) *Tighten the air hose fitting and air hose union bolt to the torque
     listed in this Chapter's Specifications.*

Air distributor

Refer to illustration 8.7
6   Remove the left saddlebag and the trunk (see Chapter 8).
7   Follow the wiring harness from the air pump to its connector, then
unplug the connector **(see illustration)**.
8   Remove the union bolt from the outlet air hose fitting. Disconnect
the hose from the air distributor, then remove the air distributor from
the fender.
9   Remove the union bolt from the inlet air hose fitting, then detach
the hose and remove the steel ball, spring seat and spring.
10   Disconnect the drain tube from the relief valve to separate the air
distributor from the motorcycle.

11   Check the passages in the air distributor for clogging. Blow them
out with compressed air.
12   Installation is the reverse of the removal steps, with the following
additions:
  a) *Use new O-rings on the air hose fittings and lubricate them with
     automatic transmission fluid.*
  b) *If the air pressure sensor or solenoids were removed the air dis-
     tributor, use new O-rings on installation.*
  c) *Tighten the air hose union bolts (and the solenoid screws and air
     pressure sensor, if removed) to the torques listed in this Chapter's
     Specifications.*

9   Final drive unit - removal, inspection and installation

Removal

Refer to illustrations 9.2a, 9.2b and 9.2c
1   Place the bike on its centerstand and remove the rear wheel (see
Chapter 7).
2   Remove the final drive unit mounting nuts and separate the unit
from the swingarm **(see illustrations)**.
3   To remove the driveshaft from the final drive unit, slip the axle and

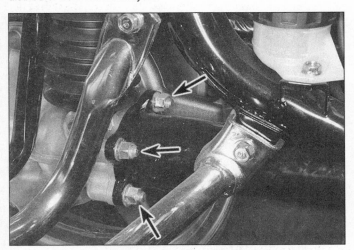

**9.2a Remove the four mounting nuts (arrows); one nut is hidden
behind the swingarm**

9.2b Pull the final drive unit and driveshaft rearward

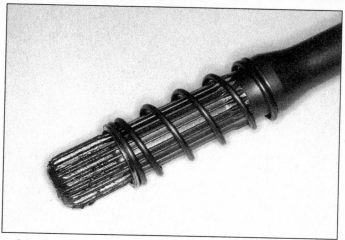

9.2c At the front of the driveshaft, remove the snap-ring and spring seat, then slide the spring off

9.5 Check the final drive unit oil seal for leaks; on installation, make sure the spacer is in position

spacer back into the final drive unit. Grasp the forward end of the driveshaft and wiggle it in a circle while pulling it away from the final drive unit. The stopper ring will provide some resistance, then the driveshaft should pull free of the final drive unit.

4   Remove the snap-ring from the forward end of the driveshaft, then slip the spring seat, spring and oil seal off the driveshaft.

Inspection

Refer to illustrations 9.5 and 9.7

5   Look into the axle holes and check for obvious signs of wear or damage such as broken gear teeth **(see illustration)**. Also check the seals for signs of leakage. Slip the driveshaft into its splines (if it was removed) and turn the pinion by hand.

6   Differential overhaul is a complicated procedure that requires several special tools, for which there are no readily available substitutes. If there's visible wear or damage, or if the differential rotation is rough or noisy, take it to a Honda dealer for disassembly and further inspection.

7   Check the coupling flange in the rear wheel for wear or damage **(see illustration)**. If necessary, remove the nuts and separate the flange from the wheel.

Installation

8   Installation is the reverse of the removal steps, with the following additions:

a) *Install a new driveshaft oil seal if you removed the driveshaft from the final drive unit. The stopper ring was used for initial assembly and need not be reinstalled.*

b) *On all models, lubricate the splines of the coupling and the final drive unit with Honda moly 60 grease or equivalent.*

c) *If you're working on a 1988 or 1989 model, lubricate the inside diameter of the coupling and the flange pins (if the flange was removed from the wheel) with Honda moly 60 or equivalent.*

d) *If you're working on a 1990 or later model, DO NOT lubricate the flange pins. They ride in aluminum collars and grease will increase wear, not reduce it.*

e) *Be sure the spacer is in the final drive unit* **(see illustration 9.5)**.

f) *Install the final drive unit loosely. Tighten to the torque listed in this Chapter's Specifications after the rear axle is installed.*

g) *Check the final drive unit oil level (see Chapter 1).*

0   Swingarm bearings - check

Remove the rear wheel and detach the brake hose and line from the swingarm (see Chapter 7). Unbolt the rear master cylinder, but eave its hose connected.

Remove the shock absorbers (Section 7). Leave the air hose con-

9.7 Coupling lubrication procedures differ according to model year; see text for details

nected to the right shock and keep it upright. Remove the final drive unit (Section 9).

3   Grasp the rear of the swingarm with one hand and place your other hand at the junction of the swingarm and the frame. Try to move the rear of the swingarm from side-to-side. Any wear (play) in the bearings should be felt as movement between the swingarm and the frame at the front. The swingarm will actually be felt to move forward and backward at the front (not from side-to-side). If any play is noted, the bearings should be replaced with new ones (see Section 12).

4   Next, move the swingarm up and down through its full travel. It should move freely, without any binding or rough spots. If it does not move freely, refer to Section 12 for servicing procedures.

11   Swingarm - removal and installation

Note: *Loosening and tightening the pivot bolt locknut on the left side of the swingarm requires a special wrench for which there is no alternative. If you don't have the special Honda tool or an exact equivalent, the locknut must be unscrewed (and later tightened) by a Honda dealer.*

Removal

Refer to illustrations 11.4a, 11.4b, 11.4c, 11.5 and 11.6

1   Perform Steps 1 and 2 of Section 10.

2   Remove the battery, battery case and resistor pack (see Chapter 9).

3   Remove the exhaust chamber and its heat shield (see Chapter 4).

6

11.4a Use this tool to loosen and tighten the swingarm locknut

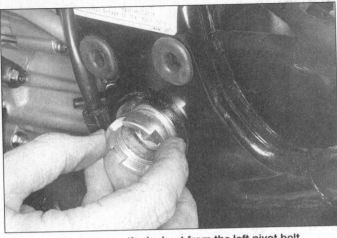

11.4b Unscrew the locknut from the left pivot bolt

11.4c Use a 17 mm Allen bolt bit in a socket to hold the left pivot bolt while you loosen and tighten the locknut and to unscrew both pivot bolts

11.5 On installation, grease the pivot bolt tips and make sure they engage the swingarm bearings

4   Undo the locknut on the left pivot bolt, using Honda tool KS-HBA-08-469 or equivalent **(see illustrations)**. While you're undoing the locknut, hold the pivot bolt from turning with a 17 mm Allen bolt bit. These are available from tool stores.

5   Unscrew the swingarm pivot bolts with the Allen bolt bit **(see illustration)**.

6   Pull the swingarm back and remove it from the frame, separating the universal joint from the output shaft as you pull **(see illustration)**.

7   Check the pivot bearings in the swingarm for dryness or deterioration (See Section 12). Lubricate or replace them as necessary.

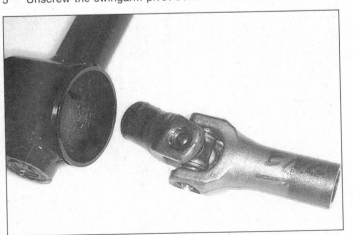

11.6 The long end of the universal joint goes toward the engine

11.8 The universal joint passes through the boot and fits over the splines on the output shaft

Installation

Refer to illustration 11.8

8   Lubricate the universal splines with moly-based grease. Make sure the universal joint boot is in place, then install the universal joint in the swingarm with its long end toward the engine **(see illustration 11.6 and the accompanying illustration)**.

9   Place the swingarm in its installed position in the frame, but don't install the universal joint on the output shaft yet. Grease the tips of the pivot bolts and thread them into their holes, making sure the tips fit into the swingarm bearings. Don't tighten the pivot bolts yet.

10   Slide the universal joint forward onto the output shaft.

11   **Note:** *The swingarm pivot bolts and locknut must be tightened in the specified sequence and to the correct torque settings.* Tighten the right pivot bolt to the torque listed in this Chapter's Specifications. Tighten the left pivot bolt after tightening the right pivot bolt. The left pivot bolt's specified torque is much lower than that of the right pivot bolt.

12   Raise and lower the swingarm several times to seat the bearings, then retighten the left pivot bolt to its specified torque.

13   Thread the locknut onto the left pivot bolt as far as you can with fingers. Then place the special wrench on the locknut and install a torque wrench in the special wrench's square hole. Hold the pivot bolt with the 17 mm Allen bit so it won't turn, then tighten the locknut to the torque listed in this Chapter's Specifications. **Note:** *The special wrench increases the torque applied to the nut, so the specified torque is less than the actual applied torque.*

14   The remainder of installation is the reverse of the removal steps.

12 Swingarm bearings - replacement

Refer to illustration 12.3

1   The swingarm rides in a pair of tapered roller bearings.

2   Remove the swingarm from the motorcycle (see Section 11).

3   Take the bearings and outer seals out of the swingarm **(see illustration)**.

4   Clean all the parts with solvent and dry them thoroughly, using compressed air, if available. If you do use compressed air, don't let the bearings spin as they're dried - it could ruin them. Wipe the old grease out of the swingarm and bearing races.

12.3 The swingarm rides on a pair of tapered roller bearings

5   Examine the races in the swingarm for cracks, dents, and pits. If even the slightest amount of wear or damage is evident, the races should be replaced with new ones. If one race (or one bearing) needs to be replaced, replace both of the bearings, as well as their races and seals, as a set.

6   To remove the bearing races, drive them out of the swingarm with a hammer and long rod. A slide hammer with the proper internal-jaw puller will also work. Remove the internal grease retainers as well.

7   Since the races are an interference fit in the swingarm, installation will be easier if the new races are left overnight in a refrigerator. This will cause them to contract and slip into place in the frame with very little effort. When installing the races, tap them gently into place with a hammer and a bearing driver, punch or a large socket. Do not strike the bearing surface or the race will be damaged.

8   Check the bearings for wear. Look for cracks, dents, and pits in the rollers and flat spots on the bearings. Replace any defective parts with new ones. If a new bearing is required, replace both of them, and the bearing races and seals, as a set.

6

Notes

Chapter 7
Brakes, wheels and tires

Contents

Specifications

Brakes

Brake lever free-play and pedal position	See Chapter 1
Brake fluid type	See Chapter 1
Front brake disc thickness	
Standard	5.8 to 6.2 mm (0.23 to 0.24 inch)
Minimum*	5.0 mm (0.20 inch)
Rear brake disc thickness	
Standard	7.3 to 7.7 mm (0.29 to 0.30 inch)
Minimum*	6.0 mm (0.24 inch)

*Refer to marks stamped into the disc (they supersede information printed here)

Disc runout limit	0.3 mm (0.01 inch)
Pad friction material thickness	
Front	
Standard	5.5 mm (0.22 inch)
Minimum	1.0 mm (0.04 inch)
Rear	
Standard	6.5 mm (0.26 inch)
Minimum	1.0 mm (0.04 inch)
Front caliper-to-bracket gap	0.7 mm (0.028 inch)

Wheels and tires

Wheel runout limit	
Radial (up-and-down)	2.0 mm (0.08 inch)
Axial (side-to-side)	2.0 mm (0.08 inch)
Axle runout limit	0.2 mm (0.01 inch)
Tire pressures	See Chapter 1
Tire sizes	See Chapter 1

7

Torque specifications

Front calipers
Mounting bolts
Bracket bolt (with anti-dive) .... 23 Nm (17 ft-lbs)
Anti-dive piston bolt.. 12 Nm (9 ft-lbs)
Lower bracket bolt (without anti-dive) .... 31 Nm (22 ft-lbs)
Pad retaining pins .... 18 Nm (13 ft-lbs)
Pad retaining pin plugs .... 2.5 Nm (22 inch-lbs)
Caliper bleed valve .... 6 Nm (53 in-lbs)
Rear caliper
Pin bolt .... 28 Nm (20 ft-lbs)
Mounting bolt .... 23 Nm (17 ft-lbs)
Pad pin retainer bolt .... 11 Nm (8 ft-lbs)
Brake disc mounting bolts... 40 Nm (29 ft-lbs)
Union (banjo fitting) bolts
1988 through 1990 .... 30 Nm (22 ft-lbs)
1991-on .... 35 Nm 25 ft-lbs)
Metal line flare nuts... 17 Nm (12 ft-lbs)
Master cylinder mounting bolts
Front .... 12 Nm (9 ft-lbs)
Rear .... 12 Nm (9 ft-lbs)
Front axle
Axle bolt .... 90 Nm (65 ft-lbs)
Axle pinch bolts... 22 Nm (16 ft-lbs)
Rear axle
Axle nut .... 110 Nm (80 ft-lbs)
Axle pinch bolt... 32 Nm (23 ft-lbs)
Damper segment retainer plate bolts... 20 Nm (14 ft-lbs)

1   General information

The models covered by this manual are equipped with hydraulic disc brakes on the front and rear. All models use a pair of four-piston calipers at the front and one dual-piston caliper at the rear. The rear brake and left front brake are operated by the brake pedal; the right front brake is operated by the brake lever on the left handlebar independently of the left front brake.

All models are equipped with cast aluminum wheels, which require very little maintenance and allow tubeless tires to be used.

Caution: *Disc brake components rarely require disassembly. Do not disassemble components unless absolutely necessary. If any hydraulic brake line connection in the system is loosened, the entire system should be disassembled, drained, cleaned and then properly filled and bled upon reassembly. Do not use solvents on internal brake components. Solvents will cause seals to swell and distort. Use only clean brake fluid, brake cleaner or alcohol for cleaning. Use care when working with brake fluid as it can injure your eyes and it will damage painted surfaces and plastic parts.*

2   Brake pads - replacement

Front calipers

Refer to illustrations 2.2a, 2.2b, 2.3a, 2.3b, 2.4a, 2.4b and 2.6

Warning: *When replacing the front brake pads always replace the pads in BOTH calipers - never just on one side. Replace the anti-squeal shims and pad spring whenever the pads are replaced. Also, the dust created by the brake system may contain asbestos, which is harmful to your health. Never blow it out with compressed air and don't inhale any of it. An approved filtering mask should be worn when working on the brakes.*

1   Place the bike on its centerstand. Refer to Chapter 8 and remove the brake disc covers.

2   Unscrew the pad pin plugs, then unscrew the pad pins **(see illustrations)**.

3   Unbolt the caliper bracket from the fork and pull the caliper off the bracket **(see illustrations)**.

4   Lift the pads out of the caliper **(see illustrations)**.

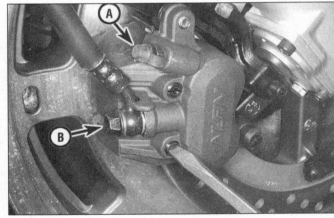

2.2a Unscrew the pad pin plugs

A   *Bleed valve*   B   *Banjo fitting bolt*

2.2b Unscrew the pad pins with an Allen wrench

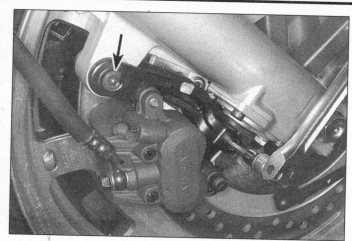

2.3a Unscrew the caliper bracket upper bolt (arrow) and the anti-dive piston bolt (or the lower bracket bolt on fork legs without anti-dive)

2.3b Take the bracket off and slide the caliper off the bracket

5   Check the condition of the brake discs (see Section 4). If they are in need of machining or replacement, follow the procedure in that Section to remove them. If they are okay, deglaze them with sandpaper or emery cloth, using a swirling motion.

6   Check the rubber pin bushings in the caliper and bracket **(see illustration 2.4b and the accompanying illustration)**. Replace them if they're deteriorated or damaged.

7   Remove the cap from the master cylinder reservoirs (front reservoir for the right caliper and rear reservoir for the left caliper) and siphon out some fluid. Push the pistons into the caliper as far as possible, while checking the master cylinder reservoirs to make sure they don't overflow. If you can't depress the pistons with thumb pressure, try using a pry bar or C-clamp. If the pistons stick, remove the caliper and overhaul it as described in Section 3.

8   Make sure the shim is in place on the outer pad and the steel shield is in place on the bracket **(see illustration 2.6)**. Lubricate the pin bushings with silicone grease and install the caliper on the bracket.

9   Install the pad spring in the caliper, then install the pads **(see illustrations 2.4b and 2.4a)**. Press the pads down against the spring and install the pad pins. Thread the pins partway in, but wait until the caliper is installed to torque them.

10   If the fork leg has an antidive unit, lubricate its needle bearing with multi-purpose grease. Install the bracket bolt and antidive unit bolt (or both bracket bolts if the fork leg doesn't have an antidive unit).

11   Tighten the bracket bolts to the torque listed in this Chapter's Specifications. Tighten the pad pins to the specified torque, then install

2.4a Pull the pads out of the caliper . . .

the pad pin plugs and tighten them to their specified torque.

12   Refill the master cylinder reservoir (see Chapter 1) and install the diaphragm and cover. Operate the brake lever several times to bring the pads into contact with the disc.

13   Reinstall the disc brake covers (see Chapter 8).

14   Check the operation of the brakes carefully before riding the motorcycle.

2.4b . . . remove the pad spring (arrow) and check the condition of the pin bushing (arrow)

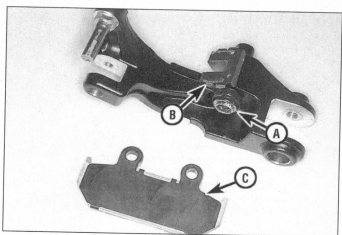

2.6 Inspect the bracket's pin bushing (A); be sure the bracket shield (B) and pad shim (C) are in place

7

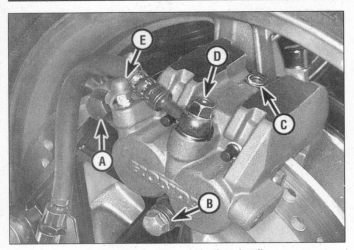

2.16a Rear caliper mounting details

A   Pin bolt
B   Mounting bolt
C   Pad pin retainer bolt
    position

D   Brake hose union bolt
E   Bleed valve

2.16b Lift the caliper off and remove the pad pin retainer (arrow)

Rear calipers

Refer to illustrations 2.16a, 2.16b, 2.17a, 2.17b, 2.20a, 2.20b and 2.20c

Warning: *The dust created by the brake system may contain asbestos, which is harmful to your health. Never blow it out with compressed air and don't inhale any of it. An approved filtering mask should be worn when working on the brakes. Replace the anti-squeal shims and pad spring whenever the pads are replaced.*

15   Place the bike on its centerstand. Refer to Chapter 8 and remove the left saddlebag.

16   Undo the pad pin retainer bolt, then remove the mounting bolts and take the caliper off the bike **(see illustrations)**.

17   Remove the pad pin retainer and pull out the pins, then take the pads out of the caliper **(see illustrations)**.

18   Perform Step 7 above to inspect the disc and prepare the caliper for pad installation.

19   Make sure the pad spring is in position with its tabs toward the wheel side of the caliper, then install the pads **(see illustration 2.17b)**.

20   Align the pin holes in the pads with the holes in the caliper, then install the pad pins. Slip the retainer over the ends of the pins so it engages the pin grooves, then bolt the retainer to the caliper **(see illustrations)**. Tighten the retainer bolt slightly at this point.

21   Lubricate the caliper pin bolt with silicone grease, then position the caliper on the bracket and install the pin bolt and mounting bolt.

2.17a Pull out the pad pins . . .

Tighten the pin bolt, mounting bolt and pad pin retainer bolt to th torque listed in this Chapter's Specifications.

22   Refill the master cylinder reservoir (see Chapter 1).

23   Operate the brake pedal to bring the pads back into contact wit the disc. Check the operation of the brakes carefully before riding th motorcycle.

24   Refer to Chapter 8 and install the left saddlebag.

2.17b . . . lift out the pads and remove the pad spring (arrow)

2.20a Align the pin holes in the caliper and pad

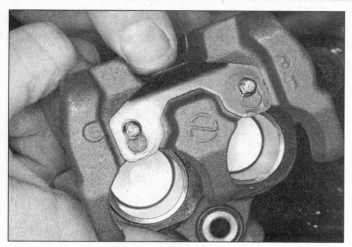

2.20b Engage the retainer holes with the grooves in the pad pins

2.20c Bolt the retainer to the caliper

3 Brake caliper - removal, overhaul and installation

Warning: *If a front caliper indicates the need for an overhaul (usually due to leaking fluid or sticky operation), BOTH front calipers should be overhauled and all old brake fluid flushed from the system. Also, the dust created by the brake system may contain asbestos, which is harmful to your health. Never blow it out with compressed air and don't inhale any of it. An approved filtering mask should be worn when working on the brakes. Do not, under any circumstances, use petroleum-based solvents to clean brake parts. Use brake cleaner or denatured alcohol only!*

Removal

1   Support the bike securely so it can't be knocked over during this procedure.

2   With a clean rag handy to catch spills, remove the brake hose banjo fitting bolt and separate the hose from the caliper **(see illustrations 2.2a and 2.16a)**. Discard the sealing washers. Place the end of the hose in a container and operate the brake lever to pump out the fluid. Once this is done, wrap a clean shop rag tightly around the hose fitting to soak up any drips and prevent contamination.

3   Unscrew the caliper mounting bolts **(see illustrations 2.3a and 2.16a)**.

4   Lift off the caliper and remove the brake pads (see Section 2).

Overhaul

Refer to illustration 3.8

5   Clean the exterior of the caliper with denatured alcohol or brake system cleaner.

6   If the bike's hydraulic system is in reasonably good condition, it can be used to remove the pistons from the calipers. Leave the fluid hose connected and remove the caliper and pads. Place a drain pan under the caliper to catch the brake fluid that will run out. **Caution:** *Place rags or plastic over nearby painted or plated parts to protect them from brake fluid splashes. Wash off any splashes immediately with soap and water to prevent damage to the surfaces.* Pump the lever or pedal a few times to force the pistons out of the caliper. If one piston comes out faster than the other one, slip a piece of wood into the pad area to block that piston until the other one is forced out.

7   If the hydraulic system isn't in good enough condition to push the pistons out, you'll need to use compressed air. Disconnect the hose from the caliper. Place a few rags between the pistons and the caliper frame to act as a cushion, then use compressed air, directed into the fluid inlet, to remove the pistons. Use only enough air pressure to ease the pistons out of the bore. If a piston is blown out, even with the cushion in place, it may be damaged. **Warning:** *Never place your fingers in front of the piston in an attempt to catch or protect it when applying compressed air, as serious injury could occur.*

8   Using a wood or plastic tool, remove the dust seals and piston seals **(see illustration)**. Metal tools may cause bore damage.

9   Clean the pistons and the bores with denatured alcohol, clean brake fluid or brake system cleaner and blow dry them with filtered, unlubricated compressed air. Inspect the surfaces of the pistons for nicks and burrs and loss of plating.

10   Check the caliper bores. If surface defects are present, the caliper must be replaced. If the caliper is in bad shape, the master cylinder should also be checked.

11   Lubricate new piston seals with clean brake fluid and install them in their grooves in the caliper bore. Make sure they aren't twisted and seat completely.

12   Lubricate new dust seals with clean brake fluid and install them in their grooves, making sure they seat correctly.

13   Lubricate the pistons with clean brake fluid and install them into the caliper bores. Using your thumbs, push the pistons all the way in, making sure they don't get cocked in the bores.

Installation

14   Refer to Section 2 and install the brake pads and caliper.

15   Connect the brake hose to the caliper, using new sealing washers on each side of the fitting. Align the banjo fitting with its tab and tighten the bolt to the torque listed in this Chapter's Specifications.

16   Fill the master cylinder with the recommended brake fluid (see Chapter 1) and bleed the system (see Section 8). Check for leaks.

17   Check the operation of the brakes carefully before riding the motorcycle.

7

3.8 Remove the pistons, then the dust seals (upper arrow) and piston seals (lower arrow)

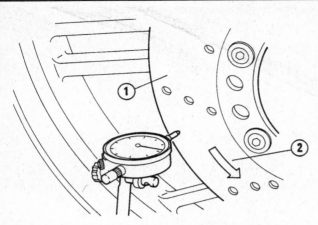

4.3 Set up a dial indicator against the brake disc (1) and turn the disc in its normal direction of rotation (2) to measure runout

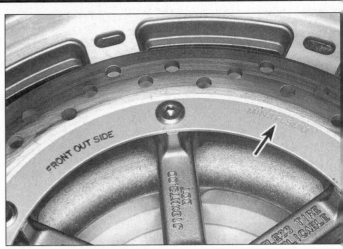

4.4 The minimum thickness is stamped into the disc (arrow)

4   Brake discs - inspection, removal and installation

Inspection

Refer to illustrations 4.3 and 4.4

1   Support the bike securely so it can't be knocked over during this procedure, with the wheel to be checked off the ground.

2   Visually inspect the surface of the disc(s) for score marks and other damage. Light scratches are normal after use and won't affect brake operation, but deep grooves and heavy score marks will reduce braking efficiency and accelerate pad wear. If the discs are badly grooved they must be machined or replaced.

3   To check disc runout, mount a dial indicator to a fork leg or the swingarm, with the plunger on the indicator touching the surface of the disc about 1/2-inch from the outer edge **(see illustration)**. Slowly turn the wheel and watch the indicator needle, comparing your reading with the limit listed in this Chapter's Specifications. If the runout is greater than allowed, check the hub bearings for play (see Section 9). If the bearings are worn, replace them and repeat this check. If the disc runout is still excessive, it will have to be replaced.

4   The disc must not be machined or allowed to wear down to a thickness less than the minimum allowable thickness, stamped on the disc and listed in this Chapter's Specifications **(see illustration)**. The thickness of the disc can be checked with a micrometer. If the thickness of the disc is less than the minimum allowable, it must be replaced.

Removal

Refer to illustration 4.6

5   Remove the wheel (see Section 11 for front wheel removal or Section 12 for rear wheel removal). **Caution:** *Don't lay the wheel down and allow it to rest on one of the discs - the disc could become warped. Set the wheel on wood blocks so the disc doesn't support the weight of the wheel.*

6   Mark the relationship of the disc to the wheel, so it can be installed in the same position. Look for L and R marks on the left and right front discs. If you don't see them, make your own. Remove the Allen head bolts that retain the disc to the wheel **(see illustration)**. Loosen the bolts a little at a time, in a criss-cross pattern, to avoid distorting the disc. Once all the bolts are loose, take the disc off.

Installation

7   Position the disc on the wheel, aligning the previously applied matchmarks (if you're reinstalling the original disc). Make sure the FRONT OUT SIDE or REAR OUT SIDE mark on the disc faces away from the wheel **(see illustration 4.6)**. If you're installing a front disc, make sure the disc with the L mark goes on the left side of the bike and the disc with the R mark goes on the right side.

4.6 Front discs are marked L for left or R for right (arrow)

8   Install the Allen bolts, tightening them a little at a time, in a criss-cross pattern, until the torque listed in this Chapter's Specifications is reached. Thoroughly clean off all grease from the brake disc(s) using acetone or brake system cleaner.

9   Install the wheel.

10   Operate the brake lever or pedal several times to bring the pads into contact with the disc. Check the operation of the brakes carefully before riding the motorcycle.

5   Front brake master cylinder - removal, overhaul and installation

1   If the master cylinder is leaking fluid, or if the lever does not produce a firm feel when the brake is applied, and bleeding the brakes does not help, master cylinder overhaul is recommended. Before disassembling the master cylinder, read through the entire procedure and make sure that you have the correct rebuild kit. Also, you will need some new, clean brake fluid of the recommended type, some clean rags and internal snap-ring pliers. **Note:** *To prevent damage to the paint from spilled brake fluid, always cover plastic or plated parts when working on the master cylinder.*

2   **Caution:** *Disassembly, overhaul and reassembly of the brake master cylinder must be done in a spotlessly clean work area to avoid contamination and possible failure of the brake hydraulic system components.*

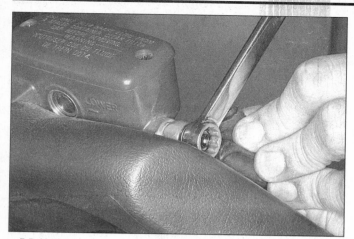

5.5 Undo the union bolt at the master cylinder; on installation, use a new sealing washer on each side of the hose fitting

5.7 Remove the Allen bolts to separate the clamp from the master cylinder; on installation, align the mark on the handlebar trim (arrow) with the split between the clamp and master cylinder

5.9 Remove the rubber boot

Removal

Refer to illustrations 5.5 and 5.7

3   Loosen but do not remove the screws holding the reservoir cover in place.

4   Disconnect the electrical connectors from the brake light switch and the cruise cancel switch if equipped (see Chapter 9).

5   Remove the banjo fitting bolt **(see illustration)** and separate the brake hose from the master cylinder. Wrap the end of the hose in a clean rag and suspend the hose in an upright position or bend it down carefully and place the open end in a clean container. The objective is

to prevent excessive loss of brake fluid, fluid spills and system contamination.

6   Remove the locknut from the underside of the lever pivot bolt, then unscrew the bolt.

7   Remove the plastic cover from the master cylinder mounting bolts (if equipped). Remove the master cylinder mounting bolts **(see illustration)** and separate the master cylinder from the handlebar.

Overhaul

Refer to illustrations 5.9, 5.10a, 5.10b and 5.10c

8   Detach the cover and the rubber diaphragm, then drain the brake fluid into a suitable container. Remove the plate from the bottom of the reservoir (if equipped), then wipe any remaining fluid out of the reservoir with a clean rag.

9   Carefully remove the rubber dust boot from the end of the piston **(see illustration)**.

10   Using snap-ring pliers, remove the snap-ring **(see illustration)** and slide out the piston assembly and the spring **(see illustrations)**. Lay the parts out in the proper order to prevent confusion during reassembly.

11   Clean all of the parts with brake system cleaner (available at auto parts stores), isopropyl alcohol or clean brake fluid. **Caution:** *Do not, under any circumstances, use a petroleum-based solvent to clean brake parts. If compressed air is available, use it to dry the parts thoroughly (make sure it's filtered and unlubricated). Check the master cylinder bore for corrosion, scratches, nicks and score marks. If damage is evident, the master cylinder must be replaced with a new one. If the master cylinder is in poor condition, then the calipers should be checked as well.*

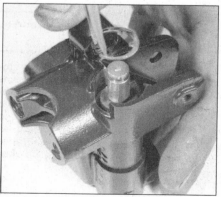

5.10a Remove the snap-ring from the cylinder bore . . .

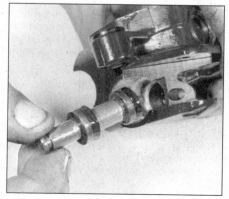

5.10b . . . then pull out the piston assembly . . .

5.10c . . . and spring

7

12   The piston assembly and spring are included in the rebuild kit. Use all of the new parts, regardless of the apparent condition of the old ones.
13   Before reassembling the master cylinder, soak the piston and the rubber cup seals in clean brake fluid for ten or fifteen minutes. Lubricate the master cylinder bore with clean brake fluid, then carefully insert the piston and related parts in the reverse order of disassembly. Make sure the lips on the cup seals do not turn inside out when they are slipped into the bore.
14   Push the piston into the bore against the spring pressure, then install the snap-ring (make sure the snap-ring is properly seated in the groove). Install the rubber dust boot (make sure the lip is seated properly in the piston groove).

Installation

15   Attach the master cylinder to the handlebar, aligning the split in the clamp with the pointer cast in the handlebar trim **(see illustration 5.7)** and tighten the bolts to the torque listed in this Chapter's Specifications.
16   Connect the brake hose to the master cylinder, using new sealing washers. Tighten the banjo fitting bolt to the torque listed in this Chapter's Specifications. Refer to Section 8 and bleed the air from the system.

6   Rear brake master cylinder - removal, overhaul and installation

1   If the master cylinder is leaking fluid, or if the pedal does not produce a firm feel when the brake is applied, and bleeding the brakes does not help, master cylinder overhaul is recommended. Before disassembling the master cylinder, read through the entire procedure and make sure that you have the correct rebuild kit. Also, you will need some new, clean brake fluid of the recommended type, some clean rags and internal snap-ring pliers.
2   **Caution:** *Disassembly, overhaul and reassembly of the brake master cylinder must be done in a spotlessly clean work area to avoid contamination and possible failure of the brake hydraulic system components.*

Removal

Refer to illustration 6.7
3   Support the bike securely so it can't be knocked over during this procedure.
4   Remove both mufflers, the exhaust chamber, the left exhaust pipe assembly and the right heat protector (see Chapter 4).
5   Remove the battery and its tray (see Chapter 8).
6   If you're working on a bike with cruise control, follow the wiring harness from the switch at the rear master cylinder to the two-pin red electrical connector behind the engine control module, then unplug it.
7   Remove the cotter pin from the clevis pin on the master cylinder pushrod **(see illustration)**. Remove the clevis pin.
8   Have a container and some rags ready to catch spilling brake fluid. Remove the union bolt and seals from the banjo fitting on the rear of the master cylinder. Direct the end of the hose into the container, unscrew the cap on the master cylinder reservoir and allow the fluid to drain.
9   Follow the metal line for the front caliper from the master cylinder to its flare nut on the frame, then undo the nut with a flare nut wrench.
10   Remove the mounting bolts **(see illustration 6.7)**. Lift the master cylinder out far enough for access to the reservoir hose clamp, then loosen the clamp and disconnect the reservoir hose from the master cylinder.

Overhaul

11   Pull the boot away from the end of the master cylinder. Depress the pushrod and, using snap-ring pliers, remove the snap-ring. Slide out the piston assembly, separate cup and spring. Lay the parts out in the proper order to prevent confusion during reassembly.
12   Clean all of the parts with brake system cleaner (available at auto parts stores), isopropyl alcohol or clean brake fluid. **Caution:** *Do not, under any circumstances, use a petroleum-based solvent to clean brake parts. If compressed air is available, use it to dry the parts thoroughly (make sure it's filtered and unlubricated).* Check the master cylinder bore

6.7   Remove the clevis pin (A), brake hose union bolt (B) and mounting bolts (C); on installation, use a new sealing washer on each side of the hose fitting

for corrosion, scratches, nicks and score marks. If damage is evident, the master cylinder must be replaced with a new one. If the master cylinder is in poor condition, then the caliper should be checked as well.
13   A new piston, separate cup and spring are included in the rebuild kit. Use them regardless of the condition of the old ones.
14   Before reassembling the master cylinder, soak the piston and the rubber cup seals in clean brake fluid for ten or fifteen minutes. Lubricate the master cylinder bore with clean brake fluid, then carefully insert the parts in the reverse order of disassembly. The flat side of the separate cup faces out of the bore (toward the piston). Make sure the lips on the cup seals do not turn inside out when they are slipped into the bore.
15   Depress the pushrod, then install the snap-ring (make sure the snap-ring is properly seated in the groove). Install the rubber dust boot (make sure the lip is seated properly in the groove).

Installation

16   Connect the reservoir hose to the master cylinder.
17   Thread the flare nut on the front caliper line into its fitting with fingers, then tighten it with a flare nut wrench. Connect the banjo fitting to the end of the master cylinder, using a new sealing washer on each side of the fitting. Tighten the union bolt to the torque listed in this Chapter's Specifications.
18   Connect the fluid feed hose to the inlet fitting and install the hose clamp.
19   Bolt the master cylinder to the frame and tighten its bolts to the torque listed in this Chapter's Specifications.
20   Connect the clevis to the brake pedal and secure the clevis pin with a new cotter pin.
21   Fill the fluid reservoir with the specified fluid (see Chapter 1) and bleed the system following the procedure in Section 8.
22   Check the position of the brake pedal (see Chapter 1) and adjust it if necessary. Check the operation of the brakes carefully before riding the motorcycle.
23   The remainder of installation is the reverse of the removal steps.

7   Brake hoses - inspection and replacement

Inspection

Refer to illustrations 7.2a through 7.2e
1   Periodically check the condition of the brake hoses.
2   Twist and flex the rubber hoses **(see illustrations 2.2a and the accompanying illustrations)** while looking for cracks, bulges and seeping fluid. Check extra carefully around the areas where the hoses connect with the banjo fittings, as these are common areas for hose failure.
3   Inspect the metal banjo fittings connected to brake hoses. If the fittings are rusted, scratched or cracked, replace them.

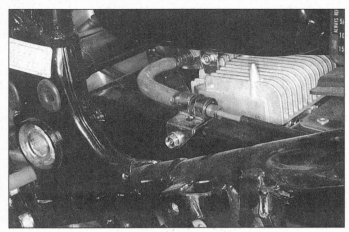

7.2a There's a brake hose on the left side of the swingarm forward of the resistor pack

7.2b The rear caliper brake hose meets a metal line at this bracket

Replacement

4   Most brake hoses have banjo fittings on each end of the hose. Cover the surrounding area with plenty of rags and unscrew the union bolts on either end of the hose. Detach the hose from any clips that may be present and remove the hose.

5   Position the new hose, making sure it isn't twisted or otherwise strained, between the two components. Make sure the metal tube portion of the banjo fitting is positioned next to the stop on the component it's connected to, if equipped **(see illustrations 2.2a and 2.16a)**. On the front master cylinder, the hose should be inclined toward the front of the bike at a 30-degree angle from vertical. Install the union bolts, using new sealing washers on both sides of the fittings, and tighten them to the torque listed in this Chapter's Specifications.

6   Flush the old brake fluid from the system, refill the system with the recommended fluid (see Chapter 1) and bleed the air from the system (see Section 8). Check the operation of the brakes carefully before riding the motorcycle.

8   Brake system bleeding

1   Bleeding the brake is simply the process of removing all the air bubbles from the brake fluid reservoirs, the lines and the brake calipers. Bleeding is necessary whenever a brake system hydraulic connection is loosened, when a component or hose is replaced, or when the master cylinder or caliper is overhauled. Leaks in the system may also allow air to enter, but leaking brake fluid will reveal their presence and warn you of the need for repair.

7.2c The front brake hoses are secured by retainers just forward of the ignition switch (arrows) . . .

2   To bleed the brakes, you will need some new, clean brake fluid of the recommended type (see Chapter 1), a length of clear vinyl or plastic tubing, a small container partially filled with clean brake fluid, some rags and a wrench to fit the brake caliper bleeder valves.

3   Cover the fuel tank and other painted components to prevent damage in the event that brake fluid is spilled.

4   Remove the reservoir cap or cover and slowly pump the brake

7

7.2d . . . and by these retainers near each fender

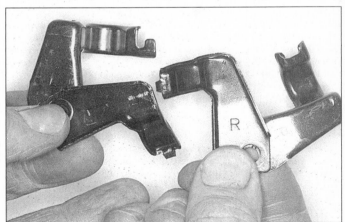

7.2e The retainers are labeled R and L for right and left sides of the bike

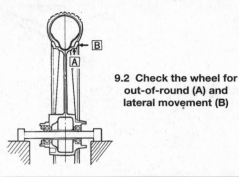

9.2 Check the wheel for out-of-round (A) and lateral movement (B)

lever or pedal a few times, until no air bubbles can be seen floating up from the holes at the bottom of the reservoir. Doing this bleeds the air from the master cylinder end of the line. Reinstall the reservoir cap or cover.

5   Pull back the rubber cover and slip a box wrench over the caliper bleed valve **(see illustration 2.2a or 2.16a)**. Attach one end of the clear vinyl or plastic tubing to the bleeder valve and submerge the other end in the brake fluid in the container.

6   Remove the reservoir cap or cover and check the fluid level. Do not allow the fluid level to drop below the lower mark during the bleeding process.

7   Carefully pump the brake lever or pedal three or four times and hold it while opening the caliper bleeder valve. When the valve is opened, brake fluid will flow out of the caliper into the clear tubing and the lever will move toward the handlebar or the pedal will move down.

8   Retighten the bleeder valve, then release the brake lever or pedal gradually. Repeat the process until no air bubbles are visible in the brake fluid leaving the caliper and the lever or pedal is firm when applied. **Note:** *The brake pedal operates two calipers, the rear and the left front. Bleed the left front caliper first, then the rear caliper.* Remember to add fluid to the reservoir as the level drops. Use only new, clean brake fluid of the recommended type. Never reuse the fluid lost during bleeding.

9   Replace the reservoir cover, wipe up any spilled brake fluid and check the entire system for leaks. **Note:** *If bleeding is difficult, it may be necessary to let the brake fluid in the system stabilize for a few hours (it may be aerated). Repeat the bleeding procedure when the tiny bubbles in the system have settled out.*

9   Wheels - inspection and repair

Refer to illustration 9.2

1   Support the motorcycle securely upright, then clean the wheels thoroughly to remove mud and dirt that may interfere with the inspection procedure or mask defects. Make a general check of the wheels and tires as described in Chapter 1.

2   Raise the wheel to be checked off the ground, then attach a dial indicator to the fork slider or the swingarm and position the stem against the side of the rim. Spin the wheel slowly and check the side-to-side (axial) runout of the rim, then compare your readings with the value listed in this Chapter's Specifications **(see illustration)**. In order to accurately check radial runout with the dial indicator, the wheel would have to be removed from the machine and the tire removed from the wheel. With the axle clamped in a vise, the wheel can be rotated to check the runout.

3   An easier, though slightly less accurate, method is to attach a stiff wire pointer to the fork or the swingarm and position the end a fraction of an inch from the wheel (where the wheel and tire join). If the wheel is true, the distance from the pointer to the rim will be constant as the wheel is rotated. **Note:** *If wheel runout is excessive, refer to the appropriate Section in this Chapter and check the wheel bearings very carefully before replacing the wheel.*

4   The wheels should also be visually inspected for cracks, flat spots on the rim and other damage. Since tubeless tires are involved, look very closely for dents in the area where the tire bead contacts the rim.

Dents in this area may prevent complete sealing of the tire against the rim, which leads to deflation of the tire over a period of time.

5   If damage is evident, or if runout in either direction is excessive, the wheel will have to be replaced with a new one. Never attempt to repair a damaged cast aluminum wheel.

10   Wheels - alignment check

1   Misalignment of the wheels, which may be due to a cocked rear wheel or a bent frame or triple clamps, can cause strange and possibly serious handling problems. If the frame or triple clamps are at fault, repair by a frame specialist or replacement with new parts are the only alternatives.

2   To check the alignment you will need an assistant, a length of string or a perfectly straight piece of wood and a ruler graduated in 1/64 inch increments. A plumb bob or other suitable weight will also be required.

3   Support the motorcycle in a level position, then measure the width of both tires at their widest points. Subtract the smaller measurement from the larger measurement, then divide the difference by two. The result is the amount of offset that should exist between the front and rear tires on both sides.

4   If a string is used, have your assistant hold one end of it about half way between the floor and the rear axle, touching the rear sidewall of the tire.

5   Run the other end of the string forward and pull it tight so that it is roughly parallel to the floor. Slowly bring the string into contact with the front sidewall of the rear tire, then turn the front wheel until it is parallel with the string. Measure the distance from the front tire sidewall to the string.

6   Repeat the procedure on the other side of the motorcycle. The distance from the front tire sidewall to the string should be equal on both sides.

7   As was previously pointed out, a perfectly straight length of wood may be substituted for the string. The procedure is the same.

8   If the distance between the string and tire is greater on one side, or if the rear wheel appears to be cocked, refer to Chapter 6, Swingarm bearings - check, and make sure the swingarm is tight.

9   If the front-to-back alignment is correct, the wheels still may be out of alignment vertically.

10   Using the plumb bob, or other suitable weight, and a length of string, check the rear wheel to make sure it is vertical. To do this, hold the string against the tire upper sidewall and allow the weight to settle just off the floor. When the string touches both the upper and lower tire sidewalls and is perfectly straight, the wheel is vertical. If it is not, place thin spacers under one leg of the centerstand.

11   Once the rear wheel is vertical, check the front wheel in the same manner. If both wheels are not perfectly vertical, the frame and/or major suspension components are bent.

11   Front wheel - removal, inspection and installation

Removal

Refer to illustrations 11.5a, 11.5b, 11.6, 11.7, 11.8a and 11.8b

1   Place the bike on its centerstand. Raise the front wheel off the ground by placing a floor jack, with a wood block on the jack head, under the engine. Don't place the jack under the oil filter.

2   Remove the brake disc covers (see Chapter 8).

3   Disconnect the speedometer cable from the drive unit (see Chapter 9).

4   Unbolt the caliper bracket on either side of the bike (it isn't necessary to remove both calipers) and remove the caliper, leaving the brake hose connected. Tie the caliper to a support such as the handlebars with a piece of wire so it doesn't hang by the brake hose. **Note:** *Slip a piece of wood between the pads of the removed caliper so the pads won't be squeezed together if the brake lever is accidentally pulled.*

5   Loosen the axle bolt, then remove the axle pinch bolts and the

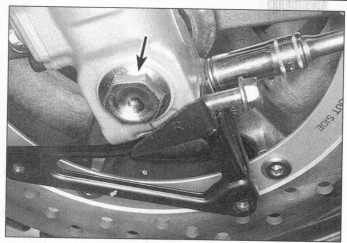

11.5a Loosen the axle bolt (arrow), undo the pinch bolts and remove the brake disc cover bracket

11.5b Remove the left side disc cover bracket; it also secures the speedometer cable (note the L and R marks on the disc cover brackets)

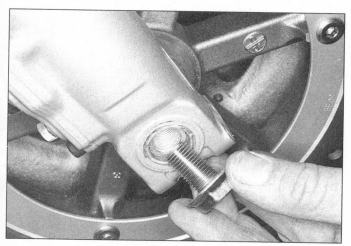

11.6 Remove the axle bolt

11.7 Slip a rod into the axle hole and pull the axle out

brake disc cover brackets **(see illustrations)**.
6   Unscrew the axle bolt **(see illustration)**.
7   Support the wheel, then pull out the axle **(see illustration)** and carefully lower the wheel away from the forks.
8   Remove the collar from the right side and the speedometer drive

assembly from the left side **(see illustrations)**. Set the wheel aside. **Caution:** *Don't lay the wheel down and allow it to rest on one of the discs - the disc could become warped. Set the wheel on wood blocks so the disc doesn't support the weight of the wheel.* **Note:** *Don't operate the front brake lever with the wheel removed.*

11.8a Remove the spacer from the right side of the wheel . . .

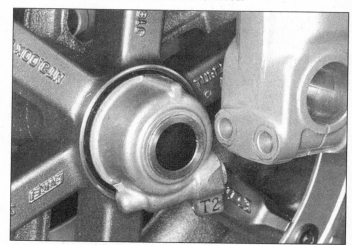

11.8b . . . and the speedometer gearbox from the left side

7

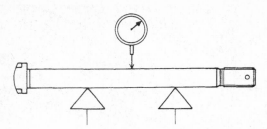

11.9 Check the axle for runout using a dial indicator and V-blocks (divide the reading by two to obtain the actual runout)

Inspection

Refer to illustration 11.9

9   Set the axle in a pair of V-blocks, rotate it and check run out with a dial indicator **(see illustration)**. If the axle is corroded, remove the corrosion with fine emery cloth.

10   Check the condition of the wheel bearings (see Section 13).

Installation

Refer to illustrations 11.11a and 11.11b

11   Apply a thin coat of grease to the seal lip, then slide the axle into the hub. Slide the wheel into place. Make sure the lugs in the speedometer drive clutch line up with the notches in the speedometer drive gear **(see illustration)**. Make sure the cast boss on the speedometer gear housing rests against the back of the tab on the left fork leg **(see illustration)**.

12   Install the front axle bolt and tighten it loosely.

13   Reinstall the disc cover brackets, making sure to place the bracket marked R on the right side and the bracket marked L on the left. Tighten the axle pinch bolts to the torque listed in this Chapter's Specifications, then tighten the axle bolt to the specified torque.

14   Install the brake caliper (see Section 3). Once the caliper is installed, measure the gap between the left brake disc (both sides) and the caliper bracket. If the gap is less then listed in this Chapter's Specifications, loosen the axle pinch bolts and reposition the fork leg until the gap is as specified. Tighten the axle pinch bolts to the specified torque, then spin the wheel, apply the left front brake several times and recheck the clearance between the brake disc and bracket. Don't operate the motorcycle until the gap is correct or the brake disc may be damaged.

15   Reconnect the speedometer cable (see Chapter 9).

16   Apply the front brake, pump the forks up and down several times and check for binding and proper brake operation.

17   Once the brakes work properly, refer to Chapter 8 and install the disc covers.

12   Rear wheel - removal, inspection and installation

Removal

Refer to illustrations 12.3, 12.5, 12.6a, 12.6b, 12.7 and 12.8

1   Place the bike on its centerstand and support it with the rear wheel off the ground. The support must be stable, so the bike can't be knocked over, and located so it won't interfere with removal of the wheel.

2   Remove the trunk and saddlebags (see Chapter 8).

3   Remove the axle nut **(see illustration)**.

4   Remove the left shock absorber's lower mounting bolt (see Chapter 6).

5   Loosen the axle pinch bolt **(see illustration)**.

6   Support the wheel. Slip a screwdriver or punch into the axle hole, pull the axle part way out and remove the washer **(see illustrations)**.

7   Lift the brake caliper and bracket out of the way and tie them up so the caliper doesn't hang by the brake hose **(see illustration)**. **Note:** *Slip a piece of wood between the pads of the removed caliper so the*

11.11a On installation, make sure the speedometer drive lugs (arrows) engage the notches in the gear box

11.11b Place the speedometer drive gear's boss (arrow) against the rear side of the tab on the fork leg; this keeps the drive gearbox from spinning with the wheel

pads won't be squeezed together if the brake lever is accidentally pulled.

8   Remove the spacer from the left side of the wheel **(see illustration)**.

9   Lower the wheel and remove it from the swingarm. **Caution:** *Don't lay the wheel down and allow it to rest on the disc or the sprocket*

12.3 Unscrew the axle nut

12.5 Loosen the axle pinch bolt . . .

12.6a pull the axle part way out . . .

12.6b . . . and remove the washer

11   Check the condition of the wheel bearings (see Section 13).

12   Pull the coupling out of the wheel (see Chapter 6). Unbolt the retainer plate that secures the rubber dampers in the wheel and turn it clockwise so the arrows on the plate and wheel are aligned. Lift the plate off and pull the rubber damper segments out of the wheel. Check the segments for damage and for wear where the coupling pins pass through them. Replace the segments as a set if problems are found. Install the new ones (or the old ones, if they're being reinstalled) with the OUTSIDE mark facing away from the wheel. Install the retainer plate with its arrow marks aligned, turn it counterclockwise and install the bolts. Tighten them to the torque listed in this Chapter's Specifications.

Installation

13   If you're working on a 1988 or 1989 model, lubricate the coupling pins with Pro Honda Moly 60 grease or equivalent. If you're working on a 1990 or later bike, don't lubricate the pins; they ride in aluminum collars and grease will cause increased wear.

14   Make sure the coupling O-rings are in place (one on each side of the coupling), then push the coupling pins into the rubber segments. Lubricate the splines with Pro Honda Moly 60 grease or equivalent.

15   The remainder of installation is the reverse of the removal steps. Tighten all fasteners to the torques listed in this Chapter's Specifications and the Chapter 6 Specifications.

16   Check the operation of the brakes carefully before riding the motorcycle.

- they could become warped. Set the wheel on wood blocks so the disc or the sprocket doesn't support the weight of the wheel. Do not operate the brake pedal with the wheel removed.

Inspection

10   Refer to Section 11 and inspect the axle.

12.7 Lift the caliper and bracket away from the bike and support the caliper so it doesn't hang by the brake hose

12.8 Remove the spacer from the left side of the wheel

7

13.3a Pry out the grease seal . . .

13.3b . . . and remove the speedometer drive

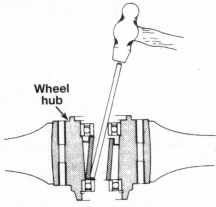

13.5a If there's enough room to tilt a metal rod so it will catch the bearing inner races, drive the bearings from the hub with a metal rod and hammer

13   Wheel bearings - replacement

Refer to illustrations 13.3a, 13.3b, 13.5a, 13.5b, 13.5c, 13.5d and 13.8

1   Support the bike securely so it can't be knocked over during this procedure and remove the wheel (see Section 11 (front wheel) or 12 (rear wheel).

2   Set the wheel on blocks so as not to allow the weight of the wheel rest on the brake disc.

3   If you're working on a front wheel, pry the grease seal out of the left side and remove the speedometer drive **(see illustrations)**. Turn the wheel over and pry the grease seal out of the other side.

4   If you're working on a rear wheel, pry the grease seal out of the left side.

5   A common method of removing wheel bearings is to insert a metal rod (preferably a brass drift punch) inserted through the center of one hub bearing and tap evenly around the inner race of the opposite bearing to drive it from the hub **(see illustration)**. The bearing spacer will also come out. On these motorcycles, it's generally not possible to tilt the rod enough to catch the opposite bearing's inner race. In this case, use a bearing remover tool consisting of a shaft and re-mover head **(see illustration)**. The head fits inside the bearing **(see illustration)**, then the wedge end of the shaft is tapped into the groove in the head to expand the head and lock it inside the bearing. Tapping on the shaft from this point will force the bearing out of the hub **(see illustration)**.

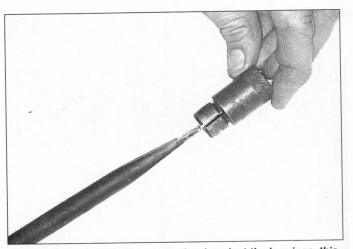

13.5b If you can't position a metal rod against the bearings, this tool can be used instead - place the split portion inside the bearing and pass the wedged rod through the hub in the split; tapping on the end of the rod will spread the split portion, locking it to the bearing, so the split portion and bearing can be driven out together

13.5c The tool can be used for front or rear bearings - place the split portion in the bearing like this . . .

13.5d . . . and pass the wedge end of the rod through the hub into the split portion

TIRE CHANGING SEQUENCE - TUBELESS TIRES

Deflate tire. After releasing beads, push tire bead into well of rim at point opposite valve. Insert lever next to valve and work bead over edge of rim.

Use two levers to work bead over edge of rim. Note use of rim protectors.

When first bead is clear, remove tire as shown.

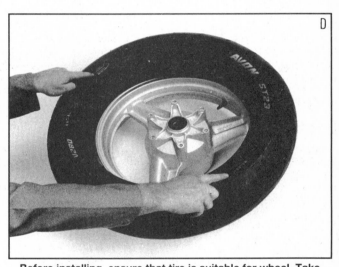

Before installing, ensure that tire is suitable for wheel. Take note of any sidewall markings such as direction of rotation arrows.

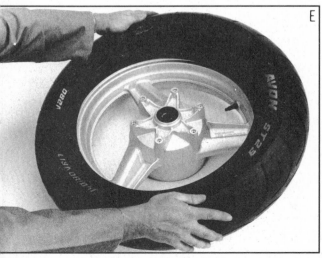

Work first bead over the rim flange.

Use a tire lever to work the second bead over rim flange.

6   Lay the wheel on its other side and remove the remaining bearing using the same technique. **Note:** *The bearings must be replaced with new ones whenever they're removed, as they're almost certain to be damaged during removal.*

7   If you're installing bearings that aren't sealed on both sides, pack the new bearings with grease from the open side. Rotate the bearing to work the grease in between the bearing balls.

8   Thoroughly clean the hub area of the wheel. Install the bearing into the recess in the hub, with the sealed side facing out. Using a bearing driver or a socket large enough to contact the outer race of the bearing, drive it in until it's completely seated **(see illustration)**. **Note:** *The right rear wheel bearing is a dual type; the left rear wheel bearings is a single type.*

9   Turn the wheel over and install the bearing spacer and bearing, driving the bearing into place as described in Step 8. Install the speedometer drive on the left side of the front wheel **(see illustration 13.3a)**.

10   Coat new grease seals with grease, then install them (on both sides of the front wheel and on the left side of the rear wheel). It should be possible to push the seals in with even finger pressure, but if necessary use a seal driver, large socket or a flat piece of wood to drive the seals into place.

11   Clean off all grease from the brake disc(s) using acetone or brake system cleaner.

12   Refer to Section 11 or 12 and install the wheel.

13.8 Drive in the new bearings and seals with a driver like this one or with a socket the same size as the bearing outer races

14 Tubeless tires - general information

1   Tubeless tires are used as standard equipment on this motorcycle. They are generally safer than tube-type tires but if problems do occur they require special repair techniques.

2   The force required to break the seal between the rim and the bead of the tire is substantial, and is usually beyond the capabilities of an individual working with normal tire irons.

3   Also, repair of the punctured tire and replacement on the wheel rim requires special tools, skills and experience that the average do-it-yourselfer lacks.

4   For these reasons, if a puncture or flat occurs with a tubeless tire, the wheel should be removed from the motorcycle and taken to a dealer service department or a motorcycle repair shop for repair or replacement of the tire. The accompanying illustrations can be used to replace a tubeless tire in an emergency.

Chapter 8 Fairing and bodywork

Contents

1   General information

Refer to illustration 1.2

This Chapter covers the procedures necessary to remove and install the fairing and other body parts. Since many service and repair operations on these motorcycles require removal of the fairing and/or other body parts, the procedures are grouped here and referred to from other Chapters.

In the event of damage to the fairing or other body part, it is usually necessary to remove the broken component and replace it with a new (or used) one. The material that the fairings are composed of doesn't lend itself to conventional repair techniques. There are, however, some shops that specialize in "plastic welding," so it would be advantageous to check around first before throwing the damaged part away. When you order new body parts, refer to the color label inside the filler cap lid **(see illustration)** to make sure the new parts match the bike.

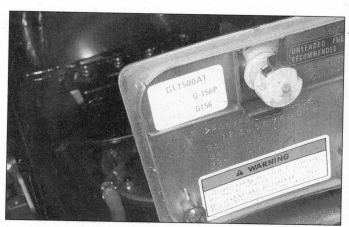

1.2 Refer to the color label inside the gas filler cap cover when you order body parts

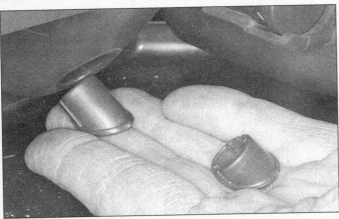

2.1 Remove the bolt caps; the longer cap goes at the rear

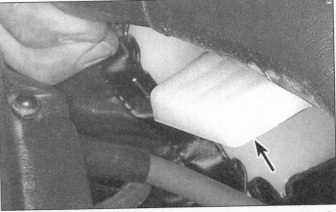

2.2 Disengage the seat hook (arrow) from the top compartment

2   Seat - removal and installation

Refer to illustrations 2.1, 2.2 and 2.3

1   Pry the bolt caps out of the passenger grab handles, then undo the Allen bolts and take the handles off **(see illustration)**.

2   Lift up the back of the seat and pull it rearward to disengage the hook at the front from the top compartment **(see illustration)**.

3   Installation is the reverse of the removal steps. It's possible to install the grab handles upside down, so refer to the R and L (right and left) marks to make sure they're installed on the correct sides of the bike **(see illustration)**. The grip area on each grab handle should be horizontal, not vertical.

3   Footrests - removal and installation

Refer to illustrations 3.1 and 3.2

1   To remove a front footrest, either unbolt its bracket from the frame or remove the clip and slide out the pivot pin **(see illustration)**.

2   To remove a rear footrest, remove the clip and pivot pin **(see illustration)**.

3   Installation is the reverse of the removal steps.

4   Brake disc covers - removal and installation

Refer to illustrations 4.1a, 4.1b, 4.2 and 4.3

1   Reach inside the fender trim cover and pull its tab out of the grommet in the fender **(see illustration)**. Disengage the tabs at the front edge

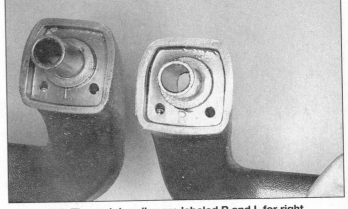

2.3 The grab handles are labeled R and L for right and left sides of the bike

of the cover from the fender and take the cover off **(see illustration)**.

2   Remove the upper disc brake cover bolt and the brake hose retainer **(see illustration)**.

3   Remove the two lower bolts and collars, then take the cover off **(see illustration)**.

4   Installation is the reverse of the removal steps, with the following additions:

a) *Be sure to install the collars in the two lower bolt holes and secure the brake hose retainer with the upper bolt.*

3.1 Undo the bolts or remove the clip and pivot pin (arrow) to remove a front footrest

3.2 Remove the clip and pivot pin (arrow) to remove a rear footrest

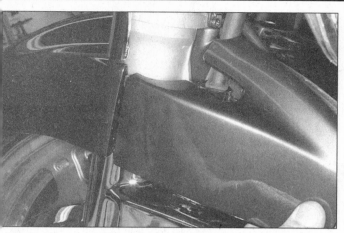

4.1a Pull the rear of the cover carefully outward to disengage the tab from the grommet

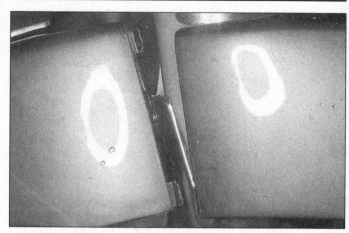

4.1b Disengage the tabs at the front of the cover from the fender

4.2 The fender cover tab fits in this grommet (arrow); the upper cover bolt secures a brake hose retainer

4.3 The two lower bolts (arrows) have collars

b) *Route the speedometer cable between the fender and the cover, not outside the cover.*
c) *The tabs at the front of the fender cover hook onto the fender; they don't just slide into the holes.*
d) *When you push the fender cover tab into the grommet, support the fender from the inside so the grommet isn't pushed out of its hole.*

5 Front fender - removal and installation

Refer to illustrations 5.2a, 5.2b, 5.3a, 5.3b, 5.4a, 5.4b and 5.5
1   Remove the fender covers and disc brake covers (Section 4).
2   Pry the plugs out of the fender upper trim cover, then remove the Allen bolts and take the cover off **(see illustrations)**.

8

5.2a Pry the trim plugs out of the holes . . .

5.2b . . . and remove the Allen bolts and collars to free the fender top trim piece

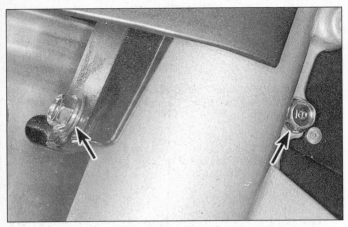

5.3a Remove the two bolts (arrows) at the side of each fender . . .

5.3b . . . the forward bolts have collars

5.4a Remove the Allen bolts that pass through the fork legs and fender sections into the fork stay

5.4b Lower the fork stay and remove the fender sections

3   Unbolt the sides of the front and rear fender sections from the fork legs **(see illustrations)**.

4   Remove the Allen bolts that pass through the fender into the fork stay **(see illustrations)**. Lower the fork stay and remove the fender sections.

5   Installation is the reverse of the removal steps, with the following addition: Be sure the integral dowels on top of the fork stay are inside the holes in the fender sections **(see illustration)**.

6   Fairing front and under covers and radiator shrouds - removal and installation

Refer to illustrations 6.1a, 6.1b, 6.2a, 6.2b, 6.2c, 6.2d and 6.3

1   Push in on the center of the front cover and at the same time p▨ the posts at its upper corners free of their grommets **(see illustratio**▨ Disengage the tabs along the bottom edge from their grooves in t▨

5.5 Be sure the integral dowels on top of the fork stay fit all the way into the fender holes, or the fender sections won't be properly supported

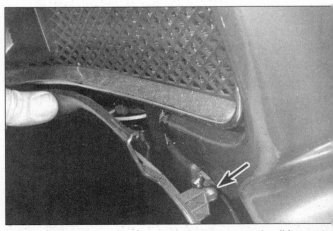

6.1a Push in on the center of the front cover and pull its posts▨ (arrow) free of the grommets (there's one at each upper corner▨

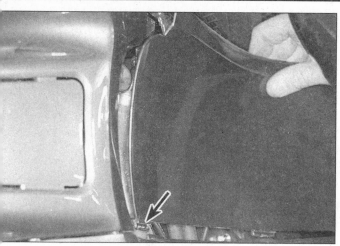

6.1b Disengage the lower tabs (arrow) from the under cover
(there's one at each corner and one in the center)

6.2a Remove the lower screw on each side of the under cover . . .

6.2b . . . and the two upper screws . . .

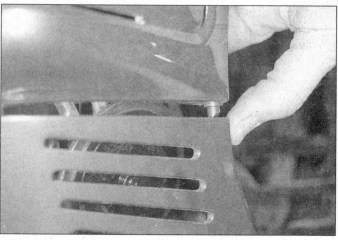

6.2c . . . lower the under cover clear of the stopper
pin on each side . . .

nder cover and lift the front cover out (see illustration).

Remove the screw from under each side of the under cover and
ne from the center (see illustrations). Disengage the under cover
rom the stopper pin and hooks of the lower fairing cover (see illustra-

tions) and take the under cover out.
3   Remove the cap nut just outside of each fork tube (see illustration). Take the radiator shroud out.
4   Installation is the reverse of the removal steps.

6.2d . . . and disengage the under cover from the tabs of the
lower fairing cover

6.3 Remove the cap nuts (arrows) to free the radiator shroud

8

7.1a Remove the lower bolts (arrows) . . .

7.1b . . . and the upper bolt to detach the front crash bars

7.2 Rear crash bar bolts

8.2a Remove the chamber protector bolts (left side shown) . . .

7   Crash bars - removal and installation

Refer to illustrations 7.1a, 7.1b and 7.2

1   To remove front crash bars, remove the lower fairing cover (Section 12). Undo two lower bolts and one upper bolt and take the bars off **(see illustrations)**.

2   To remove rear crash bars, undo the front and rear side covers and, if necessary, the saddlebag (Sections 10, 11 and 23). Unbolt the bars and take them off the frame **(see illustration)**.

3   Installation is the reverse of the removal steps.

8   Exhaust chamber protector - removal and installation

Refer to illustrations 8.2a and 8.2b

1   The chamber protectors (one on each side of the bike) protect the exhaust chamber.

2   Undo the chamber protector bolts **(see illustration)**. Lower the chamber protector clear of the footrest inner cover, disengaging the rubber tabs **(see illustration)**.

3   If it's difficult to separate the chamber protector from the footrest inner cover, remove the footrest (see Section 5) and lift the inner cover away from the chamber protector.

9   Exhaust pipe protectors - removal and installation

Refer to illustrations 9.1a, 9.1b and 9.3

1   To remove the left rear protector, start by placing a piece of duct tape over its concave surface so it won't be scratched by the side-stand on removal **(see illustration)**. Remove two bolts at the rear of the protector and one at the top front **(see illustration)**, then take the protector out.

2   To remove the left front protector, remove the fairing front cover

8.2b . . . and lower the chamber protector away from the footrest inner cover; on installation, line up the rubber tabs (arrows)

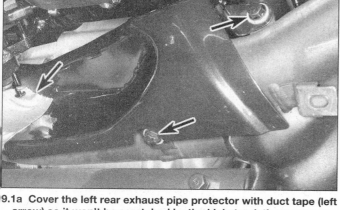

9.1a Cover the left rear exhaust pipe protector with duct tape (left arrow) so it won't be scratched by the kickstand, then remove the two rear bolts (right arrows) . . .

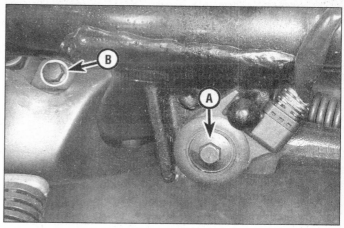

9.1b . . . and one bolt at the top front

A   Top front bolt   B   Sidestand cover bolt

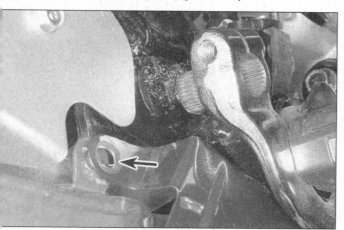

9.3 Pull the brake pedal part way off and remove the rear bolt (arrow), the top center and forward bolts and the three lower nuts

10.2 Slowly pull the rear side covers free to prevent the rear posts from breaking

and under cover (Section 6). Refer to Chapter 2 and remove the gearshift pedal. Remove one bolt at the front of the protector which was exposed when the under cover was removed. Remove one bolt at the rear of the protector. Remove three nuts along the bottom of the protector and take it off the bike.
3   To remove the right side protector, remove the brake pedal pinch

bolt and pull the pedal part way off **(see illustration)**. Remove one bolt at the rear, one bolt at the top center and one bolt at the front. Remove three nuts and washer along the bottom and take the protector off the bike.
4   Installation is the reverse of the removal steps.

10 Rear side covers - removal and installation

Refer to illustration 10.2
1   Refer to Section 2 and remove the seat.
2   Reach behind the cover and slowly pull the two rear posts out of the rubber grommets on the frame. Pull the rubber grommet in the front of the side cover off the post on the frame **(see illustration)**.
3   Installation is the reverse of the removal steps.

11 Front side covers - removal and installation

Refer to illustrations 11.2a and 11.2b
1   Remove the seat and the rear side cover (Sections 2 and 10).
2   Pull the side cover's rear post out of the grommet on the frame **(see illustration)**. Slide the cover rearward to disengage the tabs from the grommets at the front, then take the cover off **(see illustration)**.
3   Remove the screws from the inside to separate the upper and lower parts of the cover.
4   Installation is the reverse of the removal steps.

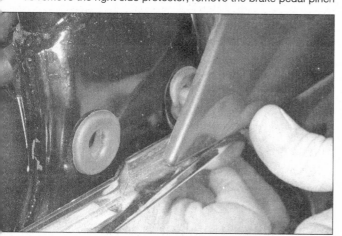

11.2a Slowly pull the front side cover's rear post free of its grommet (right side shown) . . .

8

11.2b . . . and slide the cover back to free the tabs from the upper and lower grommets (arrows)

12.3a The fairing lower covers provide an outlet for the airflow from the radiators; the deflector (arrow) wraps around the rear and lower edges

12.3b Pull the trim cover off the screw at the lower rear corner of the deflector . . .

12.3c . . . and pull the deflector off the edge of the fairing lower cover

12.4a At the upper edge of the cover, remove the trim cap from the rear end of the reflector lens to expose the rear upper screw . . .

12 Fairing lower covers - removal and installation

Refer to illustrations 12.3a, 12.3b, 12.3c, 12.4a, 12.4b and 12.5

1   Refer to Section 6 and remove the fairing front cover. Separate the fairing under cover and lower cover vertically so the front cover

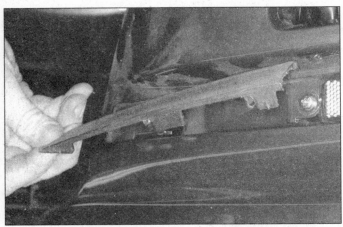

12.4b . . . and remove the trim cap at the front of the lens to expose the center and front (longer) screws; remove all three screws and take the lens off . . .

stopper pin clears the under cover **(see illustration 6.2c)**.

2   Disengage the tab at the front of the lower cover from the stoppe pin on the lower edge of the radiator shroud.

3   Pry the trim cover off the deflector retaining screw, the pull th deflector off the edge of the fairing lower cover **(see illustrations)**.

4   Pry the trim caps off the reflector lens above the lower cover **(se illustrations)**. Remove one screw from behind each trim cover and on center screws, then take off the reflector lens.

5   Pull the lower cover off the bike **(see illustration)**. Disconnect th electrical connector for the cornering light (if equipped).

6   Installation is the reverse of the removal steps.

13 Fairing top components and radio - removal and installation

Removal

Fairing pockets

Refer to illustrations 13.2 and 13.3

1   Unsnap the left pocket cover or use the ignition key to remove th right pocket cover.

2   Remove the pocket screws and lift the pocket out of the fairin **(see illustration)**.

3   The brace inside the right pocket cover tends to vibrate. This ca be stopped by taping the brace to the cover with duct tape or foa tape **(see illustration)**.

12.5 . . . then take the cover off

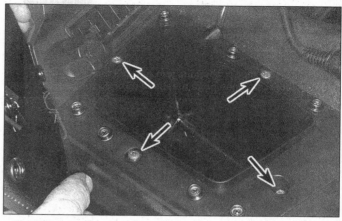

13.2 Remove the screws (arrows) and lift the pocket out of the fairing (left pocket shown)

13.3 Taping the right pocket's cover brace to the cover will keep it from vibrating

13.4a Lift the rear of the ignition switch cover free of the grommets . . .

Ignition switch cover

Refer to illustrations 13.4a and 13.4b

4 Lift slowly on the rear of the cover to pull its two posts from the rubber grommets, then disengage the tab at the front of the cover **(see illustrations)**.

5 The circular trim piece that fits around the key cylinder can be removed from the cover by turning clockwise so its tabs align with the cover slots.

Top inner covers

Refer to illustration 13.6

6 Disengage the cover tabs from the slots in the fairing and lift it out **(see illustration)**.

Top compartment and radio

Refer to illustrations 13.9, 13.10a, 13.10b, 13.11a and 13.11b

7 Refer to Section 2 and remove the seat.

13.4b . . . and disengage the tab at the front

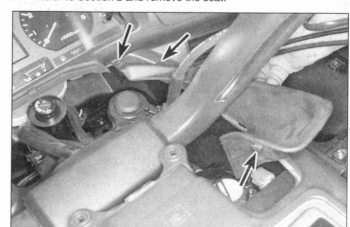

13.6 Disengage the tabs (arrows) from the fairing slots and lift the top inner cover out

8

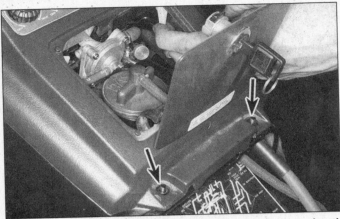

13.9 Remove the cap nuts from the top cover studs (arrows) and push the release levers forward (there's one on each side)

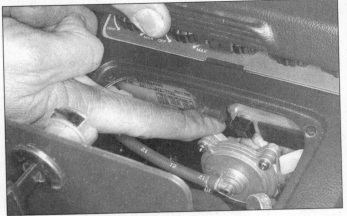

13.10a Pull up on the inside tab . . .

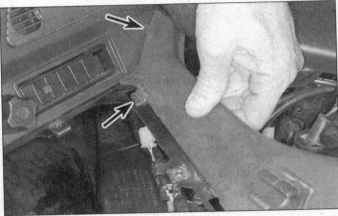

13.10b . . . and disengage the tabs on each side at the front (arrows)

13.11a Squeeze the harness retainer and slip it out of the hole; don't lose the washer

8   Remove the fairing pockets, ignition switch cover and top inner covers as described above.

9   Unlock the top compartment cover and raise the lid. Remove the cap nuts from the top compartment studs, then reach inside the cover and push the release levers forward **(see illustration)**.

10   Lift the top compartment up, disengaging the tabs at the front **(see illustrations)**.

11   If the bike has a radio, free the harness retainer from the cover **(see illustration)**. Pull the rubber boot away from the radio to expose the electrical connector and antenna plug, then disconnect them **(see illustration)**.

12   To detach the radio from the cover, remove its four mounting screws.

Installation

13   Installation is the reverse of the removal steps. **Warning:** *When reinstalling the top compartment, make sure the radio wiring harness doesn't block the air intake for the cruise valve (bikes equipped with cruise control). If the air intake is blocked, the cruise control won't disengage.*

14 Fairing inner covers - removal and installation

Refer to illustrations 14.5, 14.6a, 14.6b and 14.6c

1   Remove the seat (Section 2).

2   Remove the fairing lower cover on the side you plan to remove the inner cover from (Section 12).

3   Remove the fairing pockets, ignition switch cover, top inner

covers and top compartment (Section 13).

4   If you plan to remove the left inner cover, disconnect the CB radio wires (if equipped) and refer to Chapter 2 and remove the reverse lever (if equipped).

5   Unscrew the combined bolt/grommet post at the rear of the cover **(see illustration)**.

6   Remove one screw at the side of the cover and two screws at the top front **(see illustration)**. Lift the cover off the bike **(see illustrations)**.

7   Installation is the reverse of the removal steps.

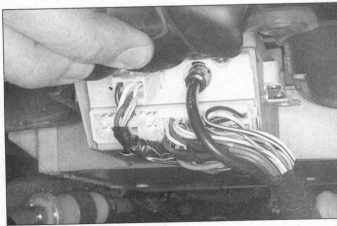

13.11b Pull back the rubber boot and disconnect the power and antenna leads

14.5 Unscrew the bolt/grommet post at the rear
of the fairing inner cover

14.6a Remove one screw on the side . . .

14.6b . . . and two screws on the top . . .

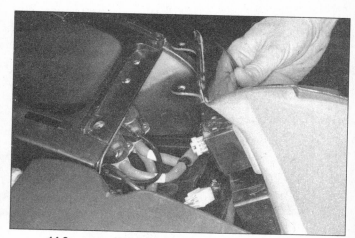

14.6c . . . and lift the fairing inner cover off the bike

15 Air ducts - removal and installation

Refer to illustrations 15.5a, 15.5b and 15.7

1   Remove the seat (Section 2).
2   Remove the fairing lower cover on the side you plan to remove
the air duct from (Section 12).
3   Remove the fairing pockets, ignition switch cover, top inner

covers and top compartment (Section 13).
4   Remove the fairing inner cover on the side you plan to remove the
air ducts from (Section 14).
5   Remove the lower duct rear screw from the side of the fairing **(see
illustration)**. Reach into the fairing pocket hole and remove the lower
duct front screw **(see illustration)**.
6   Pull the lower duct out, then pull the upper duct out.

15.5a Remove the screw at the rear of the lower duct . . .

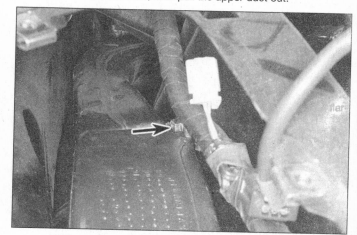

15.5b . . . and the one at the front (arrow), then take
the ducts out of the fairing

8

7   Installation is the reverse of the removal steps. Before you install the upper duct, make sure the nut clip to the side of it is in place **(see illustration)**. If the clip has been removed or has fallen out of position (during removal of the fairing, for example), the duct will be in the way, so there won't be enough room to install it.

16   Mirrors - removal and installation

Refer to illustrations 16.1 and 16.2
1   Pull the mirror cover tabs free of the fairing and pull back the cover to expose the screws **(see illustration)**.
2   Undo the mirror screws and take the mirror off the bike **(see illustration)**.
3   Installation is the reverse of the removal steps.

17   Windshield - removal and installation

Refer to illustrations 17.2a, 17.2b and 17.3
1   Pull back the mirror covers (see Section 16).
2   Remove the screw from each end of the windshield trim **(see illustration)**. Shift the trim toward the left side of the bike to free it from the tabs on the fairing, then lift it up and off **(see illustration)**.
3   Remove the windshield screws and lift the windshield off the bike **(see illustration)**.
4   Installation is the reverse of removal, with the following additions:
  a) *Install the two larger retainers in the outermost slots. The larger retainers use the black screws.*
  b) *Position all of the screws in the upper or lower position.*
  c) *Make sure the windshield height adjuster levers (if equipped) operate smoothly.*

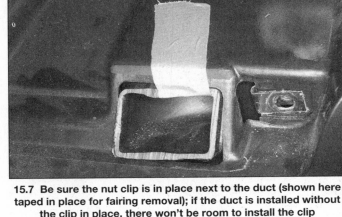

15.7 Be sure the nut clip is in place next to the duct (shown here taped in place for fairing removal); if the duct is installed without the clip in place, there won't be room to install the clip

18   Windshield height adjuster levers - removal and installation

Refer to illustrations 18.1 and 18.3
1   Check the line stamped in the end of the height adjuster shaft **(see illustration)**. It should align with the slit in the lever.
2   Remove the nut and screw and pull the lever off the shaft.
3   If necessary, remove the screw and take the adjuster plate off **(see illustration)**.
4   Installation is the reverse of the removal steps. Refer to Section 19 and adjust the levers.

16.1 Pull the mirror cover tabs free. . .

16.2 . . . and pull the cover back to expose the screws (arrows)

17.2a Remove the screw at each end of the windshield trim . . .

17.2b . . . then slide the trim to the left side of the bike (to your right when viewed from the front of the bike) to free it from the tabs (arrow) and lift it off

17.3 Remove the screws and lift the windshield off; on installation, the larger retainers with the black screws go in the two outer slots

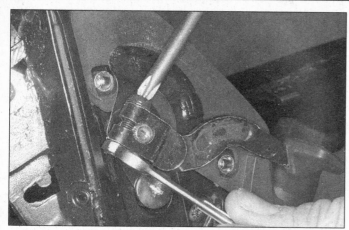

18.1 Remove the nut and screw and pull the lever off; on installation, the line in the end of the shaft aligns with the slit in the lever

18.3 Remove the screw and take the plate off

19 Windshield height levers - adjustment

Refer to illustration 19.2

1   Remove the rearview mirrors (Section 16).
2   Loosen the adjusting screw on each side of the bike **(see illustration)**.

19.2 Raise the lever all the way and loosen the adjusting screw (arrow)

3   Retighten the screw on one side only, then start the adjustment on the other side of the bike (where the screw is still loose).
4   Raise the lever on the side being adjusted all the way. Push the large chrome trim piece below the windshield backward toward the bike, then hold it in this position and tighten the screw.
5   Move the lever on the far side of the bike to the lower position.
6   Come back to the side of the bike being adjusted. Pull the lever down with a spring scale and note the amount of force required to move the lever. If it's not between 11 ad 14 pounds, repeat Step 4 until it is.
7   Repeat Steps 4 through 6 on the far side of the bike to adjust the other lever.
8   Operate both levers and make sure they move smoothly.
9   Place both levers in the lower position. Grasp the windshield and try to pull it up and push it down (don't apply more than 40 pounds of force). The windshield should not move.

20 Fairing - removal and installation

Refer to illustrations 20.3a, 20.3b, 20.3c, 20.6a and 20.6b

1   Remove the fairing inner covers and the left air ducts (Sections 14 and 15).
2   Remove the headlight assembly (see Chapter 8).
3   Remove the air solenoid bracket inside each fairing pocket opening **(see illustrations)**. If the bike has cruise control, you may need to unbolt the throttle cable junction for access to the bracket nut **(see illustration)**.

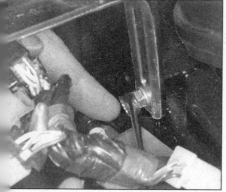

20.3a Remove the solenoid bracket from the fairing pocket opening . . .

20.3b . . . there's one on each side of the bike

20.3c If necessary, unbolt the cruise control throttle cable junction (arrow) for access to the solenoid bracket on the left side of the bike

8

20.6a **Remove two lower bolts at the front of the fairing . . .**

20.6b **. . . and two upper bolts**

21.1 **Remove four screws from along the rear edge of the trunk lower cover . . .**

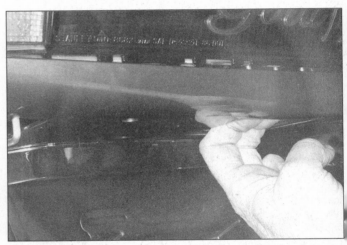

21.2a **Lower the cover away from the tabs around its edge . . .**

4   Follow the wiring harness from the instrument cluster to the electrical connectors and disconnect them. Disconnect any remaining electrical connectors and vacuum lines that connect the fairing to the bike.

5   Remove one nut and bolt from each side of the fairing just outboard of the fork legs.

6   Remove four bolts at the front of the fairing **(see illustrations)**. Lift the fairing off the frame. **Note:** *The fairing is bulky. There will be less chance of scratching it if you have an assistant to help lift.*

7   Installation is the reverse of removal. Tighten all fasteners securely, but don't overtighten them and crack the fairing.

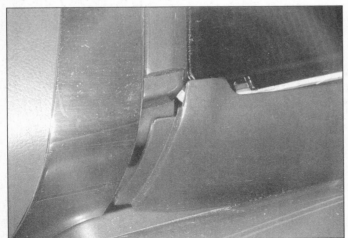

21.2b **. . . and pull the cover back to disengage its front tabs**

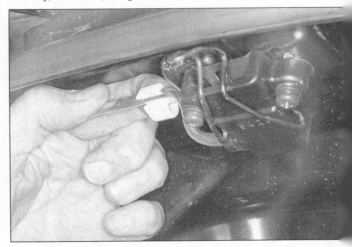

21.3a **Unclip the cable stopper in each saddlebag from its opener bar . . .**

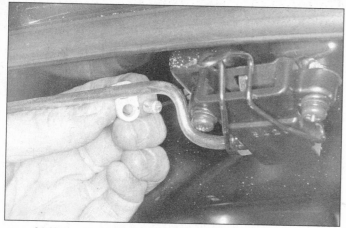

21.3b . . . then slip the cable end out of the stopper . . .

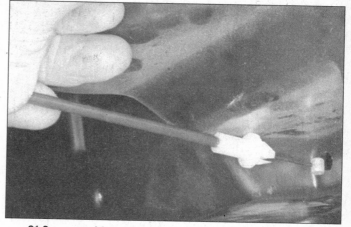

21.3c . . . and free the cable end from the saddlebag hole

21 Trunk - removal and installation

Removal

Refer to illustrations 21.1, 21.2a and 21.2b

1   Working from below and behind the trunk, remove four screws from the rear of the trunk lower cover **(see illustration)**.
2   Pull each side of the trunk lower cover rearward. Disengage the tabs at the front of the cover (one on each side) and work the cover slots free of the tabs on the lenses **(see illustrations)**.

Interstate and Aspencade

Refer to illustrations 21.3a, 21.3b and 21.3c

3   Open the saddlebag on each side of the bike. Pop each saddle-bag opener cable stopper off the opener bar, then disconnect the cable from the stopper **(see illustrations)**. Free the opener cable grommet from the saddlebag and pull the cable through the hole **(see illustration)**. The saddlebag opener cables will be removed together with the trunk.

SE

4   Remove the seat (Section 2).
5   Inside the trunk, remove the three screws that secure the right side pocket. Take the side pocket off the trunk from the outside.

All models

Refer to illustrations 21.6a, 21.6b and 21.6c

6   Disconnect the single-pin ground wire connector below the trunk

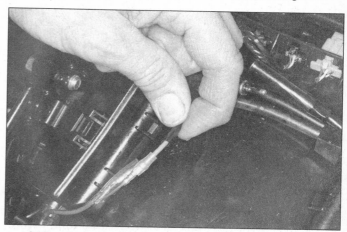

21.6a Disconnect the single ground wire below the trunk

(see illustration). Disconnect the brake and taillight connectors and unplug the antenna cable **(see illustrations)**. If you're working on an SE, disconnect the connectors for the rear speakers, high mount lights and CB antenna.
7   Pull up the helmet holder knobs. Remove four screws, one from each corner of the trunk floor. Remove the plain washer and rubber washer from beneath each screw.
8   Lift the trunk off the motorcycle.

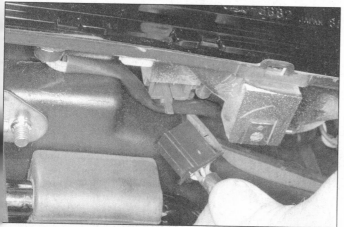

21.6b Unplug the brake and taillight connectors (one on each side of the opener levers) . . .

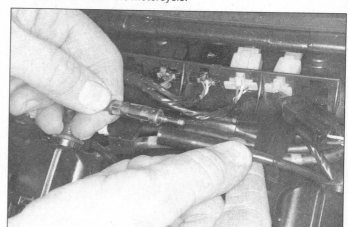

21.6c . . . and unplug the antenna cable

21.9 The helmet holder shafts engage their mechanisms like this (trunk removed for clarity)

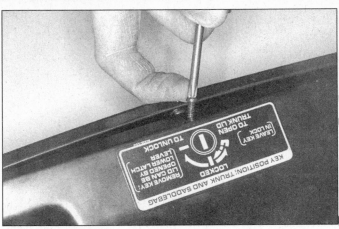

22.1a Remove one screw from the top of the catch assembly . . .

22.1b . . . and one on each side of the latch

| A | Latch screw | | B | Opener screws |

22.1c Remove four catch assembly screws from outside the trunk

| A | Catch assembly screws | | B | Latch screw |

Installation

Refer to illustration 21.9

9   Installation is the reverse of the removal steps, with the following addition: Make sure the helmet holder shafts engage the slots in the opener mechanisms **(see illustration)**.

22 Trunk latch - removal and installation

Refer to illustrations 22.1a, 22.1b, 22.1c, 22.2a, 22.2b, 22.3 and 22.4

1   Open the trunk and remove one screw from the top of the opener catch assembly **(see illustration)**. Inside the trunk lid, remove one screw on each side of the latch **(see illustration)**. Remove four more screws from the outside and take the catch assembly out **(see illustration)**.

2   Open the taillight bulb access covers inside the trunk. Remove the taillight assembly screws and nuts and take the assembly off **(see illustrations)**.

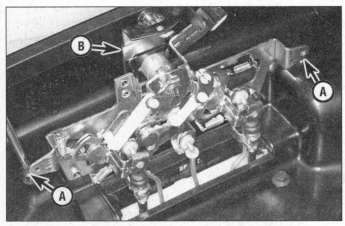

22.2a Remove the taillight assembly screws and nuts

| A | Taillight assembly center screws | B | Lock cylinder clip |

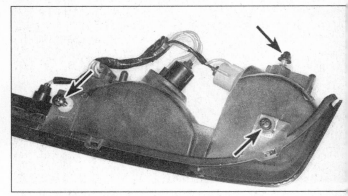

22.2b The taillight assembly is held in place by screws and nuts

22.3 Remove two latch screws from outside

22.4 Latch and opener assembly

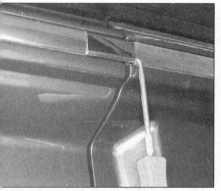

23.1a Pry off the trim covers . . .

23.1b . . . remove the screws . . .

23.1c and separate the lower saddlebag cover from the bike

3   Remove two opener screws from the floor of the trunk and two latch screws from the outside **(see illustration 22.1b and the accompanying illustration)**.

4   Pull out the lock cylinder clip and remove the latch and opener assembly from the trunk **(see illustration 22.2a and the accompanying illustration)**.

23 Saddlebags - removal and installation

Refer to illustrations 23.1a, 23.1b, 23.1c, 23.4 and 23.5

1   Pry the trim covers off the lower cover screws, then undo the screws and take off the saddlebag lower cover **(see illustrations)**.

2   Remove the trunk lower cover (Section 21). Disconnect the tail and brake light connectors.

3   Disconnect the saddlebag opener cable from the opener bar (Section 21).

4   If you're removing the right saddlebag on a bike equipped with an onboard air compressor, remove the outlet valve **(see illustration)**.

5   Remove the mounting screws from the sides and floor of the saddlebag **(see illustration)**. Lift the saddlebag off the motorcycle.

6   Installation is the reverse of the removal steps.

8

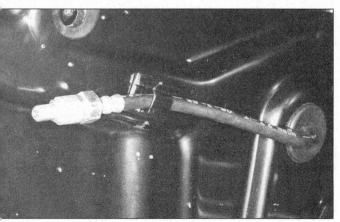

23.4 Unhook the onboard compressor hose, remove its grommet and push it through the saddlebag opening

23.5 Remove the side and bottom mounting bolts

24 Rear fender - removal and installation

Refer to illustration 24.2

1   Remove the trunk and saddlebags (Sections 21 and 23).
2   To remove the rear portion of the fender, undo its mounting bolts **(see illustration)**. Take off the fender and license plate bracket.
3   To remove the center portion of the fender, remove the reverse unit and auto cruise unit from the top of the fender (if equipped) (see Chapter 9).
4   If the bike has an onboard compressor system, detach the air distributor from the fender, leaving the air hoses connected (see Chapter 6). Unbolt the air distributor ground wire from the top of the fender.
5   Remove two bolts, one on top and one on the left side, and remove the center portion of the rear fender.
6   To remove the front portion of the rear fender, remove the left

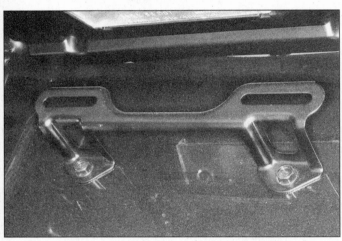

24.2 The rear fender bolts secure the license plate bracket

shock absorber (see Chapter 6) and the relay and fuse box (see Chapter 9). If the bike has cruise control, remove the speed limiter relay from its location near the relay box.
7   Unhook the fender tab from the frame, then remove the forward portion of the rear fender.
8   Installation is the reverse of the removal steps

25 Sidestand and centerstand - maintenance

Refer to illustrations 25.1a, 25.1b and 25.1c

1   The sidestand and centerstand are attached to the frame. An extension spring(s) anchored to the bracket ensures that the stand is held in the retracted position **(see illustrations)**.
2   Make sure the pivot bolt(s) is tight and the extension spring is in good condition and not overstretched. An accident is almost certain to occur if the stand extends while the machine is in motion.

26 Frame - inspection and repair

1   The frame should not require attention unless accident damage has occurred. In most cases, frame replacement is the only satisfactory remedy for such damage. A few frame specialists have the jigs and other equipment necessary for straightening the frame to the required standard of accuracy, but even then there is no simple way of assessing to what extent the frame may have been overstressed.
2   After the machine has accumulated a lot of miles, the frame should be examined closely for signs of cracking or splitting at the welded joints. Corrosion can also cause weakness at these joints. Loose engine mount bolts can cause ovaling or fracturing of the mounting tabs. Minor damage can often be repaired by welding, depending on the extent and nature of the damage.
3   Remember that a frame which is out of alignment will cause handling problems. If misalignment is suspected as the result of an accident, it will be necessary to strip the machine completely so the frame can be thoroughly checked.

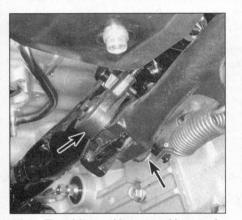

25.1a The sidestand is secured by a main bolt under the cover (left arrow) and nut (right arrow)

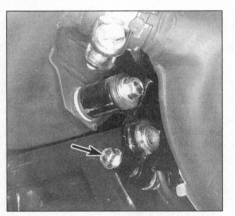

25.1b The centerstand pivot is secured by this clamp (arrow)

25.1c The centerstand spring hooks to a post on the centerstand (arrow)

Chapter 9   Electrical system

Contents

Specifications

Battery

Capacity/type	12 volts, 20 amp-hours
Specific gravity	See Chapter 1

Charging system

Leakage	0.5 mA maximum
Output	
900 rpm	Zero to 2 amps, 13.5 to 15.5 volts
1850 rpm	1.5 amps minimum, 13.5 to 15.5 volts
Stator coil resistance	0.1 to 0.3 ohms
Field coil resistance	2.9 to 4.0 ohms
Brush length	
Standard	18.0 mm (0.71 inch)
Minimum	To wear line

Starter motor

Brush length	
Standard	12.5 mm (0.49 inch)
Minimum	6.0 mm (0.24 inch)

9

Torque specifications

Oil pressure switch	12 Nm (9 ft-lbs)
Reverse switch	12 Nm (9 ft-lbs)
Alternator coupling nut	58 Nm (42 ft-lbs)
Alternator mounting bolts	Not specified
Starter mounting bolts	Not specified

1   General information

The motorcycles covered by this manual are equipped with a 12-volt electrical system.

The charging system uses a three-phase alternator with an integrated circuit regulator built in. The regulator maintains the charging system output within the specified range to prevent overcharging. The alternator diodes (rectifier) convert the AC (alternating current) output of the alternator to DC (direct current) to power the lights and other components and to charge the battery. The alternator is similar to an automotive alternator, with the field current being produced electromagnetically, rather than by permanent magnets as is common on smaller motorcycles.

An electric starter mounted to the back of the engine is standard equipment. The starting system includes the motor, the battery, the relay and the various wires and switches. If the engine kill switch and the ignition switch are both in the On position, the starting circuit allows the starter motor to operate only if the transmission is in Neutral (gear position switch indicating Neutral) or the clutch lever is pulled to the handlebar (clutch switch on) and the sidestand is up (sidestand switch on).

Note: *Keep in mind that electrical parts, once purchased, can't be returned. To avoid unnecessary expense, make very sure the faulty component has been positively identified before buying a replacement part.*

2   Electrical troubleshooting

A typical electrical circuit consists of an electrical component, the switches, relays, etc. related to that component and the wiring and connectors that hook the component to both the battery and the frame. To aid in locating a problem in any electrical circuit, refer to the wiring diagrams at the end of this Chapter.

Before tackling any troublesome electrical circuit, first study the appropriate diagrams thoroughly to get a complete picture of what makes up that individual circuit. Trouble spots, for instance, can often be narrowed down by noting if other components related to that circuit are operating properly or not. If several components or circuits fail at one time, chances are the fault lies in the fuse or ground connection, as several circuits often are routed through the same fuse and ground connections.

Electrical problems often stem from simple causes, such as loose or corroded connections or a blown fuse. Prior to any electrical troubleshooting, always visually check the condition of the fuse, wires and connections in the problem circuit. Intermittent failures can be especially frustrating, since you can't always duplicate the failure when it's convenient to test. In such situations, a good practice is to clean all connections in the affected circuit, whether or not they appear to be good. All of the connections and wires should also be wiggled to check for looseness which can cause intermittent failure. Unplug the electrical connectors in the circuit completely, then clean the terminals and reconnect them securely.

If testing instruments are going to be utilized, use the diagrams to plan where you will make the necessary connections in order to accurately pinpoint the trouble spot. The basic tools needed for electrical troubleshooting include a test light or voltmeter, a continuity tester (which includes a bulb, battery and set of test leads) and a jumper wire, preferably with a circuit breaker incorporated, which can be used to bypass electrical components. Specific checks described later in this Chapter may also require an ohmmeter.

Voltage checks should be performed if a circuit is not functioning properly. Connect one lead of a test light or voltmeter to either the negative battery terminal or a known good ground. Connect the other lead to a connector in the circuit being tested, preferably nearest to the battery or fuse. If the bulb lights, voltage is reaching that point, which means the part of the circuit between that connector and the battery is problem-free. Continue checking the remainder of the circuit in the same manner. When you reach a point where no voltage is present, the problem lies between there and the last good test point. Most of the time the problem is due to a loose connection. Keep in mind that some circuits only receive voltage when the ignition key is in the On position.

One method of finding short circuits is to remove the fuse and connect a test light or voltmeter in its place to the fuse terminals. There should be no load in the circuit (it should be switched off). Move the wiring harness from side-to-side while watching the test light. If the bulb lights, there is a short to ground somewhere in that area, probably where insulation has rubbed off a wire. The same test can be performed on other components in the circuit, including the switch.

A ground check should be done to see if a component is grounded properly. Disconnect the battery and connect one lead of a self-powered test light (continuity tester) to a known good ground. Connect the other lead to the wire or ground connection being tested. If the bulb lights, the ground is good. If the bulb does not light, the ground is not good.

A continuity check is performed to see if a circuit, section of circuit or individual component is capable of passing electricity through it. Disconnect the battery and connect one lead of a self-powered test light (continuity tester) to one end of the circuit being tested and the other lead to the other end of the circuit. If the bulb lights, there is continuity, which means the circuit is passing electricity through it properly. Switches can be checked in the same way.

Remember that all electrical circuits are designed to conduct electricity from the battery, through the wires, switches, relays, etc. to the electrical component (light bulb, motor, etc.). From there it is directed to the frame (ground) where it is passed back to the battery. Electrical problems are basically an interruption in the flow of electricity from the battery or back to it.

3   Battery - inspection and maintenance

Refer to illustration 3.4

1   Most battery damage is caused by heat, vibration, and/or low electrolyte levels, so keep the battery securely mounted, check the electrolyte level frequently and make sure the charging system is functioning properly.

2   Refer to Chapter 1 for electrolyte level and specific gravity checking procedures.

3   Check around the base inside of the battery for sediment, which is the result of sulfation caused by low electrolyte levels. These deposits will cause internal short circuits, which can quickly discharge the battery. Look for cracks in the case and replace the battery if either of these conditions is found.

4   Check the battery terminals and cable ends for tightness and corrosion. If corrosion is evident, remove the cables from the battery (see illustration) and clean the terminals and cable ends with a wire brush or knife and emery paper. Reconnect the cables and apply a thin coat of petroleum jelly to the connections to slow further corrosion.

5   The battery case should be kept clean to prevent current leakage, which can discharge the battery over a period of time (especially when it sits unused). Wash the outside of the case with a solution of baking

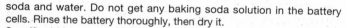

3.4 Undo the negative cable first, then the positive cable (shown); the plastic cover on the positive terminal prevents accidental contact with metal

4.5a Unbolt the battery retainer . . .

soda and water. Do not get any baking soda solution in the battery cells. Rinse the battery thoroughly, then dry it.

6   If acid has been spilled on the frame or battery box, neutralize it with the baking soda and water solution, dry it thoroughly, then touch up any damaged paint. Make sure the battery vent tube (if equipped) is directed away from the frame and is not kinked or pinched.

7   If the motorcycle sits unused for long periods of time, disconnect the cables from the battery terminals. Refer to Section 4 and charge the battery approximately once every month.

4   Battery - removal, charging and installation

Refer to illustrations 4.5a, 4.5b and 4.5c

1   If the machine sits idle for extended periods or if the charging system malfunctions, the battery can be charged from an external source.

2   To properly charge the battery, you will need a charger of the correct rating, a hydrometer, a clean rag and a syringe for adding distilled water to the battery cells.

3   The maximum charging rate for any battery is 1/10 of the rated amp/hour capacity. As an example, the maximum charging rate for a 12 amp/hour battery would be 1.2 amps and the maximum charging rate for a 14 amp/hour battery would be 1.4 amps. If the battery is charged at a higher rate, it could be damaged.

4   Do not allow the battery to be subjected to a so-called quick charge (high rate of charge over a short period of time) unless you are prepared to buy a new battery.

5   When charging the battery, always remove it from the machine **(see illustrations)** and be sure to check the electrolyte level before hooking up the charger. Add distilled water to any cells that are low.

6   Loosen the cell caps, hook up the battery charger leads (red to positive, black to negative), cover the top of the battery with a clean rag, then, and only then, plug in the battery charger. **Warning:** *Remember, the gas escaping from a charging battery is explosive, so keep open flames and sparks well away from the area. Also, the electrolyte is extremely corrosive and will damage anything it comes in contact with.*

7   Allow the battery to charge until the specific gravity is as specified (refer to Chapter 1 for specific gravity checking procedures). The charger must be unplugged and disconnected from the battery when making specific gravity checks. If the battery overheats or gases excessively, the charging rate is too high. Either disconnect the charger or lower the charging rate to prevent damage to the battery.

8   It's time for a new battery if:

a) *One or more of the cells is significantly lower in specific gravity than the others after a long slow charge;*

b) *The battery as a whole doesn't seem to want to take a charge;*

c) *Battery voltage won't increase;*

d) *The electrolyte doesn't bubble;*

e) *The plates are white (indicating sulfation) or debris has accumulated in the bottom of a cell;*

f) *The plates or insulators are warped or buckled.*

9   When the battery is fully charged, unplug the charger first, then disconnect the leads from the battery. Install the cell caps and wipe any electrolyte off the outside of the battery case.

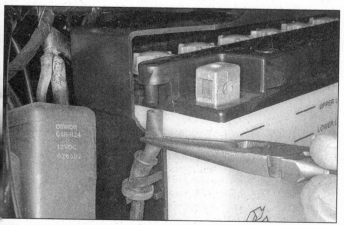

4.5b . . . and pull the vent tube off the fitting to remove the battery

4.5c If you need to remove the battery tray, undo its nut (upper arrow), plain bolt (right arrow) and shouldered bolt (left arrow)

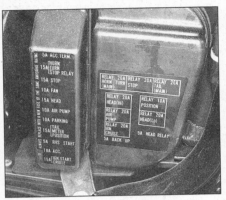  

5.1a The accessory fuses and relays are beneath covers on the side of the motorcycle ...

5.1b ... lift the covers off for access

5.1c The two main fuses (arrows) are forward of the battery tray

5 Fuses and relays - check and replacement

Fuses

Refer to illustrations 5.1a, 5.1b, 5.1c and 5.1d

1   These motorcycles have a fuse block containing accessory fuses and spares **(see illustration)**. Fuse ratings and functions are printed on the cover. There are also two main fuses on the right side of the motorcycle and a speed limiter fuse on top of the frame behind the fuel tank **(see illustrations)**. A pair of reverse fuses are located behind the battery tray.

2   If you have a test light, the accessory fuses can be checked without removing them. Turn the ignition key to the On position, connect one end of the test light to a good ground, then probe each terminal on top of the fuse. If the fuse is good, there will be voltage available at both terminals. If the fuse is blown, there will only be voltage present at one of the terminals.

3   A blown main fuse can be identified by a break in the element.

4   The accessory and main fuses can also be tested with an ohmmeter or self-powered test light. Remove the fuse and connect the tester to the ends of the fuse. If the ohmmeter shows continuity or the test lamp lights, the fuse is good. If the ohmmeter shows infinite resistance or the test lamp stays out, the fuse is blown.

5   The accessory fuses can be removed and checked visually. If you can't pull the fuse out with your fingertips, use a pair of needle-nose pliers. A blown fuse is easily identified by a break in the element.

6   If a fuse blows, be sure to check the wiring harnesses very carefully for evidence of a short circuit. Look for bare wires and chafed, melted or burned insulation. If a fuse is replaced before the cause is located, the new fuse will blow immediately.

7   Never, under any circumstances, use a higher rated fuse or bridge the fuse block terminals, as damage to the electrical system, including fire, could result.

8   Occasionally a fuse will blow or cause an open circuit for no obvious reason. Corrosion of the fuse ends and fuse block terminals may occur and cause poor fuse contact. If this happens, remove the corrosion with a wire brush or emery paper, then spray the fuse end and terminals with electrical contact cleaner.

Relays

Refer to illustrations 5.9, 5.10 and 5.11

9   The accessory relays are located in a block next to the accessory fuse block **(see illustrations 5.1 a and 5.1b)**. The speed limiter relay and power control relays are mounted on the right side of the bike behind the battery tray **(see illustration)**. The reverse relay (bikes with reverse) is mounted on the frame next to the gas tank **(see illustration 5.1d)**. The turn signal and hazard relays are mounted on top of the rear fender. You'll need to remove the trunk for access (see Chapter 8).

10   Several of the accessory relays, the two power control relays and the turn signal and hazard flasher relays have the same part numbers

5.1d The speed limiter fuse is mounted behind the gas tank

| A | Speed limiter fuse | B | Reverse relay |

printed on them **(see illustration)**. These relays are interchangeable with each other. The quickest way to test them is to remove the suspect relay and switch one of the other relays (with the same part number) into the suspect relay's position. The black relays have a slot in the case opposite the terminal lock. The blue relay has no slot to prevent it from being installed in a black relay's position.

11   Other relays can be tested with an ohmmeter and 12-volt battery. Connect the battery between the relay's power terminals with a pair of

5.9 The speed limiter relay and power control relays are mounted behind the battery tray

| A | Speed limiter relay | C | No. 2 power control relay |
| B | No. 1 power control relay (behind frame) | | |

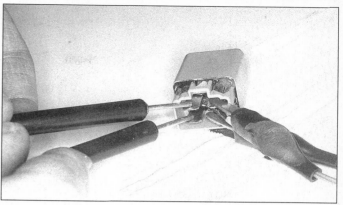

5.10 The turn signal and hazard flasher relays are mounted on top of the rear fender

jumper wires **(see illustration)**.
a) *Black relays - there should be continuity (little or no resistance) with the battery connected, and no continuity (infinite resistance) with the battery disconnected.*
b) *Blue relay - there should be no continuity with the battery connected, and continuity with the battery disconnected.*

6 Lighting system - check

1 The battery provides power for operation of the headlight, position light, taillight, brake light, license plate light, instrument cluster lights and optional accessory lights. If none of the lights operate, always check battery voltage before proceeding. Low battery voltage indicates either a faulty battery, low battery electrolyte level or a defective charging system. Refer to Chapter 1 for battery checks and Sections 28 and 29 for charging system tests. Also, check the condition of the fuses and relays and replace any that are blown or not working correctly.

Headlight

2 If the headlight is out when the engine is running, check the fuse first with the key On (see Section 5), then unplug the electrical connector for the headlight and use jumper wires to connect the bulb directly to the battery terminals. If the light comes on, the problem lies in the wiring or one of the switches or relays in the circuit. Refer to Section 12 for the switch testing procedures, and also the wiring diagrams at the end of this Chapter.

Taillight/license plate light

3 If the taillight fails to work, check the bulbs and the bulb terminals first, then check for battery voltage at the taillight electrical connector. If voltage is present, check the ground circuit for an open or poor connection.

7.2 Remove the screw at each end and take off the front grille

5.11 To test a relay, connect a 12-volt battery to its power terminals and an ohmmeter between the remaining terminals

4 If no voltage is indicated, check the fuse and the wiring between the taillight and the ignition switch, then check the switch. Check the taillight relay as well.

Brake light

5 See Section 11 for the brake light switch checking procedure.

Neutral indicator light

6 If the neutral light fails to operate when the transmission is in Neutral, check the fuses and the bulb (see Section 25 for bulb removal procedures). If the bulb and fuses are in good condition, check for battery voltage at the connector attached to the gearshift sensor. Remove the fairing lower cover from the right side of the bike; the connector is the six-pin black connector mounted in the connector bracket on the right cooling fan housing. If battery voltage is present, refer to Section 18 for the gearshift sensor check and replacement procedures.

7 If no voltage is indicated, check the wiring between the switch and the bulb for open circuits and poor connections.

7 Headlight and position light bulbs - replacement

Refer to illustrations 7.2, 7.3a, 7.3b, 7.3c, 7.7a and 7.7b
Warning: *If the bulb has just burned out, allow it to cool. It will be hot enough to burn your fingers.*
1 Remove the trim panel below the windshield (see Chapter 8).
2 Remove the screw at each side of the front grille and take it off **(see illustration)**.
3 Remove the headlight assembly mounting bolts and take the assembly off **(see illustrations)**.

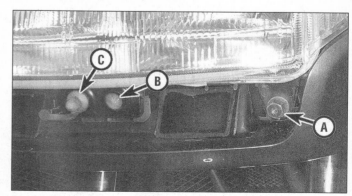

7.3a Remove the lower screw on each side . . .

A Lower headlight assembly screw
B Major horizontal adjustment screw
C Minor horizontal adjustment screw

9

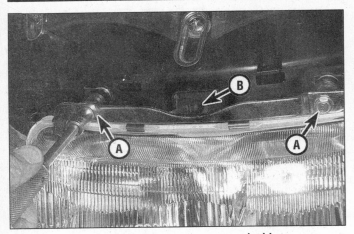

7.3b . . . and the upper screw on each side . . .

A   *Headlight assembly upper mounting screws*
B   *Minor vertical adjustment screw*

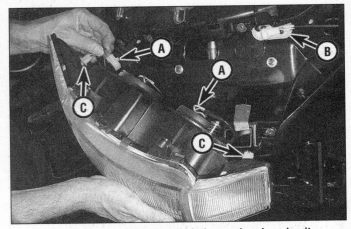

7.3c . . . then pull the assembly forward and unplug its
electrical connectors

A   *Headlight electrical connectors*
B   *Aiming cable*
C   *Position light electrical connectors*

4   Unplug the electrical connector from the headlight. Note the position of any Top markings for reinstallation and remove the rubber dust cover from the headlight assembly.

5   Lift up the retaining clip and swing it out of the way, then remove the bulb.

6   When installing the new bulb, reverse the removal procedure. Be sure not to touch the bulb with your fingers - oil from your skin will cause the bulb to overheat and fail prematurely. If you do touch the bulb, wipe it off with a clean rag dampened with rubbing alcohol.

7   To remove the aiming knob and cable, undo the screw, pull off the knob and remove the nut and washers **(see illustrations)**. Detach the front end of the cable from the fairing and remove it from the bike **(see illustration 7.3c)**.

8   To replace a position light bulb, turn its socket counterclockwise and remove it from the headlight housing **(see illustration 7.3c)**.

8   Headlight aim - check and adjustment

1   An improperly adjusted headlight may cause problems for oncoming traffic or provide poor, unsafe illumination of the road ahead. Before adjusting the headlight, be sure to consult with local traffic laws and regulations.

2   The headlight beam can be adjusted both vertically and horizontally. Before performing the adjustment, make sure the fuel tank is at least half full, and have an assistant sit on the seat.

3   Vertical adjustments can be made with the aiming knob above the

left fairing pocket **(see illustration 7.7a)**.

4   Minor vertical adjustments can be made with the screw above the top center of the headlight assembly **(see illustration 7.3b)**.

5   Horizontal adjustments can be made with the screws below the bottom center of the headlight assembly **(see illustration 7.3a)**.

9   Turn signals and taillight bulbs - replacement

Front turn signal/marker bulbs

Refer to illustration 9.1

1   To replace a front turn signal/marker bulb, remove the screw that holds the lens/lamp housing to the fairing **(see illustration)**. Pull out the lens/lamp housing.

2   Turn the bulb socket counterclockwise and remove it from the housing.

3   Push the bulb in and turn it counterclockwise to remove it. Check the socket terminals for corrosion and clean them if necessary. Line up the pins on the new bulb with the slots in the socket, push in and turn the bulb clockwise until it locks in place. **Note:** *The pins on some bulbs are offset so it can only be installed one way. It is a good idea to use a paper towel or dry cloth when handling the new bulb to prevent injury if the bulb should break and to increase bulb life.*

4   Position the lens in the fairing and install the screw. Be careful not to overtighten it.

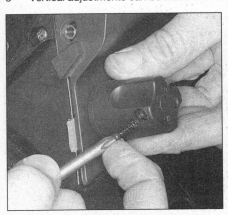

7.7a **Remove the screw and pull off the knob . . .**

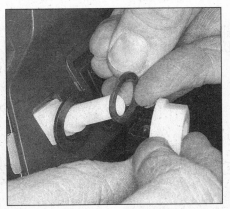

7.7b **. . . then unscrew the plastic nut and remove the washers to free the rear end of the aiming cable from the fairing**

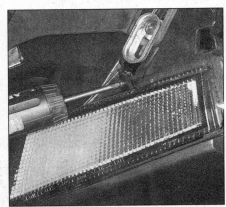

9.1 **Remove the screw at the top of the lens and pull the lens and housing forward out of the fairing**

Trunk-mounted brake and taillights

Refer to illustrations 9.5 and 9.6

5 Pry the covers loose from the bulb access holes inside the trunk **(see illustration)**.

6 Turn the bulb socket counterclockwise and remove it from the trunk **(see illustration)**.

7 Push the bulb in and turn it counterclockwise to remove it. Check the socket terminals for corrosion and clean them if necessary. Line up the pins on the new bulb with the slots in the socket, push in and turn the bulb clockwise until it locks in place. **Note:** *The pins on some bulbs are offset so it can only be installed one way. It is a good idea to use a*

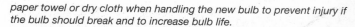

paper towel or dry cloth when handling the new bulb to prevent injury if the bulb should break and to increase bulb life.

Saddlebag-mounted brake and taillights

Refer to illustration 9.9

8 Remove the saddlebag lower cover (see Chapter 8).

9 Turn the bulb socket counterclockwise and remove it from the housing **(see illustration)**.

10 Push the bulb in and turn it counterclockwise to remove it. Check the socket terminals for corrosion and clean them if necessary. Line up the pins on the new bulb with the slots in the socket, push in and turn the bulb clockwise until it locks in place. **Note:** *The pins on some bulbs are offset so it can only be installed one way. It is a good idea to use a paper towel or dry cloth when handling the new bulb to prevent injury if the bulb should break and to increase bulb life.*

Accessory light

Refer to illustration 9.12

11 Remove the trunk lower cover (see Chapter 8).

12 Pull the accessory light socket out of the bottom of the trunk **(see illustration)**. Pull the bulb out of the socket and push a new one in. Push the socket back into the trunk, then refer to Chapter 8 and install the trunk lower cover.

License plate light

Refer to illustrations 9.13 and 9.14

13 If the trunk is installed on the bike, remove the lens screws and take off the lens **(see illustration)**. Pull the bulb out of the socket, push in a new one and reinstall the lens.

14 If the trunk has been removed, twist the socket counterclockwise and remove it from the housing **(see illustration)**. Pull the bulb out of the socket, push in a new one and reinstall the socket in the housing.

9.5 Remove the light covers; note the R and L marks (for right and left)

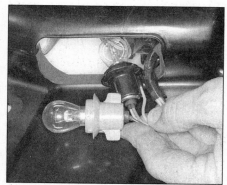

9.6 Twist the sockets and remove them from the trunk, then pull them through the holes for access to the bulbs

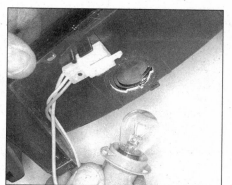

9.9 Twist the socket and remove it from the lamp housing, then push the bulb into the socket and turn counterclockwise to remove

9.12 Pull the socket out of the trunk floor, then pull the bulb out of the socket

9.13 Remove the screws and take off the license plate lens, then pull the bulb out of its socket

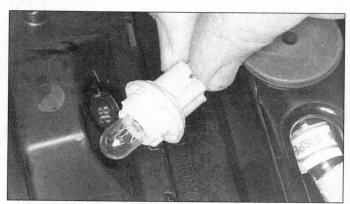

9.14 Twist the bulb socket and remove it from the lamp body, then pull the bulb out of the socket

9

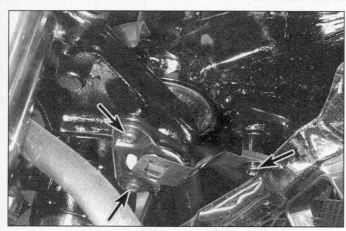

10.15 Remove the self-canceling unit's screws (arrows) and lower it out of the steering stem

10 Turn signal circuit - check

1   The battery provides power for operation of the signal lights, so if they do not operate, always check the battery voltage and specific gravity first. Low battery voltage indicates either a faulty battery, low electrolyte level or a defective charging system. Refer to Chapter 1 for battery checks and Sections 28 and 29 for charging system tests.

2   Most turn signal problems are the result of a burned out bulb or corroded socket. This is especially true when the turn signals function properly in one direction, but fail to flash in the other direction. Check the bulbs and the sockets (see Section 9).

3   Check the fuses and relays (see Section 5). The turn signal relay can be tested by switching the hazard relay into its position.

4   If the fuses and relays are okay, check the wiring in the turn signal circuit (see the wiring diagrams at the end of this Chapter). Make sure the connectors are clean and tight.

Self-canceling turn signal unit circuit check (Aspencade and Interstate)

5   Make sure the battery is fully charged and the fuses and wiring are in good condition before starting this test.

6   Remove the lower left fairing cover (see Chapter 8). Unplug the six-pin brown connector from the bracket on the cooling fan housing.

7   Connect a voltmeter between the white-green terminal in the harness side of the connector and ground. When the ignition switch is turned on, the voltmeter should indicate battery voltage.

8   Connect an ohmmeter between the pink terminal and ground. With the turn signal switch in the left or right position, there should be continuity (little or no resistance). With the turn signal in the pushed

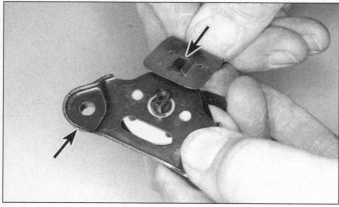

10.16 Install the boss (left arrow) with its flanges upward; fit the sensor plate (right arrow) securely over the end of the control unit

position, there should be no continuity (infinite resistance).

9   Move the ohmmeter to the light green-white terminal. Now there should be no continuity with the turn signal switch on the right or left position, and continuity with the switch pushed.

10   Support the bike with the front wheel slightly off the ground. Connect a voltmeter between the white-black terminal and ground. Turn the ignition switch on, then spin the front wheel slowly. The voltmeter should cycle between zero and 10 volts.

11   Reconnect the six-pin brown connector. Connect the voltmeter between the back side of the blue-black terminal and ground and turn the ignition switch on. With the turn signal switch in the right or left position, the voltmeter should indicate zero volts. In the pushed position, it should indicate battery voltage.

12   Connect the ohmmeter between the green wire terminal and ground. It should indicate continuity.

13   If the circuit performed as described in the preceding steps, it's okay. If not, check the wiring and turn signal switch.

Self-canceling turn signal unit removal and installation

Refer to illustrations 10.15 and 10.16

14   Refer to the steering stem removal procedure in Chapter 6 and disconnect the self-canceling unit's electrical connector.

15   Remove the self-canceling unit's retaining screws and take it off the bike **(see illustration)**.

16   Take the sensor plate and boss off the control unit **(see illustration)**. Check all parts for wear and damage and replace the unit if problems are found.

17   Installation is the reverse of the removal steps, with the following additions:

a) *Install the boss with its raised flanges upward (toward the control unit)* **(see illustration 10.16)**.

b) *Make sure the angle sensor plate fits tightly over the boss.*

11 Brake light switches - check and replacement

Circuit check

Refer to illustration 11.2a and 11.2b

1   Before checking any electrical circuit, check the fuses and relays (see Section 5).

2   Using a test light connected to a good ground, check for voltage at the brake light switch **(see illustrations)**. If there's no voltage present, check the wire between the switch and the fuse box (see the

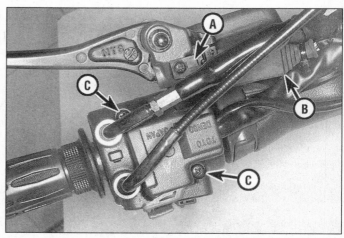

11.2a The front brake light switch is mounted next to the master cylinder

A   *Brake light switch*
B   *Cruise cancel switch connector (with cruise control)*
C   *Handlebar switch screws*

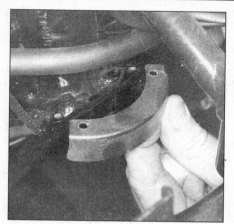

17.8 Remove the switch cover

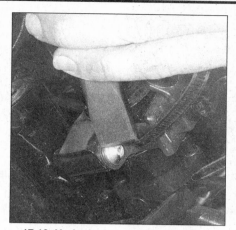

17.10 Undo the break-off bolts with a hammer and cold chisel

19.7 Remove the switch mounting bolt (lower arrow) and disengage the slot from the pin (upper arrow)

4   With the reverse lever in the on position, there should be no continuity (infinite resistance).

5   If the switch has tested OK to this point, unscrew it from the engine. Connect the ohmmeter between the switch wire terminal and the plunger on the inner end of the switch. There should be continuity.

6   If the switch fails any test, replace it. If it's good, check the reverse system wiring for breaks or bad connections. Refer to Chapter 2 and check the reverse system mechanical components.

Replacement

7   Unscrew the switch if you haven't already done so.

8   Install a new sealing washer on the switch and screw it into the engine. Tighten it to the torque listed in this Chapter's Specifications.

17   Ignition main (key) switch - check and replacement

Check

1   Remove the lower left fairing cover (see Chapter 8). Disconnect the eight-pin black electrical connector from the connector bracket on the cooling fan housing.

2   Using an ohmmeter, check the continuity between the terminal pairs indicated in the following steps. Test the switch side of the connector, not the wiring harness side.

3   Lock or off position - no continuity.

4   Acc position - continuity between red and light-green black.

5   On position - continuity between red, black, light green-blue and blue orange; also continuity between brown-white and brown.

6   P position - Continuity between red, light green-black and yellow-black.

7   If the switch fails any of the tests, replace it.

Replacement

Refer to illustrations 17.8 and 17.10

8   Remove the front fairing (see Chapter 8) and the switch cover **(see illustration)**.

9   Unplug the switch electrical connector.

10   The switch is secured by two break-off bolts. These are tightened on installation until the head snaps off, making it hard for a potential thief to remove the ignition switch. Undo the break-off bolts by turning them counterclockwise with a hammer and chisel **(see illustration)**. An alternative is to make a screwdriver slot in the ends of the bolts with the hammer and chisel, then use an impact driver to unscrew the bolts.

11   Attach the new switch to the bracket with two new break-off bolts. Tighten them until the heads snap off.

12   The remainder of installation is the reverse of the removal procedure.

18   Gear position switch (gearshift sensor) - check, removal and installation

Check

1   Remove the right lower cover from the fairing (see Chapter 8). Unplug the switch connector (it's the black six-pin connector in the bracket on the right fan housing).

2   Shift the transmission through the gears and check for continuity between the pairs of terminals listed in the following steps.

3   Neutral - light green-red and ground.

4   Second gear - black-yellow and ground.

5   Third gear - white-red and ground.

6   Fourth gear - red-white and ground.

7   Overdrive (fifth) gear - green-orange and ground.

Replacement

8   The switch is mounted inside the front engine cover. Refer to Chapter 2 for removal and installation procedures.

19   Sidestand switch - check and replacement

Check

1   Remove the inner cover from the left side of the fairing (see Chapter 8).

2   Follow the wiring harness from the switch to the three-pin green connector on the bracket behind the cruise control unit, then unplug the connector. Use an ohmmeter or test lamp to check for continuity between the pairs of terminals listed in the following steps (test the switch side of the connector, not the harness side).

3   Sidestand down - no continuity between green-white and green; continuity between yellow-black and green.

4   Sidestand up - continuity between green-white and green; no continuity between yellow-black and green.

5   If the switch fails either of these tests, replace it.

Replacement

Refer to illustration 19.7

6   Refer to Chapter 8 and remove the left front side cover.

7   Undo the switch mounting bolt **(see illustration)**. Free the harness from its retainers and disengage it from the locating pin, then take it off the motorcycle.

8   Installation is the reverse of the removal procedure. Engage the switch slot with the locating pin.

9

20.1 Disconnect the wires and remove the bolt to detach the horn

21.2 Remove the screw and detach the speedometer cable from the drive gear

20 Horn - check and replacement

Check

Refer to illustration 20.1

1   Unplug the electrical connectors from the horn **(see illustration)**. Using two jumper wires, apply battery voltage directly to the terminals on the horn. If the horn sounds, check the switch (see Section 13) and the wiring between the switch and the horn (see the wiring diagrams at the end of this Chapter).

2   If the horn doesn't sound, replace it.

Replacement

3   Unbolt the horn bracket from the frame **(see illustration 20.1)** and detach the electrical connectors.

4   Unbolt the horn from the bracket and transfer the bracket to the new horn.

5   Installation is the reverse of removal.

21 Speedometer cable - removal and installation

Refer to illustrations 21.2, 21.4, 21.5a and 21.5b

1   Remove the front fender cover from the left side of the fender and remove the left front brake disc cover (see Chapter 8).

2   Remove the retaining screw from the speedometer drive unit at the bottom of the left front fork **(see illustration)**. Pull the cable out and disengage it from the bracket.

3   Pull the cable through the retainer loop on the fender.

4   Unscrew the nut from the bottom of the speedometer and pull the cable free **(see illustration)**.

5   Pass the cable down through the fairing retainer and disengage it from the wire retainer at the front fork **(see illustrations)**. Pass the cable through the retainer that's part of the front fender and take it off the bike.

Installation

6   Installation is the reverse of the removal procedure, with the following additions:

a) *Be sure the speedometer cable is routed so it doesn't cause the steering to bind or interfere with other components.*

b) *Route the cable outside of the front fender and inside the left fender cover.*

c) *Be sure the squared-off ends of the cable fit into their spindles in the speedometer and drive gear.*

22 Instrument cluster - removal and installation

Refer to illustrations 22.7a and 22.7b

1   Remove the mirrors, the large chrome trim panel below the windshield and the top compartment (see Chapter 8).

2   Remove the headlight aiming knob and the plastic nut and washers **(see illustrations 7.7a and 7.7b)**.

3   Squeeze the retainers and remove the fresh air ducts from the outer ends of the instrument panel.

21.4 Unscrew the knurled nut and pull the upper end of the cable out of the speedometer

21.5a The cable passes through this retainer on the frame . . .

21.5b . . . and this one on the fork leg

22.7a Remove the mounting screw from each corner of the cluster . . .

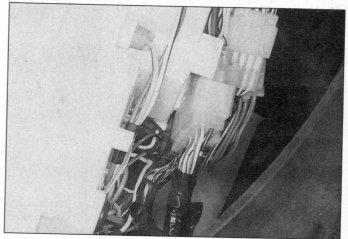

22.7b . . . then lift it up and disconnect the electrical connectors

4   If you're working on an SE, remove the opener for the exhaust pipe protector lid from the instrument panel.
5   Detach the instrument panel from the fairing and lift it off.
6   Disconnect the speedometer cable from the speedometer (Section 21).
7   Remove the mounting screw from each corner of the instrument

cluster, then lift the cluster and disconnect the electrical connectors **(see illustrations)**.
8   Installation is the reverse of the removal steps.

23   Meters and gauges - check

Coolant temperature gauge

1   Refer to Chapter 4 for coolant temperature gauge checking procedures.

Tachometer and speedometer

2   Special instruments are required to properly check the operation of these meters. Take the instrument cluster to a Honda dealer service department or other qualified repair shop for diagnosis.

24   Instrument cluster - disassembly and reassembly

Refer to illustrations 24.2a through 24.2i
1   Remove the cluster (see Section 22).
2   The accompanying photos show the disassembly of a 1996 Aspencade instrument cluster. Other models are similar. To disassemble the cluster and replace individual gauges, refer to the photos **(see illustrations)**.
3   Reassembly is the reverse of the disassembly procedure.

24.2a Remove six screws and the cluster lens . . .

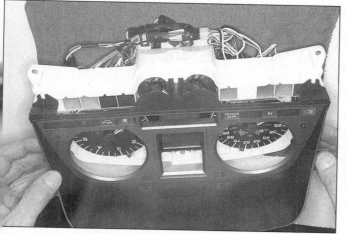

24.2b . . . lift off the cluster face . . .

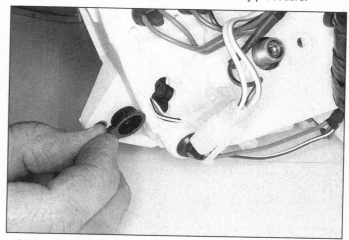

24.2c . . . pull the speedometer connector grommet out of the cluster housing and unplug the connector . . .

9

24.2d Remove the speedometer screws from the back of the housing and lift out the speedometer

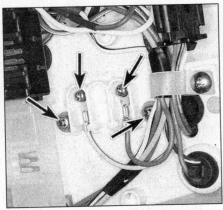

24.2e Remove the tachometer terminal and mounting screws and lift out the tachometer

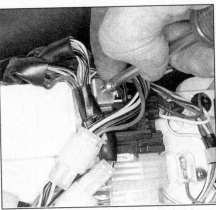

24.2f Remove the harness retainer screw

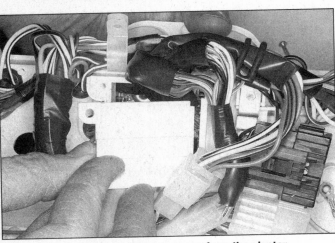

24.2g Remove the rear cover from the cluster

24.2h These screws secure the assembly of liquid crystal display, temperature gauge and fuel gauge; to separate the gauges and LCD, remove the screws from the back side of the assembly

3   Carefully push the new bulb into position, then push the socket into the cluster housing.
4   Reinstall the instrument panel.

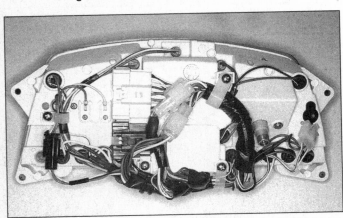

24.2i The assembled instrument cluster should look like this

25   Instrument and warning light bulbs - replacement

Refer to illustration 25.2

1   Remove the instrument cluster (see Section 22).
2   To replace a bulb, pull the appropriate rubber socket out of the back of the instrument cluster housing **(see illustration)**, then pull the bulb out of the socket. If the socket contacts are dirty or corroded, they should be scraped clean and sprayed with electrical contact cleaner before new bulbs are installed.

26   Starter relays (Aspencade and SE) - check and replacement

Check

1   Make sure the battery is fully charged and the relay wiring connections are clean and tight.

Starter relay A

Refer to illustration 26.3

2   Remove the right rear side cover (see Chapter 8).
3   Locate starter relay A next to the battery **(see illustration)**. Turn the ignition switch to the on position, then press the starter-reverse button. The relay should click as the wire is connected and disconnected.
4   If the relay doesn't click, disconnect the wires and remove it from its mount. Connect an ohmmeter to the two threaded posts on the relay. The ohmmeter should indicate no continuity (infinite resistance).
5   Connect the motorcycle's battery to the two flat terminals nearest the threaded posts. The ohmmeter should now indicate continuity (little or no resistance).
6   If the relay doesn't test correctly, replace it.

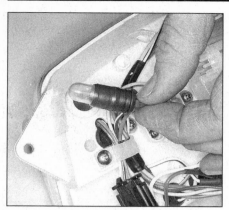

25.2 Pull the socket out of the cluster, then pull the bulb out of the socket

26.3 Starter relay A is mounted near the battery (arrow)

26.8 Starter relay B is mounted near the oil filler cap

Starter relay B

Refer to illustration 26.8

7   Remove the right front side cover (see Chapter 8).

8   Turn the ignition switch to the on position, then press the starter-reverse button. The relay should click as the button is pressed and released **(see illustration)**.

9   If the relay doesn't click, disconnect the wires and remove it from its mount. Connect an ohmmeter to the two threaded posts on the relay. The ohmmeter should indicate no continuity (infinite resistance).

10   Connect the motorcycle's battery to the two terminals in the relay's wiring harness. The ohmmeter should now indicate continuity (little or no resistance).

11   If the relay doesn't test correctly, replace it.

---

27 Starter motor - removal and installation

Refer to illustrations 27.2, 27.3 and 27.5

27.2 Detach the connector from the retainer (lower arrow) and disconnect the cable (upper arrow)

Removal

1   Remove the right front side cover (see Chapter 8). Remove the battery and battery tray (Section 3).

2   Detach the electrical connector from the connector holder on the rear end of the starter. Pull back the rubber cover, remove the nut retaining the starter cable to the starter and disconnect the cable **(see illustration)**.

3   Remove the starter mounting bolts **(see illustration)**.

4   Lift the rear end of the starter up a little bit and slide the starter backward out of the engine case. Rotate the front of the starter outward, then pull it away from the bike.

5   Check the condition of the O-ring on the end of the starter and replace it if necessary **(see illustration)**. Also check the starter pinion gear and the driven gear inside the engine for chipped or worn teeth.

Installation

6   Apply a little engine oil to the O-ring and install the starter by reversing the removal procedure.

27.3 Remove the three starter mounting bolts (outer bolt shown)

27.5 Inspect the starter pinion gear and O-ring

9

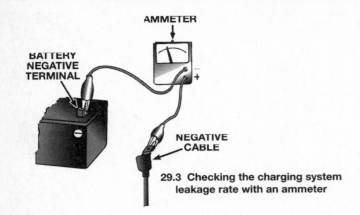

29.3 Checking the charging system leakage rate with an ammeter

28 Charging system testing - general information and precautions

1   If the performance of the charging system is suspect, the system as a whole should be checked first, followed by testing of the individual alternator components (the brushes, slip rings and coils). **Note:** *Before beginning the checks, make sure the battery is fully charged and that all system connections are clean and tight.*

2   Checking the output of the charging system and the performance of the various components within the charging system requires the use of special electrical test equipment. A voltmeter and ammeter or a

29.11a Pull back the rubber boot and remove the nut to disconnect the white wire

29.11b Free the black-light green wire from the retainer . . .

multimeter are the absolute minimum tools required. In addition, an ohmmeter is generally required for checking the remainder of the system.

3   When making the checks, follow the procedures carefully to prevent incorrect connections or short circuits, as irreparable damage to electrical system components may result if short circuits occur. Because of the special tools and expertise required, it is recommended that the job of checking the charging system be left to a dealer service department or a reputable motorcycle repair shop. **Caution:** *Never disconnect the battery cables from the battery while the engine is running. If the battery is disconnected, the alternator will be damaged.*

29 Charging system - leakage and output test

1   If a charging system problem is suspected, perform the following checks. Start by removing the left rear side cover for access to the battery (see Chapter 8).

Leakage test

Refer to illustration 29.3

2   Turn the ignition switch off and disconnect the cable from the battery negative terminal.

3   Set the multimeter to the mA (milliamps) function and connect its negative probe to the battery negative terminal, and the positive probe to the disconnected negative cable **(see illustration)**. **Caution:** *Don't connect the ammeter between the battery terminals or the ammeter will be ruined.* Compare the reading to the value listed in this Chapter's Specifications.

4   If the reading is too high there is probably a short circuit in the wiring. Thoroughly check the wiring between the various components (see the wiring diagrams at the end of the book).

5   If the reading is satisfactory, disconnect the meter and connect the negative cable to the battery, tightening it securely. Check the alternator output as described below.

Output test

6   Warm the engine to normal operating temperature, then shut it off.

7   Remove the 55-amp main fuse **(see illustration 5.1c)**. Connect an ammeter between the fuse holder terminals. **Note:** *The ammeter should be able to measure current flow in both directions.*

8   Connect the positive terminal of a voltmeter to the battery positive terminal and the voltmeter's negative terminal to the battery negative terminal (leave the cables connected to the battery).

9   Start the engine and let it idle. If the cooling fans are running, wait until they shut off. Compare the ammeter and voltmeter readings to the values listed in this Chapter's Specifications. If they're not within the specified ranges, perform the wiring harness check below.

29.11c . . . and unplug its connector at the bracket

30.3a Remove the alternator mounting bolts and move the hose bracket aside

30.3b Remove the alternator from the engine and inspect its O-ring

Wiring harness check

Refer to illustrations 29.11a, 29.11b and 29.11c

10 Disconnect the negative cable from the battery. This is necessary to prevent sparks when the wires are disconnected in the next step.

11 Disconnect the white wire from the alternator and unplug the connector for the black-light green wire **(see illustrations)**.

12 Reconnect the negative cable to the battery.

13 Connect a voltmeter between the battery terminals and note the reading(battery voltage).

14 Connect the voltmeter between the disconnected white wire and ground. It should indicate battery voltage at all times.

15 Connect the voltmeter between the black-light green wire and ground. It should indicate battery voltage when the ignition switch is turned to the on position.

16 If you don't get the correct voltmeter readings, check the wires for breaks or poor connections.

30 Alternator and coupling - removal and installation

Refer to illustrations 30.3a, 30.3b, 30.5, 30.6a and 30.6b

1 Remove the left rear side cover (see Chapter 8). Disconnect the cable from the negative terminal of the battery.

2 Disconnect the alternator wires **(see illustrations 29.11a, 29.11b and 29.11c)**.

3 Remove the alternator mounting bolts and push the hose bracket out of the way **(see illustration)**. Move the alternator rearward into the

frame, then rotate the front of it to the left and pull it forward out of the bike **(see illustration)**.

4 Inspect the alternator O-ring and replace if it's damaged or brittle.

5 Pull the rubber damper segments out of the coupling **(see illustration)**. If they're crushed or deteriorated, replace them.

6 Check the coupling itself for damaged vanes and make sure its nut is tight **(see illustration)**. If necessary, remove the nut, washer and coupling **(see illustration)**.

7 If the alternator bearing is loose, rough or noisy, refer to Chapter 2 and replace it.

8 Installation is the reverse of the removal steps with the following additions:

a) *Coat the O-ring with multi-purpose grease **(see illustration)**.*

b) *Tighten the coupling nut (if removed) and alternator mounting bolts to the torques listed in this Chapter's Specifications.*

31 Bank angle sensor (Aspencade and SE) removal and installation

Refer to illustration 31.2

Warning: *The bank angle sensor is designed to shut off the fuel pump if the bike is tipped over. If it's defective, it can shut off the engine during a turn, possibly causing a crash. Have the sensor tested by a Honda dealer if there's any doubt about its condition.*

1 Remove the seat, right saddlebag and trunk (see Chapter 8).

2 Locate the bank angle sensor and follow its wiring harness to the

30.5 Pull the damper segments out of the alternator coupling

30.6a Inspect the coupling

30.6b Take off the nut, washer and coupling

9

connector on the bracket. Unplug the connector **(see illustration)**.

3   Take the air pressure sensor off the rear fender stay, then undo the bank angle sensor mounting screws and take it off the bike.

4   Installation is the reverse of the removal steps. Don't install the bank angle sensor upside down or the starter motor won't operate.

32 Radio antenna - check, removal and installation

Removal

Refer to illustrations 32.1 and 32.2

1   To separate the antenna from the base pole, loosen the locknut and unscrew the antenna **(see illustration)**.

2   To remove the base pole from the bike, remove three screws and take the right side pocket off the trunk. Free the antenna cable and ground wire from their retainers, then follow them to the jack and connector and unplug them. Remove the base mounting bolts and take the base off **(see illustration)**.

Check

3   Using an ohmmeter, check for continuity at the following points:

a) *Top of antenna base pole to antenna cable tip - continuity (little or no resistance).*

b) *Antenna base pole to thin section of antenna jack - No continuity (infinite resistance).*

c) *Antenna base pole to thick section of antenna jack - continuity.*

d) *Antenna base pole to tip of ground wire - continuity.*

Installation

4   Installation is the reverse of the removal steps. Tighten the base bolts securely, but don't overtighten them and crack the base.

33 Speakers - removal, check and installation

Refer to illustrations 33.2a and 33.2b

1   To remove a front speaker, remove the instrument panel (see Chapter 8). To remove a rear speaker on an SE, remove the side pocket from the trunk.

2   Undo the speaker mounting screws **(see illustration)**. Pull the speaker out, disconnect its wires and remove it **(see illustration)**.

Check

3   Select the smallest range on an ohmmeter, then connect it to the speaker wire terminals. The speaker should click instantly when the ohmmeter is connected.

Installation

4   Installation is the reverse of the removal steps. Position the drain slots in the edge of the speaker at top and bottom.

31.2 The bank angle sensor (arrow) is mounted on the right rear of the bike

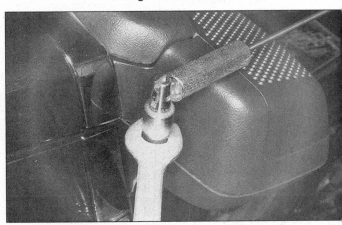

32.1 Loosen the locknut and unscrew the antenna from the base pole

34 Wiring diagrams

Prior to troubleshooting a circuit, check the fuses to make sure they're in good condition. Make sure the battery is fully charged and check the cable connections.

When checking a circuit, make sure all connectors are clean, with no broken or loose terminals or wires. When unplugging a connector, don't pull on the wires; pull only on the connector housings themselves.

32.2 Disconnect the antenna cable and ground wire, remove the bolts (arrows) and take the antenna off

33.2a The drain slots in the outer edge of the speaker go at top and bottom

33.2b Pull the speaker out and disconnect its wires

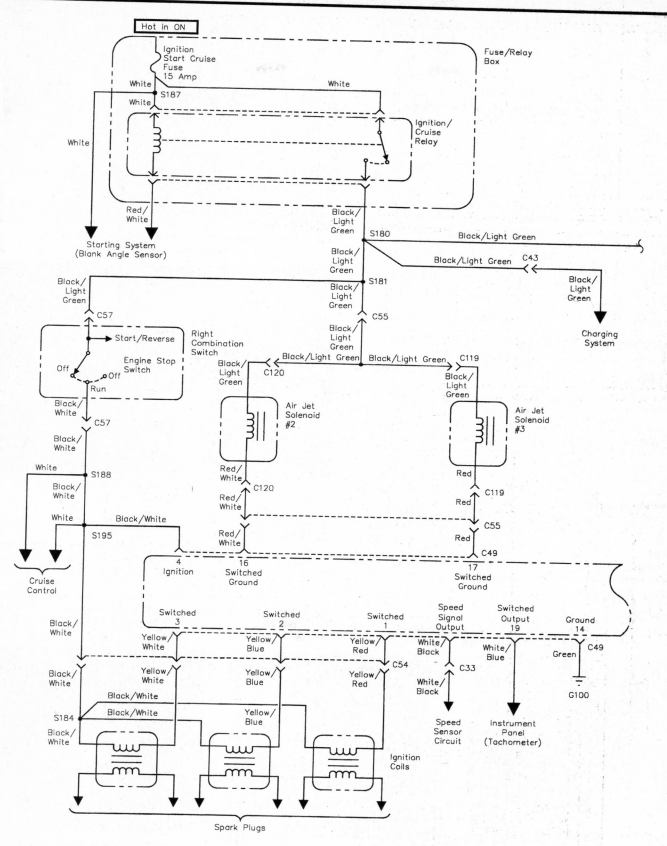

Engine control system - 1993-on (1 of 3)

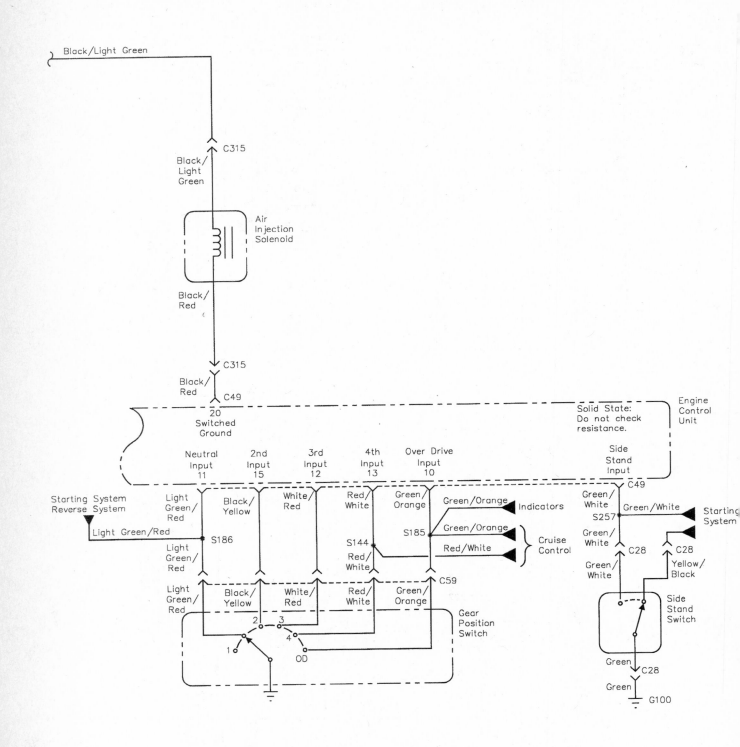

Engine control system - 1993-on (2 of 3)

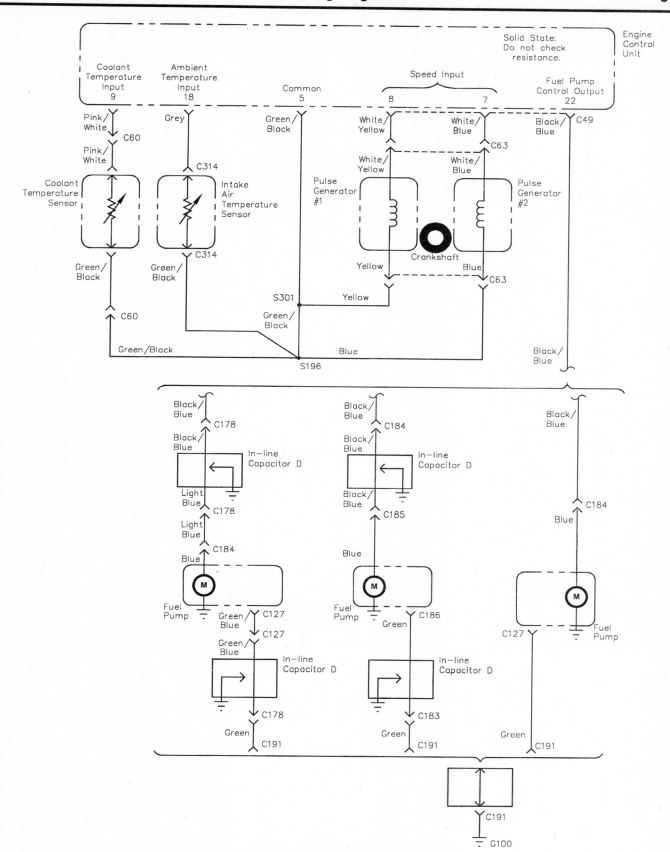

Engine control system - 1993-on (3 of 3)

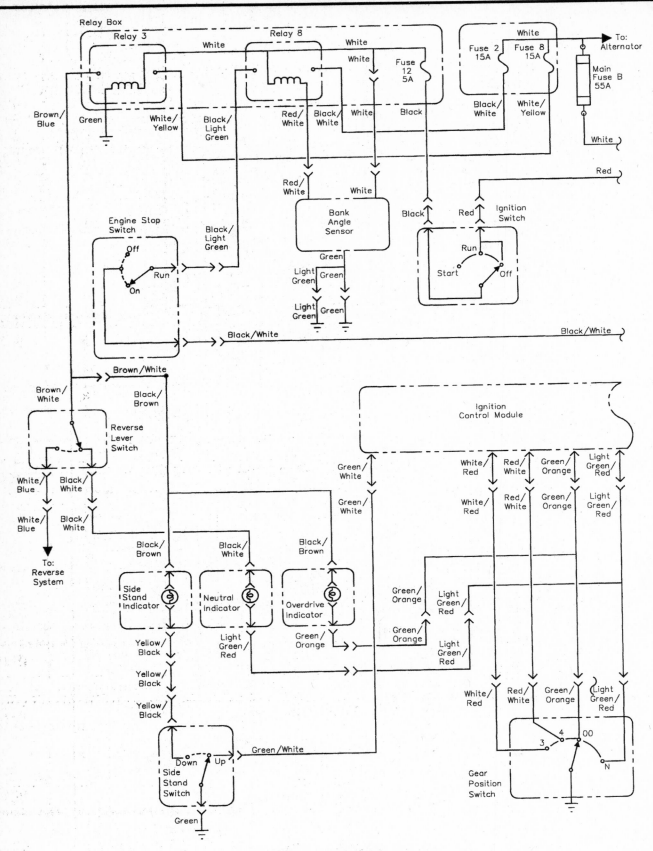

Ignition circuit - 1988 and 1989 (1 of 2)

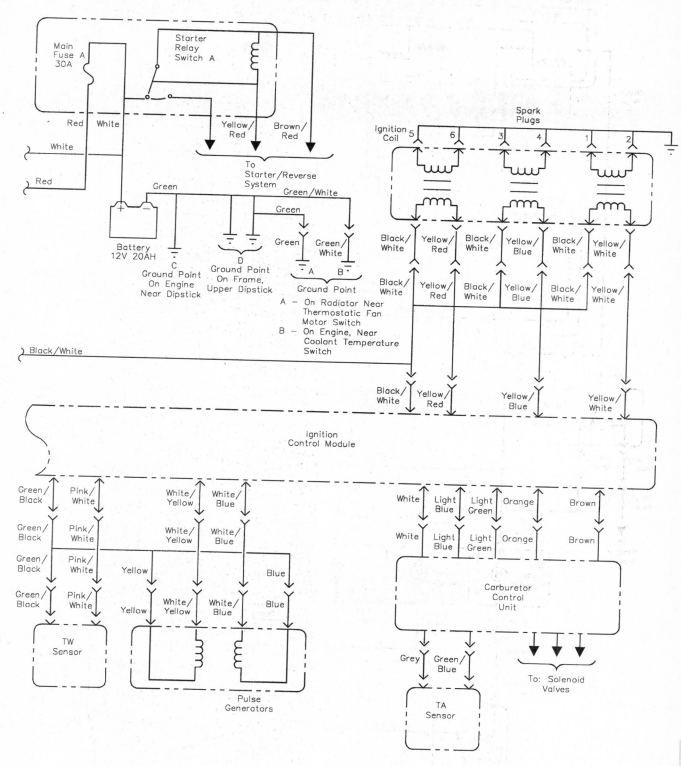

Ignition circuit - 1988 and 1989 (2 of 2)

9

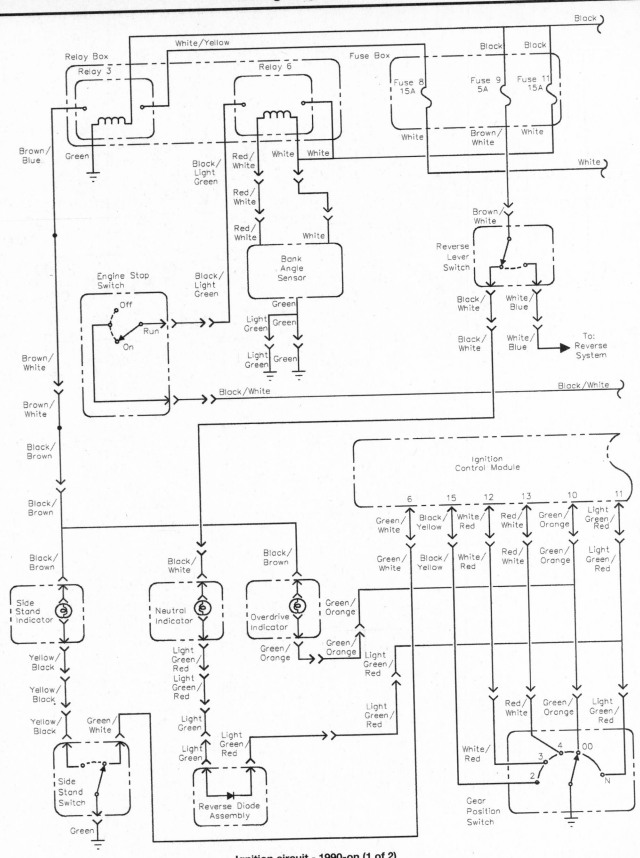

Ignition circuit - 1990-on (1 of 2)

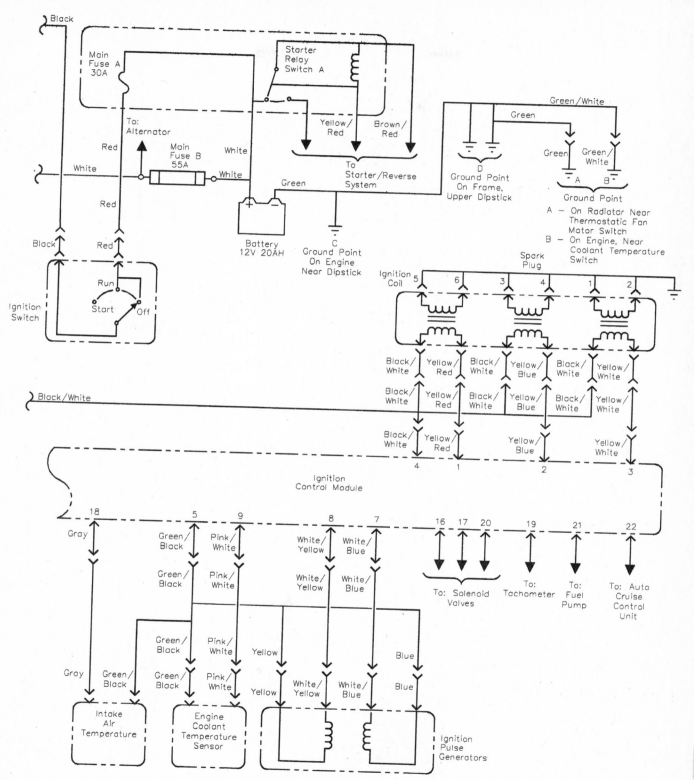

Ignition circuit - 1990-on (2 of 2)

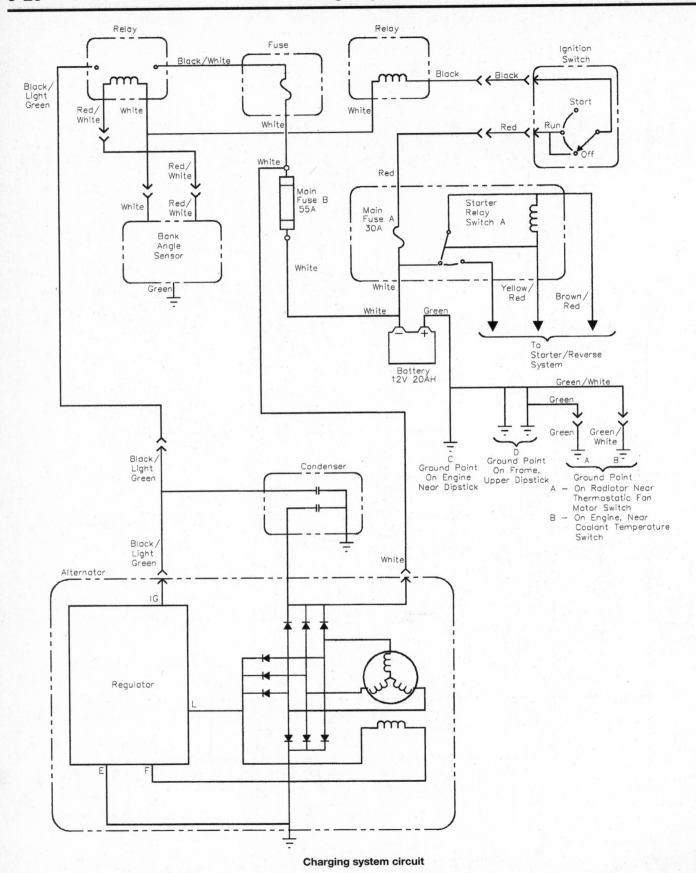

Charging system circuit

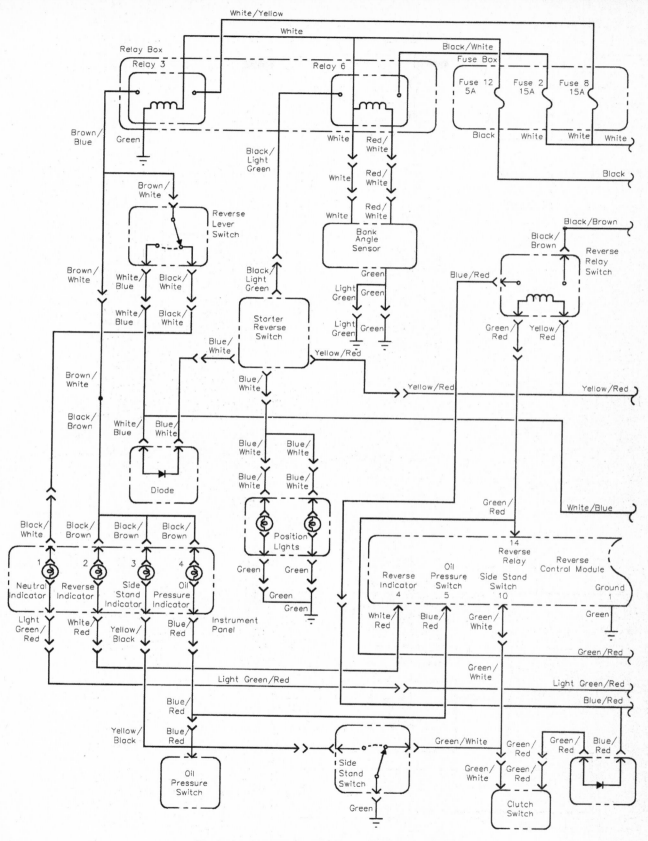

Starter/reverse circuit - 1988 and 1989 models (1 of 2)

9

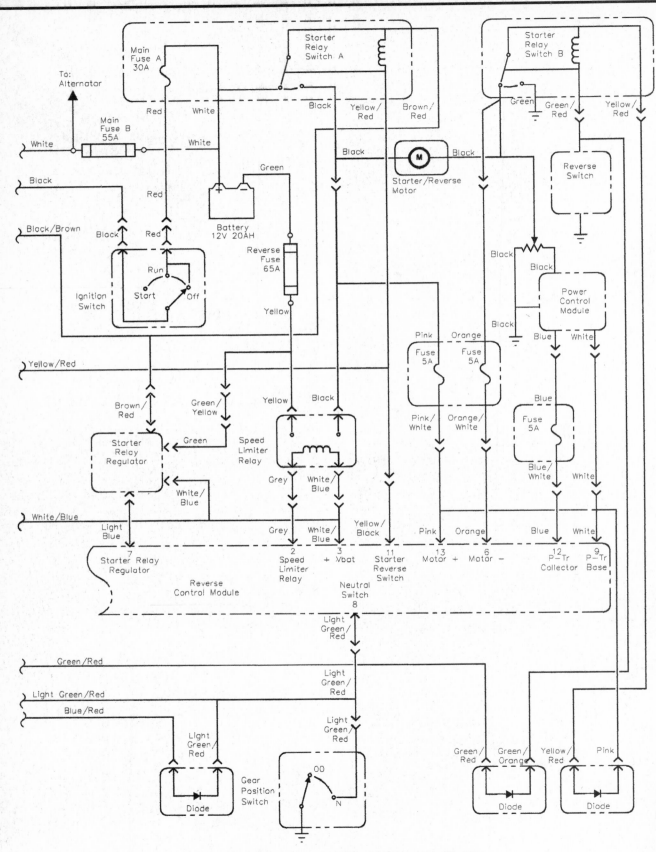

Starter/reverse circuit - 1988 and 1989 models (2 of 2)

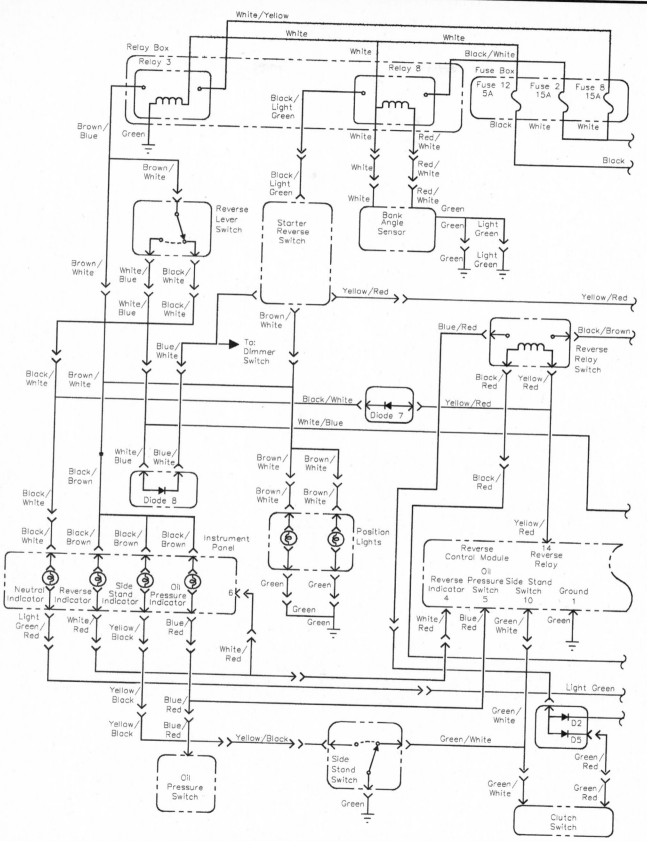

Starter/reverse circuit - 1990 and later Aspencade/SE (1 of 2)

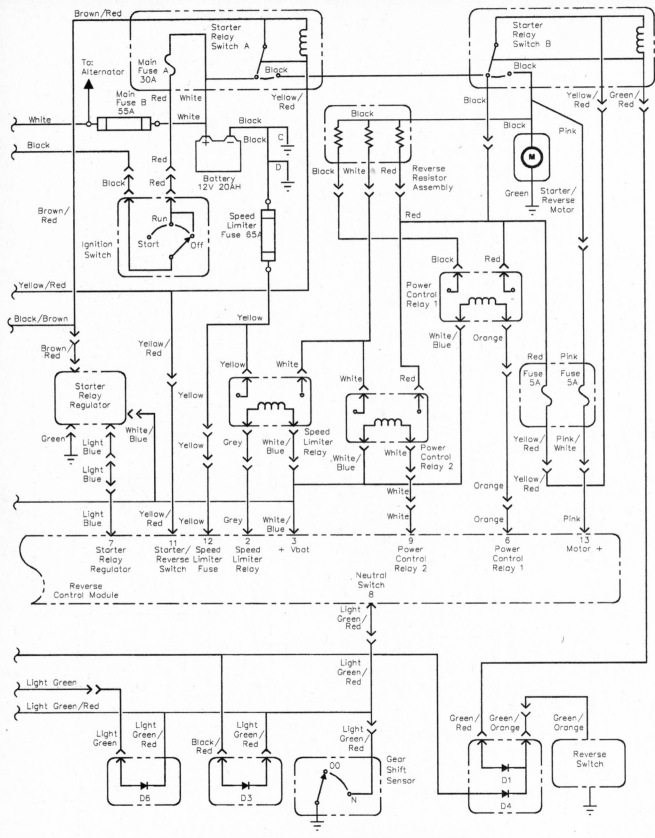

Starter/reverse circuit - 1990 and later Aspencade/SE (2 of 2)

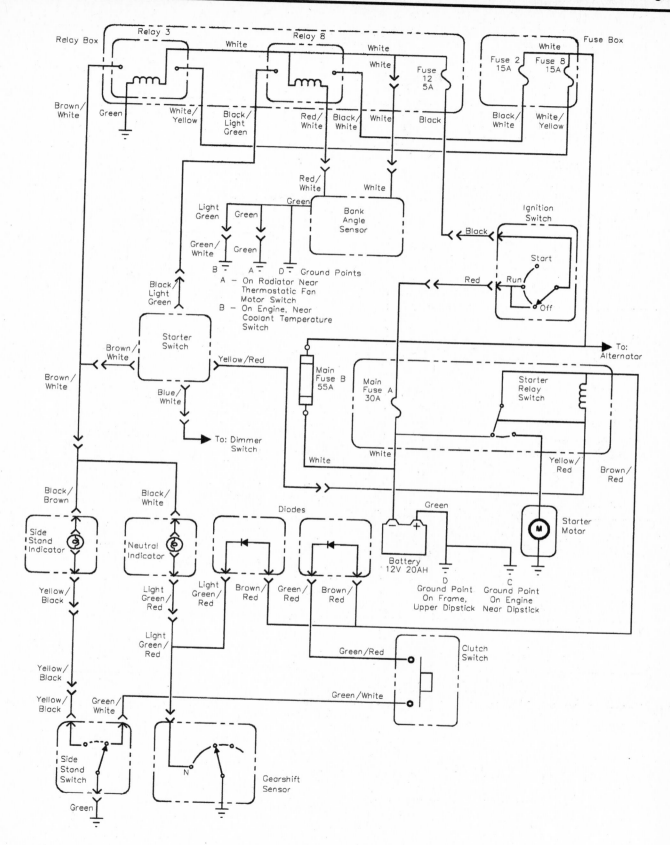

Starter circuit - 1990 and later Interstate

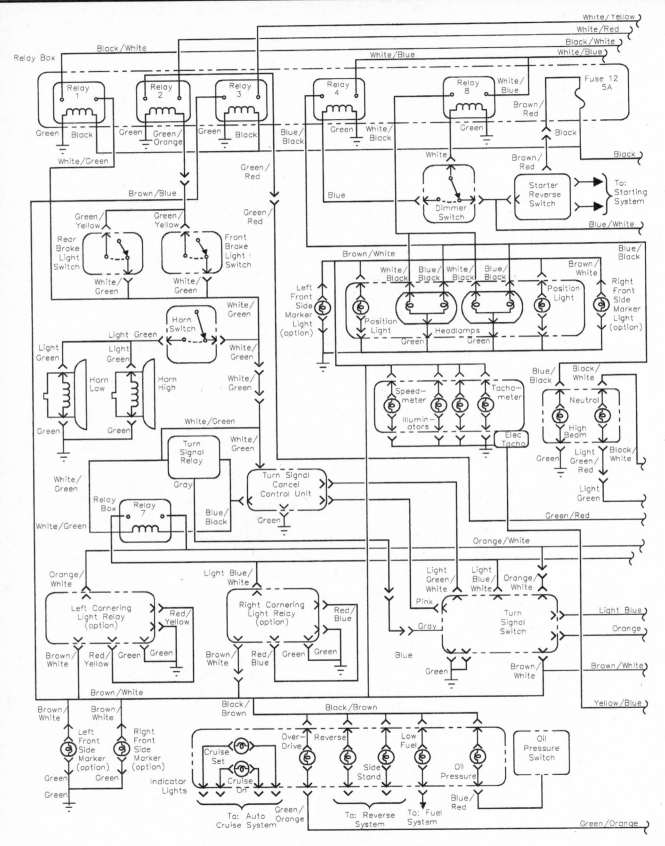

Wiring diagram - A model (1 of 2)

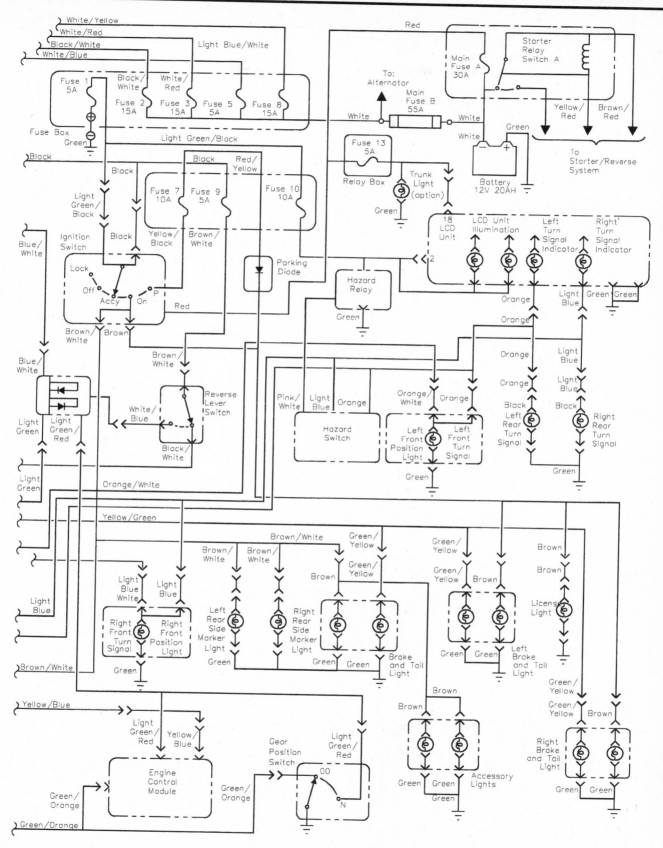

Wiring diagram - A model (2 of 2)

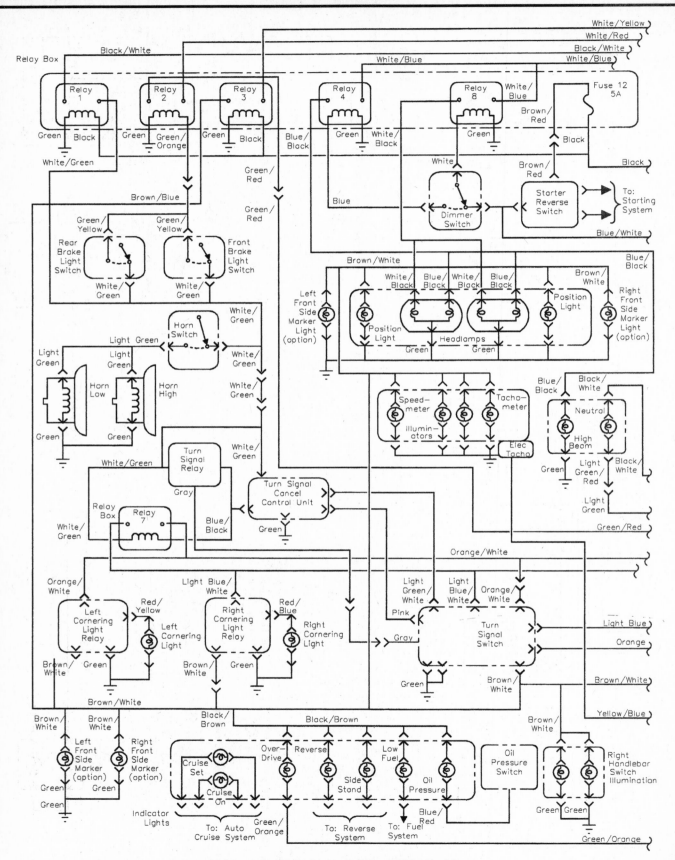

Lights, switches and instruments - typical (1 of 2)

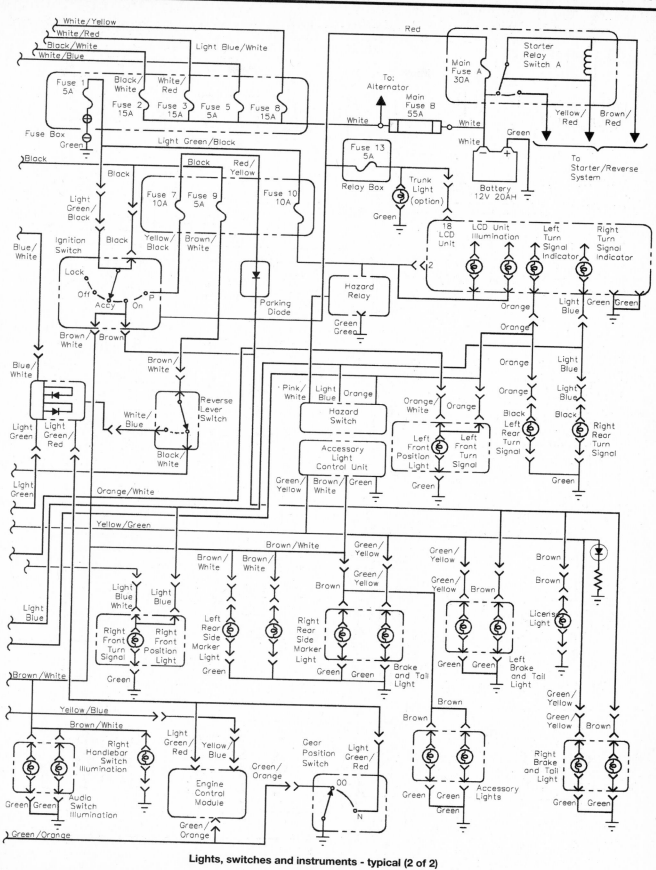

Lights, switches and instruments - typical (2 of 2)

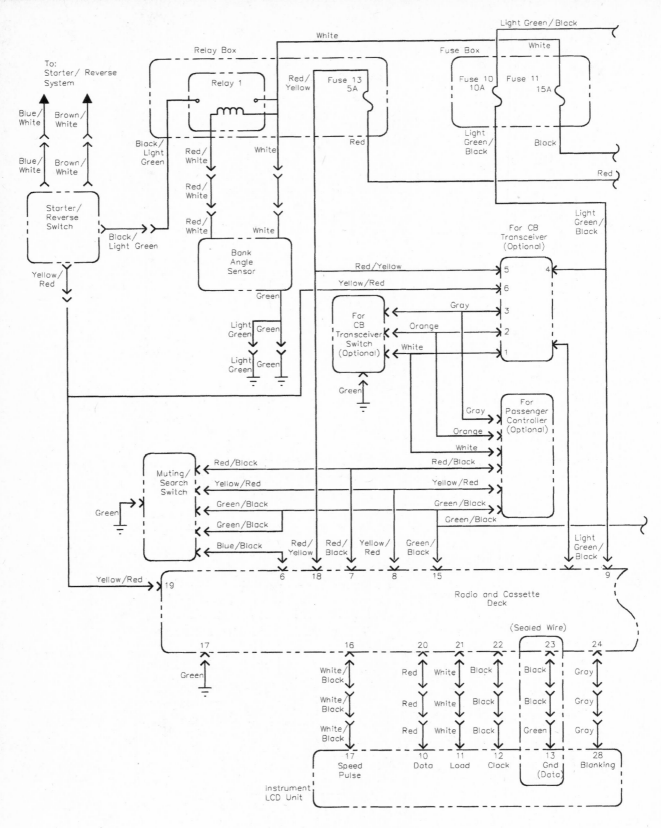

Wiring diagram - A and SE models (1 of 2)

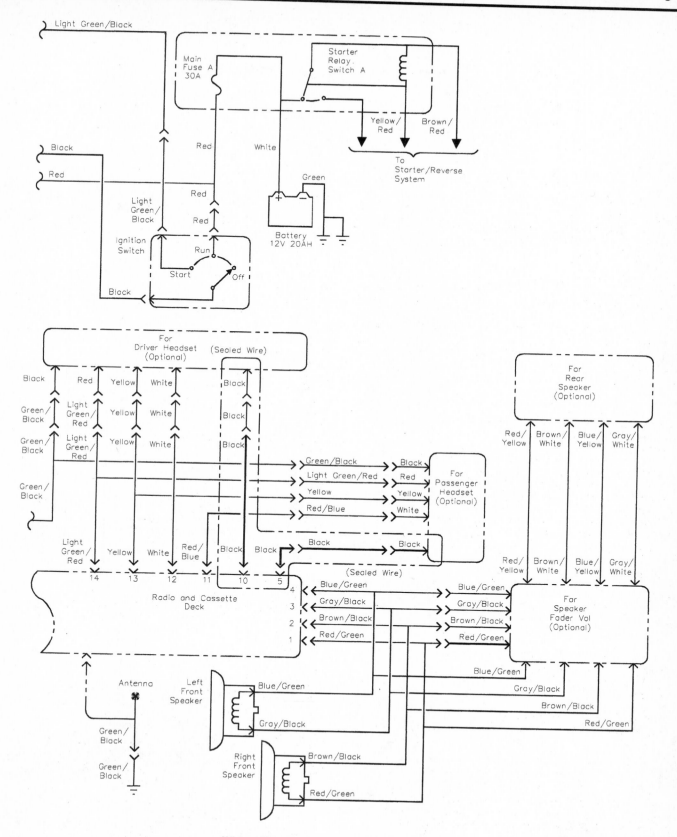

Wiring diagram - A and SE models (2 of 2)

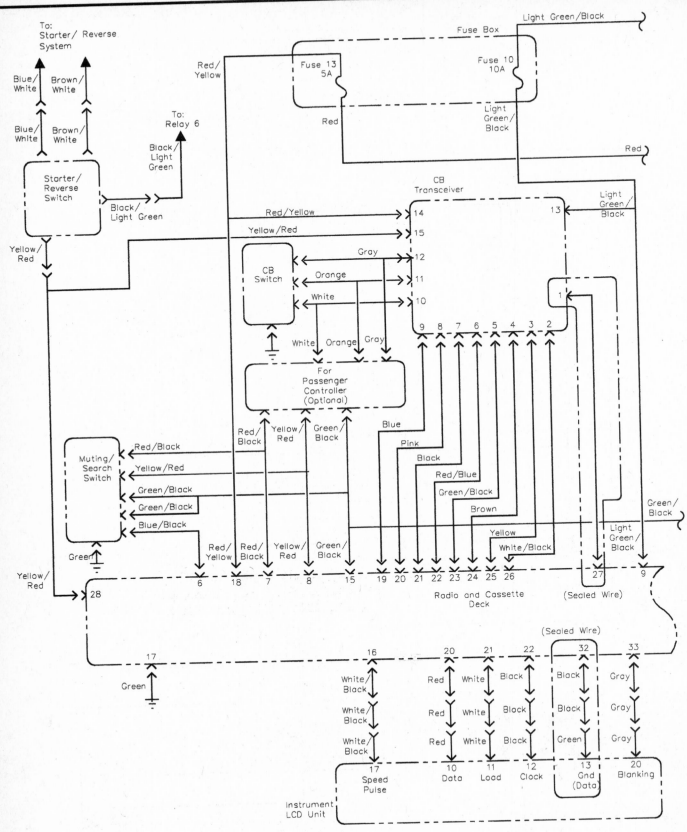

Audio system circuit - typical (1 of 2)

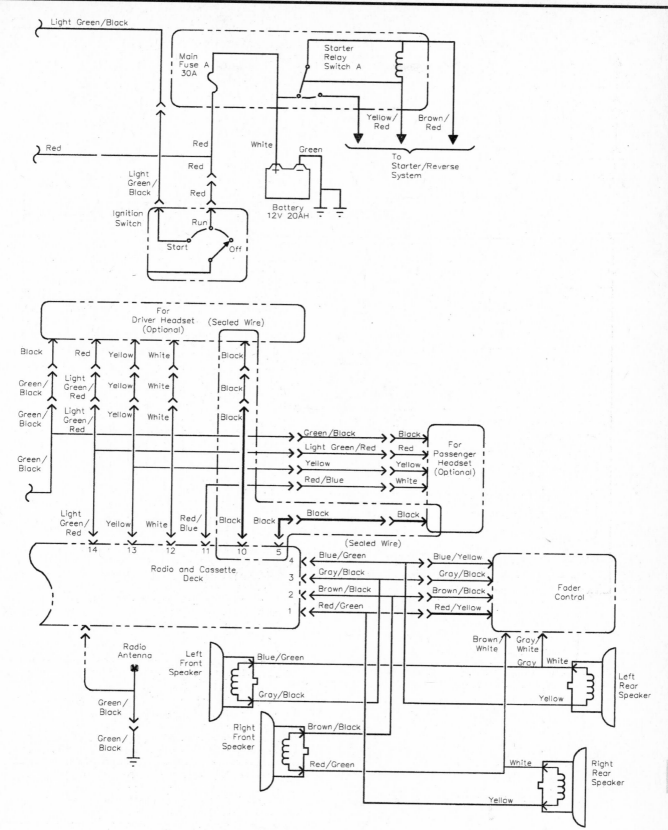

Audio system circuit - typical (2 of 2)

Conversion factors

Length (distance)
Inches (in)	X	25.4	= Millimetres (mm)	X 0.0394	= Inches (in)
Feet (ft)	X	0.305	= Metres (m)	X 3.281	= Feet (ft)
Miles	X	1.609	= Kilometres (km)	X 0.621	= Miles

Volume (capacity)
Cubic inches (cu in; in³)	X	16.387	= Cubic centimetres (cc; cm³)	X 0.061	= Cubic inches (cu in; in³)
Imperial pints (Imp pt)	X	0.568	= Litres (l)	X 1.76	= Imperial pints (Imp pt)
Imperial quarts (Imp qt)	X	1.137	= Litres (l)	X 0.88	= Imperial quarts (Imp qt)
Imperial quarts (Imp qt)	X	1.201	= US quarts (US qt)	X 0.833	= Imperial quarts (Imp qt)
US quarts (US qt)	X	0.946	= Litres (l)	X 1.057	= US quarts (US qt)
Imperial gallons (Imp gal)	X	4.546	= Litres (l)	X 0.22	= Imperial gallons (Imp gal)
Imperial gallons (Imp gal)	X	1.201	= US gallons (US gal)	X 0.833	= Imperial gallons (Imp gal)
US gallons (US gal)	X	3.785	= Litres (l)	X 0.264	= US gallons (US gal)

Mass (weight)
Ounces (oz)	X	28.35	= Grams (g)	X 0.035	= Ounces (oz)
Pounds (lb)	X	0.454	= Kilograms (kg)	X 2.205	= Pounds (lb)

Force
Ounces-force (ozf; oz)	X	0.278	= Newtons (N)	X 3.6	= Ounces-force (ozf; oz)
Pounds-force (lbf; lb)	X	4.448	= Newtons (N)	X 0.225	= Pounds-force (lbf; lb)
Newtons (N)	X	0.1	= Kilograms-force (kgf; kg)	X 9.81	= Newtons (N)

Pressure
Pounds-force per square inch (psi; lbf/in²; lb/in²)	X	0.070	= Kilograms-force per square centimetre (kgf/cm²; kg/cm²)	X 14.223	= Pounds-force per square inch (psi; lbf/in²; lb/in²)
Pounds-force per square inch (psi; lbf/in²; lb/in²)	X	0.068	= Atmospheres (atm)	X 14.696	= Pounds-force per square inch (psi; lbf/in²; lb/in²)
Pounds-force per square inch (psi; lbf/in²; lb/in²)	X	0.069	= Bars	X 14.5	= Pounds-force per square inch (psi; lbf/in²; lb/in²)
Pounds-force per square inch (psi; lbf/in²; lb/in²)	X	6.895	= Kilopascals (kPa)	X 0.145	= Pounds-force per square inch (psi; lbf/in²; lb/in²)
Kilopascals (kPa)	X	0.01	= Kilograms-force per square centimetre (kgf/cm²; kg/cm²)	X 98.1	= Kilopascals (kPa)

Torque (moment of force)
Pounds-force inches (lbf in; lb in)	X	1.152	= Kilograms-force centimetre (kgf cm; kg cm)	X 0.868	= Pounds-force inches (lbf in; lb in)
Pounds-force inches (lbf in; lb in)	X	0.113	= Newton metres (Nm)	X 8.85	= Pounds-force inches (lbf in; lb in)
Pounds-force inches (lbf in; lb in)	X	0.083	= Pounds-force feet (lbf ft; lb ft)	X 12	= Pounds-force inches (lbf in; lb in)
Pounds-force feet (lbf ft; lb ft)	X	0.138	= Kilograms-force metres (kgf m; kg m)	X 7.233	= Pounds-force feet (lbf ft; lb ft)
Pounds-force feet (lbf ft; lb ft)	X	1.356	= Newton metres (Nm)	X 0.738	= Pounds-force feet (lbf ft; lb ft)
Newton metres (Nm)	X	0.102	= Kilograms-force metres (kgf m; kg m)	X 9.804	= Newton metres (Nm)

Vacuum
Inches mercury (in. Hg)	X	3.377	= Kilopascals (kPa)	X 0.2961	= Inches mercury
Inches mercury (in. Hg)	X	25.4	= Millimeters mercury (mm Hg)	X 0.0394	= Inches mercury

Power
Horsepower (hp)	X	745.7	= Watts (W)	X 0.0013	= Horsepower (hp)

Velocity (speed)
Miles per hour (miles/hr; mph)	X	1.609	= Kilometres per hour (km/hr; kph)	X 0.621	= Miles per hour (miles/hr; mph)

Fuel consumption*
Miles per gallon, Imperial (mpg)	X	0.354	= Kilometres per litre (km/l)	X 2.825	= Miles per gallon, Imperial (mpg)
Miles per gallon, US (mpg)	X	0.425	= Kilometres per litre (km/l)	X 2.352	= Miles per gallon, US (mpg)

Temperature
Degrees Fahrenheit = (°C x 1.8) + 32

Degrees Celsius (Degrees Centigrade; °C) = (°F - 32) x 0.56

*It is common practice to convert from miles per gallon (mpg) to litres/100 kilometres (l/100km),
where mpg (Imperial) x l/100 km = 282 and mpg (US) x l/100 km = 235

Fraction/Decimal/Millimeter Equivalents

DECIMALS TO MILLIMETERS

Decimal	mm	Decimal	mm
0.001	0.0254	0.500	12.7000
0.002	0.0508	0.510	12.9540
0.003	0.0762	0.520	13.2080
0.004	0.1016	0.530	13.4620
0.005	0.1270	0.540	13.7160
0.006	0.1524	0.550	13.9700
0.007	0.1778	0.560	14.2240
0.008	0.2032	0.570	14.4780
0.009	0.2286	0.580	14.7320
0.010	0.2540	0.590	14.9860
0.020	0.5080		
0.030	0.7620		
0.040	1.0160	0.600	15.2400
0.050	1.2700	0.610	15.4940
0.060	1.5240	0.620	15.7480
0.070	1.7780	0.630	16.0020
0.080	2.0320	0.640	16.2560
0.090	2.2860	0.650	16.5100
0.100	2.5400	0.660	16.7640
0.110	2.7940	0.670	17.0180
0.120	3.0480	0.680	17.2720
0.130	3.3020	0.690	17.5260
0.140	3.5560		
0.150	3.8100		
0.160	4.0640	0.700	17.7800
0.170	4.3180	0.710	18.0340
0.180	4.5720	0.720	18.2880
0.190	4.8260	0.730	18.5420
0.200	5.0800	0.740	18.7960
0.210	5.3340	0.750	19.0500
0.220	5.5880	0.760	19.3040
0.230	5.8420	0.770	19.5580
0.240	6.0960	0.780	19.8120
0.250	6.3500	0.790	20.0660
0.260	6.6040		
0.270	6.8580	0.800	20.3200
0.280	7.1120	0.810	20.5740
0.290	7.3660	0.820	21.8280
		0.830	21.0820
0.300	7.6200	0.840	21.3360
0.310	7.8740	0.850	21.5900
0.320	8.1280	0.860	21.8440
0.330	8.3820	0.870	22.0980
0.340	8.6360	0.880	22.3520
0.350	8.8900	0.890	22.6060
0.360	9.1440		
0.370	9.3980		
0.380	9.6520		
0.390	9.9060	0.900	22.8600
0.400	10.1600	0.910	23.1140
0.410	10.4140	0.920	23.3680
0.420	10.6680	0.930	23.6220
0.430	10.9220	0.940	23.8760
0.440	11.1760	0.950	24.1300
0.450	11.4300	0.960	24.3840
0.460	11.6840	0.970	24.6380
0.470	11.9380	0.980	24.8920
0.480	12.1920	0.990	25.1460
0.490	12.4460	1.000	25.4000

FRACTIONS TO DECIMALS TO MILLIMETERS

Fraction	Decimal	mm	Fraction	Decimal	mm
1/64	0.0156	0.3969	33/64	0.5156	13.0969
1/32	0.0312	0.7938	17/32	0.5312	13.4938
3/64	0.0469	1.1906	35/64	0.5469	13.8906
1/16	0.0625	1.5875	9/16	0.5625	14.2875
5/64	0.0781	1.9844	37/64	0.5781	14.6844
3/32	0.0938	2.3812	19/32	0.5938	15.0812
7/64	0.1094	2.7781	39/64	0.6094	15.4781
1/8	0.1250	3.1750	5/8	0.6250	15.8750
9/64	0.1406	3.5719	41/64	0.6406	16.2719
5/32	0.1562	3.9688	21/32	0.6562	16.6688
11/64	0.1719	4.3656	43/64	0.6719	17.0656
3/16	0.1875	4.7625	11/16	0.6875	17.4625
13/64	0.2031	5.1594	45/64	0.7031	17.8594
7/32	0.2188	5.5562	23/32	0.7188	18.2562
15/64	0.2344	5.9531	47/64	0.7344	18.6531
1/4	0.2500	6.3500	3/4	0.7500	19.0500
17/64	0.2656	6.7469	49/64	0.7656	19.4469
9/32	0.2812	7.1438	25/32	0.7812	19.8438
19/64	0.2969	7.5406	51/64	0.7969	20.2406
5/16	0.3125	7.9375	13/16	0.8125	20.6375
21/64	0.3281	8.3344	53/64	0.8281	21.0344
11/32	0.3438	8.7312	27/32	0.8438	21.4312
23/64	0.3594	9.1281	55/64	0.8594	21.8281
3/8	0.3750	9.5250	7/8	0.8750	22.2250
25/64	0.3906	9.9219	57/64	0.8906	22.6219
13/32	0.4062	10.3188	29/32	0.9062	23.0188
27/64	0.4219	10.7156	59/64	0.9219	23.4156
7/16	0.4375	11.1125	15/16	0.9375	23.8125
29/64	0.4531	11.5094	61/64	0.9531	24.2094
15/32	0.4688	11.9062	31/32	0.9688	24.6062
31/64	0.4844	12.3031	63/64	0.9844	25.0031
1/2	0.5000	12.7000	1	1.0000	25.4000

Index

Index

Index